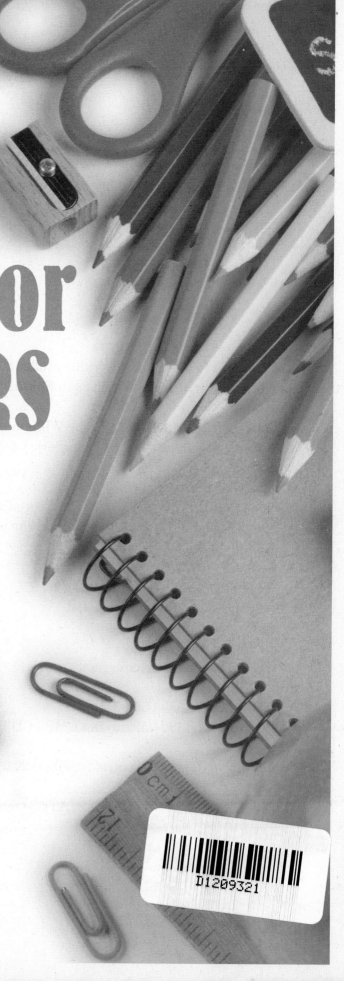

SPANISH for EDUCATORS

Third Edition

William C. Harvey, M.S.

BARRON'S

Dedicated to all the hardworking students and staff at
Whittier Christian High School in Southern California.

All inquiries should be addressed to:
Barron's Educational Series, Inc.
250 Wireless Boulevard
Hauppauge, NY 11788
www.barronseduc.com

ISBN: 978-1-4380-0506-5 (Book)
ISBN: 978-1-4380-7522-8 (Book/MP3 CD Package)

Library of Congress Control Number: 2015937267

PRINTED IN THE UNITED STATES OF AMERICA

9 8 7 6 5 4 3 2 1

10%
POST-CONSUMER
WASTE
Paper contains a minimum
of 10% post-consumer
waste (PCW). Paper used
in this book was derived
from certified, sustainable
forestlands.

TABLE OF CONTENTS

A NOTE FROM THE AUTHOR

Years ago, while teaching at a middle school in Southern California, I was frequently interrupted by other staff members who needed some quick Spanish instruction. All over campus, from the principal to the custodian, there was a demand for foreign language skills. I later discovered that the problem was nationwide. Spanish-speaking children were enrolling in schools, and English-speaking educators needed to talk to them.

This guidebook is designed for anyone involved in education who needs to communicate regularly with Spanish speakers. I have discovered that once the language and cultural barriers are removed between schools and the community, Hispanic students find greater success in the classroom. Moreover, learning Spanish often leads to exciting new experiences, as well as personal satisfaction and valuable professional growth. Trust me, fellow educators, reading through this guidebook will truly be worth your time and effort.

Good luck! ¡Buena suerte! (*'bweh-nah 'swehr-teh*)

Bill Harvey

HOW TO USE THIS GUIDEBOOK

Spanish for Educators teaches English-speaking educators, along with related professionals, how to understand and speak Spanish. This book provides readers with all the Spanish vocabulary and phrases needed to communicate key messages to Spanish-speaking students of all ages, as well as to converse socially with Hispanic visitors, co-workers, family members, and friends. To accelerate the learning process, all skills are taught gradually and are systematically reinforced through practice and review.

To get the most out of this book, either use the convenient specialized dictionary in the back, or try focusing on the icons provided on the next page. They can be helpful when you are working on a specific skill or topic of interest. Simply scan the pages for the corresponding icon, and read up on whatever you need.

MÁS INFORMACIÓN *(mahs een-fohr-mah-see·'ohn)*
(Information, tips, and suggestions)

 DIFERENCIAS CULTURALES
(dee-feh-'rehn-see·ahs kool-too-'rahl-ehs) (Insights into Hispanic culture)

 ¡ÓRDENES! *('ohr-deh-nehs)*
(Spanish command words)

 ¡ACCIÓN! *(ahk-see·'ohn)*
(Basic Spanish verb tenses)

 ¿LISTOS PARA PRACTICAR? *('lee-stohs 'pah-rah prahk-tee-'kahr)*
(Review practice exercises. Answers are not provided)

GREAT NEWS!

If you're a little fearful about learning Spanish, here's some exciting news:

➤ Grammar and pronunciation don't have to be "perfect" in order to be understood.

➤ Thousands of words are similar in both English and Spanish, which makes it easier for you to remember vocabulary.

➤ Messages in Spanish can be communicated with only a few simple expressions.

Believe me. By following the proven suggestions mentioned in this guidebook, you can pick up lots of español *(eh-spah-'nyohl)* in no time at all!

CHAPTER ONE
Capítulo Uno
(kah-'pee-too-loh 'oo-noh)

BEFORE YOU BEGIN
Antes de que usted comience
('ahn-tes deh keh oo-'stehd koh-mee-'ehn-seh)

THE SOUNDS OF SPANISH

Los sonidos del español *(lohs soh-'nee-dohs dehl eh-spah-'nyohl)*

As a beginner in the language, your first step is to learn what Spanish sounds like. Fortunately, you don't have to pronounce everything correctly in order to be understood. Not only are people generally forgiving, but in reality there aren't that many differences between the two sound systems. In fact, you'll need to remember only *five* sounds to speak well enough to be understood. These are the vowels, and unlike their English equivalents, each one is pronounced the way it is written. Go ahead—read each letter aloud, and follow the corresponding pronunciation guide:

a *(ah)*   as in yacht
e *(eh)*   as in met
i *(ee)*   as in keep
o *(oh)*   as in open
u *(oo)*   as in tool

Now, let's learn how to pronounce all the other letters. And, remember—each letter has its own unique sound:

Spanish Letter	English Sound
c (after an e or i)	s as in sit (**cigarro**) *(see-'gah-rroh)*
g (after an e or i)	h as in hop (**general**) *(heh-neh-'rahl)*
h	silent, like k in knives (**hombre**) *('ohm-breh)*
j	h as in hat (**Julio**) *('hoo-lee·oh)*
ll	y as in yes (**pollo**) *('poh-yoh)*
ñ	ny as in canyon (**señor**) *(seh-'nyohr)*
qu	k as in kit (**tequila**) *(teh-'kee-lah)*
rr	the rolled r sound (**burro**) *('boo-rroh)*
v	v as in volt (**viva**) *('vee-vah)*
z	s as in son (**zapato**) *(sah-'pah-toh)*

Although some dialects may vary slightly, the rest of the letters in Spanish are similar to their equivalents in English:

b	bueno *('bweh-noh)*	p	pronto *('prohn-toh)*
d	dinero *(dee-'neh-roh)*	r	tres *(trehs)*
f	flan *(flahn)*	s	sí *(see)*
l	loco *('loh-koh)*	t	taco *('tah-koh)*
m	mucho *('moo-choh)*	x	éxito *('ehk-see-toh)*
n	nada *('nah-dah)*		

Now, read the following words aloud, and then guess at their meanings. Don't forget that each letter needs to be pronounced the way it was introduced earlier:

amigo	*(ah-'mee-goh)*
burro	*('boo-rroh)*
Cinco de Mayo	*('seen-koh deh 'mah-yoh)*
escuela	*(eh-'skweh-lah)*
español	*(eh-'spah-'nyohl)*
estudiante	*(eh-stoo-dee-'ahn-teh)*
excelente	*(ehk-seh-'lehn-teh)*
Feliz Navidad	*(feh-'lees nah-vee-'dahd)*
problema	*(proh-'bleh-mah)*
profesor	*(proh-feh-'sohr)*
televisión	*(teh-leh-vee-see-'ohn)*
tortilla	*(tohr-'tee-yah)*

MÁS INFORMACIÓN

➤ Any part of a word with an accent mark (´) needs to be pronounced LOUDER and with more emphasis (i.e., María) *(mah-'ree·ah)*. If there's no accent mark, say the last part of the word louder and with more emphasis (i.e., Beatriz) *(beh-ah-'trees)*. For words ending in a vowel, or in n or s, the next to the last syllable is stressed (i.e., Fernando) *(fehr-'nahn-doh)*.

➤ In some cases, the letter u doesn't make the "oo" sound (i.e., guitarra *[gee-'tah-rrah]* or guerra *['geh-rrah]*).

In the world of education, there are occasions when the best way to communicate is through the written word. In those cases, you may have to depend on your spelling skills in Spanish. Fortunately, the language is spelled the way it is pronounced. So, if you know your alphabet in Spanish, you are in pretty good shape. Try practicing these letters aloud:

a *(ah)*	f *('eh-feh)*
b *(beh 'grahn-deh)*	g *(heh)*
c *(seh)*	h *('ah-cheh)*
ch *(cheh)*	i *(ee)*
d *(deh)*	j *('hoh-tah)*
e *(eh)*	k *(kah)*

l (*'eh-leh*)	rr (*'eh-rreh*)
ll (*'eh-yeh*)	s (*'eh-seh*)
m (*'eh-meh*)	t (*teh*)
n (*'eh-neh*)	u (*oo*)
ñ (*'eh-nyeh*)	v (*'veh 'chee-kah*)
o (*oh*)	w (*veh 'doh-bleh*)
p (*peh*)	x (*'eh-kees*)
q (*koo*)	y (*ee-gree-'eh-gah*)
r (*'eh-reh*)	z (*'seh-tah*)

 ¿LISTOS PARA PRACTICAR?

If you're having problems with the sounds of Spanish, try listening to the language for a few minutes each day. Spanish radio and TV stations (as well as all the great stuff found on the Internet) are fun yet effective ways to become familiar with your new pronunciation patterns.

KEY EXPRESSIONS
Las expresiones claves (*lahs ehk-spreh-see-'oh-nehs 'klah-vehs*)

The best way to get started in Spanish is to try out your new sounds in everyday conversations. Regardless of your situation, these basic expressions are a must for every Spanish student.

Excuse me!	¡Con permiso! *(kohn pehr-'mee-soh)*
Go ahead!	¡Pase! *('pah-seh)*
I'm sorry!	¡Lo siento! *(loh see-'ehn-toh)*
Thanks a lot!	¡Muchas gracias! *('moo-chahs 'grah-see·ahs)*
Please!	¡Por favor! *(pohr fah-'vohr)*
Yes!	¡Sí! *(see)*
You're welcome!	¡De nada! *(deh 'nah-dah)*
Hi!	¡Hola! *('oh-lah)*
Good morning!	¡Buenos días! *('bweh-nohs 'dee·ahs)*
Good afternoon!	¡Buenas tardes! *('bweh-nahs 'tahr-dehs)*
Good evening!/Good night!	¡Buenas noches! *('bweh-nahs 'noh-chehs)*
Good-bye!	¡Adiós! *(ah-dee-'ohs)*
See you later!	¡Hasta luego! *('ah-stah loo-'eh-goh)*
How are you!	¿Cómo está? *('koh-moh eh-'stah)*
What's happening?	¿Qué pasa? *('keh 'pah-sah)*
How's it going?	¿Qué tal? *(keh tahl)*
Nice to meet you!	¡Mucho gusto! *('moo-choh 'goo-stoh)*
Fine, thanks!	¡Bien, gracias! *('bee·ehn 'grah-see·ahs)*
And you?	¿Y usted? *(ee oo-'stehd)*
Very good!	¡Muy bien! *('moo·ee 'bee·ehn)*
Nothing much!	¡Sin novedad! *('seen noh-veh-'dahd)*
Same to you!	¡Igualmente! *(ee-gwahl-'mehn-teh)*
Me, too!	¡Yo tambien! *(yoh tahm-bee-'ehn)*

 MÁS INFORMACIÓN

➤ Several words in English are spelled the same in Spanish, and they usually have the same meaning. But, watch out! They are NOT pronounced the same!

chocolate *(choh-koh-'lah-teh)*
color *(koh-'lohr)*
final *(fee-'nahl)*
idea *(ee-'deh-ah)*
natural *(nah-too-'rahl)*
terror *(teh-'rrohr)*

➤ The upside down exclamation point (¡) and question mark (¿) are found at the beginning of sentences, and must be used when you write in Spanish.

➤ Scan these other "excuse me" phrases:

Excuse me! (if you cough or sneeze) ¡Perdón! *(pehr-'dohn)*
Excuse me! (if you need someone's attention) ¡Disculpe! *(dees-'kool-peh)*

➤ Look! Some words change meanings if you drop the accent mark:

yes	sí (see)	if	si (see)
how	cómo *('koh-moh)*	I eat	como *('koh-moh)*
give	dé *(deh)*	from	de *(deh)*
what?	¿Qué? *(keh)*	that	que *(keh)*

DIFERENCIAS CULTURALES

Friendly greetings in Spanish are used all day long. Being courteous is the key to establishing trust with your students and their families. Throughout the Spanish-speaking world, a smile and a pleasant word can lead to respect and complete cooperation.

¿LISTOS PARA PRACTICAR?

Practice this dialogue with a friend:

Hola. *('oh-lah)*
¿Qué pasa? *('keh 'pah-sah)*
¿Cómo está? *('koh-moh eh-'stah)*

Muy bien. Hasta luego.
*('moo·ee 'bee·ehn. 'ah-stah
loo-'eh-goh)*

Buenas tardes. *('bweh-nahs 'tahr-dehs)*
Sin novedad. *(seen noh-veh-'dahd)*
Bien, gracias. ¿Y usted? *('bee·ehn,
'grah-see·ahs. ee oo-'stehd)*
Adiós. *('ah-dee-'ohs)*

MORE ESSENTIAL PHRASES
Más frases esenciales *(mahs 'frah-sehs eh-sehn-see-'ah-lehs)*

Spanish is full of common expressions that are used regularly in normal conversations. A lot can be communicated simply by saying a few short phrases. Interject one of these whenever it is appropriate:

Don't worry.	**No se preocupe.** *(noh seh preh-oh-'koo-peh)*
Good idea.	**Buena idea.** *('bweh-nah ee-'deh-ah)*
I see.	**Ya veo.** *(yah 'veh-oh)*
I think so.	**Creo que sí.** *('kreh-oh keh see)*
Maybe.	**Quizás.** *(kee-'sahs)*
More or less.	**Más o menos.** *(mahs oh 'meh-nohs)*
Not yet.	**Todavía no.** *(toh-dah-'vee·ah noh)*
Ready?	**¿Listo?** *('lee-stoh)*
Sure.	**Claro.** *('klah-roh)*
That depends.	**Depende.** *(deh-'pehn-deh)*

Put a little more emotion into these!

Bless you!	**¡Salud!** *(sah-'lood)*
Congratulations!	**¡Felicitaciones!** *(feh-lee-see-tah-see-'oh-nehs)*
Good luck!	**¡Buena suerte!** *('bweh-nah 'swehr-teh)*
Happy Birthday!	**¡Feliz cumpleaños!** *(feh-'lees koom-pleh-'ah-nyohs)*
Welcome!	**¡Bienvenidos!** *('bee·ehn veh-'nee-dohs)*
Wow!	**¡Caramba!** *(kah-'rahm-bah)*
For heaven's sake!	**¡Dios mío!** *('dee·ohs 'mee·oh)*

Bear in mind that most idiomatic expressions cannot be translated word for word. Therefore, try to memorize each phrase as one long string of individual sounds.

MÁS INFORMACIÓN

➤ The word **Qué** *(keh)* is often part of an emotional comment:

What a shame!	**¡Qué lástima!** *(keh 'lah-stee-mah)*
That's great!	**¡Qué bueno!** *(keh 'bweh-noh)*
How funny!	**¡Qué chistoso!** *(keh chee-'stoh-soh)*

➤ And don't forget these holidays:

Merry Christmas!	¡Feliz Navidad! *(feh-'lees nah-vee-'dahd)*
Happy New Year!	¡Feliz año nuevo! *(feh-'lees 'ah-nyoh noo-'eh-voh)*
Happy Easter!	¡Felices pascuas! *(feh-'lee-sehs 'pah-skwahs)*

➤ There are several ways to say good-bye in Spanish, so continue to wave and shout:

Have a nice day!	¡Que le vaya bien! *(keh leh vah-yah bee-'ehn)*
We'll see you!	¡Nos vemos! *(nohs 'veh-mohs)*
Go with God!	¡Vaya con Dios! *('vah-yah kohn dee-'ohs)*

¿LISTOS PARA PRACTICAR?

Connect each phrase with its appropriate response. No answers are provided in this section, so you'll have to look them up on your own!

Qué lástima. *(keh 'lah-stee-mah)*	Todavía no. *(toh-dah-'vee·ah noh)*
Mucho gusto. *('moo-choh 'goo-stoh)*	Nos vemos. *(nohs 'veh-mohs)*
¿Cómo está? *('koh-moh eh-'stah)*	Salud. *(sah-'lood)*
Gracias. *('grah-see·ahs)*	De nada. *(deh 'nah-dah)*
¡Ah-choo! *(ah-'choo)*	Bien. ¿Y usted? *('bee·ehn ee oo-'stehd)*
Hasta luego. *('ah-stah loo-'eh-goh)*	Igualmente. *(ee-gwahl-'mehn-teh)*
¿Listo? *('lee-stoh)*	Lo siento. *(loh see-'ehn-toh)*

DO YOU SPEAK SPANISH?
¿Habla usted español? *('ah-blah oo-'stehd eh-spah-'nyohl)*

Once you finish with the greetings and common courtesies, you will face the inevitable problem of not being able to understand one another. To make things easier, try to pronounce a few of these one-liners. They send the message that you are doing the best you can!

Again.	Otra vez. *('oh-trah vehs)*
Do you understand?	¿Entiende? *(ehn-tee-'ehn-deh)*
How do you say it?	¿Cómo se dice? *('koh-moh seh'dee-seh)*
How do you spell it?	¿Cómo se deletrea? *('koh-moh seh deh-leh-'treh-ah)*

I don't understand!	¡No entiendo! *(noh ehn-tee-'ehn-doh)*
I'm learning Spanish.	Estoy aprendiendo español. *(eh-'stoh-ee ah-prehn-dee-'ehn-doh eh-spah-'nyohl)*
I speak a little Spanish.	Hablo poquito español. *('ah-bloh poh-'kee-toh eh-spah-'nyohl)*
More slowly!	¡Más despacio! *(mahs deh-'spah-see·oh)*
Thanks for your patience.	Gracias por su paciencia. *('grah-see·ahs pohr soo pah-see-'ehn-see·ah)*
What does it mean?	¿Qué significa? *(keh seeg-nee-'fee-kah)*
Word by word!	¡Palabra por palabra! *(pah-'lah-brah pohr pah-'lah-brah)*
Please repeat.	Repita, por favor. *(reh-'pee-tah, pohr fah-'vohr)*

Seriously consider posting these expressions nearby. They can help you out if you ever get into trouble!

NECESSARY VOCABULARY
El vocabulario necesario *(ehl voh-kah-boo-'lah-ree·oh neh-seh-'sah-ree·oh)*

It's impossible to carry on intelligent conversations in Spanish without the basic vocabulary words. To learn them quickly, let's list the terms under specific categories. And, as you read each series, try to pronounce everything correctly. Good luck!

Everyday Things	Las cosas diarias *(lahs 'koh-sahs dee-'ah-ree·ahs)*
bed	la cama *(lah 'kah-mah)*
book	el libro *(ehl 'lee-broh)*
car	el carro *(ehl 'kah-rroh)*
chair	la silla *(lah 'see-yah)*
classroom	la clase *(lah 'klah-seh)*
computer	la computadora *(lah kohm-poo-tah-'doh-rah)*
desk	el escritorio *(ehl ehs-kree-'toh-ree·oh)*
door	la puerta *(lah 'pwehr-tah)*
floor	el piso *(ehl 'pee-soh)*
food	la comida *(lah koh-'mee-dah)*
homework	la tarea *(lah tah-'reh-ah)*
house	la casa *(lah 'kah-sah)*
light	la luz *(lah loos)*
office	la oficina *(lah oh-fee-'see-nah)*
paper	el papel *(ehl pah-'pehl)*

pen	el lapicero *(ehl lah-pee-'seh-roh)*
pencil	el lápiz *(ehl 'lah-pees)*
restroom	el servicio *(ehl sehr-'vee-see·oh)*
room	el cuarto *(ehl 'kwahr-toh)*
school	la escuela *(lah eh-'skweh-lah)*
table	la mesa *(lah 'meh-sah)*
telephone	el teléfono *(ehl teh-'leh-foh-noh)*
trash can	el cesto de basura *(ehl 'sehs-toh deh bah-'soo-rah)*
water	el agua *(ehl 'ah-gwah)*
window	la ventana *(lah vehn-'tah-nah)*
work	el trabajo *(ehl trah-'bah-hoh)*

People	La gente *(la 'hehn-teh)*
baby	el/la bebé *(ehl/la beh-'beh)*
boy	el niño *(ehl 'nee-nyoh)*
brother	el hermano *(ehl ehr-'mah-noh)*
daughter	la hija *(lah 'ee-hah)*
father	el padre *(ehl 'pah-dreh)*
girl	la niña *(lah 'nee-nyah)*
man	el hombre *(ehl 'ohm-breh)*
mother	la madre *(lah 'mah-dreh)*
person	la persona *(lah pehr-'soh-nah)*
sister	la hermana *(lah ehr-'mah-nah)*
son	el hijo *(ehl 'ee-hoh)*
student	el estudiante *(ehl eh-stoo-dee-'ahn-teh)*
teacher	el maestro *(ehl mah-'eh-stroh)*
teenager (female)	la muchacha *(lah moo-'chah-chah)*
teenager (male)	el muchacho *(ehl moo-'chah-choh)*
woman	la mujer *(lah moo-'hehr)*

The Colors	Los colores *(lohs koh-'loh-rehs)*
black	negro *('neh-groh)*
blue	azul *(ah-'sool)*
brown	café *(kah-'feh)*
green	verde *('vehr-deh)*
orange	anaranjado *(ah-nah-rahn-'hah-doh)*
purple	morado *(moh-'rah-doh)*
red	rojo *('roh-hoh)*
white	blanco *('blahn-koh)*
yellow	amarillo *(ah-mah-'ree-yoh)*

More Important Words	Más palabras importantes *(mahs pah-'lah-brahs eem-pohr-'tahn-tehs)*
a few	pocos *('poh-kohs)*
a little	poco *('poh-koh)*
all	todo *('toh-doh)*
bad	malo *('mah-loh)*
big	grande *('grahn-deh)*
good	bueno *('bweh-noh)*
less	menos *('meh-nohs)*
many	muchos *('moo-chohs)*
more	más *(mahs)*
much	mucho *('moo-choh)*
small	pequeño *(peh-'keh-nyoh)*

 ## MÁS INFORMACIÓN

➤ Notice that the names for people, places, and things are either masculine or feminine, and so have either el *(ehl)* or la *(lah)* in front. El and la mean "the." Generally, if the word ends in the letter o there's an el in front; i.e., el cuarto *(ehl 'kwahr-toh)*, el niño *(ehl 'nee-nyoh)*. Conversely, if the word ends in an a there's a la in front; i.e., la mesa *(lah 'meh-sah)*, la persona *(lah pehr-'soh-nah)*. Some Spanish words are exceptions: el agua *(ehl 'ah-gwah)*, el sofá *(ehl soh-'fah)*.

➤ Words not ending in either an o or a need to be memorized; i.e., el amor *(ehl ah-'mohr)*, la luz *(lah loos)*. In the case of single objects, use el and la much like the word "the" in English: The house is big (la casa es grande) *(lah 'kah-sah ehs 'grahn-deh)*.

➤ Remember, too, that el and la are used in Spanish to indicate a person's gender. El maestro *(ehl mah-'eh-stroh)* is a male teacher, while la maestra *(lah mah-'ehs-trah)* is a female teacher. Words ending in e usually do not change on account of gender: you usually identify them by putting el or la in front. La estudiante *(lah eh-stoo-dee-'ahn-teh)* is a female student, whereas el estudiante is a male student.

➤ One effective method to remember the names for things is to write their names on removable stickers and then place them on the objects you are trying to remember.

➤ Be aware that there are other names in Spanish for the items listed below. Here are a few synonyms you should know:

teacher   el profesor *(ehl proh-feh-'sohr)* or
                 la profesora *(lah proh-feh-'soh-rah)*

desk   el pupitre *(ehl poo-'peeh-treh)*

student   el alumno *(ehl ah-'loom-noh)* or
                 la alumna *(lah ah'loom-nah)*

young person   el chico *(ehl 'chee-koh)* or
                 la chica *(lah'chee-kah)*

man   el señor *(ehl seh-'nyohr)*

woman   la señora *(lah seh-'nyoh-rah)*

pen   la pluma *(lah 'ploo-mah)*

car   el coche *(ehl 'koh-cheh)*

 ## ¿LISTOS PARA PRACTICAR?

Fill in the blank with an English translation:

el lápiz *(ehl 'lah-pees)*   _____

el libro *(ehl 'lee-broh)*   _____

la mesa *(lah 'meh-sah)*   _____

el trabajo *(ehl trah-'bah-hoh)*   _____

la escuela *(lah eh-'skweh-lah)*   _____

Now match the opposites:

padre *('pah-dreh)*   maestro *(mah-'eh-stroh)*
pequeño *(peh-'keh-nyoh)*   mujer *(moo-'hehr)*
hombre *('ohm-breh)*   negro *('neh-groh)*
blanco *('blahn-koh)*   grande *('grahn-deh)*
estudiante *(eh-stoo-dee-'ahn-teh)*   madre *('mah-dreh)*

NUMBERS

Los números *(lohs 'noo-meh-rohs)*

No one can survive in Spanish without the numbers, so say each of these words more than once:

0	cero *('seh-roh)*	14	catorce *(kah-'tohr-seh)*
1	uno *('oo-noh)*	15	quince *('keen-seh)*
2	dos *(dohs)*	16	dieciséis *(dee-ehs-ee-'seh·ees)*
3	tres *(trehs)*	17	diecisiete *(dee-ehs-ee-see-'eh-teh)*
4	cuatro *('kwah-troh)*	18	dieciocho *(dee-ehs-ee-'oh-choh)*
5	cinco *('seen-koh)*	19	diecinueve *(dee-ehs-ee-noo-'eh-veh)*
6	seis *('seh·ees)*	20	veinte *('veh·een-teh)*
7	siete *(see-'eh-teh)*	30	treinta *('treh·een-tah)*
8	ocho *('oh-choh)*	40	cuarenta *(kwah-'rehn-tah)*
9	nueve *(noo-'eh-veh)*	50	cincuenta *(seen-'kwehn-tah)*
10	diez *(dee-'ehs)*	60	sesenta *(seh-'sehn-tah)*
11	once *('ohn-seh)*	70	setenta *(seh-'tehn-tah)*
12	doce *('doh-seh)*	80	ochenta *(oh-'chehn-tah)*
13	trece *('treh-seh)*	90	noventa *(noh-'vehn-tah)*

For all the numbers in-between, just add "y" (ee), which means "and":

21 veinte y uno *('veh·een-teh ee 'oo-noh)*
22 veinte y dos *('veh·een-teh ee dohs)*
21 veinte y tres *('veh·een-teh ee trehs)*

Sooner or later, you'll also need to know how to say the larger numbers in Spanish. They aren't that difficult, so practice aloud:

100	cien *('see-ehn)*
200	doscientos *(dohs-see-'ehn-tohs)*
300	trescientos *(trehs-see-'ehn-tohs)*
400	cuatrocientos *(kwah-troh-see-'ehn-tohs)*
500	quinientos *(keen-ee-'ehn-tohs)*
600	seiscientos *(seh·ees-see-'ehn-tohs)*
700	setecientos *(seh-teh-see-'ehn-tohs)*
800	ochocientos *(oh-choh-see-'ehn-tohs)*
900	novecientos *(noh-veh-see-'ehn-tohs)*
1000	mil *(meel)*

And here's how you put them together: 3.756 = tres mil setecientos cincuenta y seis

➤ The ordinal numbers are valuable, too! Practice:

first	**primero** (*pree-'meh-roh*)
second	**segundo** (*seh-'goon-doh*)
third	**tercero** (*tehr-'seh-roh*)
fourth	**cuarto** (*'kwahr-toh*)
fifth	**quinto** (*'keen-toh*)
sixth	**sexto** (*'sehks-toh*)
seventh	**séptimo** (*'sehp-tee-moh*)
eighth	**octavo** (*ohk-'tah-voh*)
ninth	**noveno** (*noh-'veh-noh*)
tenth	**décimo** (*'deh-see-moh*)

➤ Look at what you can say now. By the way, "first" and "third" lose a letter when they go before a noun:

first grade	**primer grado** (*pree-'mehr 'grah-doh*)
second grade	**segundo grado** (*seh-'goon-doh 'grah-doh*)
third grade	**tercer grado** (*tehr-'sehr 'grah-doh*)

➤ Are you ready to form a few phrases? You'll need the following:

for	**para** (*'pah-rah*)	**para la clase** (*'pah-rah lah 'klah-seh*)
in, on, at	**en** (*ehn*)	**en el cuarto** (*ehn ehl 'kwahr-toh*)
of, from	**de** (*deh*)	**de la persona** (*deh lah pehr-'soh-nah*)
to	**a** (*ah*)	**a la oficina** (*ah lah oh-fee-'see-nah*)
with	**con** (*kohn*)	**con el agua** (*kohn ehl 'ah-gwah*)
without	**sin** (*seen*)	**sin el carro** (*seen ehl 'kah-rroh*)

➤ There are only two contractions in Spanish:

to the	**al** (*ahl*)	**al hombre** (*ahl 'ohm-breh*)
of the, from the	**del** (*dehl*)	**del libro** (*dehl 'lee-broh*)

➤ Use these words to link everything together:

and = y *(ee)*   or = o *(oh)*   but = pero *('peh-roh)*

Thank you and good-bye!
¡Gracias y adiós! *('grah-see·ahs ee ah-dee-'ohs)*

DIFERENCIAS CULTURALES

If you get stuck in the middle of a phrase or sentence, don't be afraid to send messages using hand gestures or facial expressions. Body signals are used frequently in conversations throughout the Spanish-speaking world. And remember, there's nothing wrong with repeating your message several times until you're understood!

FOLLOW THE RULES!
¡Siga las reglas! *('see-gah lahs 'reh-glahs)*

Certain grammatical rules must be followed. In Spanish, these two should always be taken seriously:

1) The Reverse Order Rule:

As you begin to link your Spanish words together, you will find that sometimes words are positioned in reverse order (as compared to English). This Reverse Rule is applied when you give a description. The descriptive word goes after the word being described. Study these examples.

The big house.	La casa grande. *(lah 'kah-sah 'grahn-deh)*
The green chair.	La silla verde. *(lah 'see-yah 'vehr-deh)*
The important teacher.	El maestro importante. *(ehl mah-'eh-stroh eem-pohr-'tahn-teh)*

2) The Agreement Rule:

Here's another rule that must be followed when you are referring to more than one item in Spanish. First, the words el *(ehl)* and la *(lah)* (see page 11), become los *(lohs)* and las *(lahs)*, respectively.

15

el estudiante *(ehl eh-stoo-dee-'ahn-teh)*	los estudiantes *(lohs eh-stoo-dee-'ahn-tehs)*
la mesa *(lah 'meh-sah)*	las mesas *(lahs 'meh-sahs)*
la silla *(lah 'see-yah)*	las sillas *(lahs 'see-yahs)*
el servicio *(ehl sehr-'vee-see·oh)*	los servicios *(lohs sehr-'vee-see·ohs)*

Second, not only do all nouns and adjectives need to end in **s** or **es** to make the sentence plural, but when they are used together, the genders (the **o** and **a** endings), must match as well.

two white doors	**dos puertas blancas** *(dohs 'pwehr-tahs 'blahn-kahs)*
many red cars	**muchos carros rojos** *('moo-chohs 'kah-rrohs 'roh-hohs)*
six little children	**seis niños pequeños** *('seh·ees 'nee-nyohs peh-'keh-nyohs)*

By the way, to say "a" or "an" in Spanish, use **un** *(oon)* or **una** *('oo-nah)*:

a student	**un estudiante** *(oon eh-stoo-dee-'ahn-teh)*
	un estudiante americano *(oon eh-stoo-dee-'ahn-teh ah-meh-ree-'kah-noh)*
a window	**una ventana** *('oo-nah vehn-'tah-nah)*
	una ventana blanca *('oo-nah vehn-'tah-nah 'blahn-kah)*

And to say "some" or "a few," use **unos** *('oo-nohs)* or **unas** *('oo-nahs)*:

some students	**unos estudiantes** *('oo-nohs eh-stoo-dee-'ahn-tehs)*
	unos estudiantes americanos *('oo-nohs eh-stoo-dee-'ahn-tehs ah-meh-ree-'kah-nohs)*
a few windows	**unas ventanas** *('oo-nahs vehn-'tah-nahs)*
	unas ventanas blancas *('oo-nahs vehn-'tah-nahs 'blahn-kahs)*

Remember that a combined group of males and females always take the masculine article:

Dos profesores y tres profesoras *(dohs proh-feh-'soh-rehs ee trehs proh-feh-'soh-rahs)*	→ **unos profesores** *('oo-nohs proh-feh-'soh-rehs)*
El niño y la niña *(ehl 'neen-yoh ee lah 'neen-yah)*	→ **los niños** *(lohs 'neen-yohs)*

Fill in the missing number in each series:

treinta, cuarenta, _____, sesenta *('treh·een-tah, kwah-'rehn-*

tah, _____, seh-'sehn-tah)

primero, segundo, tercero, _____, *(pree-'meh-roh, seh-'goon-*

doh, tehr-'seh-roh, _____)

_____, cinco, seis, siete *(_____, 'seen-koh,*

'seh·ees, see-'eh-teh)

Write the Spanish translation for these words:

with _____

on _____

to the _____

Follow the example. Change these from the singular to the plural:

el carro grande
(ehl 'kah-rroh 'grahn-deh)

los carros grandes
(lohs 'kah-rrohs 'grahn-dehs)

la silla roja
('lah 'see-yah 'roh-hah)

_____

un hombre importante
(oon 'ohm-breh eem-pohr-'tahn-teh)

_____

la oficina blanca
(lah oh-fee-'see-nah 'blahn-kah)

_____

una clase pequeña
('oo-nah 'klah-seh peh-'keh-nyah)

_____

THE QUESTIONS
Las preguntas *(lahs preh-'goon-tahs)*

The following set of Spanish questions should be memorized right away. See if you can recognize any of these from the expressions we learned earlier:

How many?	¿Cuántos? *('kwahn-tohs)*
How much?	¿Cuánto? *('kwahn-toh)*
How?	¿Cómo? *('koh-moh)*
What?	¿Qué? *(keh)*
When?	¿Cuándo? *('kwahn-doh)*
Where?	¿Dónde? *('dohn-deh)*
Which?	¿Cuál? *(kwahl)*
Who?	¿Quién? *(kee-'ehn)*
Whose?	¿De quién? *(deh kee-'ehn)*
Why?	¿Por qué? *(pohr keh)*

Now, cover up the right column and try to translate without looking. How many can you remember?

MÁS INFORMACIÓN

➤ A few questions are actually common one-liners used regularly in simple conversations. Notice how they are not literal translations.

How's it going?	¿Qué tal? *(keh tahl)*
What's your name?	¿Cómo se llama? *('koh-moh seh 'yah-mah)*
How old are you?	¿Cuántos años tiene? *('kwahn-tohs 'ah-nyohs tee-'eh-neh)*

POWERFUL PRONOUNS!
¡Los pronombres poderosos! *(lohs proh-'nohm-brehs poh-deh-'roh-sohs)*

Students and their families will ask who everybody is. This is the quickest way to respond:

I	Yo *(yoh)*
We	Nosotros *(noh-'soh-trohs)*
You	Usted *(oo-'stehd)*
You (plural)	Ustedes *(oo-'steh-dehs)*
She	Ella *('eh-yah)*
He	El *(ehl)*
They (feminine)	Ellas *('eh-yahs)*
They (masculine)	Ellos *('eh-yohs)*

Practice:

She's from Mexico.	Ella es de Mexico. *('eh-yah ehs deh 'meh-hee-koh)*
How are you?	¿Cómo está usted? *('koh-moh eh-'stah oo-'stehd)*
I am learning.	Yo estoy aprendiendo. *(yoh eh-'stoh-ee ah-prehn-dee-'ehn-doh)*

The *TÚ* Form

The word **tú** *(too)* is the informal way of saying "you" in Spanish. This casual form is generally used among family and friends, but can be used when an adult addresses a child. Here are some examples:

You are my friend.	Tú eres mi amigo. *(too 'eh-rehs mee ah-'mee-goh)*
Do you speak Spanish?	¿Tú hablas español? *(too 'ah-blahs ehs-pah-'nyohl)*
How are you?	¿Cómo estás tú? *('koh-moh ehs-'tahs too)*
And you?	¿Y tú? *(ee too)*
Do you understand?	¿Entiendes tú? *(ehn-tee-'ehn-dehs too)*

MÁS INFORMACIÓN

➤ Nosotras *(noh-'soh-trahs)* is "We" feminine:

   ¿Ustedes? *(oo-'steh-dehs)*   ¡Sí, nosotras! *(see, noh-'soh-trahs)*

➤ Would any of the following words be helpful? Of course! Think of ways these can be used to answer school-related questions:

someone	alguien *('ahl-gee·ehn)*
something	algo *('ahl-goh)*
somewhere	por alguna parte *(pohr ahl-'goo-nah 'pahr-teh)*

anyone	cualquiera *(kwahl-kee-'eh-rah)*
anything	cualquier cosa *(kwahl-kee-'ehr 'koh-sah)*
anywhere	en cualquier parte *(ehn kwahl-kee-'ehr 'pahr-teh)*

everyone	todos *('toh-dohs)*
everything	todo *('toh-doh)*
everywhere	por todas partes *(pohr 'toh-dahs 'pahr-tehs)*

no one	nadie *('nah-dee·eh)*
nothing	nada *('nah-dah)*
nowhere	por ninguna parte *(pohr neen-'goo-nah 'pahr-teh)*

Yo soy excelente maestro. Estoy aprendiendo mucho español.

WHOSE IS IT?
¿De quién es? *(deh kee-'ehn ehs)*

A similar group of Spanish words is used to indicate possession. They tell us "whose" it is:

It's my desk.	Es mi escritorio. *(ehs mee eh-skree-'toh-ree·oh)*
It's your, his, her, or their desk.	Es su escritorio. *(ehs soo eh-skree-'toh-ree·oh)*
It's our desk.	Es nuestro escritorio. *(ehs noo-'eh-stroh eh-skree-'toh-ree·oh)*

Notice what happens to pronouns when you talk about more than one:

mi escritorio *(mee eh-skree-'toh-ree·oh)*	mis escritorios *(mees eh-skree-'toh-ree·ohs)*
su escritorio *(soo eh-skree-'toh-ree·oh)*	sus escritorios *(soos eh-skree-'toh-ree·ohs)*
nuestro escritorio *(noo-'eh-stroh eh-skree-'toh-ree·oh)*	nuestros escritorios *(noo-'eh-strohs eh-skree-'toh-ree·ohs)*

The informal way to express *your* (adjective) is tu, which is spelled the same way as the personal pronoun *you* (tú), but without the accent.

It's your desk.	Es tu escritorio *(ehs too ehs-kree-'toh'ree·oh)*

Now try these other possessive words. Are you able to translate the sentences?

mine	mío or mía *('mee·oh, 'mee·ah)* Es mío. *(ehs 'mee·oh)*
yours, his, hers, theirs	suyo or suya *('soo-yoh, 'soo-yah)* Es suya. *(ehs 'soo-yah)*
yours (inf. sing.)	tuyo or tuya *('too-yoh, 'too-yah)* Es tuyo. *(ehs 'too-yoh)*

By the way, if something belongs to someone else, you can also use de to indicate possession:

It's Mary's.	Es de María. *(ehs deh mah-'ree·ah)*
It's the school's.	Es de la escuela. *(ehs deh lah ehs-'kweh-lah)*
It's his.	Es de él. *(ehs deh ehl)*

➤ Don't be afraid to answer simple questions with brief, effective responses. Notice these examples:

¿Cuántos? *('kwahn-tohs)*	Muchos. *('moo-chohs)*
¿Quién? *(kee-'ehn)*	Ella. *('eh-yah)*
¿Dónde? *('dohn-deh)*	San Antonio. *(sahn ahn-'toh-nee·oh)*

¿LISTOS PARA PRACTICAR?

Connect the names with the corresponding pronouns:

Laura	ustedes *(oo-'steh-dehs)*
Francisco	nosotros *(noh-'soh-trohs)*
Carolina y yo	ellos *('eh-yohs)*
Raul y Paula	él *(ehl)*
Samuel y usted	ella *('eh-yah)*

ESTÁ and ES
(eh-'stah) and *(ehs)*

Now that you can form short phrases on your own, it's time to join all of your words together. To accomplish this, you'll need to understand the difference between está *(eh-'stah)* and es *(ehs)*. Both words mean "is," but they're used differently.

The word está *(eh-'stah)* expresses a temporary state, condition, or location:

The girl is fine.	La niña está bien.
	(lah 'nee-nyah eh-'stah 'bee·ehn)
The girl is in the room.	La niña está en el cuarto.
	(lah 'nee-nyah eh-'stah ehn ehl 'kwahr-toh)

The word es *(ehs)* expresses an inherent characteristic or quality, including origin and ownership.

The girl is small.	**La niña es pequeña.**
	(lah 'nee-nyah ehs peh-'keh-nyah)
The girl is Maria.	**La niña es María.**
	(lah 'nee-nyah ehs mah-'ree·ah)
The girl is American.	**La niña es americana.**
	(lah 'nee-nyah ehs ah-meh-ree-'kah-nah)
The girl is my friend.	**La niña es mi amiga.**
	(lah 'nee-nyah ehs mee ah-'mee-gah)

Can you see how helpful these two words can be? Countless comments can be made with only a minimum of vocabulary. You'll also need to talk about more than one person, place, or thing. To do so, replace está *(eh-'stah)* with están *(eh-'stahn)*, and es *(ehs)* with son *(sohn)*. And don't forget that words must agree when you change to plurals.

The book is on the table.	**El libro está en la mesa.**
	(ehl 'lee-broh eh-'stah ehn
	lah 'meh-sah)
The books are on the table.	**Los libros están en la mesa.**
	(lohs 'lee-brohs eh-'stahn
	ehn lah 'meh-sah)
The book is important.	**El libro es importante.**
	(ehl 'lee-broh ehs eem-pohr-
	'tahn-teh)
The books are important.	**Los libros son importantes.**
	(lohs 'lee-brohs sohn eem-
	pohr-'tahn-tehs)

Check out these other examples. Read them aloud as you focus on their structure and meaning:

The chairs are black.	**Las sillas son negras.**
	(lahs 'see-yahs sohn 'neh-grahs)
The papers are at my house.	**Los papeles están en mi casa.**
	(lohs pah-'peh-lehs eh-'stahn ehn
	mee 'kah-sah)
They are not friends.	**No son amigos.**
	(noh sohn ah-'mee-gohs)

Are they good?   ¿Están buenos?
                                        (eh-'stahn 'bweh-nohs)

The best way to learn how to use these words correctly is to listen to Spanish speakers in real-life conversations. They constantly use **es** *(ehs),* **está** *(eh-'stah),* **son** *(sohn),* and **están** *(eh-'stahn)* to communicate everyday messages.

MÁS INFORMACIÓN

➤ A lot more can be said when you learn these vocabulary terms. Remember that they change according to gender:

that	**ese** *('eh-seh)* or **esa** *('eh-sah)*
	Ese muchacho está aquí.
	('eh-seh moo-'chah-choh ehs-'tah ah-'kee)
these	**estos** *('eh-stohs)* or **estas** *('eh-stahs)*
	Estos tacos están malos.
	('eh-stohs 'tah-kohs ehs-'tahn 'mah-lohs)
this	**este** *('eh-steh)* or **esta** *('eh-stah)*
	Este es mi papel amarillo.
	('eh-steh ehs mee pah-'pehl ah-mah-'ree-yoh)
those	**esos** *('eh-sohs)* or **esas** *('eh-sahs)*
	Esos son hombres buenos.
	('eh-sohs sohn 'ohm-brehs 'bweh-nohs)

I AM and WE ARE

Estoy-Soy and Estamos-Somos *(eh-'stoh·ee / 'soh·ee and eh-'stah-mohs / 'soh-mohs)*

To say "I am" and "We are" in Spanish, you must also acquire their different forms. As with **está** *(eh-'stah)* and **están** *(eh-'stahn),* the words **estoy** *(eh-'stoh·ee)* and **estamos** *(eh-'stah-mohs)* refer to the location or condition of a person, place, or thing. And just like **es** *(ehs)* and **son** *(sohn),* the words **soy** *('soh·ee)* and **somos** *('soh-mohs)* are used with everything else.

I am fine.	Estoy bien.
	(eh-'stoh·ee 'bee·ehn)
We are in the room.	Estamos en el cuarto.
	(eh-'stah-mohs ehn ehl 'kwahr-toh)
I am Lupe.	Soy Lupe.
	('soh·ee 'loo-peh)
We are Cuban.	Somos cubanos.
	('soh-mohs koo-'bah-nohs)

Now let's group all of these forms together. Look at these present tense forms of the verbs ESTAR *(eh-'stahr)* and SER *(sehr)*:

To be	Estar	Ser
I'm	estoy *(eh-'stoh·ee)*	soy *('soh·ee)*
You're *(informal)*	estás *(eh-'stahs)*	eres *('eh-rehs)*
You're *(formal)*, He's, She's	está *(eh-'stah)*	es *(ehs)*
You're *(pl.)*, They're	están *(eh-'stahn)*	son *(sohn)*
We're	estamos *(eh-'stah-mohs)*	somos *('soh-mohs)*

MÁS INFORMACION

➤ Notice that Spanish has both formal and informal verb forms (check the verb estar on the previous page). However, the informal plural form is rarely used in Latin America.

➤ You don't have to use the subject pronouns in every sentence. It's usually understood who's involved:

Nosotros somos *(noh-'soh-trohs 'soh-mohs)* and Somos *('soh-mohs)* both mean "We are."

➤ "There is" and "There are" are very easy in Spanish. In both cases you use the little word, hay *('ah·ee)* (pronounced "I").

| There's one class. | Hay una clase. *('ah·ee 'oo-nah 'klah-seh)* |
| There are two classes. | Hay dos clases. *('ah·ee dohs 'klah-sehs)* |

Join the subject pronouns with their possessive forms:

Ella *('eh-yah)*   mi *(mee)*
Yo *(yoh)*   nuestro *(noo-'eh-stroh)*
Nosotros *(noh-'soh-trohs)*   su *(soo)*

Translate into English:

¿Quién? *(kee-'ehn)*   _____

¿Cuántos? *('kwahn-tohs)*   _____

¿Dónde? *('dohn-deh)*   _____

Fill in each blank with the appropriate verb form:

está, son, hay, estoy, somos *(eh-'stah, sohn, 'ah·ee, eh-'stoh·ee, 'soh-mohs)*

Estos _____ muy buenos. *('eh-stohs _____ 'moo·ee 'bweh-nohs)*

Pedro _____ en la oficina. *('peh-droh _____ ehn lah oh-fee-'see-nah)*

Ella y yo _____ amigas. *('eh-yah ee yoh _____ ah-'mee-gahs)*

No _____ problema. *(noh _____ proh-'bleh-mah)*

Yo _____ bien. *('yoh _____ 'bee·ehn)*

TO HAVE
Tener *(teh-'nehr)*

Tener (to have) is another common linking word in Spanish, and its forms will become more necessary as you begin to create Spanish sentences on your own. Here are the basics to get you started:

I have	tengo *('tehn-goh)*
You *(informal)* have	tienes *(tee-'eh-nehs)*
You *(formal)* have, He has, She has	tiene *(tee-'eh-neh)*
You have (pl.), They have	tienen *(tee-'eh-nehn)*
We have	tenemos *(teh-'neh-mohs)*

Study these examples:

I have a pen.   **Tengo un lapicero.** *('tehn-goh oon lah-pee-'seh-roh)*

She has a white book.   **Tiene un libro blanco.** *(tee-'eh-neh oon 'lee-broh 'blahn-koh)*

They have twenty students.   **Tienen veinte estudiantes.** *(tee-'eh-nehn 'veh·een-teh eh-stoo-dee-'ahn-tehs)*

We have a big school.   **Tenemos una escuela grande.** *(teh-'neh-mohs 'oo-nah eh-'skweh-lah 'grahn-deh)*

 MÁS INFORMACIÓN

➤ Even though **tener** literally means to "have," sometimes it is used instead of the verb **estar** to express a temporary condition. Review these expressions as often as you can:

(I am) afraid	**(tengo) miedo** *('tehn-goh mee-'eh-doh)*
(we are) at fault	**(tenemos) la culpa** *(teh-'neh-mohs lah 'kool-pah)*
(they are) cold	**(tienen) frío** *(tee-'eh-nehn 'free·oh)*
(she is) 15 years old	**(tiene) quince años** *(tee-'eh-neh 'keen-seh 'ah-nyohs)*
(I am) hot	**(tengo) calor** *('tehn-goh kah-'lohr)*
(They are) hungry	**(tienen) hambre** *(tee-'eh-nehn 'ahm-breh)*
(he is) sleepy	**(tiene) sueño** *(tee-'eh-neh 'sweh-nyoh)*
(we are) thirsty	**(tenemos) sed** *(teh-'neh-mohs sehd)*

➤ To say *not* in Spanish, interject the word no in front of the verb:

Mr. Smith is not my teacher.	El Sr. Smith no es mi maestro. *(ehl seh-'nyohr eh-'smeeth noh ehs mee mah-'eh-stroh)*
I do not have the paper.	No tengo el papel. *(noh 'tehn-goh ehl pah-'pehl)*
There are no more chairs.	No hay más sillas. *(noh 'ah·ee mahs 'see-yahs)*

➤ Tienes *(tee-'eh-nehs)* is the informal way to say "you have":

My friend, do you have a car?	¿Amigo, tienes un carro? *(ee-'mee-goh, tee-'eh-nehs oon 'kah-rroh)*

MORE SPANISH VERBS

Más verbos en español *(mahs 'vehr-bohs ehn eh-spah-'nyohl)*

Putting a few words together in a new language is a thrilling experience, but real communication begins once you start using verbs or action words. Although estar, ser, and tener *(eh-'stahr, sehr, teh-'nehr)* are extremely useful, they do not express action. Learning how to use Spanish verbs will allow us to talk about what's going on in the world around us.

Spend a few moments memorizing this brief list of helpful beginning verbs. Notice that Spanish action words end in the letters -ar, -er, or -ir:

to come	venir *(veh-'neer)*
to drink	beber *(beh-'behr)*
to drive	manejar *(mah-neh-'hahr)*
to eat	comer *(koh-'mehr)*
to follow	seguir *(seh-'geer)*
to go	ir *(eer)*
to learn	aprender *(ah-prehn-'dehr)*
to listen	escuchar *(eh-skoo-'chahr)*
to look	mirar *(mee-'rahr)*
to play	jugar *(hoo-'gahr)*
to read	leer *(leh-'ehr)*
to run	correr *(koh-'rrehr)*
to sleep	dormir *(dohr-'meer)*
to speak	hablar *(ah-'blahr)*

to study	**estudiar** *(ehs-too-dee-'ahr)*
to understand	**entender** *(ehn-tehn-'dehr)*
to wait	**esperar** *(eh-speh-'rahr)*
to walk	**caminar** *(kah-mee-'nahr)*
to work	**trabajar** *(trah-bah-'hahr)*
to write	**escribir** *(eh-skree-'beer)*

 MÁS INFORMACIÓN

➤ You can never learn enough action words in Spanish. Over one hundred verbs are listed in the specialized dictionary at the end of this book, so use it as a reference tool. When you come across a verb as you study and practice, look it up in Spanish or English to learn its base form and meaning.

➤ Many Spanish verb infinitives that relate to education are similar to English. Look at these examples:

to communicate	**comunicar** *(koh-moo-nee-'kahr)*
to consult	**consultar** *(kohn-sool-'tahr)*
to converse	**conversar** *(kohn-vehr-'sahr)*
to observe	**observar** *(ohb-sehr-'vahr)*
to organize	**organizar** *(ohr-gah-nee-'sahr)*
to plan	**planear** *(plah-neh-'ahr)*
to practice	**practicar** *(prahk-tee-'kahr)*

THE SHORTCUTS
Los atajos *(lohs ah-'tah-hohs)*

Let's combine verbs with simple phrases to create complete sentences. For example, look what happens when you add these verb infinitives to **Favor de...** *(fah-'vohr deh),* which implies, "Would you please...":

Please ...	**Favor de...** *(fah-'vohr deh)*
write everything.	**escribir todo.** *(eh-skree-'beer 'toh-doh)*
read the paper.	**leer el papel.** *(leh-'ehr ehl pah-'pehl)*
speak in English.	**hablar en inglés.** *(ah-'blahr ehn een-'glehs)*

Here are some other shortcuts. By adding these formal phrases to verb infinitives or vocabulary, you can make statements, ask questions, or give commands. First read the phrase, and then try out the sample sentence:

Don't	No *(noh)*
Don't run.	No correr. *(noh koh-'rrehr)*
You have to	Tiene que *(tee-'eh-neh keh)*
You have to study.	Tiene que estudiar. *(tee-'eh-neh keh eh-stoo-dee-'ahr)*
You should	Debe *('deh-beh)*
You should read.	Debe leer. *('deh-beh leh-'ehr)*
I'm going to	Voy a *('voh·ee ah)*
I'm going to eat.	Voy a comer. *('voh·ee ah koh-'mehr)*
You need	Necesita *(neh-seh-'see-tah)*
You need to learn.	Necesita aprender. *(neh-seh-'see-tah ah-prehn-'dehr)*

You're doing great! This time, work on a few question phrases:

Do you want	Quiere *(kee-'eh-reh)*
Do you want to come?	¿Quiere venir? *(kee-'eh-reh veh-'neer)*
Can you	Puede *('pweh-deh)*
Can you wait?	¿Puede esperar? *('pweh-deh eh-speh-'rahr)*
Do you like	Le gusta *(leh 'goo-stah)*
Do you like to play?	¿Le gusta jugar? *(leh 'goo-stah hoo-'gahr)*

 MÁS INFORMACIÓN

➤ *Spanish For Educators* is full of these shortcut phrases, so jot them down now and start practicing right away!

➤ Check out these other one-liners. Add them to the verbs above if you need to:

One must	Hay que *('ah·ee keh)*
Do you prefer	Prefiere *(preh-fee-'eh-reh)*

I would like	Quisiera *(kee-see-'eh-rah)*
Let's	Vamos a *('vah-mohs ah)*
Could you	Podría *(poh-'dree·ah)*

➤ The informal verbal phrases are included in Chapter Three as educators communicate with younger children.

¿LISTOS PARA PRACTICAR?

Use forms of tener *(teh-'nehr)* to translate the following:

They are cold. _____

I don't have the book. _____

We are hungry. _____

Insert the verb infinitive that best fits each sentence:

comer, hablar, escribir, leer, escuchar *(koh-'mehr, ah-'blahr, eh-skree-'beer, leh-'ehr, eh-skoo-'chahr)*

Favor de _____ en el papel. *(fah-'vohr deh _____ ehn ehl pah-'pehl)*

Tiene que _____ el libro. *(tee-'eh-neh keh _____ ehl 'lee-broh)*

Necesita _____ inglés. *(neh-seh-'see-tah _____ een-'glehs)*

¿Quiere _____ en el restaurante? *(kee-'eh-reh _____ ehn ehl reh-stah·oo-'rahn-teh)*

Voy a _____ el radio. *('voh·ee ah _____ ehl 'rah-dee·oh)*

¡ACCIÓN!

To express clearly your thoughts in Spanish, you'll need to learn as many verb tenses as possible. Throughout this book, in sections entitled ¡ACCIÓN!, you will be introduced to a variety of conjugated verb forms. By practicing the patterns, you'll soon be able to discuss past, present, and future events.

Let's begin with one of the easiest verb forms to use. It's the present progressive tense, and it refers to actions that are taking place at this moment. It is similar to our "ing" form in English. Simply change the base verb ending slightly, and then combine the new form with the four forms of the verb estar (eh-'stahr). The -ar verbs become -ando ('ahn-doh), while the -er and -ir verbs become -iendo ('yehn-doh). Study these examples closely:

work	trabajar (trah-bah-'hahr)
working	trabajando (trah-bah-'hahn-doh)
We're working.	Estamos trabajando. (eh-'stah-mohs trah-bah-'hahn-doh)
eat	comer (koh-'mehr)
eating	comiendo (koh-mee-'ehn-doh)
He is eating.	Está comiendo. (eh-'stah koh-mee-'ehn-doh)
write	escribir (eh-skree-'beer)
writing	escribiendo (eh-skree-bee-'ehn-doh)
I'm writing.	Estoy escribiendo. (eh-'stoh·ee eh-skree-bee-'ehn-doh)

MÁS INFORMACIÓN

➤ Some verbs change in spelling and pronunciation when you add the -ndo ending. Look at these examples:

sleep	dormir (dohr-'meer)
sleeping	durmiendo (duhr-mee-'ehn-doh)
read	leer (leh-'ehr)
reading	leyendo (leh-'yehn-doh)

¡ÓRDENES!

As long as we're talking about working with Spanish speakers, why not spend some time reviewing the following important command or request words. They are unique forms of verbs that can be used all by themselves. Try using them in work-related situations—and always say por favor *(pohr fah-'vohr):*

Please...	Por favor... *(pohr fah-vohr)*
come	venga *('vehn-gah)*
follow	siga *('see-gah)*
go	vaya *('vah-yah)*
listen	escuche *(eh-'skoo-cheh)*
run	corra *('koh-rrah)*

These are considered formal commands. The informal forms are different and will be presented in Chapter Three.

wait	espere *(eh-'speh-reh)*
walk	camine *(kah-'mee-neh)*
watch	mire *('mee-reh)*

MÁS INFORMACIÓN

➤ Any vocabulary item can be learned quickly if it's practiced in conjunction with a command word. For example, to pick up the names for furniture, have a native Spanish speaker command you to touch, look at, or point to things throughout the home. This exercise really works, and more importantly, it can be fun:

Touch...	Toque... *('toh-keh)*	...the table	...la mesa *(lah 'meh-sah)*
Look at...	Mire... *('mee-reh)*	...the book	...el libro *(ehl 'lee-broh)*
Point to...	Señale... *(seh-'nyah-leh)*	...the chair	...la silla *(lah 'see-yah)*

➤ Several important command words have the word se at the end. Notice the pattern in these formal commands:

Hurry up!	¡Apúrese! *(ah-'poo-reh-seh)*
Sit down!	¡Siéntese! *(see-'ehn-teh-seh)*
Stand up!	¡Levántese! *(leh-'vahn-teh-seh)*
Stop!	¡Párese! *('pah-reh-seh)*
Stay!	¡Quédese! *('keh-deh-seh)*

➤ There's no better way to learn than by doing. That's why each chapter includes a section entitled ¡ÓRDENES! where you receive new lists of command words, followed by tips on how to practice them with Spanish speakers.

 ## DIFERENCIAS CULTURALES

Commands are practical and easy to use, but try not to overdo it. Those teachers who tend to be overbearing have problems earning respect. Try to give your orders sparingly and always add por favor *(pohr fah-'vohr)*.

 ## ¿LISTOS PARA PRACTICAR?

Follow the pattern as you practice:

caminar *(kah-mee-'nahr)*	caminando *(kah-mee-'nahn-doh)*	Estoy caminando *(eh-'stoh·ee kah-mee-'nahn-doh)*
trabajar *(trah-bah-'hahr)*	_____	_____
hablar *(ah-'blahr)*	_____	_____
estudiar *(eh-stoo-dee-'ahr)*	_____	_____
comer *(koh-'mehr)*	_____	_____
escribir *(eh-skree-'beer)*	_____	_____
aprender *(ah-prehn-'dehr)*	_____	_____
dormir *(dohr-'meer)*	_____	_____

Connect the opposites:

Siéntese *(see-'ehn-teh-seh)* Vaya *('vah-yah)*

Venga *('vehn-gah)*   Camine *(kah-'mee-neh)*

Corra *('koh-rrah)*   Levántese *(leh-'vahn-teh-seh)*

CHAPTER TWO
Capítulo Dos
(kah-'pee-too-loh dohs)

AT SCHOOL
En la escuela
(ehn lah eh-'skweh-lah)

WHERE DO YOU WORK?

¿Dónde trabaja usted? *('dohn-deh trah-'bah-hah oo-'stehd)*

Now that you've learned some of the fundamental skills in Spanish, it's time to tackle those words that relate to the workplace. This next list of terms should help to get you started. Use the opening phrase as you practice reading aloud:

Where's (the)...?	¿Dónde está...? *('dohn-deh eh-'stah...)*
academy	la academia *(ah-kah-'deh-mee·ah)*
agency	la agencia *(lah ah-'hehn-see·ah)*
branch	la sucursal *(lah soo-koor-'sahl)*
building	el edificio *(ehl eh-dee-'fee-see·oh)*
campus	el campo *(ehl 'kahm-poh)*
center	el centro *(ehl 'sehn-troh)*
class	la clase *(lah 'klah-seh)*
college	la universidad *(lah oo-nee-vehr-see-'dahd)*
department	el departamento *(ehl deh-pahr-tah-'mehn-toh)*
district	el distrito *(ehl dee-'stree-toh)*
division	la división *(lah dee-vee-see-'ohn)*
institute	el instituto *(ehl een-stee-'too-toh)*
institution	la institución *(lah een-stee-too-see-'ohn)*
large room	el salón *(ehl sah-'lohn)*
office	la oficina *(lah oh-fee-'see-nah)*
organization	la organización *(lah ohr-gah-nee-sah-see-'ohn)*
room	el cuarto *(ehl 'kwahr-toh)*
school	la escuela *(lah eh-'skweh-lah)*
site	el sitio *(ehl 'see-tee·oh)*
university	la universidad *(lah oo-nee-vehr-see-'dahd)*

Now, mention a few more key parts of the campus. Try out this new pattern while you review:

Go to (the)...	Vayan a... *('vah-yahn ah...)*
auditorium	el auditorio *(ehl ow-dee-'toh-ree·oh)*
cafeteria	la cafetería *(lah kah-feh-teh-'ree·ah)*
courtyard	la plaza *(lah 'plah-sah)*
dormitory	el dormitorio *(ehl dohr-mee-'toh-ree·oh)*
gym	el gimnasio *(ehl heem-'nah-see·oh)*
hall	el pasillo *(ehl pah-'see-yoh)*

laboratory	el laboratorio (ehl lah-boh-rah-'toh-ree·oh)
library	la biblioteca (lah bee-blee·oh-'teh-kah)
lobby	el vestíbulo(ehl veh-'stee-boo-loh)
locker	el armario (ehl ahr-'mah-ree·oh)
mailbox	el buzón (ehl boo-'sohn)
parking lot	el estacionamiento (ehl eh-stah-see·oh-nah-mee-'ehn-toh)
playground	el campo de recreo (ehl 'kahm-poh deh reh-'kreh-oh)
restroom	el servicio (ehl sehr-'vee-see·oh)
theater	el teatro (ehl teh-'ah-troh)
warehouse	el almacén (ehl ahl-mah-'sehn)
workshop	el taller (ehl tah-'yehr)

The following vocabulary words will come in handy almost immediately. Notice how they fit into phrases:

It's in the _____ room.	Está en el salón de _____ . (eh-'stah ehn ehl sah-'lohn deh _____)
music	la música (lah 'moo-see-kah)
art	el arte (ehl 'ahr-teh)
study	el estudio (ehl eh-'stoo-dee·oh)
computer	la computadora (lah kohm-poo-tah-'doh-rah)
copy	la copiadora (lah koh-pee·ah-'doh-rah)
It's in the _____ office.	Está en la oficina de _____ . (eh-'stah ehn lah oh-fee-'see-nah deh _____)
administration	la administración (lah ahd-mee-nee-strah-see·'ohn)
health	la salud (lah sah-'lood)
attendance	la asistencia (lah ah-see-'stehn-see·ah)
athletic	la educación física (lah eh-doo-kah-see·'ohn 'fee-see-kah)
admissions	las admisiones (lahs ahd-mee-see·'oh-nehs)

It's in the _____ building.	**Está en el edificio de** _____. *(eh-'stah ehn ehl eh-dee-'fee-see·oh deh _____)*
conference	**las conferencias** *(lahs kohn-feh-'rehn-see·ahs)*
storage	**el depósito** *(ehl deh-'poh-see-toh)*
science	**las ciencias** *(lahs see-'ehn-see·ahs)*
humanities	**las humanidades** *(lahs oo-mah-nee-'dah-dehs)*
security	**la seguridad** *(lah seh-goo-ree-'dahd)*
It's in the _____ center.	**Está en el centro de** _____. *(eh-'stah ehn ehl 'sehn-troh deh _____)*
assessment	**la evaluación** *(lah eh-vah-loo-ah-see·'ohn)*
media	**los medios de comunicación** *(lohs 'meh-dee·ohs deh koh-moo-nee-kah-see·'ohn)*
training	**el entrenamiento** *(ehl ehn-treh-nah-mee-'ehn-toh)*
supplies	**las provisiones** *(lahs proh-vee-see·'oh-nehs)*
communications	**las comunicaciones** *(lahs koh-moo-nee-kah-see·'oh-nehs)*

MÁS INFORMACIÓN

➤ Words change meanings depending on where a student is from.

In most countries, "college" is **la universidad** *(lah oo-nee-vehr-see-'dahd)*, while **el colegio** *(ehl koh-'leh-hee·oh)* means "high school."

➤ There are all kinds of educational institutions:

monastery	**el monasterio** *(ehl moh-nah-'steh-ree·oh)*
convent	**el convento** *(ehl kohn-'vehn-toh)*
seminary	**el seminario** *(seh-mee-'nah-ree·oh)*

boarding school	el internado *(ehl een-tehr-'nah-doh)*	
parochial school	la escuela parroquial *(lah eh-'skweh-lah pah-rroh-kee-'ahl)*	

➤ Could these terms help you out in your situation? Notice the practice sentences:

zone	la zona *(lah 'soh-nah)*	¿Dónde está la zona roja? *('dohn-deh eh-'stah lah 'soh-nah 'roh-hah)*
area	el área (f) *(ehl 'ah-reh-ah)*	Son áreas importantes. *(sohn 'ah-reh-ahs eem-pohr-'tahn-tehs)*
place	el lugar *(ehl loo-'gahr)*	Este es el lugar. *('eh-steh ehs ehl loo-'gahr)*
property	la propiedad *(lah proh-pee·eh-'dahd)*	La propiedad es grande. *(lah proh-pee·eh-'dahd ehs 'grahn-deh)*
space	el espacio *(ehl eh-'spah-see·oh)*	No hay espacio. *(noh 'ah·ee eh-'spah-see·oh)*
corner	la esquina *(lah eh-'skee-nah)*	Está en la esquina. *(eh-'stah ehn lah eh-'skee-nah)*

WORDS THAT TELL *WHERE*
Palabras que expresan *dónde* *(pah-'lah-brahs keh ehk-'spreh-sahn 'dohn-deh)*

To find what you're looking for, these "where" words will be required. Pay attention to how they can be used:

It's...	Está... *(eh-'stah)*
above, on top	encima *(ehn-'see-mah)*
against	contra *('kohn-trah)*
at the bottom	en el fondo *(ehn ehl 'fohn-doh)*
behind	detrás *(deh-'trahs)*
down	abajo *(ah-'bah-hoh)*
far	lejos *('leh-hohs)*
here	aquí *(ah-'kee)*
in front of	en frente de *(ehn 'frehn-teh deh)*
inside	adentro *(ah-'dehn-troh)*
next to	al lado de *(ahl 'lah-doh deh)*
opposite	de frente de *(deh 'frehn-teh deh)*

outside	**afuera** *(ah-'fweh-rah)*
over	**sobre** *('soh-breh)*
over there	**allá** *(ah-'yah)*
straight ahead	**adelante** *(ah-deh-'lahn-teh)*
there	**allí** *(ah-'yee)*
to the left	**a la izquierda** *(ah lah ees-kee-'ehr-dah)*
near	**cerca** *('sehr-kah)*
to the right	**a la derecha** *(ah lah deh-'reh-chah)*
up	**arriba** *(ah-'rree-bah)*

If a map is required, send everybody this way:

It's on the _____ side.	**Está en el lado _____ .** *(eh-'stah ehn ehl 'lah-doh)*
east	**este** *('eh-steh)*
north	**norte** *('nohr-teh)*
south	**sur** *(soor)*
west	**oeste** *(oh-'eh-steh)*

MÁS INFORMACIÓN

➤ Be specific! The class is on the corner, next to the office:

La clase está en la esquina, al lado de la oficina. *(lah 'klah-seh eh-'stah ehn lah eh-'skee-nah, ahl 'lah-doh deh lah oh-fee-'see-nah)*

➤ You'll need these for larger facilities:

first floor	**primer piso** *(pree-'mehr 'pee-soh)*
second floor	**segundo piso** *(seh-'goon-doh 'pee-soh)*
third floor	**tercer piso** *(tehr-'sehr 'pee-soh)*

➤ By the way, **en** *(ehn)* (in, on, at) is one of the most commonly used words in Spanish. Watch:

She's in her office,
on the second floor,
at her desk.

Está en su oficina *(eh-'stah ehn soo oh-fee-'see-nah),*
en el segundo piso *(ehn ehl seh-'goon-doh 'pee-soh).*
en su escritorio. *(ehn soo eh-skree-'toh-ree·oh).*

➤ And always use **estar** *(eh-'stahr)* instead of **ser** *(sehr)* to tell where someone is located:

The man is here. **El hombre está aquí.**
(ehl 'ohm-breh eh-'stah ah-'kee)

➤ Be familiar with as many location words as you can:

It's... **Está...** *(eh-'stah)*

face down	**boca abajo** *('boh-kah ah-'bah-hoh)*
face up	**boca arriba** *('boh-kah ah-'rree-bah)*
on its way	**en camino** *(ehn kah-'mee-noh)*
backwards, inside out, or upside down	**al revés** *(ahl reh-'vehs)*
in back	**atrás** *(ah-'trahs)*
in front	**al frente** *(ahl 'frehn-teh)*
in the middle	**al medio** *(ahl 'meh-dee·oh)*
underground	**subterráneo** *(soob-teh-'rrah-neh-oh)*

¿LISTOS PARA PRACTICAR?

Can you name three important buildings on a school campus?

_____

_____

_____

Translate these sentences as fast as you can:

La clase está adelante y a la derecha. *(lah 'klah-seh eh-'stah ah-deh-'lahn-teh ah lah deh-'reh-chah)*

Los servicios están allí, arriba. *(lohs sehr-'vee-see·ohs eh-'stahn ah-'yee, ah-'rree-bah)*

El edificio no está muy lejos. *(ehl eh-dee-'fee-see·oh noh eh-'stah 'moo·ee 'leh-hohs)*

La oficina de asistencia está al sur del centro de comunicaciones. *(lah oh-fee-'see-nah deh ah-see-'stehn-see·ah eh-'stah ahl soor dehl 'sehn-troh deh koh-moo-nee-kah-see·'oh-nehs)*

El cuarto está en el tercer piso, al lado del salón de música. *(ehl 'kwahr-toh eh-'stah ehn ehl tehr-'sehr 'pee-soh ahl 'lah-doh dehl sah-'lohn deh 'moo-see-kah)*

This group of opposites should be simple. Just draw a line to connect each pair:

adentro *(ah-'dehn-troh)*   derecha *(deh-'reh-chah)*
abajo *(ah-'bah-hoh)*   arriba *(ah-'rree-bah)*
izquierda *(ees-kee-'ehr-dah)*   norte *('nohr-teh)*
sur *(soor)*   cerca *('sehr-kah)*
lejos *('leh-hohs)*   afuera *(ah-'fweh-rah)*
detrás *(deh-'trahs)*   al frente *(ahl 'frehn-teh)*

INSIDE THE BUILDING
Adentro del edificio *(ah-'dehn-troh dehl eh-dee-'fee-see·oh)*

Once you're inside the building, start to point out those things you recognize. By pointing at each item as you name it, your Spanish is acquired much faster:

It's near (the)...   Está cerca de... *(eh-'stah 'sehr-kah deh...)*

elevator   el ascensor *(ehl ah-sehn-'sohr)*
entrance   la entrada *(lah ehn-'trah-dah)*
escalator   la escalera mecánica *(lah eh-skah-'leh-rah meh-'kah-nee-kah)*
exit   la salida *(lah sah-'lee-dah)*
stairs   las escaleras *(lahs eh-skah-'leh-rahs)*
steps   los escalones *(lohs eh-skah-'loh-nehs)*

OK, now give details:

double doors	**las puertas dobles** *(lahs 'pwehr-tahs 'doh-blehs)*
front counter	**el mostrador principal** *(ehl moh-strah-'dohr preen-see-'pahl)*
It's in front of (the)...	**Está en frente de...** *(eh-'stah ehn 'frehn-teh deh...)*
reception desk	**la recepción** *(lah reh-sehp-see-'ohn)*
trash can	**el bote de basura** *(ehl 'boh-teh deh bah-'soo-rah)*
water fountain	**la fuente de agua** *(lah 'fwehn-teh deh 'ah-gwah)*

Check all around the grounds. How many of these words can you put into practice?

Walk to (the)...	**Camine a...** *(kah-'mee-neh ah)*
balcony	**el balcón** *(ehl bahl-'kohn)*
bridge	**el puente** *(ehl 'pwehn-teh)*
deck	**la terraza** *(lah teh-'rrah-sah)*
driveway	**la entrada para carros** *(lah ehn-'trah-dah 'pah-rah 'kah-rrohs)*
fence	**la cerca** *(lah 'sehr-kah)*
garden	**el jardín** *(ehl hahr-'deen)*
gate	**el portón** *(ehl pohr-'tohn)*
lot	**el lote** *(ehl 'loh-teh)*
porch	**el portal** *(ehl pohr-'tahl)*
ramp	**la rampa** *(lah 'rahm-pah)*
sidewalk	**la acera** *(lah ah-'seh-rah)*
tower	**la torre** *(lah 'toh-rreh)*
wall	**la pared** *(lah pah-'rehd)*

MÁS INFORMACIÓN

➤ When giving instructions to younger students, be sure to tell them about the restroom:

Please use (the)...   Favor de usar... *(fah-'vohr deh oo-'sahr)*

    dispenser   el distribuidor *(ehl dees-tree-boo-ee-'dohr)*

    mirror   el espejo *(ehl eh-'speh-hoh)*
    paper towel   la toalla de papel *(lah toh-'ah-yah deh pah-'pehl)*

    sink   el lavamanos *(ehl lah-vah-'mah-nohs)*
    soap   el jabón *(ehl hah-'bohn)*
    toilet   el excusado *(ehl ehk-skoo-'sah-doh)*
    toilet paper   el papel higiénico *(ehl pah-'pehl ee-hee-'eh-nee-koh)*

    urinal   el orinal *(ehl oh-ree-'nahl)*

¿LISTOS PARA PRACTICAR?

How would you say these in Spanish?

The stairs are next to the elevator.
There's no toilet paper in the restroom.
Where is the water fountain?

Connect the words that are related:

el jabón *(ehl hah-'bohn)*   el portón *(ehl pohr-'tohn)*
la terraza *(lah teh-'rrah-sah)*   el lavamanos *(ehl lah-vah-'mah-nohs)*
la cerca *(lah 'sehr-kah)*   el portal *(ehl pohr-'tahl)*

Trust is very important in the Hispanic culture, especially in student-teacher relationships. Throughout the education process, feel free to open up about yourself, your family, your work, and your home. Since language is a barrier, begin by showing your students where everything is located. Don't be shy, always be honest, and make them feel at home.

WORDS THAT TELL *WHEN*

Palabras que expresan *cuándo* *(pah-'lah-brahs keh ehk-'spreh-sahn 'kwahn-doh)*

One of the most frequently asked questions in the field of education is "when?" Be prepared when the time to answer in Spanish comes. Begin by learning a few of the most popular responses:

afterward	después *(deh-'spwehs)*
always	siempre *(see-'ehm-preh)*
before	antes *('ahn-tehs)*
early	temprano *(tehm-'prah-noh)*
late	tarde *('tahr-deh)*
later	más tarde *(mahs 'tahr-deh)*
lots of times	muchas veces *('moo-chahs 'veh-sehs)*
never	nunca *('noon-kah)*
now	ahora *(ah-'oh-rah)*
once	una vez *('oo-nah vehs)*
right now	ahorita *(ah-oh-'ree-tah)*
sometimes	a veces *(ah 'veh-sehs)*
soon	pronto *('prohn-toh)*
then	entonces *(ehn-'tohn-sehs)*
today	hoy *('oh·ee)*
tomorrow	mañana *(mah-'nyah-nah)*
tonight	esta noche *('eh-stah 'noh-cheh)*
yesterday	ayer *(ah-'yehr)*

Notice this pattern:

usually	usualmente *(oo-soo-ahl-'mehn-teh)*
generally	generalmente *(heh-neh-rahl-'mehn-teh)*
frequently	frecuentemente *(freh-kwehn-teh-'mehn-teh)*

46

➤ All sorts of time expressions are needed in a school setting. A good way to learn is to group your related phrases into sets of three:

last month	**el mes pasado** (*ehl mehs pah-'sah-doh*)
last night	**anoche** (*ah-'noh-cheh*)
last week	**la semana pasada** (*lah seh-'mah-nah pa-'sah-dah*)
next month	**el próximo mes** (*ehl 'prohk-see-moh mehs*)
next week	**la próxima semana** (*lah 'prohk-see-mah seh-'mah-nah*)
next year	**el próximo año** (*ehl 'prohk-see-moh 'ah-nyoh*)
tomorrow morning	**mañana por la mañana** (*mah-'nyah-nah pohr lah mah-'nyah-nah*)
the day before yesterday	**anteayer** (*ahn-teh-ah-'yehr*)
the day after tomorrow	**pasado mañana** (*pah-'sah-doh mah-'nyah-nah*)
in a moment	**en un momento** (*ehn oon moh-'mehn-toh*)
in a while	**en un rato** (*ehn oon 'rah-toh*)
in a minute	**en un minuto** (*ehn oon mee-'noo-toh*)
at dawn	**a la madrugada** (*ah lah mah-droo-'gah-dah*)
at dusk	**al anochecer** (*ahl ah-noh-cheh-'sehr*)
at sunset	**a la puesta del sol** (*ah lah'pweh-stah dehl sohl*)
each day	**cada día** (*'kah-dah 'dee·ah*)
every day	**todos los días** (*'toh-dohs lohs 'dee·ahs*)
daily	**a diario** (*ah dee-'ah-ree·oh*)
yet	**todavía** (*toh-dah-'vee·ah*)
just	**apenas** (*ah-'peh-nahs*)
already	**ya** (*yah*)

➤ Understanding and using words like **dónde** (*'dohn-deh*) and **cuándo** (*'kwahn-doh*) is crucial in gathering information. The best way to learn how to use question words is to focus on the first word of each sentence and then try to get a general feel for what the person might be asking. Attempting to translate every word will only lead to frustration.

TIME TELLING!

¡Decir la hora! *(deh-'seer lah 'oh-rah)*

You can't discuss school activities without mentioning the clock. To read the clock in Spanish, simply give the hour, followed by the word **y** *(ee)* (and), and the minutes. For example, 8:15 is **ocho y quince** *('oh-choh ee 'keen-seh)*. Read through these other questions and answers:

What time is it?	¿Qué hora es? *(keh 'oh-rah ehs)*
At what time?	¿A qué hora? *(ah keh 'oh-rah)*
It's...	Son las... *(sohn lahs)*
At...	A las... *(ah lahs)*
10:40	diez y cuarenta
	(dee-'ehs ee kwah-'rehn-tah)
3:25	tres y veinte y cinco
	(trehs ee 'veh·een-teh ee 'seen-koh)
12:05 A.M.	doce y cinco de la mañana
	('doh-seh ee 'seen-koh deh lah mah-'nyah-nah)
4:00 P.M.	cuatro de la tarde
	('kwah-troh deh lah 'tahr-deh)
9:30 P.M.	nueve y treinta de la noche
	(noo-'eh-veh ee 'treh·een-tah deh lah 'noh-cheh)

➤ Are you picking up on everyday expressions as you review? Don't forget that "time" vocabulary can be practiced whenever you like:

noon	**mediodía** *(meh-dee·oh-'dee·ah)*
midnight	**medianoche** *(meh-dee·ah-'noh-cheh)*
on time	**a tiempo** *(ah tee-'ehm-poh)*
A.M.	**de la mañana** *(deh lah mah-'nyah-nah)*
P.M.	**de la tarde** *(deh lah 'tahr-deh)* or
	de la noche *(deh lah 'noh-cheh)*

➤ For 1:00–1:59, use **Es la...** *(ehs lah)* instead of **Son las...** *(sohn lahs)*. For example:

It's one o' clock.	**Es la una.** *(ehs lah 'oo-nah)*
At one-thirty.	**A la una y treinta.** *(ah lah 'oo-nah ee 'treh-een-tah)*

Continue to practice by reading aloud:

At two o'clock sharp.	**A las dos en punto.** *(ah lahs dohs ehn 'poon-toh)*
At around six o'clock.	**A eso de las seis.** *(ah 'eh-soh deh lahs 'seh-ees)*
At half past three.	**A las tres y media.** *(ah lahs trehs ee 'meh-dee·ah)*
At ten fifteen.	**A las diez y cuarto.** *(ah lahs dee-'ehs ee 'kwahr-toh)*
At five minutes to eight.	**A las ocho menos cinco.** *(ah lahs 'oh-choh 'meh-nohs 'seen-koh)*

WHAT DAY?
¿Qué día? *(keh 'dee·ah)*

Spend a few minutes looking over the following Spanish words. They'll allow you to say things about the calendar and making schedules. Then stress each sound as you pronounce them aloud:

The days of the week	**Los días de la semana** *(lohs 'dee·ahs deh lah seh-'mah-nah)*
Monday	**lunes** *('loo-nehs)*
Tuesday	**martes** *('mahr-tehs)*
Wednesday	**miércoles** *(mee-'ehr-koh-lehs)*

Thursday	**jueves** *(hoo-'eh-vehs)*
Friday	**viernes** *(vee-'ehr-nehs)*
Saturday	**sábado** *('sah-bah-doh)*
Sunday	**domingo** *(doh-'meen-goh)*

Now, read these questions and answers. See how **los días** *(lohs 'dee·ahs)* function as one-word responses to "when" questions:

When is there school?	**¿Cuándo hay escuela?** *('kwahn-doh 'ah·ee eh-'skweh-lah)*
Tuesday and Thursday	**Martes y jueves** *('mahr-tehs ee hoo-'eh-vehs)*
When is the class?	**¿Cuándo es la clase?** *('kwahn-doh ehs lah 'klah-seh)*
Monday	**Lunes** *('loo-nehs)*
When are we going there?	**¿Cuándo vamos ahí?** *('kwahn-doh 'vah-mohs ah-'ee)*
Friday	**Viernes** *(vee-'ehr-nehs)*

MÁS INFORMACIÓN

➤ Most students of Spanish get confused when using the words **por** *(pohr)* and **para** *('pah-rah)* because they are similar in meaning. The differences between the two are not easy to explain, so it may be best to listen to Spanish speakers as they use them, and then try them out in short, practical phrases.

by Friday	**para el viernes** *('pah-rah ehl vee-'ehr-nehs)*
for two days	**por dos días** *(pohr dohs 'dee·ahs)*
in order to go	**para ir** *('pah-rah eer)*
throughout the afternoon	**por la tarde** *(pohr lah 'tahr-deh)*

➤ "On Friday" is **el viernes** *(ehl vee-'ehr-nehs)* but "on Fridays" is **los viernes** *(lohs vee-'ehr-nehs)*.

➤ If you want, you can interject the following expressions:

the next one	**el próximo** *(ehl 'prohk-see-moh)*
the past one	**el pasado** *(ehl pah-'sah-doh)*
the weekend	**el fin de semana** *(ehl feen deh-seh-'mah-nah)*

➤ Use **¿Hace cuánto?** *('ah-seh 'kwahn-toh)* for "How long ago?"

How long ago?	**¿Hace cuánto?** *('ah-seh 'kwahn-toh)*
Two weeks ago.	**Hace dos semanas.**
	('ah-seh dohs seh-'mah-nahs)

WHAT MONTH?
¿Qué mes? *(keh mehs)*

As far as the months are concerned, just remember that most words are similar in both Spanish and English.

The Months of the Year	**Los meses del año** *(lohs 'meh-sehs dehl 'ah-nyoh)*
January	**enero** *(eh-'neh-roh)*
February	**febrero** *(feh-'breh-roh)*
March	**marzo** *('mahr-soh)*
April	**abril** *(ah-'breel)*
May	**mayo** *('mah-yoh)*
June	**junio** *('hoo-nee·oh)*
July	**julio** *('hoo-lee·oh)*
August	**agosto** *(ah-'goh-stoh)*
September	**septiembre** *(sehp-tee-'ehm-breh)*
October	**octubre** *(ohk-'too-breh)*
November	**noviembre** *(noh-vee-'ehm-breh)*
December	**diciembre** *(dee-see-'ehm-breh)*

WHAT'S THE DATE?

¿Cuál es la fecha? *(kwahl ehs lah 'feh-chah)*

To give the date, reverse the order of your words. For example, February 2nd is **el dos de febrero** *(ehl dohs deh feh-'breh-roh)*.

And this is how you say "the first" in Spanish:
el primero *(ehl pree-'meh-roh)*
January 1st
el primero de enero *(ehl pree-'meh-roh deh eh-'neh-roh)*
The year is often read as one large number:

2016   **dos mil dieciséis** *(dohs meel dee·ehs-ee-'seh·ees)*

Can you give today's date in Spanish? Use a calendar to practice your new vocabulary!

 ¿LISTOS PARA PRACTICAR?

All set to translate? Good luck!

¿Está caminando Carlos a la escuela hoy? *(eh-'stah kah-mee-'nahn-doh 'kahr-lohs ah lah eh-'skweh-lah 'oh·ee)*
¡Venga ahora! *('vehn-gah ah-'oh-rah)*
A veces tengo problemas con mi trabajo. *(ah 'veh-sehs 'tehn-goh proh-'bleh-mahs kohn mee trah-'bah-hoh)*

Choose the best word to complete each series:

mes   **ayer**   **a veces** *(mehs, ah-'yehr, ah 'veh-sehs)*

siempre, nunca, _____ *(see-'ehm-preh, 'noon-kah)*

hoy, mañana, _____ *('oh·ee, mah-'nyah-nah)*

día, semana, _____ *('dee·ah, seh-'mah-nah)*

Try to complete these lists, but without any help:
lunes, martes, miércoles, _____ *('loo-nehs, 'mahr-tehs, mee-'ehr-koh-lehs)*
enero, febrero, marzo, _____ *(eh-'neh-roh, feh-'breh-roh, 'mahr-soh)*

Say these dates and times in Spanish:

At 6:00 A.M. _____

June 6, 1999 _____

It's 9:30 P.M. _____

 DIFERENCIAS CULTURALES

Not all folks panic when it comes to tardiness—some cultures put less emphasis on beating the clock than others. Be direct and explain the importance of punctuality in school functions and activities.

You have to arrive early.
Tiene que llegar temprano.
(tee-'eh-neh keh yeh-'gahr tehm-'prah-noh)

Don't be late!
¡No llegue tarde!
(noh 'yeh-geh 'tahr-deh)

If you're late again, I'll have to call your home.
Si llega tarde otra vez, tendré que llamar a su casa.
(see 'yeh-gah 'tahr-deh 'oh-trah vehs, tehn-'dreh keh yah-'mahr ah soo 'kah-sah)

WHO IS IT?
¿Quién es? *(kee-'ehn ehs)*

Once you feel comfortable responding to "where" and "when" questions in Spanish, attempt to focus on "who" it is you're talking about. Perhaps the best place to start is among your fellow employees. Do any of these job titles sound familiar? Note that the "/a" indicates the feminine ending. Titles that do not have it are unisex.

Who's the...	¿Quién es el/la...? *(kee-'ehn ehs ehl/lah...)*
administrator	administrador/a *(ahd-mee-nee-strah-'dohr/ah)*
assistant	asistente *(ah-see-'stehn-teh)*
board member	miembro/a de la junta directiva *(mee-'ehm-broh/ah deh lah 'hoon-tah dee-rehk-'tee-vah)*
cashier	cajero/a *(kah-'heh-roh/ah)*
clerk	dependiente *(deh-pehn-dee-'ehn-teh)*
cook	cocinero/a *(koh-see-'neh-roh/ah)*
director	director/a *(dee-rehk-'tohr/ah)*
gardener	jardinero/a *(hahr-dee-'neh-roh/ah)*
instructor	instructor/a *(een-strook-'tohr/ah)*
janitor	bedel *(beh-'dehl)*
nurse	enfermero/a *(ehn-fehr-'meh-roh/ah)*
principal	director/a *(dee-rehk-'tohr/ah)*
secretary	secretario/a *(seh-kreh-'tah-ree·oh/ah)*
security guard	guardia de seguridad *('gwahr-dee·ah deh seh-goo-ree-'dahd)*
superintendent	superintendente *(soo-pehr-een-tehn-'dehn-teh)*
supervisor	supervisor/a *(soo-pehr-vee-'sohr/ah)*
teacher	maestro/a *(mah-'eh-stroh/ah)*
teacher's aide	ayudante/a de maestro *(ah-yoo-'dahn-teh/ah deh mah-'eh-stroh)*
trainer	entrenador/a *(ehn-treh-nah-'dohr/ah)*
tutor	tutor *(too-'tohr)*

You haven't mentioned everyone, so continue to practice:

Listen to (the)...	Escuche al/a la... *(eh-'skoo-cheh ahl/ah lah...)*
assistant superintendent	asistente/a del superintendente *(ah-see-'stehn-teh/ah dehl soo-pehr-een-tehn-'dehn-teh)*
bus driver	chofer de autobús *(choh-'fehr deh ow-toh-'boos)*
chairperson	director/a del departamento *(dee-rehk-'tohr/ah dehl deh-pahr-tah-'mehn-toh)*
consultant	consultor/a *(kohn-sool-'tohr/ah)*
counselor	consejero/a *(kohn-seh-'heh-roh/ah)*
crossing guard	guardia del tráfico *('gwahr-dee·ah dehl 'trah-fee-koh)*

educator	educador/a *(eh-doo-kah-'dohr/ah)*
helper	ayudante/a *(ah-yoo-'dahn-teh/ah)*
interpreter	intérprete *(een-'tehr-preh-teh)*
leader	líder *('lee-dehr)*
librarian	bibliotecario/a *(bee-blee·oh-teh-'kah-ree·oh/ah)*
official	oficial *(oh-fee-see-'ahl)*
operator	operador/a *(oh-peh-rah-'dohr/ah)*
psychologist	psicólogo/a *(see-'koh-loh-goh/ah)*
receptionist	recepcionista *(reh-sehp-see·oh-'nee-stah)*
specialist	especialista *(eh-speh-see·ah-'lee-stah)*
speech pathologist	patólogo del habla *(pah'toh-log-goh dehl 'ah-blah)*
technician	técnico/a *('tehk-nee-koh/ah)*
therapist	terapista *(teh-rah-'pee-stah)*
translator	traductor/a *(trah-dook-'tohr/ah)*
vice-principal	subdirector/a *(soob-dee-rehk-'tohr/ah)*
volunteer	voluntario/a *(voh-loon-'tah-ree·oh/ah)*

For the sake of convenience, the masculine form will be used for generic titles in the remainder of this guidebook.

➤ Not every job title can be translated. Notice the shortcut method:

office professionals or clerical staff =		secretarios *(seh-kreh-'tah-ree·ohs)*
instructional assistants	=	ayudantes *(ah-yoo-'dahn-tehs)*
campus caterers	=	cocineros *(koh-see-'neh-rohs)*

➤ In most cases, administrative positions are translated in reverse word order in Spanish. If you work as a specialist, learn how to give your unique title in Spanish:

Migrant Education Director
Director de educación para los inmigrantes *(dee-rehk-'tohr deh eh-doo-kah-see·'ohn 'pah-rah lohs een-mee-'grahn-tehs)*

Special Education Teacher
Profesor/a de educación especial *(proh-feh-'sohr / ah deh eh-doo-kah-see·'ohn ehs-peh-see-'ahl)*

Bilingual Education Specialist
Especialista de educación bilingüe *(eh-speh-see·ah-'lee-stah deh eh-doo-kah-see·'ohn bee-'leen-gweh)*

➤ And these are very general terms to define the people you work with:

staff	los funcionarios *(lohs foonk-see·oh-'nah-ree·ohs)*
personnel	el personal *(ehl pehr-soh-'nahl)*
employees	los empleados *(lohs ehm-pleh-'ah-dohs)*
paraprofessional	el/la paraprofesional *(ehl/lah pah-rah-proh-feh-see·oh-'nahl)*

➤ Look up the names of all unique titles on your own!

Dean of Student Life, Vocational Consultant, Network Engineer

MORE OCCUPATIONS
Más ocupaciones *(mahs oh-koo-pah-see-'oh-nehs)*

A variety of professionals are called to help out on campus, so learn the following job titles as well. Can you fill in the blank with a person's name? *Don't forget to change these when you refer to a female:*

_____ is (the)...   _____ es... *(ehs)*

architect	el arquitecto *(ehl ahr-kee-'tehk-toh)*
carpenter	el carpintero *(ehl kahr-peen-'teh-roh)*
dentist	el dentista *(ehl dehn-'tee-stah)*
doctor	el doctor *(ehl dohk-'tohr)*
engineer	el ingeniero *(ehl een-heh-nee-'eh-roh)*
firefighter	el bombero *(ehl bohm-'beh-roh)*
lawyer	el abogado *(ehl ah-boh-'gah-doh)*
mail carrier	el cartero *(ehl kahr-'teh-roh)*
mechanic	el mecánico *(ehl meh-'kah-nee-koh)*
painter	el pintor *(ehl peen-'tohr)*
plumber	el plomero *(ehl ploh-'meh-roh)*
police officer	el policía *(ehl poh-lee-'see·ah)*

HOW CAN I HELP YOU?

¿En qué puedo servirle? *(ehn keh 'pweh-doh sehr-'veer-leh)*

Do you know enough Spanish to ask questions by yourself? This first one is a classic, and usually follows an introduction or friendly greeting:

Are you...?   ¿Está usted...? *(eh-'stah oos-'tehd...)*

available	disponible *(dee-spoh-'nee-bleh)*
bored	aburrido *(ah-boo-'rree-doh)*
busy	ocupado *(oh-koo-'pah-doh)*
comfortable	cómodo *('koh-moh-doh)*
excited	emocionado *(eh-moh-see·oh-'nah-doh)*
fine	bien *('bee·ehn)*
happy	contento *(kohn-'tehn-toh)*
lost	perdido *(pehr-'dee-doh)*
nervous	nervioso *(nehr-vee-'oh-soh)*
OK	regular *(reh-goo-'lahr)*
prepared	preparado *(preh-pah-'rah-doh)*
ready	listo *('lee-stoh)*
relaxed	relajado *(reh-lah-'hah-doh)*
sad	triste *('tree-steh)*
sick	enfermo *(ehn-'fehr-moh)*
sure	seguro *(seh-'goo-roh)*
surprised	sorprendido *(sohr-prehn-'dee-doh)*
tired	cansado *(kahn-'sah-doh)*
upset	enojado *(eh-noh-'hah-doh)*
worried	preocupado *(preh-oh-koo-'pah-doh)*

Now, try one of these formal questions as you offer to help, and then focus on any key words that may sound familiar:

How can I help you?	¿En qué puedo servirle? *(ehn keh 'pweh-doh sehr-'veer-leh)*
What do you need?	¿Qué necesita usted? *(keh neh-seh-'see-tah oo-'stehd)*
Where are you going?	¿Adónde va usted? *(ah-'dohn-deh vah oo-'stehd)*

Who would you like to speak to?	**¿Con quién quisiera hablar?** *(kohn kee-'ehn kee-see-'eh-rah ah-'blahr)*
What is the problem?	**¿Cual es el problema?** *(kwahl ehs ehl proh-'bleh-mah)*

Keep going; however, this time find out who they are:

Are you (the) _____?	**¿Es usted _____?** *(ehs oo-'stehd ____)*

employee	**el empleado** *(ehl ehm-pleh-'ah-doh)*
guest	**el huésped** *(ehl 'weh-spehd)*
member	**el miembro** *(ehl mee-'ehm-broh)*
mother	**la madre** *(lah 'mah-dreh)*
neighbor	**el vecino** *(ehl veh-'see-noh)*
owner	**el dueño** *(ehl 'dweh-nyoh)*
parent	**el padre** *(ehl 'pah-dreh)*
relative	**el pariente** *(ehl pah-ree-'ehn-teh)*
salesperson	**el vendedor** *(ehl vehn-deh-'dohr)*
student	**el estudiante** *(ehl eh-stoo-dee-'ahn-teh)*
visitor	**el visitante** *(ehl vee-see-'tahn-teh)*

➤ Note that **padres** means "parents," whereas **parientes** means "relatives." This is a source of endless mistakes.

To find out what's going on, ask a simple formal question, and worry about the details later:

Do you have (the)...?	**¿Tiene...?** *(tee-'eh-neh)*
appointment	**la cita** *(lah 'see-tah)*
meeting	**la reunión** *(lah reh-oo-nee-'ohn)*
class	**la clase** *(lah 'klah-seh)*
conference	**la conferencia** *(lah kohn-feh-'rehn-see·ah)*
seminar	**el seminario** *(ehl seh-mee-'nah-ree·oh)*

Do you want (the)...?	**¿Quiere...?** *(kee-'eh-reh)*
schedule	**el horario** *(eh oh-'rah-ree·oh)*
map	**el mapa** *(ehl 'mah-pah)*
pass	**el permiso** *(ehl pehr-'mee-soh)*
application	**la solicitud** *(lah soh-lee-see-'tood)*

form	el formulario *(ehl fohr-moo-'lah-ree·oh)*
website	el sitio web *(ehl 'see-tee·oh web)*

Do you need...?	¿Necesita...? *(neh-seh-'see-tah)*
to attend	asistir *(ah-see-'steer)*
to enroll	matricularse *(mah-tree-koo-'lahr-seh)*
to call	llamar *(yah-'mahr)*
to park	estacionar *(eh-stah-see·oh-'nahr)*
to deliver	entregar *(ehn-treh-'gahr)*
to visit	visitar *(vee-see-'tahr)*
to sign	firmar *(feer-'mahr)*

MÁS INFORMACIÓN

➤ Some things might require a little more explanation:

There's a...	Hay un... *('ah·ee oon...)*
plan	plan *(plahn)*
procedure	procedimiento *(proh-seh-dee-mee-'ehn-toh)*
process	proceso *(proh-'seh-soh)*

➤ Bear in mind that adjectives that are masculine often end in o. When the adjective is feminine, in most cases you delete the o and add an a (aburrido—aburrida, contento—contenta) *(ah-boo-'rree-doh, ah-boo-'rree-dah, kohn-'tehn-toh, kohn-'tehn-tah)*.

➤ These terms all refer to some kind of meeting. You'll run across them several times in this guidebook:

la reunión *(lah reh-oo-nee-'ohn)*
la junta *(lah 'hoon-tah)*
la conferencia *(lah kohn-feh-'rehn-see·ah)*

PERSONAL INFORMATION

La información personal *(lah een-fohr-mah-see·'ohn pehr-soh-'nahl)*

At times, it's necessary to gather personal information in order to assist others more efficiently. These next questions and answers are also useful for filling out documents or forms. Notice that both the formal and informal questions are provided:

| What is your...? | ¿Cuál es su...? *(kwahl ehs soo....?)* |
| | ¿Cuál es tu...? *(kwahl ehs too....?)* |

address	dirección *(dee-rehk-see·'ohn)*
age	edad *(eh-'dahd)*
area code	código telefónico *('koh-dee-goh teh-leh-'foh-nee-koh)*
date of birth	fecha de nacimiento *('feh-chah deh nah-see-mee-'ehn-toh)*
email	correo electrónico *(koh'reh-oh eh-lehk-'troh-nee-koh)*
first language	lengua materna *('lehn-gwah mah-'tehr-nah)*
first name	primer nombre *(pree-'mehr 'nohm-breh)*
full name	nombre y apellido *('nohm-breh ee ah-peh-'yee-doh)*
last name	apellido *(ah-peh-'yee-doh)*
maiden name	nombre de soltera *('nohm-breh deh sohl-'teh-rah)*
middle initial	segunda inicial *(seh-'goon-dah een-nee-see-'ahl)*
nationality	nacionalidad *(nah-see·oh-nah-lee-'dahd)*
nickname	apodo *(ah-'poh-doh)*
place of birth	lugar de nacimiento *(loo-'gahr deh nah-see-mee-'ehn-toh)*
relationship	relación *(reh-lah-see·'ohn)*
zip code	zona postal *('soh-nah poh-'stahl)*

Here's another useful pattern:

What's the _____ number?	¿Cuál es el número de _____ ? *(kwahl ehs ehl 'noo-meh-roh deh...?)*
apartment	apartamento *(ah-pahr-tah-'mehn-toh)*
cellular	celular *(seh-loo-'lahr)*
code	código *('koh-dee-goh)*
I.D.	identificación *(ee-dehn-tee-fee-kah-see·'ohn)*
license	licencia *(lee-'sehn-see·ah)*
office	oficina *(oh-fee-'see-nah)*

60

password	**contraseña** *(kohn-trah-'seh-nyah)*
room	**cuarto** *('kwahr-toh)*
social security	**seguro social** *(seh-'goo-roh soh-see-'ahl)*
telephone	**teléfono** *(teh-'leh-foh-noh)*

MÁS INFORMACIÓN

➤ Take note:

male	**masculino** *(mah-skoo-'lee-noh)*
female	**femenino** *(feh-meh-'nee-noh)*

DIFERENCIAS CULTURALES

When referring to others by name, it really helps if you are able to pronounce people's names correctly, as it makes them feel much more at ease. Always remember that Spanish is pronounced the way it is written. Also, it is not uncommon for someone in Spain or Latin America to have two last names. Don't get confused. Here's the order:

First name	Father's last name	Mother's last name
primer nombre	**apellido paterno**	**apellido materno**
(pree-'mehr	*(ah-peh-'yee-doh*	*(ah-'peh-'yee-doh*
'nohm-breh)	*pah-'tehr-noh)*	*mah-'tehr-noh)*
Juan Carlos	**Espinoza**	**García**
(wahn 'kahr-lohs)	*(eh-spee-'noh-sah)*	*(gahr-'see·ah)*

61

WHAT KIND OF SCHOOL?

¿Qué tipo de escuela? *(keh 'tee-poh deh eh-'skweh-lah)*

As the Spanish-speaking public begins to inquire about your educational program or facility, make sure you can give a description effectively.

It's a/an _____ school. **Es una escuela** _____ . *(ehs 'oo-nah eh-'skweh-lah* _____ *)*

accelerated	**de estudiantes avanzados** *(deh eh-stoo-dee-'ahn-tehs ah-vahn-'sah-dohs)*
alternative	**alternativa** *(ahl-tehr-nah-'tee-vah)*
boys'	**para niños** *('pah-rah 'nee-nyohs)*
commuter	**para viajeros abonados** *('pah-rah vee·ah-'heh-rohs ah-boh-'nah-dohs)*
continuation	**de continuación** *(deh kohn-tee-noo-ah-see-'ohn)*
correctional	**correccional** *(koh-rrehk-see·oh-'nahl)*
correspondence	**de correspondencia** *(deh koh-rreh-spohn-'dehn-see·ah)*
court	**de la corte** *(deh lah 'kohr-teh)*
day	**diurna** *(dee-'oor-nah)*
girls'	**para niñas** *('pah-rah 'nee-nyahs)*
grammar	**primaria** *(pree-'mah-ree·ah)*
high	**secundaria** *(seh-koon-'dah-ree·ah)*
home	**domiciliaria** *(doh-mee-see-lee-'ah-ree·ah)*
military	**militar** *(mee-lee-'tahr)*
night	**nocturna** *(nohk-'toor-nah)*
nursery	**guardería** *('gwahr-deh-'ree·ah)*
parochial	**parroquial** *(pah-rroh-kee-'ahl)*
preschool	**preescolar** *(preh-eh-skoh-'lahr)*
private	**privada** *(pree-'vah-dah)*
public	**pública** *('poo-blee-kah)*
religious	**religiosa** *(reh-lee-hee-'oh-sah)*
trade	**de artes y oficios** *(deh 'ahr-tehs ee oh-'fee-see·ohs)*
training	**de entrenamiento** *(deh ehn-treh-nah-mee-'ehn-toh)*

MÁS INFORMACIÓN

➤ Acquire all the buzz words related to your professional field:

It's...   Es... *(ehs...)*

elementary education   la enseñanza primaria *(lah ehn-seh-'nyahn-sah
                             pree-'mah-ree·ah)*

secondary education   la enseñanza secundaria *(lah ehn-seh-'nyahn-sah
                             seh-koon-'dah-ree·ah)*

higher education   la enseñanza superior *(lah ehn-seh-'nyahn-sah
                             soo-peh-ree-'ohr)*

It's a...   Es una escuela... *(ehs oo-nah eh-'skweh-lah)*

home school   casera *(kah-'seh-rah)*
magnet school   imán *(ee-'mahn)*
model school   modelo *(moh-'deh-loh)*
pilot school   piloto *(pee-'loh-toh)*
satellite school   satélite *(sah-'teh-lee-teh)*

DIFERENCIAS CULTURALES

Grade levels seldom translate exactly from one country to the next, or from one U.S. school system to another. The following translations should provide a basic guide:

nursery school   jardín infantil básico *(hahr-'deen een-fahn-'teel
                            'bah-see-koh)*

kindergarten   jardín infantil superior *(hahr-'deen een-fahn-'teel
                            soo-peh-ree-'ohr)*

grade school   escuela primaria *(eh-'skweh-lah pree-'mah-ree·ah)*

middle school ⎫
intermediate school ⎬   escuela intermedia *(eh-'skweh-lah een-tehr-'meh-
junior high school ⎭   dee·ah)*

high school   escuela superior, escuela de segunda enseñanza
                            *(eh-'skweh-lah soo-peh-ree-'ohr, eh-'skweh-lah deh
                            seh-'goon-dah ehn-seh-'nyahn-sah)*

63

| community college
junior college | universidad de dos años de estudios
(oo-nee-vehr-see-'dahd deh dohs 'ah-nyohs deh eh-'stoo-dee·ohs) |
| college
university | universidad de cuatro años de estudios o más
(oo-nee-vehr-see-'dahd deh 'kwah-troh 'ah-nyohs deh eh-'stoo-dee·ohs oh mahs) |

DESCRIBE THINGS

Describa las cosas *(deh-'skree-bah lahs 'koh-sahs)*

Work on expanding your descriptive vocabulary by reading the list of opposites below. Be sure to change them to the feminine form if necessary:

It's...	Es... *(ehs...)* Está... *(eh-'stah...)*
cheap expensive	barato *(bah-'rah-toh)* caro *('kah-roh)*
clean dirty	limpio *('leem-pee·oh)* sucio *('soo-see·oh)*
deep shallow	profundo *(proh-'foon-doh)* bajo *('bah-hoh)*
difficult easy	difícil *(dee-'fee-seel)* fácil *('fah-seel)*
hard soft	duro *('doo-roh)* blando *('blahn-doh)*
long short (in length)	largo *('lahr-goh)* corto *('kohr-toh)*
narrow wide	estrecho *(eh-'streh-choh)* ancho *('ahn-choh)*

pretty	bonito *(boh-'nee-toh)*
ugly	feo *('feh-oh)*
rough	áspero *('ah-speh-roh)*
smooth	liso *('lee-soh)*
dry	seco *('seh-koh)*
wet	mojado *(moh-'hah-doh)*
thin	delgado *(dehl-'gah-doh)*
thick	grueso *(groo-'eh-soh)*

Keep in mind that in Spanish, the adjective (the word used to describe anything) usually goes after the noun and they must agree in gender and number. Here are some more vocabulary words:

It's an _____ class.	Es una clase _____ . *(ehs 'oo-nah 'klah-seh)*
excellent	excelente *(ehk-seh-'lehn-teh)*
important	importante *(eem-pohr-'tahn-teh)*
interesting	interesante *(een-teh-reh-'sahn-teh)*
He's a _____ teacher.	Es un maestro _____ . *(ehs oon mah-'eh-stroh)*
bald	calvo *('kahl-voh)*
blond	rubio *('roo-bee·oh)*
dark-haired	moreno *(moh-'reh-noh)*
She is a _____ principal.	Es una directora _____ . *(ehs 'oo-nah dee-rehk-'toh-rah)*
bad	mala *('mah-lah)*
good	buena *('bweh-nah)*
prepared	preparada *(preh-pah-'rah-dah)*

MÁS INFORMACIÓN

➤ Description words that begin with **no**, **in-**, or **des-** often refer to an opposite:

qualified (**calificado**) *(kah-lee-fee-'kah-doh)*
unqualified (**no calificado**) *(noh kah-lee-fee-'kah-doh)*

correct (**correcto**) *(koh-'rrehk-toh)*
incorrect (**incorrecto**) *(een-koh-'rrehk-toh)*

employed (**empleado**) *(ehm-pleh-'ah-doh)*
unemployed (**desempleado**) *(dehs-ehm-pleh-'ah-doh)*

➤ And use these little words to compare things:

a little big	**un poco grande** *(oon 'poh-koh 'grahn-deh)*
as big as	**tan grande como** *(tahn 'grahn-deh 'koh-moh)*
bigger than	**más grande que** *(mahs 'grahn-deh keh)*
biggest	**el más grande** *(ehl mahs 'grahn-deh)*
so big	**tan grande** *(tahn 'grahn-deh)*
too big	**demasiado grande** *(deh-mah-see-'ah-doh 'grahn-deh)*
very big	**muy grande** *('moo·ee 'grahn-deh)*

Can you read and understand the following sentences?

Carlos es más grande que Samuel.
('kahr-lohs ehs mahs 'grahn-deh keh sah-moo-'ehl)

Samuel es tan grande como una casa.
(sah-moo-'ehl ehs tahn 'grahn-deh 'koh-moh 'oo-nah 'kah-sah)

Felipe es el más grande.
(feh-'lee-peh ehs ehl mahs 'grahn-deh)

Name three different kinds of schools in Spanish:

_____

_____

_____

Answer these questions about yourself in Spanish:

¿Cuál es su fecha de nacimiento? *(kwahl ehs soo 'feh-chah deh nah-see-mee-'ehn-toh)*

¿Cuál es su número de teléfono? *(kwahl ehs soo 'noo-meh-roh deh teh-'leh-foh-noh)*

¿Cuál es su nombre y apellido? *(kwahl ehs soo 'nohm-breh ee ah-peh-'yee-doh)*

Here are some more opposites to practice. You know what to do:

grueso *(groo-'eh-soh)*
moreno *(moh-'reh-noh)*
caro *('kah-roh)*
limpio *('leem-pee·oh)*
difícil *(dee-'fee-seel)*
feo *('feh-oh)*
blando *('blahn-doh)*
largo *(bah-'rah-toh)*
profundo *(proh-'foon-doh)*
mojado *(moh-'hah-doh)*

seco *('seh-koh)*
rubio *('roo-bee·oh)*
fácil *('fah-seel)*
bonito *(boh-'nee-toh)*
bajo *('bah-hoh)*
corto *('kohr-toh)*
barato *(bah-'rah-toh)*
delgado *(dehl-'gah-doh)*
sucio *('soo-see·oh)*
duro *('doo-roh)*

Fill in the blanks using the correct word:

la maestra, el cocinero, el bedel *(lah mah-'eh-strah, ehl koh-see-'neh-roh, ehl beh-'dehl)*

_____ **está esperando en la cafetería.** *(_____ eh-'stah eh-speh-'rahn-doh ehn lah kah-feh-teh-'ree·ah)*

_____ está hablando en la clase. (_____ eh-'stah ah-'blahn-doh ehn lah 'klah-seh)

_____ está trabajando en el baño. (_____ eh-'stah trah-bah-'hahn-doh ehn ehl 'bah-nyoh)

 ¡ACCIÓN!

To handle any encounter with a Spanish speaker, make sure you've set aside all the appropriate Spanish verbs. As you take on this new list of actions, utilize the short-cuts that you know:

to leave	salir *(sah-'leer)*	<u>Voy a salir a las tres.</u> *('voh·ee ah sah-'leer ah lahs trehs)*
to arrive	llegar *(yeh-'gahr)*	<u>Tiene que llegar temprano.</u> *(tee-'eh-neh keh yeh-'gahr tehm-'prah-noh)*
to enter	entrar *(ehn-'trahr)*	<u>Favor de entrar ahí.</u> *(fah-'vohr deh ehn-'trahr ah-'ee)*
to park	estacionar *(eh-stah-see·oh-'nahr)*	<u>No estacionar aquí.</u> *(noh eh-stah-see·oh-'nahr ah-'kee)*
to answer	contestar *(kohn-teh-'stahr)*	_____.
to ask	preguntar *(preh-goon-'tahr)*	_____.
to attend	asistir *(ah-see-'steer)*	_____.
to begin	empezar *(ehm-peh-'sahr)*	_____.
to bring	traer *(trah-'ehr)*	_____.
to call	llamar *(yah-'mahr)*	_____.
to close	cerrar *(seh-'rrahr)*	_____.
to deliver	entregar *(ehn-treh-'gahr)*	_____.

to do	hacer *(ah-'sehr)*	_____.
to end	terminar *(tehr-mee-'nahr)*	_____.
to find	encontrar *(ehn-kohn-'trahr)*	_____.
to look for	buscar *(boo-'skahr)*	_____.
to move	mover *(moh-'vehr)*	_____.
to open	abrir *(ah-'breer)*	_____.
to return	regresar *(reh-greh-'sahr)*	_____.
to sign	firmar *(feer-'mahr)*	_____.
to take	tomar *(toh-'mahr)*	_____.
to visit	visitar *(vee-see-'tahr)*	_____.

We have learned that our Spanish verbs change when we talk about current action:

To speak	hablar *(ah-'blahr)*
I'm speaking.	Estoy hablando. *(eh-'stoh·ee ah-'blahn-doh)*
To eat	comer *(koh-'mehr)*
We're eating.	Estamos comiendo. *(eh-'stah-mohs koh-mee-'ehn-doh)*
To write	escribir *(eh-skree-'beer)*
He's writing.	Está escribiendo. *(eh-'stah eh-skree-bee-'ehn-doh)*

The same thing happens consistently when we refer to everyday activities. However, this time the verbs shift according to who completes the action. This next pattern is the same for most action words:

To Speak	Hablar *(ah-'blahr)*
I speak	hablo *('ah-bloh)*
You speak (informal)	hablas *('ah-blahs)*
You speak (formal); he, she speaks	habla *('ah-blah)*
You (plural), they speak	hablan *('ah-blahn)*
We speak	hablamos *(ah-'blah-mohs)*

To Eat	Comer (koh-'mehr)
I eat	como ('koh-moh)
You eat (informal)	comes ('koh-mehs)
You eat (formal); he, she eats	come ('koh-meh)
You (plural), they eat	comen ('koh-mehn)
We eat	comemos (koh-'meh-mohs)

To Write	Escribir (eh-skree-'beer)
I write	escribo (eh-'skree-boh)
You write (informal)	escribes (eh-'skree-behs)
You write (formal); he, she writes	escribe (eh-'skree-beh)
You (plural), they write	escriben (eh-'skree-behn)
We write	escribimos (eh-skree-'bee-mohs)

Notice how the -ar verb, hablar (ah-'blahr), doesn't change the same as the -er and -ir verbs! This tip will be helpful as you pick up more action forms later on. By the way, always be on the lookout for verbs that require se, which indicates that the action performed reflects back to the speaker: él apura (ehl ah-'poo-rah)—he hurries (somebody), él se apura (ehl seh ah-'poo-rah)—he hurries (himself).

to stay	quedarse (keh-'dahr-seh)	He stays in class.	se queda en la clase. (seh 'keh-dah ehn lah 'klah-seh)
to stop	pararse (pah-'rahr-seh)	He stops here.	Se para aquí. (seh 'pah-rah ah-'kee)
to hurry	apurarse (ah-poo-'rahr -seh)	He hurries a lot.	Se apura mucho. (seh ah-'poo-rah 'moo-choh)
to sit	sentarse (sehn-'tahr-seh)	He sits there.	Se sienta ahí. (seh see-'ehn-tah ah-'ee)
to get up	levantarse (leh-vahn-'tahr-seh)	He gets up at six.	Se levanta a las seis. (seh leh-'vahn-tah ah lahs 'seh·ees)
to enroll	matricularse (mah-tree-koo-'lahr-seh)	He enrolls late.	Se matricula tarde. (seh mah-tree-'koo-lah 'tahr-deh)
to meet	reunirse (reh-oo-'neer-seh)	He meets with her.	Se reune con ella. (seh reh-'oo-neh kohn 'eh-yah)

70

➤ Many Spanish verbs are irregular because they don't follow the pattern above. Look at the following:

to begin	empezar *(ehm-peh-'sahr)*
I begin	Empiezo *(ehm-pee-'eh-soh)*
to think	pensar *(pehn-'sahr)*
I think	Pienso *(pee-'ehn-soh)*
to leave	salir *(sah-'leer)*
I leave	Salgo *('sahl-goh)*
to tell	decir *(deh-'seer)*
I tell	Digo *('dee-goh)*
to see	ver *(vehr)*
I see	Veo *('veh-oh)*
to give	dar *(dahr)*
I give	Doy *(doh·ee)*
to find	encontrar *(ehn-kohn-'trahr)*
I find	Encuentro *(ehn-'kwehn-troh)*
to offer	ofrecer *(oh-freh-'sehr)*
I offer	Ofrezco *(oh-'freh-skoh)*
to do	hacer *(ah-'sehr)*
I do	Hago *('ah-goh)*
to bring	traer *(trah-'ehr)*
I bring	Traigo *('trah-ee-goh)*
to understand	entender *(ehn-tehn-'dehr)*
I understand	Entiendo *(ehn-tee-'ehn-doh)*

➤ Bear in mind that the informal (tú) form may be added if you consistently talk to small children. In general, all you do is add -s to the "you" singular form:

¿Habla español? (*'ah-blah eh-spah-'nyohl*)

¿Hablas español? (*'ah-blahs eh-spah-'nyohl*)

¿Escribe mucho? (*eh-'skree-beh 'moo-choh*)

¿Escribes mucho? (*eh-'skree-behs 'moo-choh*)

¿Entiende inglés? (*ehn-tee-'ehn-deh een-'glehs*)

¿Entiendes inglés? (*ehn-tee-'ehn-dehs een-'glehs*)

➤ To describe an action word in Spanish, try one of these. Do you note any pattern?

completely	completamente (*kohm-pleh-tah-'mehn-teh*)
quickly	rápidamente (*rah-pee-dah-'mehn-teh*)
slowly	lentamente (*lehn-tah-'mehn-teh*)

➤ And this is how you ask a question in the present tense:

Are they working?
¿Están trabajando?
(*eh-'stahn trah-bah-'hahn-doh*)

Do they work?
¿Trabajan?
(*trah-'bah-hahn*)

 ## ¡ÓRDENES!

Although we've learned several valuable command words already, let's work on a few more. This group of formal commands relates to general activities around the school site:

bring	traiga (*'trah·ee-gah*)
call	llame (*'yah-meh*)
close	cierre (*see-'eh-rreh*)
enter	entre (*'ehn-treh*)
leave	salga (*'sahl-gah*)
move	mueva (*'mweh-vah*)
open	abra (*'ah-brah*)
read	lea (*'leh-ah*)

72

return	**regrese** *(reh-'greh-seh)*
sign	**firme** *('feer-meh)*
take	**tome** *('toh-meh)*
write	**escriba** *(eh-'skree-bah)*

Enter through the large gate.
Entre por el portón grande. *('ehn-treh pohr ehl pohr-'tohn 'grahn-deh)*

Return tomorrow at eight o'clock.
Regrese mañana a las ocho. *(reh-'greh-seh mah-'nyah-nah ah lahs 'oh-choh)*

 MÁS INFORMACIÓN

➤ A simple approach to forming a formal command in Spanish requires knowledge of the three different action word (verb) endings. As you know, the endings are:

-ar as in **hablar** *(ah-'blahr)*	to speak
-er as in **comer** *(koh-'mehr)*	to eat
-ir as in **escribir** *(eh-skree-'beer)*	to write

To make a formal command word, drop the last two letters of the infinitive ("to") form and replace them as follows:

-ar	=	**-e**	
hablar	=	**¡Hable!** *('ah-bleh)*	Speak!
-er	=	**-a**	
comer	=	**¡Coma!** *('koh-mah)*	Eat!
-ir	=	**-a**	
escribir	=	**¡Escriba!** *(eh-'skree-bah)*	Write!

But beware! Some verbs are special and simply have to be memorized:

ir	=	¡Vaya! *('vah-yah)*	Go!
venir	=	¡Venga! *('vehn-gah)*	Come!
decir	=	¡Diga! *('dee-gah)*	Speak!

➤ Again, remember that formal commands are generally used with adults or older students.

 ¿LISTOS PARA PRACTICAR?

Now choose the best command word!

Lea, Llame, Conteste, Firme, Traiga
('leh-ah, 'yah-meh, kohn-'teh-steh, 'feer-meh, 'trah·ee-gah)

_____ la pregunta. *(lah preh-'goon-tah)*

_____ el libro. *(ehl 'lee-broh)*

_____ su nombre. *(soo 'nohm-breh)*

_____ a su casa. *(ah soo 'kah-sah)*

_____ la silla. *(lah 'see-yah)*

Connect the opposites:

contestar *(kohn-teh-'stahr)*	encontrar *(ehn-kohn-'trahr)*
abrir *(ah-'breer)*	terminar *(tehr-mee-'nahr)*
empezar *(ehm-peh-'sahr)*	cerrar *(seh-'rrahr)*
entrar *(ehn-'trahr)*	salir *(sah-'leer)*
buscar *(boo-'skahr)*	preguntar *(preh-goon-'tahr)*

Shift from one tense to the next. Follow the example given:

Están visitando. *(eh-'stahn vee-see-'tahn-doh)*   Visitan. *(vee-'see-tahn)*

Están llamando. *(eh-'stahn yah-'mahn-doh)*   _____

Están regresando. *(eh-'stahn reh-greh-'sahn-doh)*   _____

Están llegando. *(eh-'stahn yeh-'gahn-doh)*   _____

CHAPTER THREE
Capítulo Tres
(kah-'pee-too-loh trehs)

THE YOUNGER STUDENTS
Los estudiantes menores
(lohs eh-stoo-dee-'ahn-tehs meh-'noh-rehs)

HOW ARE YOU, SWEETHEART?

¿Cómo estás tú, querido? *('koh-moh eh-'stahs too, keh-'ree-doh)*

Let's begin our classroom experiences in Spanish by exploring the world of early education. As you have seen, some of the words in Spanish change slightly when you address loved ones or young children. Here are more examples of casual or informal Spanish:

You are my friend.	Tú eres mi amigo. *(too 'eh-rehs mee ah-'mee-goh)*
Do you speak Spanish?	¿Tú hablas español? *(too 'ah-blahs eh-spah-'nyohl)*
You don't have a pencil.	Tú no tienes un lápiz. *(too noh tee-'eh-nehs oon 'lah-pees)*

Can you tell that tú *(too)* means "you"? Note that the word "your" is tu:

Where's your family?	¿Dónde está tu familia? *('dohn-deh eh-'stah too fah-'mee-lee·ah)*

All informal verb forms require changes when you talk in casual settings, and most can be recognized because they end in the letter -s.

Do you have...?	¿Tienes...? *(tee-'eh-nehs)*
Do you want...?	¿Quieres...? *(kee-'eh-rehs)*
Do you need...?	¿Necesitas...? *(neh-seh-'see-tahs)*

OK, picture a group of children as you practice:

How many do you have?	¿Cuántos tienes? *('kwahn-tohs tee-'eh-nehs)*
Which one do you want?	¿Cuál quieres? *(kwahl kee-'eh-rehs)*
What do you need?	¿Qué necesitas? *(keh neh-seh-'see-tahs)*

These comments are common around the very young:

How cute!	¡Qué precioso! *(keh pre-see-'oh-soh)*
How funny!	¡Qué cómico! *(keh 'koh-mee-koh)*
How pretty!	¡Qué bonito! *(keh boh-'nee-toh)*
What a beautiful face!	¡Qué linda cara! *(keh 'leen-dah 'kah-rah)*

What a beautiful outfit!	¡Qué linda ropa!
	(keh 'leen-dah 'roh-pah)
What a beautiful smile!	¡Qué linda sonrisa!
	(keh 'leen-dah sohn-'ree-sah)
What a beautiful voice!	¡Qué linda voz!
	(keh 'leen-dah vohs)
What beautiful hair!	¡Qué lindo pelo!
	(keh 'leen-doh 'peh-loh)

DIFERENCIAS CULTURALES

Hispanics also use the informal tú form whenever they tell children what to do. It sends a message of closeness and intimacy. We'll study these verb conjugations soon:

Come here, my darling.	Ven acá, mi querido.
	(vehn ah-'kah, mee keh-'ree-doh)
Come here, my love.	Ven acá, mi amor.
	(vehn ah-'kah, mee ah-'mohr)
Don't be afraid.	No tengas miedo.
	(noh 'tehn-gahs mee-'eh-doh)
Don't cry.	No llores.
	(noh 'yoh-rehs)
Give me a hug.	Dame un abrazo.
	('dah-meh oon ah-'brah-soh)
It's lots of fun.	Es muy divertido.
	(ehs 'moo·ee dee-vehr-'tee-doh)
It's for you.	Es para ti.
	(ehs 'pah-rah tee)

THE LITTLE ONES
Los niñitos *(lohs nee-'nyee-tohs)*

Many parents today get a jump start on their child's formal education by enrolling them in nursery schools, preschools, and child-care facilities. For those educators who teach Spanish-speaking infants and toddlers, here are some key words that can make early instruction a whole lot easier:

Let's go to (the)...	Vamos a... (*'vah-mohs ah...*)
bassinet	el bacinete (*ehl bah-see-'neh-teh*)
cradle	la cuna mecedora (*lah 'koo-nah meh-seh-'doh-rah*)
crib	la cuna (*lah 'koo-nah*)
doll house	la casa de muñecas (*lah 'kah-sah deh moo-'nyeh-kahs*)
game	el juego (*ehl 'hweh-goh*)
playpen	el corral de juego (*ehl koh-'rrahl deh 'hweh-goh*)
potty	la vasinica (*lah vah-see-'nee-kah*)
stroller	el carrito de bebé (*ehl kah-'rree-toh deh beh-'beh*)
stuffed animal	el animal de peluche (*ehl ah-nee-'mahl deh peh-'loo-cheh*)
toy	el juguete (*ehl hoo-'geh-teh*)

Take (the)...	Toma... (*'toh-mah*)
bib	el babero (*ehl bah-'beh-roh*)
blanket	la cobija (*lah koh-'bee-hah*)
nursing bottle	el biberón (*ehl bee-beh-'rohn*)
pacifier	el chupete (*ehl choo-'peh-teh*)
rattle	el sonajero (*ehl soh-nah-'heh-roh*)

THE TOY CHEST
El baúl de juguetes (*ehl bah-'ool deh hoo-'geh-tehs*)

Bring (the)...	Trae... (*'trah-eh...*)
action figure	el personaje de acción (*ehl pehr-soh-'nah-heh deh ahk-see-'ohn*)
ball	la pelota (*lah peh-'loh-tah*)
balloon	el globo (*ehl 'gloh-boh*)
bat	el bate (*ehl 'bah-teh*)
blocks	los cubitos (*lohs koo-'bee-tohs*)
coloring book	el librito de dibujos (*ehl lee-'bree-toh deh dee-'boo-hohs*)
costume	el disfraz (*ehl dees-'frahs*)
crayons	los lápices para pintar (*lohs 'lah-pee-sehs 'pah-rah peen-'tahr*)
doll	la muñeca (*lah moo-'nyeh-kah*)
drum	el tambor (*ehl tahm-'bohr*)

easel	el caballete (*ehl kah-bah-'yeh-teh*)
jump rope	la cuerda para brincar (*lah 'kwehr-dah 'pah-rah breen-'kahr*)
kite	la cometa (*lah koh-'meh-tah*)
little car	el carrito (*ehl kah-'rree-toh*)
mobile	el móvil (*ehl 'moh-veel*)
model	el modelo (*ehl moh-'deh-loh*)
monster	el monstruo (*ehl 'mohn-stroo-oh*)
puppets	los títeres (*lohs 'tee-teh-rehs*)
puzzle	el rompecabezas (*ehl rohm-peh-kah-'beh-sahs*)
skates	los patines (*lohs pah-'tee-nehs*)
sled	el trineo (*ehl tree-'neh-oh*)
spaceship	la nave espacial (*lah 'nah-veh eh-spah-see-'ahl*)
storybook	el libro de cuentos (*ehl 'lee-broh deh 'kwehn-tohs*)
transformer	el transformador (*ehl trahns-fohr-mah-'dohr*)
tricycle	el triciclo (*ehl tree-'see-kloh*)
wagon	el vagón (*ehl vah-'gohn*)
whistle	el silbato (*ehl seel-'bah-toh*)

The toy _____	_____ de juguete (_____ *deh hoo-'geh-teh*)

airplane	el avión (*ehl ah-vee-'ohn*)
animal	el animal (*ehl ah-nee'mahl*)
boat	el barco (*ehl 'bahr-koh*)
dinosaur	el dinosaurio (*ehl dee-noh-'sah-oo-ree·oh*)
dragon	el dragón (*ehl drah-'gohn*)
horn	la trompeta (*lah trohm-'peh-tah*)
soldier	el soldado (*ehl sohl-'dah-doh*)
truck	el camión (*ehl kah-mee-'ohn*)
weapon	la arma (*lah'ahr-mah*)

It's...	Es (de...) (*ehs deh ...*)

cardboard	cartón (*kahr-'tohn*)
cloth	tela (*'teh-lah*)
electronic	electrónico (*eh-lehk-'troh-nee-koh*)
metal	metal (*meh-'tahl*)
modeling clay	plastilina (*plah-stee-'lee-nah*)
plastic	plástico (*'plah-stee-koh*)
wood	madera (*mah-'deh-rah*)

➤ Most Spanish speakers have learned to use English brand names to specify their favorite playthings:

los HotWheels
el Nintendo
la Cabbage Patch
los Legos
el Spongebob

➤ There are plenty of words that relate to child's play—try these out as part of your instruction:

Do you like...?	¿Te gustan...? *(teh 'goo-stahn)*
cartoons	los dibujos animados *(lohs dee-'boo-hohs ah-nee-'mah-dohs)*
jokes	los chistes *(lohs 'chee-stehs)*
rhymes	las rimas *(lahs 'ree-mahs)*
skits	los dramas cortos *(lohs 'drah-mahs 'kohr-tohs)*
songs	las canciones *(lahs kahn-see-'oh-nehs)*
tricks	los trucos *(lohs 'troo-kohs)*

➤ A few games have their own special names in Spanish:

chess	el ajedrez *(ehl ah-heh-'drehs)*
checkers	el juego de damas *(ehl 'hweh-goh deh 'dah-mahs)*
playing cards	la baraja de juguete *(lah bah-'rah-hah deh hoo-'geh-teh)*

➤ We have...   Tenemos... *(teh-'neh-mohs)*

videos	vídeos *('vee-deh-ohs)*
video games	videojuegos *(vee-deh-oh-hoo-'eh-gohs)*
computer games	juegos para la computadora *(hoo-'eh-gohs 'pah-rah lah kohm poo-tah-'doh-rah)*

➤ The problem is...   El problema es...

wetting	orinarse *(oh-ree-'nahr-seh)*
tantrums	tener rabietas *(teh-'nehr rah-bee-'eh-tahs)*
thumb-sucking	chuparse el dedo *(choo-'pahr-seh ehl 'deh-doh)*

THE LESSONS

Las lecciones *(lahs lehk-see·'oh-nehs)*

In addition to playtime, preschool-aged children also need academic instruction. See if you can figure out what to say about these popular classroom items:

toy dishes	los platos de juguete *(lohs 'plah-tohs deh hoo-'geh-teh)*
small boxes	las cajas chicas *(lahs 'kah-hahs 'chee-kahs)*
plastic scissors	las tijeras de plástico *(lahs tee-'heh-rahs deh 'plah-stee-koh)*
work tables	las mesas de trabajo *(lahs 'meh-sahs deh trah-'bah-hoh)*
large pictures	los dibujos grandes *(lohs dee-'boo-hohs 'grahn-dehs)*
music CDs	los CDs de música *(lohs see-'dees deh 'moo-see-kah)*

And, what about the curriculum? Most schools for the very young teach basic skills in the following areas:

Let's study...	Vamos a estudiar... *('vah-mohs ah eh-stoo-dee-'ahr)*
art	el arte *(ehl 'ahr-teh)*
language	el lenguaje *(ehl lehn-'gwah-heh)*
math	las matemáticas *(lahs mah-teh-'mah-tee-kahs)*
music	la música *(lah 'moo-see-kah)*
physical education	la educación física *(lah eh-doo-kah-see-'ohn 'fee-see-kah)*
science	la ciencia *(lah see-'ehn-see·ah)*
social studies	los estudios sociales *(lohs eh-'stoo-dee·ohs soh-see·'ah-lehs)*

These topics should be covered, too:

behavior	el comportamiento *(ehl kohm-pohr-tah-mee-'ehn-toh)*
health	la salud *(lah sah-'lood)*
safety	la seguridad *(lah seh-goo-ree-'dahd)*

➤ If stuffed animals are being used for either instruction or play, learn the proper names for each one:

elephant	**el elefante** *(ehl eh-leh-'fahn-teh)*
giraffe	**la jirafa** *(lah hee-'rah-fah)*
lion	**el león** *(ehl leh-'ohn)*
monkey	**el mono** *(ehl 'moh-noh)*
tiger	**el tigre** *(ehl 'tee-greh)*

VOCABULARY LIST

Lista de vocabulario *('lee-stah deh voh-kah-boo-'lah-ree·oh)*

Besides grammar and pronunciation practice, preschool teachers teach vocabulary words to enhance language development. Look at this selection.

Let's learn about...	**Aprendamos sobre...** *(ah-prehn-'dah-mohs 'soh-breh...)*
actions	**las acciones** *(lahs ahk-see·'oh-nehs)*
animals	**los animales** *(lohs ah-nee-'mah-lehs)*
body parts	**las partes del cuerpo** *(lahs 'pahr-tehs dehl 'kwehr-poh)*
calendar	**el calendario** *(ehl kah-lehn-'dah-ree·oh)*
city	**la ciudad** *(lah see-oo-'dahd)*
clock	**el reloj** *(ehl reh-'loh)*
clothing	**la ropa** *(lah 'roh-pah)*
colors	**los colores** *(lohs koh-'loh-rehs)*
descriptions	**las descripciones** *(lahs deh-skreep-see·'oh-nehs)*
family	**la familia** *(lah fah-'mee-lee·ah)*
foods	**las comidas** *(lahs koh-'mee-dahs)*
home	**la casa** *(lah 'kah-sah)*
instruments	**los instrumentos musicales** *(lohs een-stroo-'mehn-tohs moo-see-'kah-lehs)*
nature	**la naturaleza** *(lah nah-too-rah-'leh-sah)*
numbers	**los números** *(lohs 'noo-meh-rohs)*

occupations	las ocupaciones *(lahs oh-koo-pah-see·'oh-nehs)*
outdoors	las afueras *(lahs ah-'fweh-rahs)*
school	la escuela *(lah eh-'skweh-lah)*
sports	los deportes *(lohs deh-'pohr-tehs)*
transportation	el transporte *(ehl trahns-'pohr-teh)*
weather	el clima *(ehl 'klee-mah)*

MÁS INFORMACIÓN

➤ To be more specific, break your word groups into detailed selections. For example, here's what you can share about la casa *(lah 'kah-sah)*:

They are...	Son... *(sohn...)*
appliances	los electrodomésticos *(lohs eh-lehk-troh-doh-'meh-stee-kohs)*
furniture	los muebles *(lohs 'mweh-blehs)*
rooms	los cuartos *(lohs 'kwahr-tohs)*

➤ Check out these other visual aids:

movies	las películas *(lahs peh-'lee-koo-lahs)*
paintings	los cuadros *(lohs 'kwah-drohs)*
photos	las fotos *(lahs 'foh-tohs)*
picture books	los libros ilustrados *(lohs 'lee-brohs ee-loo-'strah-dohs)*
portraits	los retratos *(lohs reh-'trah-tohs)*

DIFERENCIAS CULTURALES

What do you know about children's games from other countries? You may have to ask around for the equivalents to activities such as hopscotch, dodgeball, or tag. Their names generally differ from one country to the next.

LET'S CLEAN UP!

¡Vamos a limpiar! *('vah-mohs ah leem-pee-'ahr)*

When the lesson is over and it's time to clean their mess, many youngsters may not know what they're supposed to do. You can help:

Pick up...	Recoge... *(reh-'koh-heh)*
Move... (the)	Mueve... *('mweh-veh)*
Take...	Toma... *('toh-mah)*

basket	la canasta *(lah kah-'nah-stah)*
broom	la escoba *(lah eh-'skoh-bah)*
bucket	el balde *(ehl 'bahl-deh)*
duster	el limpiador *(ehl leem-pee·ah-'dohr)*
dustpan	el recogedor de basura *(ehl reh-koh-heh-'dohr deh bah-'soo-rah)*
mop	el trapeador *(ehl trah-peh-ah-'dohr)*
sponge	la esponja *(lah eh-'spohn-hah)*
towel	la toalla *(lah toh-'ah-yah)*

While working alongside little children during cleanup, mention a few of these common action words:

to dust	sacudir *(sah-koo-'deer)*	Estamos sacudiendo el escritorio. *(eh-'stah-mohs sah-koo-dee-'ehn-doh ehl eh-skree-'toh-ree·oh)*
to mop	trapear *(trah-peh-'ahr)*	Estamos trapeando el baño. *(eh-'stah-mohs trah-peh-'ahn-doh ehl 'bah-nyoh)*
to sweep	barrer *(bah-'rrehr)*	Estamos barriendo la basura. *(eh-'stah-mohs bah-rree-'ehn-doh lah bah-'soo-rah)*

What's going on here? Go ahead and translate these command phrases.

Escribe los números en el pizarrón. *(eh-'skree-beh lohs 'noo-meh-rohs ehn ehl pee-sah-'rrohn)*
Trae las fotos de tu familia. *('trah-eh lahs 'foh-tohs deh too fah-'mee-lee·ah)*
Toma la esponja y mueve el balde. *('toh-mah lah eh-'spohn-hah ee 'mweh-veh ehl 'bahl-deh)*

Can you name three different toys in Spanish?

_____   _____   _____

THE GRADE SCHOOL
La escuela primaria *(lah eh-'skweh-lah pree-'mah-ree·ah)*

Many children don't receive formal instruction until they enter elementary or grammar school. The traditional classroom is full of new terminology for the Spanish speaker, so consider labeling the following items in both languages:

Look at the...	Mira... *('mee-rah)*
alarm	**la alarma** *(lah ah-'lahr-mah)*
bell	**la campana** *(lah kahm-'pah-nah)*
bench	**el banco** *(ehl 'bahn-koh)*
bulletin board	**el tablero de anuncios** *(ehl tah-'bleh-roh deh ah-'noon-see·ohs)*
cabinet	**el gabinete** *(ehl gah-bee-'neh-teh)*
chair	**la silla** *(lah 'see-yah)*
clock	**el reloj** *(ehl reh-'loh)*
computer	**la computadora** *(lah kohm-poo-tah-'doh-rah)*
desk	**el escritorio** *(ehl ehs-kree-'toh-ree·oh)*
DVD player	**el tocador de DVD** *(ehl toh-kah-'dohr deh dee-vee-dee)*
filing cabinet	**el archivo** *(ehl ahr-'chee-voh)*
flag	**la bandera** *(lah bahn-'deh-rah)*

85

loudspeaker	el altoparlante *(ehl ahl-toh-pahr-'lahn-teh)*
projector	el proyector *(ehl proh-yehk-'tohr)*
pencil sharpener	el sacapuntas *(ehl sah-kah-'poon-tahs)*
screen	la pantalla *(lah pahn-'tah-yah)*
shelf	el estante *(ehl eh-'stahn-teh)*
table	la mesa *(lah 'meh-sah)*
teacher's desk	el escritorio del maestro *(ehl eh-skree-'toh-ree·oh dehl mah-'eh-stroh)*
television	el televisor *(ehl teh-leh-vee-'sohr)*
wastebasket	el cesto de basura *(ehl 'seh-stoh deh bah-'soo-rah)*
whiteboard	el pizarrón *(ehl pee-sah-'rrohn)*

As the children move through the grade school level, a variety of classroom materials will be put to use during instruction. To learn these objects quickly, try moving them around. Watch:

Bring...	Trae... *('trah-eh)*
Use... (the)	Usa... *('oo-sah)*
Pick up...	Recoge... *(reh-'koh-heh)*
book	el libro *(ehl 'lee-broh)*
brush	el pincel *(ehl peen-'sel)*
card	la tarjeta *(lah tahr-'heh-tah)*
envelope	el sobre *(ehl 'soh-breh)*
eraser	el borrador *(ehl boh-rrah-'dohr)*
folder	la libreta *(lah lee-'breh-tah)*
glue	el pegamento *(ehl peh-gah-'mehn-toh)*
marker	el marcador *(ehl mahr-kah-'dohr)*
notebook	el cuaderno *(ehl kwah-'dehr-noh)*
paint	la pintura *(lah peen-'too-rah)*
paper	el papel *(ehl pah-'pehl)*
paper clip	el clip *(ehl kleep)*
pen	el lapicero *(ehl lah-pee-'seh-roh)*
pencil	el lápiz *(ehl 'lah-pees)*
pin	el alfiler *(ehl ahl-fee-'lehr)*
ruler	la regla *(lah 'reh-glah)*
stapler	la engrapadora *(lah ehn-grah-pah-'doh-rah)*
string	el hilo *(ehl 'ee-loh)*
tape	la cinta *(lah 'seen-tah)*
thumbtack	la tachuela *(lah tah-choo-'eh-lah)*

Continue to give directions. Most of the time, all that's needed is a one-liner or two:

This way.	**De esta manera.** *(deh 'eh-stah mah-'neh-rah)*
Like this.	**Así.** *(ah-'see)*
Keep going.	**Sigue.** *('see-geh)*

 MÁS INFORMACIÓN

➤ Here's more complex vocabulary:

national anthem	**el himno nacional** *(ehl 'eem-noh nah-see·oh-'nahl)*
pledge of allegiance	**la promesa patriótica** *(lah proh-'meh-sah pah-tree·'oh-tee-kah)*
textbook	**el libro de texto** *(ehl 'lee-broh deh 'tehk-stoh)*
sheet of paper	**la hoja de papel** *(lah 'oh-hah deh pah-'pehl)*

➤ Be on the lookout for other Spanish words that refer to the objects mentioned here. Not all Spanish-speaking countries use the same vocabulary!

pen	**la pluma** *(lah 'ploo-mah)* instead of **lapicero** *(lah-pee-'seh-roh)*
notebook	**la carpeta** *(lah kahr-'peh-tah)* instead of **cuaderno** *(kwah-'dehr-noh)*

➤ Spanglish is OK with some trademarks:

el Whiteout®
el Gluestick®
el Post-it®
el Scotch® tape

MORE IMPORTANT WORDS

Más palabras importantes *(mahs pah-'lah-brahs eem-pohr-'tahn-tehs)*

All sorts of valuable phrases will be exchanged at this level, so grab hold of the most popular terms right away. Here's an easy pattern:

What's (the)...?	¿Cuál es... ? *(kwahl ehs...?)*
chapter	**el capítulo** *(ehl kah-'pee-too-loh)*
date	**la fecha** *(lah 'feh-chah)*
grade (academic)	**la nota** *(lah 'noh-tah)*
grade (level)	**el grado** *(ehl 'grah-doh)*
letter	**la letra** *(lah 'leh-trah)*
number	**el número** *(ehl 'noo-meh-roh)*
page	**la página** *(lah 'pah-hee-nah)*
story	**el cuento** *(ehl 'kwehn-toh)*
title	**el título** *(ehl 'tee-too-loh)*
word	**la palabra** *(lah pah-'lah-brah)*

¿Por qué tengo una mala nota en matemáticas?

Porque dos y dos no son cuarenta.

Throughout each lesson, feel free to stimulate responses using key Spanish words:

Let's do...(the)	**Vamos a hacer...** *('vah-mohs ah ah-'sehr...)*
activity	**la actividad** *(lah ahk-tee-vee-'dahd)*
assignment	**la tarea** *(lah tah-'reh-ah)*
course	**el curso** *(ehl 'koor-soh)*
exercise	**el ejercicio** *(ehl eh-hehr-'see-see·oh)*

lesson	la lección *(lah lehk-see·'ohn)*
program	el programa *(ehl proh-'grah-mah)*

Do all of you understand (the)...?	¿Todos entienden...? *('toh-dohs ehn-tee-'ehn-dehn...?)*

answer	la respuesta *(lah reh-'spweh-stah)*
concept	el concepto *(ehl kohn-'sehp-toh)*
idea	la idea *(lah ee-'deh-ah)*
principle	el principio *(ehl preen-'see-pee·oh)*
problem	el problema *(el proh-'bleh-mah)*
question	la pregunta *(lah preh-'goon-tah)*
reason	la razón *(lah rah-'sohn)*
result	el resultado *(ehl reh-sool-'tah-doh)*
secret	el secreto *(ehl seh-'kreh-toh)*
solution	la solución *(lah soh-loo-see·'ohn)*
theme	el tema *(ehl 'teh-mah)*
theory	la teoría *(lah teh-oh-'ree·ah)*
topic	el asunto *(ehl ah-'soon-toh)*

MÁS INFORMACIÓN

➤ As lessons are being presented, you'll emphasize the importance of learning English. Here are a few beginning skills:

We study (the)...	Estudiamos... *(eh-stoo-dee-'ah-mohs)*
alphabet	el alfabeto *(ehl ahl-fah-'beh-toh)*
handwriting	la caligrafía *(lah kah-lee-grah-'fee·ah)*
printing	la imprenta *(lah eem-'prehn-tah)*
pronunciation	la pronunciación *(lah proh-noon-see·ah-see·'ohn)*
reading	la lectura *(lah lehk-'too-rah)*
spelling	la ortografía *(lah ohr-toh-grah-'fee·ah)*

THE PLAYGROUND

El campo de recreo *(ehl 'kahm-poh deh reh-'kreh-oh)*

There's a break between classes, so the kids are dashing outside to play with their friends. Younger students will often talk about these things on the playground:

Let's run to (the)...	Corramos a... *(koh-'rrah-mohs ah...)*
bars	las barras *(lahs 'bah-rrahs)*
benches	las bancas *(lahs 'bahn-kahs)*
jungle gym	los juegos infantiles *(lohs 'hweh-gohs een-fahn-'tee-lehs)*
merry-go-round	los caballitos *(lohs kah-bah-'yee-tohs)*
poles	los postes *(lohs 'poh-stehs)*
rings	los anillos *(lohs ah-'nee-yohs)*
rope	la soga *(lah 'soh-gah)*
sandbox	el cajón de arena *(ehl kah-'hohn deh ah-'reh-nah)*
seesaw	el subibaja *(ehl soo-bee-'bah-hah)*
slide	el tobogán *(ehl toh-boh-'gahn)*
swing	el columpio *(ehl koh-'loom-pee·oh)*
tricycle	el triciclo *(ehl tree-'see-kloh)*
water fountain	el bebedero *(ehl beh-beh-'deh-roh)*

Whenever children get together to play, there are disagreements. Practice these verbs by writing full sentences:

to argue	discutir *(dee-skoo-'teer)* _____
to beat up	golpear *(gohl-peh-'ahr)* _____
to bite	morder *(mohr-'dehr)* _____
to bother	molestar *(moh-leh-'stahr)* _____
to bounce	rebotar *(reh-boh-'tahr)* _____
to break	romper *(rohm-'pehr)* _____
to climb	subir *(soo-'beer)* _____
to cry	llorar *(yoh-'rahr)* _____
to complain	quejarse *(keh-'hahr-seh)* _____
to curse	decir groserías *(deh-'seer groh-seh-'ree·ahs)* _____
to fall	caerse *(kah-'ehr-seh)* _____
to fight	pelear *(peh-leh-'ahr)* _____
to grab	agarrar *(ah-gah-'rrahr)* _____
to hide	esconder *(eh-skohn-'dehr)* _____
to hit	pegar *(peh-'gahr)* _____

to jump	saltar *(sahl-'tahr)* _____
to kick	patear *(pah-teh-'ahr)* _____
to lose	perder *(pehr-'dehr)* _____
to pull	jalar *(hah-'lahr)* _____
to push	empujar *(ehm-poo-'hahr)* _____
to roll	rodar *(roh-'dahr)* _____
to shake	sacudir *(sah-koo-'deer)* _____
to skip	dar brincos *('dahr 'breen-kohs)* _____
	¿Quiere dar brincos? *Kee-'eh-reh 'dahr 'breen-kohs)*
	_____
to spit	escupir *(eh-skoo-'peer)* _____
to throw	tirar *(tee-'rahr)* _____
to trip	tropezar *(troh-peh-'sahr)*
	Están tropezando. *(eh-'stahn troh-peh-'sahn-doh)*
	_____
to win	ganar *(gah-'nahr)* _____
to wrestle	luchar *(loo-'chahr)* _____
to yell	gritar *(gree-'tahr)* _____

MÁS INFORMACIÓN

➤ For a more extensive list of Spanish verbs, check the specialized selection at the end of the book!

➤ Do not forget this shortcut that was presented earlier:

Please don't...	Favor de no... *(fah-'vohr deh noh...)*
fight	pelear *(peh-leh-'ahr)*
push	empujar *(ehm-poo-'hahr)*
yell	gritar *(gree-'tahr)*

➤ Become familiar with any Spanish word that relates to playground activity:

You guys need (the)...	Necesitan... *(neh-seh-'see-tahn)*
ball	la pelota *(peh-'loh-tah)*
basket	la canasta *(kah-'nah-stah)*
bat	el bate *(ehl 'bah-teh)*
captain	el capitán *(ehl kah-pee-'tahn)*
coach	el entrenador *(ehl ehn-treh-nah-'dohr)*

equipment	**el equipaje** *(ehl eh-kee-'pah-heh)*
field	**el campo** *(ehl 'kahm-poh)*
glove	**el guante** *(ehl 'gwahn-teh)*
net	**la red** *(lah rehd)*
player	**el jugador** *(ehl hoo-gah-'dohr)*
racket	**la raqueta** *(lah rah-'keh-tah)*
rink	**la pista de hielo** *(lah 'pees-tah deh 'yeh-loh)*
rules	**los reglamentos** *(lohs reh-glah-'mehn-tohs)*
score	**la cuenta** *(lah 'kwehn-tah)*
stick	**el palo** *(ehl 'pah-loh)*
team	**el equipo** *(ehl eh-'kee-poh)*
tournament	**el torneo** *(ehl tohr-'neh-oh)*
uniforms	**los uniformes** *(lohs oo-nee-'fohr-mehs)*

➤ The names for major sports are very similar to English. Can you guess at the meanings of these?

el béisbol *(ehl 'beh·ees-bohl)*
el básquetbol *(ehl 'bah-skeht-bohl)*
el vólibol *(ehl 'voh-lee-bohl)*

➤ The following playtimes may vary depending on where you work:

snack time	**el descanso para comer** *(ehl deh-'skahn-soh 'pah-rah koh-'mehr)*
recess	**el recreo** *(ehl reh-'kreh-oh)*
lunchtime	**la hora de almuerzo** *(lah 'oh-rah dehl ahl-moo-'ehr-soh)*

¿LISTOS PARA PRACTICAR?

Connect the terms that belong together:

la alarma	la brocha
el televisor	el pizarrón
la pintura	la campana
el cuaderno	la libreta
el marcador	la pantalla

Translate into English:

The question is on page 5. _____

What is the title of the story? _____

The chapter has an important theme. _____

Name three things in Spanish that kids like to play during recess:

_____   _____   _____

Change these actions from one tense to the other. Then, go back and translate. See example:

Pateamos. *(pah-teh-'ah-mohs)*   <u>**Estamos pateando.**</u>
(We kick)   (We're kicking)

Saltamos. *(sahl-'tah-mohs)* _____

Empujamos. *(ehm-poo-'hah-mohs)* _____

Gritamos. *(gree-'tah-mohs)* _____

Jugamos. *(hoo-'gah-mohs)* _____

HEALTH CARE
El cuidado de la salud *(ehl kwee-'dah-doh deh lah sah-'lood)*

Educators need plenty of energy to keep up with the demands of young children, especially when it comes to emergency health care. At the preschool and elementary school levels, for example, treatment is often part of the daily routine. Look through this first list if you take care of the very little ones:

Do you want (the)...?   **¿Quieres...?** *(kee-'eh-rehs)*

Band Aid®   **la curita** *(lah koo-'ree-tah)*
cotton   **el algodón** *(ehl ahl-goh-'dohn)*
cream   **la crema** *(lah 'kreh-mah)*
diaper   **el pañal** *(ehl pah-'nyahl)*
formula   **la fórmula** *(lah 'fohr-moo-lah)*
lotion   **la loción** *(lah loh-see·'ohn)*

powder	**el talco** *(ehl 'tahl-koh)*
towelette	**la toallita** *(lah toh-ah-'yee-tah)*

You have (a)...	**Tienes...** *(tee-'eh-nehs)*
cold	**resfrío** *(rehs-'free·oh)*
colic	**cólico** *('koh-lee-koh)*
rash	**erupciones** *(eh-roop-see-'oh-nehs)*

Now help out the students who are a little older. Talk to them in private:

Is/Are there...?	**¿Hay...?** *('ah·ee...)*
bleeding	**sangramiento** *(sahn-grah-mee-'ehn-toh)*
fever	**fiebre** *(fee-'eh-breh)*
pain	**dolor** *(doh-'lohr)*

It's a...	**Es un/una...** *(ehs 'oon / 'oo-nah...)*
blister	**ampolla** *(ahm-'poh-yah)*
break	**quebradura** *(keh-brah'doo-dah)*
bruise	**contusión** *(kohn-too-see-'ohn)*
burn	**quemadura** *(keh-mah-'doo-rah)*
cut	**cortadura** *(kohr-tah-'doo-rah)*
scrape	**rasguño** *(rahs-'goo-nyoh)*
sprain	**torcedura** *(tohr-seh-'doo-rah)*

Here's (the)...	**Aquí tienes...** *(ah-'kee tee-'eh-nehs...)*
bandage	**el vendaje** *(ehl vehn-'dah-heh)*
blanket	**la cobija** *(lah koh-'bee-hah)*
ice	**el hielo** *(ehl 'yeh-loh)*
medicine	**la medicina** *(lah meh-dee-'see-nah)*
water	**el agua** *(ehl 'ah-gwah)*

➤ Don't fret if you didn't find what you're looking for. We'll talk more about health care in Chapter Eight when we discuss the school nurse.

➤ By the way, these terms are always good to know:

visually impaired	**ciego/a** *(see-'eh-goh / ah)*
hearing impaired	**sordo/a** *('sohr-doh / ah)*
physically or mentally challenged	**incapacitado/ah** *(een-kah-pah-see-'tah-doh / ah)*

➤ Bodily functions have names in Spanish, also. Read on:

burp	**el eructo** *(ehl eh-'rook-toh)*
cough	**la tos** *(lah tohs)*
hiccup	**el hipo** *(ehl 'ee-poh)*
sneeze	**el estornudo** *(ehl eh-stohr-'noo-doh)*

DIFERENCIAS CULTURALES

Throughout history, we have discovered that certain herbs and spices work wonders on common ailments. In Latin America, the practice of home remedies—**los remedios caseros** *(lohs reh-'meh-dee·ohs kah-'seh-rohs)*—is quite popular, so don't be surprised if your Hispanic students offer to prepare something when a fellow pupil gets sick or injured.

WHERE DOES IT HURT?

¿Dónde te duele? *('dohn-deh teh 'dweh-leh)*

Assisting Spanish-speaking kids is a breeze once you determine what's troubling them. The fastest way is to use "yes-no" questions. Ask them to point as you move through the list below:

Does (the) _____ hurt?   ¿Te duele _____ ? *(teh 'dweh-leh)*

ankle	el tobillo *(ehl toh-'bee-yoh)*
arm	el brazo *(ehl 'brah-soh)*
back	la espalda *(lah eh-'spahl-dah)*
body	el cuerpo *(ehl 'kwehr-poh)*
cheek	la mejilla *(lah meh-'hee-yah)*
chest	el pecho *(ehl 'peh-choh)*
chin	la barbilla *(lah bahr-'bee-yah)*
ear	la oreja *(lah oh-'reh-hah)*
elbow	el codo *(ehl 'koh-doh)*
eye	el ojo *(ehl 'oh-hoh)*
face	la cara *(lah'kah-rah)*
finger	el dedo *(ehl 'deh-doh)*
foot	el pie *(ehl 'pee-eh)*
hand	la mano *(lah 'mah-noh)*
head	la cabeza *(lah kah-'beh-sah)*
hip	la cadera *(lah kah-'deh-rah)*
knee	la rodilla *(lah roh-'dee-yah)*
leg	la pierna *(lah pee-'ehr-nah)*
lip	el labio *(ehl 'lah-bee·oh)*
mouth	la boca *(lah 'boh-kah)*
neck	el cuello *(ehl 'kweh-yoh)*
nose	la nariz *(lah nah-'rees)*
shoulder	el hombro *(ehl 'ohm-broh)*
stomach	el estómago *(ehl eh-'stoh-mah-goh)*
throat	la garganta *(lah gahr-'gahn-tah)*
toe	el dedo del pie *(ehl 'deh-doh dehl pee-'eh)*
tongue	la lengua *(lah 'lehn-gwah)*
wrist	la muñeca *(lah moo-'nyeh-kah)*

➤ Add these one-liners to your collection:

Be careful!	**¡Ten cuidado!** *(tehn kwee-'dah-doh)*
Call your mother!	**¡Llama a tu mamá!** *('yah-mah ah too mah-'mah)*
Danger!	**¡Peligro!** *(peh-'lee-groh)*
It's an emergency!	**¡Es una emergencia!** *(ehs 'oo-nah eh-mehr-'hehn-see·ah)*
Go to the nurse!	**¡Ve a la enfermera!** *(veh ah lah ehn-fehr-'meh-rah)*

➤ You'll probably hear these terms mentioned, too:

brain	**el cerebro** *(ehl seh-'reh-broh)*
hair	**el pelo** *(ehl 'peh-loh)*
heart	**el corazón** *(ehl koh-rah-'sohn)*
lungs	**los pulmones** *(lohs pool-'moh-nehs)*
skin	**la piel** *(lah pee-'ehl)*
teeth	**los dientes** *(lohs dee-'ehn-tehs)*

HOW'S THE WEATHER?
¿Cómo está el tiempo? *('koh-moh eh-'stah ehl tee-'ehm-poh)*

Some things in life we can't control. They often are the cause of our physical problems. Here's how we comment on the current weather conditions:

It's...	**Hace...** *('ah-seh...)*
cold	**frío** *('free·oh)*
hot	**calor** *(kah-'lohr)*
nice weather	**buen tiempo** *('bwehn tee-'ehm-poh)*
sunny	**sol** *(sohl)*
windy	**viento** *(vee-'ehn-toh)*

It's...	**Está...** *(eh-'stah...)*
clear	**despejado** *(dehs-'peh-'hah-doh)*
cloudy	**nublado** *(noo-'blah-doh)*
cool	**fresco** *('frehs-koh)*

drizzling	**lloviznando** *(yoh-vees-'nahn-doh)*
humid	**húmedo** *(óo-meh-doh)*
raining	**lloviendo** *(yoh-vee-'ehn-doh)*
snowing	**nevando** *(neh-'vahn-doh)*
warm	**templado** *(tehm-'plah-doh)*

Throughout the year, spend time with your students discussing health and safety concerns related to changes in the weather. If you like, consider teaching units based on the four seasons or **estaciones** *(eh-stah-see-'oh-nehs)*:

It's...	**Es...** *(ehs...)*
winter	**el invierno** *(ehl een-vee-'ehr-noh)*
spring	**la primavera** *(lah pree-mah-'veh-rah)*
summer	**el verano** *(ehl veh-'rah-noh)*
fall	**el otoño** *(ehl oh-'toh-nyoh)*

SAFETY FIRST!
¡Primero, la seguridad! *(pree-'meh-roh, lah seh-goo-ree-'dahd)*

The safety of all children is of tremendous importance, so continue to acquire all the Spanish words and phrases that you can.

You shouldn't...	**No debes...** *(noh 'deh-behs...)*
drink alcohol	**tomar alcohol** *(toh-'mahr ahl-'kohl)*
use drugs	**usar drogas** *(oo-'sahr 'droh-gahs)*
talk to strangers	**hablar con extraños** *(ah-'blahr kohn eh-'strah-nyohs)*
smoke cigarettes	**fumar cigarillos** *(foo-'mahr see-gah-'ree-yohs)*
sniff glue	**inhalar pegamento** *(een-ah-'lahr peh-gah-'mehn-toh)*
go there	**ir allí** *(eer ah·'yee)*
touch	**tocar** *(toh-'kahr)*

Let's talk about...	**Hablemos de...** *(ah-'bleh-mohs deh...)*
abandoned buildings	**los edificios abandonados** *(lohs eh-dee-'fee-see·ohs ah-bahn-doh-'nah-dohs)*
natural disasters	**los desastres naturales** *(lohs deh-'sah-strehs nah-too-'rah-lehs)*
good health	**la buena salud** *(lah 'bweh-nah sah-'lood)*

➤ Outline these important topics and present them in full detail:

attendance procedures   **los procedimientos de asistencia** *(lohs proh-seh-dee-mee-'ehn-tohs deh ah-see-'stehn-see·ah)*

fire drill   **el simulacro de incendio** *(ehl see-moo-'lah-kroh deh een-'sehn-dee·oh)*

safety rules   **las reglas de seguridad** *(lahs 'reh-glahs deh seh-goo-ree-'dahd)*

telephone use   **el uso del teléfono** *(ehl 'oo-soh dehl teh-'leh-foh-noh)*

➤ In an emergency, you might have to use several actions at once:

to breathe   **respirar** *(reh-spee-'rahr)*

to chew   **masticar** *(mah-stee-'kahr)*

to swallow   **tragar** *(trah-'gahr)*

➤ In order to disseminate information, most schools issue the following items:

Take (the)...   **Toma...** *('toh-mah)*

brochure   **el folleto** *(ehl foh-'yeh-toh)*

coupon   **el cupón** *(ehl koo-'pohn)*

envelope   **el sobre** *(ehl 'soh-breh)*

flyer   **la hoja** *(lah 'oh-hah)*

notice   **el anuncio** *(ehl ah-'noon-see·oh)*

ticket   **el boleto** *(ehl boh-'leh-toh)*

➤ A variety of school events cannot be translated easily, so you may want to announce them in English only:

Back-to-School Night
Open House
Parent Conference Day

MORE VERBS FOR TEACHERS

Más verbos para los maestros *(mahs 'vehr-bohs 'pah-rah lohs mah-'eh-strohs)*

If you're involved in elementary education, you're going to need a lot more action words in Spanish. Say each word as you practice the present tense:

to arrange   **arreglar** *(ah-rreh-'glahr)*   **Arreglamos las sillas.** *(ah-rreh-'glah-mohs lahs 'see-yahs)*

to ask for	**pedir** *(peh-'deer)*	**Pedimos la engrapadora.** *(peh-'dee-mohs lah ehn-grah-pah-'doh-rah)*
to check	**revisar** *(reh-vee-'sahr)*	**Revisamos los problemas.** *(reh-vee-'sah-mohs lohs proh-'bleh-mahs)*
to choose	**escoger** *(eh-skoh-'hehr)*	**Escogemos las pinturas.** *(eh-skoh-'heh-mohs lahs peen-'too-rahs)*
to correct	**corregir** *(koh-rreh-'heer)*	**Corregimos los papeles.** *(koh-rreh-'hee-mohs lohs pah-'peh-lehs)*
to erase	**borrar** *(boh-'rrahr)*	**Borramos el pizarrón.** *(boh-'rrah-mohs ehl pee-sah-'rrohn)*
to fill out	**llenar** *(yeh-'nahr)*	**Llenamos la página.** *(yeh-'nah-mohs lah 'pah-hee-nah)*
to pass out	**repartir** *(reh-pahr-'teer)*	**Repartimos los libros.** *(reh-pahr-'tee-mohs lohs 'lee-brohs)*
to pronounce	**pronunciar** *(proh-noon-see-'ahr)*	**Pronunciamos las letras.** *(proh-noon-see-'ah-mohs lahs 'leh-trahs)*
to remember	**recordar** *(reh-kohr-'dahr)*	**Recordamos el número.** *(reh-kohr-'dah-mohs ehl 'noo-meh-roh)*
to repeat	**repetir** *(reh-peh-'teer)*	**Repetimos las palabras.** *(reh-peh-'tee-mohs lahs pah-'lah-brahs)*
to ride	**montar** *(mohn-'tahr)*	**Montamos las bicicletas.** *(mohn-'tah-mohs lahs bee-see-'kleh-tahs)*
to see	**ver** *(vehr)*	**Vemos los dibujos.** *('veh-mohs lohs dee-'boo-hohs)*
to spell	**deletrear** *(deh-leh-treh-'ahr)*	**Deletreamos los nombres.** *(deh-leh-treh-'ah-mohs lohs 'nohm-brehs)*
to stack	**amontonar** *(ah-mohn-toh-'nahr)*	**Amontonamos los cuadernos.** *(ah-mohn-toh-'nah-mohs lohs kwah-'dehr-nohs)*
to teach	**enseñar** *(ehn-seh-'nyahr)*	**Enseñamos a los amigos.** *(ehn-seh-'nyah-mohs ah lohs ah-'mee-gohs)*

You still need more action words. Fill in the blanks by following the pattern shown.

to give	dar *(dahr)*	Damos el papel a los niños. *('dah-mohs ehl pah-'pehl ah lohs 'nee-nyohs)*
to help	ayudar *(ah-yoo-'dahr)*	Ayudamos a los estudiantes. *(ah-yoo-'dah-mohs ah lohs eh-stoo-dee-'ahn-tehs)*
to use	usar *(oo-'sahr)*	Usamos los libros rojos. *(oo-'sah-mohs lohs 'lee-brohs 'roh-hohs)*
to carry	llevar *(yeh-'vahr)*	_____.
to clean	limpiar *(leem-pee-'ahr)*	_____.
to count	contar *(kohn-'tahr)*	_____.
to cut	cortar *(kohr-'tahr)*	_____.
to draw	dibujar *(dee-boo-'hahr)*	_____.
to fold	doblar *(doh-'blahr)*	_____.
to paint	pintar *(peen-'tahr)*	_____.
to point	señalar *(seh-nyah-'lahr)*	_____.
to put	poner *(poh-'nehr)*	_____.
to put in	meter *(meh-'tehr)*	_____.
to show	mostrar *(moh-'strahr)*	_____.
to sing	cantar *(kahn-'tahr)*	_____.
to take out	sacar *(sah-'kahr)*	_____.
to tie	amarrar *(ah-mah-'rrahr)*	_____.
to touch	tocar *(toh-'kahr)*	_____.

➤ Teachers ought to remember a few verbs with se as well:

to bathe	bañarse *(bah-'nyahr-seh)*
to behave	portarse *(pohr-'tahr-seh)*
to comb one's hair	peinarse *(peh·ee-'nahr-seh)*
to complain	quejarse *(keh-'hahr-seh)*
to fall	caerse *(kah-'ehr-seh)*
to get dressed	vestirse *(veh-'steer-seh)*
to get lost	perderse *(pehr-'dehr-seh)*
to turn around	darse vuelta *('dahr-seh 'vwehl-tah)*
to wash	lavarse *(lah-'vahr-seh)*

➤ Here's a common way to recognize opposites in Spanish. Notice the prefix des- in these examples:

to dress	vestirse *(veh-'steer-seh)*
to undress	desvestirse *(dehs-veh-'steer-seh)*
to tie	amarrar *(ah-mah-'rrahr)*
to untie	desamarrar *(dehs-ah-mah-'rrahr)*
to fold	doblar *(doh-'blahr)*
to unfold	desdoblar *(dehs-doh-'blahr)*

¡ACCIÓN!

Bear in mind that all action words can be altered to communicate time-referenced messages. For example, you know that the -ndo ending indicates that actions are taking place right now:

to drive	manejar *(mah-neh-'hahr)*
I am driving	Estoy manejando *(eh-'stoh-ee mah-neh-'han-doh)*

And you know that there are at least five consistent changes that occur when action words refer to everyday activities:

I drive	Manejo *(mah-'neh-hoh)*
You (informal) drive	Manejas *(mah-'neh-hahs)*
You (formal) drive; He, She drives	Maneja *(mah-'neh-hah)*
You (pl.), They drive	Manejan *(mah-'neh-hahn)*
We drive	Manejamos *(mah-neh-'hah-mohs)*

You've also probably realized that not all action words like to follow the rules. Look at these three familiar irregular verbs. Can you tell which person these forms are referring to?

Ir (to go) *(eer)*	Tener (to have) *(teh-'nehr)*	Ser (to be) *('sehr)*
voy *('voh-ee)*	tengo *('tehn-goh)*	soy *('soh-ee)*
vas (informal) *(vahs)*	tienes (informal) *(tee-'eh-nehs)*	eres (informal) *('eh-rehs)*
va *(vah)*	tiene *(tee-'eh-neh)*	es *(ehs)*
van *(vahn)*	tienen *(tee-'eh-nehn)*	son *(sohn)*
vamos *('vah-mohs)*	tenemos *(teh-'neh-mohs)*	somos *('soh-mohs)*

See how they don't follow the regular-verb patterns? Notice the other unusual patterns below. These two verbs are used daily by teachers everywhere, so spend as much time as you need to review:

Poder (to be able) *(poh-'dehr)*		
puedo *('pweh-doh)*	I can read.	Puedo leer. *('pweh-doh leh-'ehr)*
puedes (informal) *(pweh-dehs)*	You can ski.	Puedes esquiar. *('pweh-dehs eh-skee-'ahr)*

puede *('pweh-deh)*	He (she, you) can go.	**Puede ir.** *('pweh-deh eer)*
pueden *('pweh-dehn)*	They can play.	**Pueden jugar.** *('pweh-dehn hoo-'gahr)*
podemos *(poh-'deh-mohs)*	We can study.	**Podemos estudiar.** *(poh-'deh-mohs eh-stoo-dee-'ahr)*

Querer (to want) *(keh-'rehr)*		
quiero *(kee-'eh-roh)*	I want to leave.	**Quiero salir.** *(kee-'eh-roh sah-'leer)*
quieres (informal) *(kee-'eh-rehs)*	You want to drive.	**Quieres manejar.** *(kee-'eh-rehs mah-neh-'hahr)*
quiere *(kee-'eh-reh)*	He (she) wants to walk. You want to walk.	**Quiere caminar.** *(kee-'eh-reh kah-mee-'nahr)*
quieren *(kee-'eh-rehn)*	They want to eat.	**Quieren comer.** *(kee-'eh-rehn koh-'mehr)*
queremos *(keh-'reh-mohs)*	We want to see.	**Queremos ver.** *(keh-'reh-mohs vehr)*

Many irregular verbs follow a **-ue** or **-ie** pattern that becomes familiar with practice:

Dormir (to sleep) *(dohr-'meer)*	**Entender (to understand)** *(ehn-tehn-'dehr)*
duermo *('dwehr-moh)*	entiendo *(ehn-tee-'ehn-doh)*
duermes (informal) *('dwehr-mehs)*	entiendes (informal) *(ehn-tee-'ehn-dehs)*
duerme *('dwehr-meh)*	entiende *(ehn-tee-'ehn-deh)*
duermen *('dwehr-mehn)*	entienden *(ehn-tee-'ehn-dehn)*
dormimos *(dohr-'mee-mohs)*	entendemos *(ehn-tehn-'deh-mohs)*

MÁS INFORMACIÓN

➤ Here are three other informal ways to discuss one's likes and dislikes. Note how unique each form is:

Do you like...?	¿Te gusta...? *(teh 'goo-stah...)*
Yes, I like...	Sí, me gusta... *(see, meh-'goo-stah...)*

| Would you like...? | ¿Quisieras...? *(kee-see-'eh-rahs...)* |
| Yes, I'd like... | Sí, quisiera... *(see, kee-see-'eh-rah...)* |

| Do you wish...? | ¿Deseas...? *(deh-'seh-ahs...)* |
| Yes, I wish... | Sí, deseo... *(see, deh-'seh-oh...)* |

➤ In Spanish, there are two primary ways to say "to know."

<u>To know something</u> requires the verb saber *(sah-'behr)*, while <u>to know someone</u> requires the verb conocer *(koh-noh-'sehr)*. Instead of working on all the conjugated forms of these new verbs, why not put them to practical use. Next time you need to know, pull a line from the sentences below:

I don't know.	No sé.
	(noh seh)
I don't know him.	No le conozco.
	(noh leh koh-'noh-skoh)
Do you know English?	¿Sabes inglés?
	('sah-behs een-'glehs)
Do they know her?	¿La conocen a ella?
	(lah koh-'noh-sehn ah 'eh-yah)

Obviously, saber *(sah-'behr)* works wonders in the classroom. Ask your students about anything:

Do you know how to speak English?
¿Saben hablar inglés? *('sah-behn ah-'blahr een-'glehs)*

Do you know how to read and write?
¿Saben leer y escribir? *('sah-behn leh-'ehr ee eh-skree-'beer)*

Do you know how to do it?
¿Saben hacerlo? *('sah-behn ah-'sehr-loh)*

 ## ¡ÓRDENES!

A good part of teaching involves giving commands, so don't hold back as you direct these verb forms at your students. See how the forms are informal, which means they are addressed to children, family, or friends. The form is the same as the third person singular in the present tense. Can you translate?

Arrange	Arregla las sillas. (ah-'rreh-glah lahs 'see-yahs)
Ask for	Pide mi ayuda. ('pee-deh mee ah-'yoo-dah)
Check	Revisa los problemas. (reh-'vee-sah lohs proh-'bleh-mahs)
Choose	Escoge el color. (eh-'skoh-heh ehl koh-'lohr)
Erase	Borra el pizarrón. ('boh-rrah ehl pee-sah-'rrohn)
Fill out	Llena los papeles. ('yeh-nah lohs pah-'peh-lehs)
Pass out	Reparte los lápices. (reh-'pahr-teh lohs 'lah-pee-sehs)
Remember	Recuerda el número. (reh-'kwehr-dah ehl 'noo-meh-roh)
Repeat	Repite la palabra. (reh-'pee-teh lah pah-'làh-brah)
Spell	Deletrea tu nombre. (deh-leh-'treh-ah too 'nohm-breh)
Stack	Amontona los libros. (ah-mohn-'toh-nah lohs 'lee-brohs)

Now, utilize these informal commands on the playground:

Catch!	¡Agarra! (ah-'gah-rrah)
Climb!	¡Sube! ('soo-beh)
Hit!	¡Pega! ('peh-gah)
Jump!	¡Salta! ('sahl-tah)
Throw!	¡Tira! ('tee-rah)
Win!	¡Gana! ('gah-nah)

Note the changes below in the personal form for both the singular and plural commands. You'll have to do your own translating. Be careful—a few of them are irregular!

Singular	Plural	
ayuda	ayuden	(ah-'yoo-dah, ah-'yoo-dehn)
canta	canten	('kahn-tah, 'kahn-tehn)
corta	corten	('kohr-tah, 'kohr-tehn)
cuenta	cuenten	('kwehn-tah, 'kwehn-tehn)
da	den	(dah, dehn)
dibuja	dibujen	(dee-'boo-hah, dee-'boo-hehn)
empuja	empujen	(ehm-'poo-hah, ehm-'poo-hehn)
limpia	limpien	('leem-pee·ah, 'leem-pee·ehn)
lleva	lleven	('yeh-vah, 'yeh-vehn)
muestra	muestren	('mweh-strah, 'mweh-strehn)

pinta	pinten	*('peen-tah, 'peen-tehn)*
señala	señalen	*(seh-'nyah-lah, seh-'nyah-lehn)*
toca	toquen	*('toh-kah, 'toh-kehn)*
usa	usen	*('oo-sah, 'oo-sehn)*

¡Antonio, <u>empuja</u> la puerta! *(ahn-'toh-nee·oh, ehm-'poo-hah lah 'pwehr-tah)*

¡Marcos y Antonio, <u>empujen</u> la puerta! *('mahr-kohs ee ahn-'toh-nee·oh, ehm-'poo-hehn lah 'pwehr-tah)*

 MÁS INFORMACIÓN

➤ A handful of informal commands are irregular and may have to be memorized:

Leave!	¡Sal!	*(sahl)*
Put!	¡Pon!	*(pohn)*
Do!	¡Haz!	*(ahs)*

➤ Also remember that some verbs have more than one meaning in Spanish. Look at these examples:

tocar *(toh-'kahr)*	to touch or to play a musical instrument
contar *(kohn-'tahr)*	to count or to tell a story
hacer *(ah-'sehr)*	to do or to make
tomar *(toh-'mahr)*	to take or to drink
esperar *(eh-speh-'rahr)*	to wait or to hope for
llevar *(yeh-'vahr)*	to carry or to wear

➤ Sometimes action words are actually more like phrases or expressions. Try out these informal one-liners today!

Behave!	¡Pórtate bien! *('pohr-tah-teh 'bee·ehn)*
Pay attention!	¡Presta atención! *('preh-stah ah-tehn-see·'ohn)*
Line up!	¡Ponte en fila! *('pohn-teh ehn 'fee-lah)*
Turn around!	¡Date vuelta! *('dah-teh 'vwehl-tah)*
Be quiet!	¡Silencio! *(see-'lehn-see·oh)*
Ask permission!	¡Pide permiso! *('pee-deh pehr-'mee-soh)*

➤ When the class gets noisy, utilize key phrases to keep things in order:

Only one person speaks at a time.	Solo una persona hable a la vez. *('soh-loh 'oo-nah pehr-'soh-nah 'ah-bleh ah lah vehs)*

Please raise your hand.	Levanta la mano, por favor. *(leh-'vahn-tah lah 'mah-noh, pohr fah-'vohr)*
You have to wait your turn.	Tienes que esperar tu turno. *(tee-'eh-nehs keh eh-speh-'rahr too 'toor-noh)*

¿LISTOS PARA PRACTICAR?

Name five body parts in Spanish:

_____ _____ _____ _____ _____

Look outside and answer these questions:

¿En qué estación estás ahora? *(ehn keh eh-stah-see-'ohn eh-'stahs ah-'oh-rah)*
¿Cómo está el tiempo? *('koh-moh eh-'stah ehl tee-'ehm-poh)*
¿Hace frío hoy? *('ah-seh 'free·oh 'oh·ee)*

Which words best relate to each other?

cortadura *(kohr-tah-'doo-rah)*	el hielo *(ehl 'yeh-loh)*
torcedura *(tohr-seh-'doo-rah)*	la aspirina *(lah ah-spee-'ree-nah)*
fiebre *(fee-'eh-breh)*	la curita *(lah koo-'ree-tah)*

Study the examples, and then make the changes:

ir (yo) *(eer, yoh)*	voy *('voh·ee)*
tener (nosotros) *(teh-'nehr, noh-'soh-trohs)*	_____
comer (tú) *(koh-'mehr, too)*	_____
ser (ellos) *(sehr,'eh-yohs)*	_____
poder (él) *(poh-'dehr, ehl)*	_____
querer (usted) *(keh-'rehr, oo-'stehd)*	_____
entender (ella) *(ehn-tehn-'dehr, 'eh-yah)*	_____

Alter these formal commands slightly to create informal ones:

cante *('kahn-teh)*   <u>canta</u> *('kahn-tah)*

ayude *(ah-'yoo-deh)*   _____

empuje *(ehm-'poo-heh)*   _____

limpie *('leem-pee·eh)*   _____

use *('oo-seh)*   _____

 DIFERENCIAS CULTURALES

Notice how in some cultures, male and female roles are extremely different. From childhood, many Hispanic students are raised to perform some tasks, while leaving others to the opposite sex. Over time children will learn to make their own choices, so try not to force boys and girls to participate in some events when they adamantly refuse.

CHAPTER FOUR
Capítulo Cuatro
(kah-'pee-too-loh 'kwah-troh)

THE OLDER STUDENTS
Los estudiantes mayores
(lohs eh-stoo-dee-'ahn-tehs mah-'yoh-rehs)

COURSE OF STUDY

El plan de estudios *(ehl plahn deh eh-'stoo-dee·ohs)*

At middle schools and high schools across the country, young people move quickly from classroom to classroom, taking courses in a variety of subjects. Many of their class titles are listed below. Can you identify them in Spanish?

It's a course in...	Es un curso de... *(ehs oon 'koor-soh deh...)*
algebra	el álgebra *(ehl 'ahl-heh-brah)*
art	el arte *(ehl 'ahr-teh)*
astronomy	la astronomía *(lah ah-stroh-noh-'mee·ah)*
biology	la biología *(lah bee·oh-loh-'hee·ah)*
calculus	el cálculo *(ehl 'kahl-koo-loh)*
chemistry	la química *(lah 'kee-mee-kah)*
choir	el coro *(ehl 'koh-roh)*
civics	el civismo *(ehl see-'vees-moh)*
competitive athletics	los deportes competitivos *(lohs deh-'pohr-tehs kohm-peh-tee-'tee-vohs)*
computers	las computadoras *(lahs kohm-poo-tah-'doh-rahs)*
drama	el drama *(ehl 'drah-mah)*
driver's education	la enseñanza de conducir *(lah ehn-seh-'nyahn-sah deh kohn-doo-'seer)*
earth science	la ciencia del mundo *(lah see-'ehn-see·ah dehl 'moon-doh)*
economics	la economía *(lah eh-koh-noh-'mee·ah)*
English as a second language	el inglés como segundo idioma *(ehl een-'glehs 'koh-moh seh-'goon-doh ee-dee-'oh-mah)*
English literature	la literatura inglesa *(lah lee-teh-rah-'too-rah een-'gleh-sah)*
European history	la historia de Europa *(lah ee-'stoh-ree·ah deh eh-oo-'roh-pah)*
geography	la geografía *(lah heh-oh-grah-'fee·ah)*
geometry	la geometría *(lah heh-oh-meh-'tree·ah)*
health	la salud *(lah sah-'lood)*
industrial arts	las artes industriales *(lahs 'ahr-tehs een-doo-stree·'ah-lehs)*
journalism	el periodismo *(ehl peh-ree·oh-'dees-moh)*
language arts	el lenguaje *(ehl lehn-'gwah-heh)*
Latin	el latín *(ehl lah-'teen)*

mathematics	**las matemáticas** *(lahs mah-teh-'mah-tee-kahs)*
music	**la música** *(lah 'moo-see-kah)*
philosophy	**la filosofía** *(lah fee-loh-soh-'fee·ah)*
physical education	**la educación física** *(lah eh-doo-kah-see·'ohn 'fee-see-kah)*
physics	**la física** *(lah 'fee-see-kah)*
political science	**la ciencia política** *(lah see-'ehn-see·ah poh-'lee-tee-kah)*
psychology	**la psicología** *(lah see-koh-loh-'hee·ah)*
reading	**la lectura** *(lah lehk-'too-rah)*
social studies	**los estudios sociales** *(lohs eh-'stoo-dee·ohs soh-see-'ah-lehs)*
sociology	**la sociología** *(lah soh-see·oh-loh-'hee·ah)*
special education	**la educación especial** *(lah eh-doo-kah-see·'ohn eh-speh-see-'ahl)*
speech	**el discurso** *(ehl dee-'skoor-soh)*
trigonometry	**la trigonometría** *(lah tree-goh-noh-meh-'tree·ah)*
U.S. history	**la historia de los Estados Unidos** *(lah ee-'stoh-ree·ah deh lohs eh-'stah-dohs oo-'nee-dohs)*
Western civilization	**la civilización del Occidente** *(lah see-vee-lee-sah-see·'ohn dehl ohk-see-'dehn-teh)*
world history	**la historia mundial** *(lah ee-'stoh-ree·ah moon-dee-'ahl)*
world languages	**los idiomas extranjeros** *(lohs ee-dee·'oh-mahs eks-trahn-'heh-rohs)*
writing	**la escritura** *(lah eh-skree-'too-rah)*

Using what we've already learned in Spanish, let's create a few practical sentences that can help us communicate better with our Spanish-speaking students. Think of situations where these comments would be considered appropriate:

You need to take a <u>math</u> class.
Necesitas tomar una clase de matemáticas. *(neh-seh-'see-tahs toh-'mahr 'oo-nah 'klah-seh deh mah-teh-'mah-tee-kahs)*

There is no <u>P.E.</u> today.
No hay clase de educación física hoy. *(noh 'ah·ee 'klah-seh deh eh-doo-kah-see·'ohn 'fee-see-kah 'oh·ee)*

Does your <u>English</u> class have a lot of students?
¿Hay muchos estudiantes en tu clase de inglés? *('ah·ee 'moo-chohs eh-stoo-dee-'ahn-tehs ehn too 'klah-se deh een-'glehs)*

You have to read your <u>history</u> book.
Tienes que leer tu libro de historia. *(tee-'eh-nehs keh leh-'ehr too 'lee-broh deh ee-'stoh-ree·ah)*

Are you studying <u>geography</u>?
¿Estás estudiando geografía? *(eh-'stahs eh-stoo-dee-'ahn-doh heh-oh-grah-'fee·ah)*

Now, go back and substitute the underlined word with a different class title. Continue to read aloud in Spanish.

MORE THINGS IN THE CLASSROOM
Más cosas en la clase *(mahs 'koh-sahs ehn lah 'klah-seh)*

You already know the names in Spanish for several objects in the classroom. Those words were introduced earlier when we learned about the elementary school. However, at the middle and high school levels, a number of other items need to be identified. Again, use bilingual labels whenever possible:

We have (the)...

Tenemos...*(teh-'neh-mohs)*

atlas	**el atlas** *(ehl 'aht-lahs)*
binder	**el encuadernador** *(ehl ehn-kwah-dehr-nah-'dohr)*
calculator	**la calculadora** *(lah kahl-koo-lah-'doh-rah)*
chart	**el diagrama** *(ehl dee·ah-'grah-mah)*
dictionary	**el diccionario** *(ehl deek-see·oh-'nah-ree·oh)*
digital camera	**la cámara digital** *(lah 'kah-mah-rah dee-hee'tahl)*
DVD player	**el tocador de DVDs** *(ehl toh-kah-'dohr deh dee-vee-'dees)*
easel	**el caballete** *(ehl kah-bah-'yeh-teh)*
globe	**el mundo** *(ehl 'moon-doh)*
graph	**el gráfico** *(ehl 'grah-fee-koh)*
headphones	**los audífonos** *(lohs ow-'dee-foh-nohs)*

labels	**las etiquetas** *(lahs eh-tee-'keh-tahs)*
laminations	**las hojas laminadas** *(lahs 'oh-hahs lah-mee-'nah-dahs)*
laptop	**la computadora portátil** *(lah kohm-poo-tah-'doh-rah pohr-'tah-teel)*
map	**el mapa** *(ehl 'mah-pah)*
microphone	**el micrófono** *(ehl mee-'kroh-foh-noh)*
model	**el modelo** *(ehl moh-'deh-loh)*
photocopier	**la fotocopíadora** *(lah foh-toh-koh-pee·ah-'doh-rah)*
podium	**el podio** *(ehl 'poh-dee·oh)*
recorder	**la grabadora** *(lah grah-bah-'doh-rah)*
screen	**la pantalla** *(lah pahn-'tah-yah)*
smartboard	**la pizarra interactiva** *(lah pee-'sah-rrah een-teh-rahk-'tee-vah)*
stationery	**los objetos de escritorio** *(lohs ohb-'heh-tohs dehl eh-skree-'toh-ree·oh)*
stool	**el banquillo** *(ehl bahn-'kee-yoh)*

Outside the classroom, children should be informed about school activities, policy changes, and upcoming events. Tell the Spanish speakers where they can find the information they need:

Everyone look at (the)...	**Todos miren...** *('toh-dohs 'mee-rehn)*
announcement	**el anuncio** *(ehl ah-'noon-see·oh)*
bulletin	**el boletín** *(ehl boh-leh-'teen)*
bulletin board	**el tablón de anuncios** *(ehl tah-'blohn deh ah-'noon-see·ohs)*
calendar	**el calendario** *(ehl kah-lehn-'dah-ree·oh)*
channel	**el canal** *(ehl kah-'nahl)*
film	**la película** *(lah peh-'lee-koo-lah)*
flyer	**el papel** *(ehl pah-'pehl)*
letter	**la carta** *(lah 'kahr-tah)*
memo	**el memorándum** *(ehl meh-moh-'rahn-doom)*
note	**la nota** *(lah 'noh-tah)*
notice	**el anuncio** *(ehl ah-'noon-see·oh)*
page	**la página** *(lah 'pah-hee-nah)*
poster	**el cartel** *(ehl kahr-'tehl)*
program	**el programa** *(ehl pro-'grah-mah)*
report	**el reporte** *(ehl reh-'pohr-teh)*
schedule	**el horario** *(ehl oh-'rah-ree·oh)*
sheet	**la hoja** *(lah 'oh-hah)*

sign	**el letrero** *(ehl leh-'treh-roh)*
video	**el vídeo** *(ehl 'vee-deh-oh)*

If things are filed away, make sure all students can find them:

Look in (the)...	**Busquen en...** *('boo-skehn ehn)*
bag	**la bolsa** *(lah 'bohl-sah)*
basket	**la canasta** *(lah kahn-'nahs-tah)*
box	**la caja** *(lah 'kah-hah)*
cabinet	**el gabinete** *(ehl gah-bee-'neh-teh)*
cupboard	**el armario** *(ehl ahr-'mah-ree·oh)*
drawer	**el cajón** *(ehl kah-'hohn)*
file	**el archivo** *(ehl ahr-'chee-voh)*
jar	**la jarra** *(lah 'hah-rrah)*

It's in (the)...	**Está en...** *(eh-'stah ehn...)*
aisle	**el pasillo** *(ehl pah-'see-yoh)*
group	**el grupo** *(ehl 'groo-poh)*
kit	**el estuche** *(ehl eh-'stoo-cheh)*
line	**la fila** *(lah 'fee-lah)*
pack	**el paquete** *(ehl pah-'keh-teh)*
row	**la fila** *(lah 'fee-lah)*
set	**el conjunto** *(ehl kohn-'hoon-toh)*

For those educators who keep all they can in the classroom, here's a set of words just for you:

armchair	**el sillón** *(ehl see-'yohn)*
bin	**el depósito** *(ehl deh-'poh-see-toh)*
chest	**el baúl** *(ehl bah-'ool)*
flower	**la flor** *(lah flohr)*
hanger	**el gancho** *(ehl 'gahn-choh)*
key	**la llave** *(lah 'yah-veh)*
lock	**el candado** *(ehl kahn-'dah-doh)*
mat	**el tapete** *(ehl tah-'peh-teh)*
photos	**las fotos** *(lahs 'foh-tohs)*
picture frame	**el marco** *(ehl 'mahr-koh)*
plant	**la planta** *(lah 'plahn-tah)*
rack	**el estante** *(ehl eh-'stahn-teh)*
rug	**la alfombra** *(lah ahl-'fohm-brah)*

shelf	la repisa *(lah reh-'pee-sah)*
sofa	el sofá *(ehl soh-'fah)*
stereo	el estéreo *(ehl eh-'steh-reh-oh)*
vase	el florero *(ehl floh-'reh-roh)*

Does anything need to be plugged in?

adapter	el adaptador *(ehl ah-dahp-tah-'dohr)*
air conditioner	el acondicionador de aire *(ehl ah-kohn-dee-see·oh-nah-'dohr deh 'ah·ee-reh)*
cable	el cable *(ehl 'kah-bleh)*
charger	el cargador *(ehl kahr-gah-'dohr)*
electrical outlet	el enchufe *(ehl ehn-'choo-feh)*
fan	el ventilador *(ehl vehn-tee-lah-'dohr)*
heater	el calentador *(ehl kah-lehn-tah-'dohr)*
lamp	la lámpara *(lah 'lahm-pah-rah)*
light switch	el interruptor *(ehl een-teh-rroop-'tohr)*
thermostat	el termostato *(ehl tehr-moh-'stah-toh)*

THE LABORATORY
El laboratorio *(ehl lah-boh-rah-'toh-ree·oh)*

Science class has its own vocabulary list. For starters, why not point to these items on the counters and shelves:

We'll use (the)...	Vamos a usar... *('vah-mohs ah oo-'sahr...)*
batteries	las pilas *(lahs 'pee-lahs)*
beaker	la cubeta *(lah koo-'beh-tah)*
burner	el quemador *(ehl keh-mah-'dohr)*
candle	la vela *(lah 'veh-lah)*
clamp	la abrazadera *(lah ah-brah-sah-'deh-rah)*
faucet	el grifo *(ehl 'gree-foh)*
feather	la pluma *(lah 'ploo-mah)*
filter paper	el papel filtro *(ehl pah-'pehl 'feel-troh)*
fishbowl	la pecera *(lah peh-'seh-rah)*
flask	el frasco *(ehl 'frah-skoh)*
forceps	las tenazas *(lahs teh-'nah-sahs)*
funnel	el embudo *(ehl ehm-'boo-doh)*

lens	el lente *(ehl 'lehn-teh)*
magnet	el imán *(ehl ee-'mahn)*
magnifying glass	la lupa *(lah 'loo·pah)*
match	el fósforo *(ehl 'fohs-foh-roh)*
microscope	el microscopio *(ehl mee-kroh-'skoh-pee·oh)*
model	el modelo *(ehl moh-'deh-loh)*
petri dish	el platito de muestras *(ehl plah-'tee-toh deh 'mweh-strahs)*
prism	el prisma *(ehl 'prees-mah)*
pump	la bomba *(lah 'bohm-bah)*
safety glasses	los lentes de seguridad *(lohs 'lehn-tehs deh seh-goo-ree-'dahd)*
scale	la balanza *(lah bah-'lahn-sah)*
slide	la muestra en transparencia *(lah 'mweh-strah ehn trahns-pah-'rehn-see·ah)*
stand	el soporte *(ehl soh-'pohr-teh)*
telescope	el telescopio *(ehl teh-leh-'skoh-pee·oh)*
test tube	el tubo de ensayo *(ehl 'too-boh deh ehn-'sah-yoh)*
thermometer	el termómetro *(ehl tehr-'moh-meh-troh)*
tub	la tina *(lah 'tee-nah)*
tube	el tubo *(ehl 'too-boh)*

MÁS INFORMACIÓN

➤ Each new word will help:

electricity	la electricidad *(lah eh-lehk-tree-see-'dahd)*
heating	la calefacción *(lah kah-leh-fahk-see-'ohn)*
plumbing	las tuberías *(lahs too-beh-'ree·ahs)*

➤ And, how about those appliances that may be required during scientific experiments?

Use (the)...	Usa... *('oo-sah...)*
blender	la licuadora *(lah lee-kwah-'doh-rah)*
dishwasher	el lavaplatos *(ehl lah-vah-'plah-tohs)*
dryer	la secadora *(lah seh-kah-'doh-rah)*
freezer	el congelador *(ehl kohn-heh-lah-'dohr)*

hot water heater	**el calentador de agua** *(ehl kah-lehn-tah-'dohr deh 'ah-gwah)*
microwave	**el microonda** *(ehl mee-kroh-'ohn-dah)*
oven	**el horno** *(ehl 'ohr-noh)*
refrigerator	**el refrigerador** *(ehl reh-free-heh-rah-'dohr)*
stove	**la estufa** *(lah eh-'stoo-fah)*
washer	**la lavadora** *(lah lah-vah-'doh-rah)*

¿LISTOS PARA PRACTICAR?

Name five popular high school subjects:

_____ _____ _____ _____ _____

Translate into Spanish:

Where's the lamp? _____

We need a heater. _____

The light switch is over there. _____

Can you list three common items found in a science lab?

_____ _____ _____

Use the sample sentence as you fill in the blanks:

mapa (estudiar) *('mah-pah, eh-stoo-dee-'ahr)* $\qquad$ **Estudias el mapa.** *(eh-'stoo-dee·ahs ehl 'mah-pah)*

paquete (abrir) *(pah-'keh-teh, ah-'breer)* _____

anuncio (leer) *(ah-'noon-see·oh, leh-'ehr)* _____

álgebra (entender) *('ahl-heh-brah, ehn-tehn-'dehr)* _____

THE COMPUTER

La computadora *(lah kohm-poo-tah-'doh-rah)*

The classroom computer is a common sight at schools everywhere. Assist the Spanish speakers by using the words below:

application	la aplicación *(lah ah-plee-kah-see-'ohn)*
battery	la pila *(lah'pee-lah)*
cable	el cable *(ehl 'kah-bleh)*
code	el código *(ehl 'koh-dee-goh)*
database	la base de datos *(lah 'bah-seh deh 'dah-tohs)*
disc	el disco *(ehl 'dee-skoh)*
disc drive	la disquetera *(lah dees-keh-'teh-rah)*
email	el correo electrónico *(ehl koh-'rreh-oh eh-lehk-'troh-nee-koh)*
file	el fichero *(ehl fee-'cheh-roh)*
folder	el directorio *(ehl dee-rehk-'toh-ree·oh)*
hard drive	el disco duro *(ehl 'dees-koh 'doo-roh)*
headphones	los audífonos *(lohs ah·oo-'dee-foh-nohs)*
input	la entrada de información *(lah ehn-'trah-dah deh een-fohr-mah-see-'ohn)*
keyboard	el teclado *(ehl teh-'klah-doh)*
language	el lenguaje *(ehl lehn-'gwah-heh)*
laptop	el portátil *(ehl pohr-'tah-teel)*
memory	la memoria *(lah meh-'moh-ree·ah)*
microphone	el micrófono *(ehl mee-'kroh-foh-noh)*
monitor	el monitor *(ehl moh-nee-'tohr)*
mouse	el ratón *(ehl rah-'tohn)*
output	la salida de información *(lah sah-'lee-dah deh een-fohr-mah-see·'ohn)*
password	la contaseña *(lah kohn-tah-'sehn-yah)*
printer	la impresora *(lah eem-preh-'soh-rah)*
program	el programa *(ehl proh-'grah-mah)*
programming	la programación *(lah proh-grah-mah-see·'ohn)*
scanner	el escáner *(ehl eh-'skah-nehr)*
screen	la pantalla *(lah pahn-'tah-yah)*
settings	los ajustes *(lohs ah-'hoos-tehs)*
software	el programa *(ehl proh-'grah-mah)*
speakers	los parlantes *(lohs pahr-'lahn-tehs)*
system	el sistema *(ehl see-'steh-mah)*

toolbar	la barra de herramientas *(lah 'bah-rrah deh eh-rrah-mee-'ehn-tahs)*
volume	el volumen *(ehl voh-'loo-mehn)*
website	el sitio web *(ehl 'see-tee·oh web)*
wireless connection	la conección inalámbrica *(la koh-nehk-see-'ohn een-ah-'lahm-bree-kah)*

THE INTERNET
El internet *(ehl een-tehr-'neht)*

In Spanish, computer vocabulary is often the same as in English (el airplay, el hashtag, el text, el blog, el smartphone, la podcast, la iPad, el g-mail, la MP3, la chatting, el wifi, etc.). However, these other words related to working on the web might be useful, too:

I'm going...	Voy a... *('voh-ee ah)*
to click	pulsar *(pool-'sahr)*
to connect	conectar *(koh-nehk-'tahr)*
to cut and paste	cortar y pegar *(kohr-'tahr ee peh-'gahr)*
to delete	eliminar *(eh-lee-mee-'nahr)*
to download	descargar *(dehs-kahr-gahr)*
to drag	arrastrar *(ah-rrahs-'trahr)*
to file	archivar *(ahr-chee-'vahr)*
to find	encontrar *(ehn-kohn-'trahr)*
to forward	reenviar *(reh-ehn-vee-'ahr)*
to print	imprimir *(eem-pree-'meer)*
to receive	recibir *(reh-see-'beer)*
to reply	responder *(reh-spohn-'dehr)*
to save	ahorrar *(ah-oh-'rrahr)*

to search	buscar *(boos-'kahr)*
to select	escoger *(ehs-koh-'hehr)*
to send	enviar *(ehn-vee-'ahr)*
to text	mandar texto *(mahn-'dahr 'tehks-toh)*
Where's (the)...?	¿Dónde está...? *('dohn-deh ehs-'tah)*
attachment	el adjunto *(ehl ahd-'hoon-toh)*
browser	el navegador *(ehl nah-veh-gah-'dohr)*
contact	el contacto *(ehl kohn-'tahk-toh)*
document	el documento *(ehl doh-koo-'meha-toh)*
home page	la página inicial *(lah 'pah-hee-nah ee-nee-see-'ahl)*
mailbox	el buzón *(ehl boo-'sohn)*
menu	el menú *(ehl meh-'noo)*
message	el mensaje *(ehl mehn-'sah-heh)*
preferences	las preferencias *(lahs preh-feh-'rehn-see·ahs)*
program	el programa *(ehl proh-'grah-mah)*
search engine	el buscador *(ehl boos-kah-'dohr)*
server	el servidor *(ehl sehr-vee-'dohr)*
trash	la basura *(lah bah-'soo-rah)*

The parts of an email are named as follows:

Tina	@	winner	.	provider	.	pe
nombre del usario	arroba	nombre de dominio	punto	el proveedor de acceso a la internet	punto	país
(user name)	(at)	(domain name)	(dot)	(provider)	(dot)	(country)

SCIENCE CLASS
La clase de ciencias *(lah 'klah-seh deh see-'ehn-see·ahs)*

Obviously, you are unable to teach complex scientific concepts in Spanish, but you may explain general areas:

We study (the)...	Estudiamos... *(eh-stoo-dee-'ah-mohs)*
animals	los animales *(lohs ah-nee-'mah-lehs)*
engines	los motores *(lohs moh-'toh-rehs)*
environment	el ambiente *(ehl ahm-bee-'ehn-teh)*
heat	el calor *(ehl kah-'lohr)*

human body	el cuerpo humano *(ehl 'kwehr-poh oo-'mah-noh)*
machines	las máquinas *(lahs 'mah-kee-nahs)*
motion	el movimiento *(ehl moh-vee-mee-'ehn-toh)*
plants	las plantas *(lahs 'plahn-tahs)*
sound	el sonido *(ehl soh-'nee-doh)*
universe	el universo *(ehl oo-nee-'vehr-soh)*
weather	el clima *(ehl 'klee-mah)*

Some concepts or principles, however, cannot be defined in simple terms. Here are a few examples:

Do you understand...?	¿Entiendes...? *(ehn-tee-'ehn-dehs)*
centrifugal force	la fuerza centrífuga *(lah 'fwehr-sah sehn-'tree-foo-gah)*
energy	la energía *(lah eh-nehr-'hee·ah)*
gravity	la gravedad *(lah grah-veh-'dahd)*
inertia	la inercia *(lah ee-'nehr-see·ah)*
matter	la materia *(lah mah-'teh-ree·ah)*
power	la potencia *(lah poh-'tehn-see·ah)*

By the way, can you define the object you're working with?

It's a...	Es un... *(ehs oon)*
gas	gas *(gahs)*
grain	grano *('grah-noh)*
liquid	líquido *('lee-kee-doh)*
powder	polvo *('pohl-voh)*
solid	sólido *('soh-lee-doh)*

 MÁS INFORMACIÓN

➤ Next time, ask a Spanish-speaking pupil what everyone is shouting about. Here's what to say when there's a problem in the lab:

Something's wrong!	¡Algo está mal! *('ahl-goh eh-'stah mahl)*
It looks strange!	¡Se ve raro! *(seh veh 'rah-roh)*
Let's clean it up!	¡Vamos a limpiarlo! *('vah-mohs ah leem-pee-'ahr-loh)*

Check the...!	¡Verifique...! (veh-ree-'fee-keh...)
control	el control (ehl kohn-'trohl)
cycle	el ciclo (ehl 'see-kloh)
level	el nivel (ehl nee-'vehl)
light	la luz (lah loos)
power	la potencia (lah poh-'tehn-see·ah)
speed	la velocidad (lah veh-loh-see-'dahd)
temperature	la temperatura (lah tehm-peh-rah-'too-rah)
time	la hora (lah 'oh-rah)
tune	el tono (ehl 'toh-noh)
weight	el peso (ehl 'peh-soh)

I'm going to...!	¡Voy a...! ('voh·ee ah...)
cancel it	cancelarlo (kahn-seh-'lahr-loh)
deactivate it	desactivarlo (dehs-ahk-tee-'vahr-loh)
dissect it	disecarlo (dee-seh-'kahr-loh)
pause it	pausarlo (pow-'sahr-loh)
stop it	pararlo (pah-'rahr-loh)
turn it off	apagarlo (ah-pah-'gahr-loh)

➤ Astronomy, la astronomía (lah ah-stroh-noh-'mee·ah), is generally part of the science curriculum:

I want to study (the)...	Quiero estudiar... (kee-'eh-roh eh-stoo-dee-'ahr)
moon	la luna (lah 'loo-nah)
planet	el planeta (ehl plah-'neh-tah)
solar system	el sistema solar (ehl see-'steh-mah soh-'lahr)
star	la estrella (lah eh-'streh-yah)
sun	el sol (ehl sohl)

MATH CLASS
La clase de matemáticas (lah 'klah-seh deh mah-teh-'mah-tee-kahs)

Math is full of details that need to be explained, so do what you can with this next list of words and phrases. Bear in mind that attempting to use Spanish to teach tougher material often accelerates the learning process:

area	el área *(ehl 'ah-reh-ah)*
average	el promedio *(ehl proh-'meh-dee·oh)*
bar	la barra *(lah 'bah-rrah)*
circle	el círculo *(ehl 'seer-koo-loh)*
circumference	la circunferencia *(lah seer-koon-feh-'rehn-see·ah)*
computation	la computación *(lah kohm-poo-tah-see-'ohn)*
cost	el costo *(ehl 'koh-stoh)*
cube	el cubo *(ehl 'koo-boh)*
decimal	el decimal *(ehl deh-see-'mahl)*
degree	el grado *(ehl 'grah-doh)*
denominator	el denominador *(ehl deh-noh-mee-nah-'dohr)*
depth	la profundidad *(lah proh-foon-dee-'dahd)*
diagram	el diagrama *(ehl dee·ah-'grah-mah)*
diameter	el diámetro *(ehl dee-'ah-meh-troh)*
difference	la diferencia *(lah dee-feh-'rehn-see·ah)*
digit	el dígito *(ehl 'dee-hee-toh)*
dimension	la dimensión *(lah dee-mehn-see-'ohn)*
distance	la distancia *(lah dee-'stahn-see·ah)*
equal	la igualdad *(lah ee-gwahl-'dahd)*
equation	la ecuación *(lah eh-kwah-see-'ohn)*
equivalent	el equivalente *(ehl eh-kee-vah-'lehn-teh)*
exponent	el exponente *(ehl ehks-poh-'nehn-teh)*
figure	la figura *(lah fee-'goo-rah)*
formula	la fórmula *(lah 'fohr-moo-lah)*
fraction	la fracción *(lah frahk-see-'ohn)*
height	la altura *(lah ahl-'too-rah)*
length	el largo *(ehl 'lahr-goh)*
line	la línea *(lah 'lee-neh-ah)*
logic	la lógica *(lah 'loh-hee-kah)*
mode	el modo *(ehl 'moh-doh)*
numeral	el numeral *(ehl noo-meh-'rahl)*
numerator	el numerador *(ehl noo-meh-rah-'dohr)*
operation	la operación *(lah oh-peh-rah-see-'ohn)*
percent	el porcentaje *(ehl pohr-sehn-'tah-heh)*
perimeter	el perímetro *(ehl peh-'ree-meh-troh)*
point	el punto *(ehl 'poon-toh)*
probability	la probabilidad *(lah proh-bah-bee-lee-'dahd)*
product	el producto *(ehl proh-'dook-toh)*
quadrant	el cuadrante *(ehl kwah-'drahn-teh)*
quantity	la cantidad *(lah kahn-tee-'dahd)*
quotient	el cociente *(ehl koh-see-'ehn-teh)*

radius	el radio *(ehl 'rah-dee·oh)*
rate	la tasa *(lah 'tah-sah)*
ratio	la proporción *(lah proh-pohr-see·'ohn)*
rectangle	el rectángulo *(ehl rehk-'tahn-goo-loh)*
remainder	el residuo *(ehl reh-'see-doo·oh)*
result	el resultado *(ehl reh-sool-'tah-doh)*
solution	la solución *(lah soh-loo-see·'ohn)*
speed	la velocidad *(lah veh-loh-see-'dahd)*
sphere	la esfera *(lah eh-'sfeh-rah)*
square	el cuadro *(ehl 'kwah-droh)*
statistic	la estadística *(lah eh-stah-'dee-stee-kah)*
sum	la suma *(lah 'soo-mah)*
surface	la superficie *(lah soo-pehr-'fee-see·eh)*
term	el término *(ehl 'tehr-mee-noh)*
time	el tiempo *(ehl tee-'ehm-poh)*
total	el total *(ehl toh-'tahl)*
triangle	el triángulo *(ehl tree-'ahn-goo-loh)*
unit	la unidad *(lah oo-nee-'dahd)*
value	el valor *(ehl vah-'lohr)*
volume	el volumen *(ehl voh-'loo-mehn)*
weight	el peso *(ehl 'peh-soh)*
width	el ancho *(ehl'ahn-choh)*

Continue to copy the words you need, but this time, focus on "mathematic" verbs:

to add	sumar *(soo-'mahr)*	**Estamos sumando las fracciones.** *(eh-'stah-mohs soo-'mahn-doh lahs frahk-see·'oh-nehs)*
to calculate	calcular *(kahl-koo-'lahr)*	_____
to change	cambiar *(kahm-bee-'ahr)*	_____
to compare	comparar *(kohm-pah-'rahr)*	_____
to divide	dividir *(dee-vee-'deer)*	_____
to factor	factorar *(fahk-toh-'rahr)*	_____
to guess	adivinar *(ah-dee-vee-'nahr)*	_____
to measure	medir *(meh-'deer)*	_____
to multiply	multiplicar *(mool-tee-plee-'kahr)*	_____
to omit	omitir *(oh-mee-'teer)*	_____

to practice	practicar *(prahk-tee-'kahr)*	_____
to reduce	reducir *(reh-doo-'seer)*	_____
to round off	redondear *(reh-dohn-deh-'ahr)*	_____
to simplify	simplificar *(seem-plee-fee-'kahr)*	_____
to solve	resolver *(reh-sohl-'vehr)*	_____
to subtract	restar *(reh-'stahr)*	_____

MÁS INFORMACIÓN

➤ Use the vocabulary from the right column to create sentences:

_____ number   el número _____ *(ehl 'noo-meh-roh)*

whole	entero *(ehn-'teh-roh)*
negative	negativo *(neh-gah-'tee-voh)*
mixed	mixto *('meeks-toh)*
like	mismo *('mees-moh)*
unlike	diferente *(dee-feh-'rehn-teh)*
real	real *(reh-'ahl)*
rational	racional *(rah-see·oh-'nahl)*

➤ Learn faster by grouping key words into pairs:

| sample | la muestra *(lah 'mweh-strah)* |
| example | el ejemplo *(ehl eh-'hehm-ploh)* |

| parallel | paralelo *(pah-rah-'leh-loh)* |
| perpendicular | perpendicular *(pehr-pehn-dee-koo-'lahr)* |

| plus | más *(mahs)* |
| minus | menos *('meh-nohs)* |

| times | por *(pohr)* |
| divided by | dividido por *(dee-vee-'dee-doh pohr)* |

| center | el centro *(ehl 'sehn-troh)* |
| side | el lado *(ehl 'lah-doh)* |

cone	el cono *(ehl 'koh-noh)*
cylinder	el cilindro *(ehl see-'leen-droh)*

¡Los lados del ejemplo son paralelos! *(lohs 'lah-dohs dehl eh-'hehm-ploh sohn pah-rah-'leh-lohs)*

MEASUREMENT
Las medidas *(lahs meh-'dee-dahs)*

Discussing measurements is a daily routine in math or science, so learn these powerful words and phrases in Spanish as soon as you can:

It's a/an...	Es... *(ehs)*
double	un doble *(oon 'doh-bleh)*
dozen	una docena *('oo-nah doh-'seh-nah)*
drop	una gota *('oo-nah 'goh-tah)*
gross	una gruesa *('oo-nah groo-'eh-sah)*
half	una mitad *('oo-nah mee-'tahd)*
pair	un par *(oon pahr)*
portion	una porción *('oo-nah pohr-see-'ohn)*
quarter	un cuarto *(oon 'kwahr-toh)*
third	un tercio *(oon 'tehr-see·oh)*
ton	una tonelada *('oo-nah toh-neh-'lah-dah)*
unit	una unidad *('oo-nah oo-nee-'dahd)*

Take a/an...	Tome... *('toh-meh)*
centimeter	un centímetro *(oon sehn-'tee-meh-troh)*
foot	un pie *(oon 'pee-eh)*
gallon	un galón *(oon gah-'lohn)*
gram	un gramo *(oon 'grah-moh)*
kilogram	un kilogramo *(oon kee-loh-'grah-moh)*
inch	una pulgada *('oo-nah pool-'gah-dah)*
liter	un litro *(oon'lee-troh)*
meter	un metro *(oon 'meh-troh)*
mile	una milla *('oo-nah 'mee-yah)*
millimeter	un milímetro *(oon mee-'lee-meh-troh)*
ounce	una onza *('oo-nah 'ohn-sah)*
pound	una libra *('oo-nah 'lee-brah)*

| quart | un cuarto *(oon 'kwahr-toh)* |
| yard | una yarda *('oo-nah 'yahr-dah)* |

MÁS INFORMACIÓN

➤ Stick in a word that helps describe:

only	**solamente** *(soh-lah-'mehn-teh)*	**Solamente tres pulgadas.** *(soh-lah-'mehn-teh trehs pool-'gah-dahs)*
none	**ninguno** *(neen-'goo-noh)*	**Ninguno de los dos números.** *(neen-'goo-noh deh lohs dohs 'noo-meh-rohs)*
the rest	**los demás** *(lohs deh-'mahs)*	**Los demás problemas.** *(lohs deh-'mahs proh-'bleh-mahs)*

DIFERENCIAS CULTURALES

What do you know about the metric system? You may need to post a conversion table if your class makeup is international.

5/8 mi.	=	**un kilómetro** *(oon kee-'loh-meh-troh)*
2.2 lbs.	=	**un kilógramo** *(oon kee-'loh-grah-moh)*
32° Fahrenheit	=	**O° Celsius** *('seh-roh 'sehl-see-oos)*

MORE MATHEMATICAL EXPRESSIONS

Más expresiones matemáticas

(mahs eks-preh-see-'oh-nehs mah-teh-'mah-tee-kahs)

Fractions are spelled in Spanish as in English, using a cardinal number for the numerator and an ordinal number for the denominator. The only exceptions are ½ (un medio) and ⅓ (un tercio):

¼	un cuarto *(oon 'kwahr-toh)*
⅜	· tres octavos *(trehs ohk-'tah-vohs)*
⅔	dos tercios *(dohs 'tehr-see·ohs)*

Beyond one-tenth, the cardinal number adds the suffix –avo(s) to form the smaller fractions. Exceptions include one-hundredth (un centésimo) and one-thousandth (un milésimo):

one-thirteenth	un treceavo *(oon treh-seh-'ah-voh)*
four-nineteenths	cuatro diecinueveavos *('kwah-troh dee-ehs-ee noo--eh-veh-'ah-vohs)*
three-twentieths	tres veinteavos *(trehs veh-een-teh-'ah-vohs)*
two-hundredths	dos centésimos *(dohs sehn-'teh-see-mohs)*

Mixed numbers have y *(ee)* between the whole number and the fraction. When nouns are added, they usually are written after the full amount, but are pronounced between the whole number and the fraction:

5⅔ litros	cinco litros y dos tercios *('seen-koh 'leet-rohs ee dohs 'tehr-see·ohs)*
7¼ libras	siete libras y un cuarto *(see-'eh-teh 'lee-brahs ee oon 'kwahr-toh)*
3½ manzanas	tres manzanas y media *(trehs mahn-'sah-nahs ee 'meh-dee·ah)*

When referring to percentages in Spanish, a singular masculine article is generally placed before the number. *Percent* is por ciento *(pohr see-'ehn-toh)*:

We received the twenty percent discount.	Recibimos el diez por ciento de descuento. *(reh-see-'bee-mohs ehl dee-'ehs pohr see-'ehn-toh deh dehs-'kwehn-toh)*

GLOBAL STUDIES

Los Estudios Globales *(lohs eh-'stoo-dee·ohs gloh-'bah-lehs)*

Why not set aside those vocabulary items that specifically focus on lessons in humanities. Here's a beginner's list in Spanish. Learn it and create full sentences.

politics	la política *(lah poh-'lee-tee-kah)*	¿Qué sabes tú de la política de Cuba? *(keh 'sah-behs too deh deh 'koo-bah)*

agriculture	la agricultura *(lah ah-gree-kool-'too-rah)*
ancestor	el antepasado *(ehl ahn-teh-pah-'sah-doh)*
army	el ejército *(ehl eh-'hehr-see-toh)*
battle	la batalla *(lah bah-'tah-yah)*
border	la frontera *(lah frohn-'teh-rah)*
century	el siglo *(ehl 'see-gloh)*
civilization	la civilización *(lah see-vee-lee-sah-see-'ohn)*
colony	la colonia *(lah koh-'loh-nee·ah)*
conquest	la conquista *(lah kohn-'kee-stah)*
continent	el continente *(ehl kohn-tee-'nehn-teh)*
country	el país *(ehl pah-'ees)*
culture	la cultura *(lah kool-'too-rah)*
custom	la costumbre *(lah koh-'stoom-breh)*
development	el desarrollo *(ehl dehs-ah-'rroh-yoh)*
discovery	el descubrimiento *(ehl deh-skoo-bree-mee-'ehn-toh)*
dynasty	la dinastía *(lah dee-nah-'stee·ah)*
economy	la economía *(lah eh-koh-noh-'mee·ah)*
election	la elección *(lah eh-lehk-see-'ohn)*
empire	el imperio *(ehl eem-'peh-ree·oh)*
evolution	la evolución *(lah eh-voh-loo-see-'ohn)*
expansion	la expansión *(lah ehk-spahn-see-'ohn)*
exploration	la exploración *(lah ehks-ploh-rah-see-'ohn)*
exportation	la exportación *(lah ehks-pohr-tah-see-'ohn)*
freedom	la libertad *(lah lee-behr-'tahd)*
government	el gobierno *(ehl goh-bee-'ehr-noh)*
growth	el crecimiento *(ehl kreh-see-mee-'ehn-toh)*
hunger	el hambre *(ehl 'ahm-breh)*
immigration	la inmigración *(lah een-mee-grah-see-'ohn)*
importation	la importación *(lah eem-pohr-tah-see-'ohn)*
independence	la independencia *(lah een-deh-pehn-'dehn-see·ah)*

industry	la industria *(lah een-'doo-stree·ah)*
invasion	la invasión *(lah een-vah-see·'ohn)*
law	la ley *(lah 'leh·ee)*
mining	la minería *(lah mee-neh-'ree·ah)*
monarchy	la monarquía *(lah moh-nahr-'kee·ah)*
nation	la nación *(lah nah-see·'ohn)*
origin	el origen *(ehl oh-'ree-hehn)*
peace	la paz *(lah pahs)*
pollution	la contaminación *(lah kohn-tah-mee-nah-see·'ohn)*
population	la población *(lah poh-blah-see·'ohn)*
poverty	la pobreza *(lah poh-'breh-sah)*
race	la raza *(lah 'rah-sah)*
regime	el régimen *(ehl 'reh-hee-mehn)*
reign	el reino *(ehl 'reh·ee-noh)*
religion	la religión *(lah reh-lee-hee·'ohn)*
republic	la república *(lah reh-'poo-blee-kah)*
reunification	la reunificación *(lah reh-oo-nee-fee-kah-see·'ohn)*
revolution	la revolución *(lah reh-voh-loo-see·'ohn)*
state	el estado *(ehl eh-'stah-doh)*
territory	el territorio *(ehl teh-rree-'toh-ree·oh)*
trade	el comercio *(ehl koh-'mehr-see·oh)*
voyage	el viaje *(ehl vee-'ah-heh)*
war	la guerra *(lah 'geh-rrah)*
wealth	la riqueza *(lah ree-'keh-sah)*
world	el mundo *(ehl 'moon-doh)*

MÁS INFORMACIÓN

➤ Memorize strategic times in world history:

Industrial Revolution	La Revolución industrial *(lah reh-voh-loo-see·'ohn een-doo-stree-'ahl)*
Reformation	La Reforma *(lah reh-'fohr-mah)*
Renaissance	El Renacimiento *(ehl reh-nah-see-mee-'ehn-toh)*

➤ Start a list of meaningful descriptive words. Study these examples:

ancient	antiguo *(ahn-'tee-gwoh)*
modern	moderno *(moh-'dehr-noh)*
prehistoric	prehistórico *(preh-ee-'stoh-ree-koh)*

131

➤ Use magazines or newspapers to discuss any important issue:

civil rights	los derechos humanos *(lohs deh-'reh-chohs oo-'mah-nohs)*
political parties	los partidos políticos *(lohs pahr-'tee-dohs poh-'lee-tee-kohs)*
pollution	la contaminación *(lah kohn-tah-mee-nah-see-'ohn)*

➤ Deeper concepts should be translated, so memorize these words, too:

hatred	el odio *(ehl 'oh-dee·oh)*
hope	la esperanza *(lah eh-speh-'rahn-sah)*
injustice	la injusticia *(lah een-hoo-'stee-see·ah)*
justice	la justicia *(lah hoo-'stee-see·ah)*
kindness	la bondad *(lah bohn-'dahd)*
love	el amor *(ehl ah-'mohr)*
racism	el racismo *(ehl rah-'sees-moh)*
respect	el respeto *(ehl reh-'speh-toh)*
trust	la confianza *(lah kohn-fee-'ahn-sah)*

RACE AND NATIONALITY
Raza y nacionalidad *('rah-sah ee nah-see·oh-nah-lee-'dahd)*

Identify the folks around you by race and nationality. Use these words to describe:

She's...	Ella es... *('eh-yah ehs...)*
Asian	asiática *(ah-see-'ah-tee-kah)*
African-American	afroamericana *(ah-froh-ah-meh-ree-'kah-nah)*
Hispanic	hispana *(ee-'spah-nah)*
Latin	latina *(lah-'tee-nah)*
Middle Eastern	del Oriente Medio *(dehl oh-ree-'ehn-teh 'meh-dee·oh)*
Native American	amerindia *(ah-mehr-'een-dee·ah)*
Polynesian	polinesia *(poh-lee-'neh-see·ah)*
white	blanca *('blahn-kah)*
He's...	Él es... *(ehl ehs...)*
African-American	afroamericano *(ah-froh-ah-meh-ree-'kah-noh)*
Anglo-Saxon	anglosajón *(ahn-gloh-sah-'hohn)*

| Asian-American | asiáticoamericano *(ah-see-'ah-tee-koh-ah-meh-ree-'kah-noh)* |
| Latin-American | latinoamericano *(lah-tee-noh-ah-meh-ree-'kah-noh)* |

Here's another pattern. Just insert the appropriate word:

| The boy is... | El niño es... *(ehl 'nee-nyoh ehs...)* |

African	africano *(ah-free-'kah-noh)*
Arab	árabe *('ah-rah-beh)*
Australian	australiano *(ow-strah-lee-'ah-noh)*
Canadian	canadiense *(kah-nah-dee-'ehn-seh)*
Chinese	chino *('chee-noh)*
Dutch	holandés *(oh-lahn-'dehs)*
English	inglés *(een-'glehs)*
French	francés *(frahn-'sehs)*
German	alemán *(ah-leh-'mahn)*
Greek	griego *(gree-'eh-goh)*
Iraqi	iraquí *(ee-rah-'kee)*
Irish	irlandés *(eer-lahn-'dehs)*
Italian	italiano *(ee-tah-lee-'ah-noh)*
Japanese	japonés *(hah-poh-'nehs)*
Portuguese	portugués *(pohr-too-'gehs)*
Russian	ruso *('roo-soh)*
Scottish	escocés *(ehs-koh-'sehs)*
Spanish	español *(eh-spah-'nyohl)*
Swedish	sueco *('sweh-koh)*
Swiss	suizo *('swee-soh)*
U.S.	norteamericano *(nohr-teh-ah-meh-ree-'kah-noh)*
Vietnamese	vietnamita *(vee-eht-nah-'mee-tah)*

And, how about south of the border? Allow your students to share:

| I'm _____ | Soy _____ *('soh·ee...)* |

Argentinean	argentino *(ahr-hehn-'tee-noh)*
Bolivian	boliviano *(boh-lee-vee-'ah-noh)*
Brazilian	brasileño *(brah-see-'leh-nyoh)*
Chilean	chileno *(chee-'leh-noh)*
Colombian	colombiano *(koh-lohm-bee-'ah-noh)*
Costa Rican	costarricense *(koh-stah-rree-'sehn-seh)*

Cuban	cubano *(koo-'bah-noh)*
Dominican	dominicano *(doh-mee-nee-'kah-noh)*
Ecuadorian	ecuatoriano *(eh-kwah-'toh-ree-'ah-noh)*
Guatemalan	guatemalteco *(gwah-teh-mahl-'teh-koh)*
Haitian	haitiano *(ah·ee-tee·'ah-noh)*
Honduran	hondureño *(ohn-doo-'reh-nyoh)*
Mexican	mexicano *(meh-hee-'kah-noh)*
Nicaraguan	nicaragüense *(nee-kah-rah-'gwehn-seh)*
Panamanian	panameño *(pah-nah-'meh-nyoh)*
Paraguayan	paraguayo *(pah-rah-'gwah-yoh)*
Peruvian	peruano *(peh-roo-'ah-noh)*
Puerto Rican	puertorriqueño *(pwehr-toh-rree-'keh-nyoh)*
Salvadoran	salvadoreño *(sahl-vah-doh-'reh-nyoh)*
Uruguayan	uruguayo *(oo-roo-'gwah-yoh)*
Venezuelan	venezolano *(veh-neh-soh-'lah-noh)*

 MÁS INFORMACIÓN

➤ What about political titles?

dictator	el dictador *(ehl deek-tah-'dohr)*
emperor	el emperador *(ehl ehm-peh-rah-'dohr)*
king	el rey *(ehl 'reh·ee)*
president	el presidente *(ehl preh-see-'dehn-teh)*
queen	la reina *(lah 'reh·ee-nah)*
ruler	el gobernante *(ehl goh-behr-'nahn-teh)*

➤ Now, look at these religious believers:

Buddhist	budista *(boo-'dee-stah)*
Catholic	católico *(kah-'toh-lee-koh)*
Christian	cristiano *(kree-stee·'ah-noh)*
Hindu	hindú *(een-'doo)*
Islamist	islamita *(ees-lah-'mee-tah)*
Jewish	judío *(hoo-'dee·oh)*
Mormon	mormón *(mohr-'mohn)*
Muslim	musulmán *(moo-sool-'mahn)*
Protestant	protestante *(proh-teh-'stahn-teh)*

DIFERENCIAS CULTURALES

Most of Latin America is Roman Catholic, and you may notice the religious influence during your association with some Hispanics during a crisis. Using the word God, **Dios** *('dee·ohs)* in the conversation, attending daily mass, **la misa** *(lah 'mee-sah)*, or observing Catholic traditions are common signs of their faith. Remember that respect and sensitivity are always in demand when topics center around cultural and religious beliefs.

¿LISTOS PARA PRACTICAR?

Choose the best word to fit in the blank:

continente, país, estado *(kohn-tee-'nehn-teh, pah-'ees, eh-'stah-doh)*

Los Estados Unidos es un _____. *(lohs eh-'stah-dohs oo-'nee-dohs*

ehs oon _____)

Africa es un _____. *('ah-free-kah ehs oon _____)*

California es un _____. *(kah-lee-'fohr-nee·ah ehs oon)*

Connect the math terms that closely relate to each other:

triángulo *(tree-'ahn-goo-loh)*   **mixto** *('meeks-toh)*
peso *('peh-soh)*   **restar** *(reh-'stahr)*
simplificar *(seem-plee-fee-'kahr)*   **estatura** *(eh-stah-'too-rah)*
ecuación *(eh-kwah-see-'ohn)*   **reducir** *(reh-doo-'seer)*
entero *(ehn-'teh-roh)*   **cuadrado** *(kwah-'drah-doh)*
sumar *(soo-'mahr)*   **operación** *(oh-peh-rah-see-'ohn)*

Translate:

el poder *(ehl poh-'dehr)*   _____

la energía *(lah eh-nehr-'hee·ah)*   _____

el calor *(ehl kah-'lohr)*   _____

Write in Spanish:

1/2 _____

3 ft. _____

1/3 _____

12 oz. _____

1 in. _____

List three countries and the languages spoken there:

Italia *(ee-'tah-lee·ah)*   italiano *(ee-tah-lee-'ah-noh)*

_____   _____

_____   _____

_____   _____

ENGLISH CLASS
La clase de inglés *(lah 'klah-seh deh een-'glehs)*

Due to the high numbers of non-English and limited-English-speaking children in schools across the U.S., educators are struggling to find the best methods to teach English as a second language. Older learners require plenty of explanation and practice, so be sure to present these terms to all your native Spanish speakers. They can be useful when questions arise about English:

article	el artículo *(ehl ahr-'tee-koo-loh)*
character	el personaje *(ehl pehr-soh-'nah-heh)*
composition	la composición *(lah kohm-poh-see-see·'ohn)*
essay	al ensayo *(ehl ehn-'sah-yoh)*
novel	la novela *(lah noh-'veh-lah)*
page	la página *(lah 'pah-hee-nah)*
paragraph	el párrafo *(ehl 'pah-rrah-foh)*
plot	el argumento *(ehl ahr-goo-'mehn-toh)*
poetry	la poesía *(lah poh-eh-'see·ah)*

prose	la prosa *(lah 'proh-sah)*
short story	el cuento *(ehl 'kwehn-toh)*
table of contents	el contenido *(ehl kohn-teh-'nee-doh)*

In English class, teachers communicate using grammar words found in textbooks. They're a bore, but any student of languages needs to know them. Fortunately, many of these look like English:

adjective	el adjetivo *(ehl ahd-heh-'tee-voh)*
adverb	el adverbio *(ehl ahd-'vehr-bee·oh)*
capital letter	la mayúscula *(lah mah-'yoo-skoo-lah)*
cognate	la palabra afín *(lah pah-'lah-brah ah-'feen)*
comma	la coma *(lah 'koh-mah)*
conditional	el condicional *(ehl kohn-dee-see·oh-'nahl)*
conjugation	la conjugación *(lah kohn-hoo-gah-see-'ohn)*
consonant	la consonante *(lah kohn-soh-'nahn-teh)*
dialog	el diálogo *(ehl dee-'ah-loh-goh)*
ending	el final *(ehl fee-'nahl)*
exercise	el ejercicio *(ehl eh-hehr-'see-see·oh)*
feminine	femenino *(feh-meh-'nee-noh)*
form	la forma *(lah 'fohr-mah)*
future	el futuro *(ehl foo-'too-roh)*
gerund	el gerundio *(ehl heh-'roon-dee·oh)*
grammar	la gramática *(lah grah-'mah-tee-kah)*
imperative	el imperativo *(ehl eem-peh-rah-'tee-voh)*
imperfect	el imperfecto *(ehl eem-pehr-'fehk-toh)*
infinitive	el infinitivo *(ehl een-fee-nee-'tee-voh)*
language	el idioma *(ehl ee-dee-'oh-mah)*
letter	la letra *(lah 'leh-trah)*
lower case letter	la minúscula *(lah mee-'noo-skoo-lah)*
masculine	masculino *(mah-skoo-'lee-noh)*
meaning	el significado *(ehl seeg-nee-fee-'kah-doh)*
noun	el sustantivo *(ehl soo-stahn-'tee-voh)*
object	el objetivo *(ehl ohb-heh-'tee-voh)*
participle	el participio *(ehl pahr-tee-'see-pee·oh)*
passive voice	la voz pasiva *(lah vohs pah-'see-vah)*
past	el pasado *(ehl pah-'sah-doh)*
perfect	el perfecto *(ehl pehr-'fehk-toh)*
period	el punto *(ehl 'poon-toh)*
person	la persona *(lah pehr-'soh-nah)*
possessive	el posesivo *(ehl poh-seh-'see-voh)*

present	el presente *(ehl preh-'sehn-teh)*
preterit	el pretérito *(ehl preh-'teh-ree-toh)*
progressive	el progresivo *(ehl proh-greh-'see-voh)*
pronoun	el pronombre *(ehl proh-'nohm-breh)*
pronunciation	la pronunciación *(lah proh-noon-see·ah-see·'ohn)*
radical	el radical *(ehl rah-dee-'kahl)*
reflexive	el reflexivo *(ehl reh-flehk-'see-voh)*
regular	regular *(reh-goo-'lahr)*
sentence	la frase *(lah 'frah-seh)*
singular	el singular *(ehl seen-goo-'lahr)*
sound	el sonido *(ehl soh-'nee-doh)*
speech	el habla *(ehl 'ah-blah)*
structure	la estructura *(lah eh-strook-'too-rah)*
subject	el sujeto *(ehl soo-'heh-toh)*
subjunctive	el subjuntivo *(ehl soob-hoon-'tee-voh)*
syllable	la sílaba *(lah 'see-lah-bah)*
symbol	el símbolo *(ehl 'seem-boh-loh)*
synonym	el sinónimo *(ehl see-'noh-nee-moh)*
the reading	la lectura *(lah lehk-'too-rah)*
tense	el tiempo *(ehl tee-'ehm-poh)*
test	el examen *(ehl ehk-'sah-mehn)*
theme	el tema *(ehl 'teh-mah)*
verb	el verbo *(ehl 'vehr-boh)*
vocabulary	el vocabulario *(ehl voh-kah-boo-'lah-ree·oh)*
vowel	la vocal *(lah voh-'kahl)*
word	la palabra *(lah pah-'lah-brah)*
writing	la escritura *(lah eh-skree-'too-rah)*

Now, create a few sentences:

La frase no tiene una coma. *(lah 'frah-seh noh tee-'eh-neh 'oo-nah 'koh-mah)*
Escriba el verbo en el tiempo pasado. *(eh-'skree-bah ehl 'vehr-boh ehn ehl tee-'ehm-poh pah-'sah-doh)*

_____

_____

_____

THE FINE ARTS
Las bellas artes *(lahs 'beh-yahs 'ahr-tehs)*

Young people take classes in other areas besides the basics. Let's review a few subjects that help students develop their unique talents and abilities:

Art **(el arte)** *(ehl 'ahr-teh)*

Look at (the)...	Mira... *('mee-rah)*
design	**el diseño** *(ehl dee-'seh-nyoh)*
drawing	**el dibujo** *(ehl dee-'boo-hoh)*
illustration	**la ilustración** *(lah ee-loo-strah-see-'ohn)*
painting	**la pintura** *(lah peen-'too-rah)*
photography	**la fotografía** *(lah foh-toh-grah-'fee·ah)*
pottery	**la cerámica** *(lah seh-'rah-mee-kah)*
sculpture	**la escultura** *(lah eh-skool-'too-rah)*

Theater **(el teatro)** *(ehl teh-'ah-troh)*

actor	**el actor** *(ehl ahk-'tohr)*
actress	**la actriz** *(lah ahk-'trees)*
director	**el director** *(ehl dee-rehk-'tohr)*
playwright	**el dramaturgo** *(ehl drah-mah-'toor-goh)*

We study (the)...	Estudiamos... *(eh-stoo-dee-'ah-mohs...)*
acting	**la actuación** *(lah ahk-too-ah-see-'ohn)*
audience	**el auditorio** *(ehl ow-dee-'toh-ree·oh)*
ballet	**el balet** *(ehl bah-'leh)*
choreography	**la coreografía** *(lah koh-reh-oh-grah-'fee·ah)*
comedy	**la comedia** *(lah koh-'meh-dee·ah)*
costume	**el disfraz** *(ehl dees-'frahs)*
dance	**el baile** *(ehl 'bah·ee-leh)*
improvisation	**la improvisación** *(lah eem-proh-vee-sah-see-'ohn)*
play	**el drama** *(ehl 'drah-mah)*
production	**la producción** *(lah proh-dook-see-'ohn)*
scene	**la escena** *(lah eh-'seh-nah)*
stage	**el escenario** *(ehl eh-seh-'nah-ree·oh)*
tragedy	**la tragedia** *(lah trah-'heh-dee·ah)*

Music (la música) *(lah 'moo-see-kah)*

I like (the)...	Me gusta... *(meh 'goo-stah)*
band	la banda *(lah 'bahn-dah)*
choir	el coro *(ehl 'koh-roh)*
instrument	el instrumento *(ehl een-stroo-'mehn-toh)*
note	la nota *(lah 'noh-tah)*
opera	la ópera *(lah 'oh-peh-rah)*
orchestra	la orquesta *(lah ohr-'keh-stah)*
scale	la escala *(lah eh-'skah-lah)*
song	la canción *(lah kahn-see-'ohn)*

I play (the)...	Toco... *('toh-koh)*
bass	el bajo *(ehl 'bah-hoh)*
cello	el violonchelo *(ehl vee·oh-lohn-'cheh-loh)*
clarinet	el clarinete *(ehl klah-ree-'neh-teh)*
drum	el tambor *(ehl tahm-'bohr)*
flute	la flauta *(lah 'flah-oo-tah)*
guitar	la guitarra *(lah gee-'tah-rrah)*
organ	el órgano *(ehl 'ohr-gah-noh)*
piano	el piano *(ehl pee-'ah-noh)*
saxophone	el saxófono *(ehl sahk-'soh-foh-noh)*
trombone	el trombón *(ehl trohm-'bohn)*
trumpet	la trompeta *(lah trohm-'peh-tah)*
violin	el violín *(ehl vee·oh-'leen)*

Physical Education (la educación física) *(lah eh-doo-kah-see·'ohn 'fee-see-kah)*
For a list of sports, see page 147. These words will be very useful as well:

We are...	Estamos... *(eh-'stah-mohs...)*
doing exercise	haciendo ejercicio *(ah-see-'ehn-doh eh-hehr-'see-see·oh)*
jumping	saltando *(sahl-'tahn-doh)*
lifting weights	levantando pesos *(leh-vahn-'tahn-doh 'peh-sohs)*
running	corriendo *(koh-rree-'ehn-doh)*
swimming	nadando *(nah-'dahn-doh)*

Let's...	Vamos a... *('vah-mohs ah...)*
bounce	rebotar *(reh-boh-'tahr)*
catch	agarrar *(ah-gah-'rrahr)*
hit	pegar *(peh-'gahr)*
kick	patear *(pah-teh-'ahr)*
pass	pasar *(pah-'sahr)*
pitch	lanzar *(lahn-'sahr)*
serve	servir *(sehr-'veer)*
shoot	disparar *(dee-spah-'rahr)*
throw	tirar *(tee-'rahr)*

MÁS INFORMACIÓN

➤ P.E. teachers should label some of these items in Spanish with removable stickers:

I need (the)...	Necesito... *(neh-seh-'see-toh...)*
ball	la pelota *(lah peh-'loh-tah)*
basket	la canasta *(lah kah-'nah-stah)*
bat	el bate *(ehl 'bah-teh)*
mitt	el guante *(ehl 'gwahn-teh)*
net	la red *(lah rehd)*
racket	la raqueta *(lah rah-'keh-tah)*
stick	el palo *(ehl 'pah-loh)*
treadmill	el molino *(ehl moh-'lee-noh)*
weights	las pesas *(lahs 'peh-sahs)*

➤ When exercise is the topic, be sure to explain the benefits:

You need...	Necesitas... *(neh-seh-'see-tahs...)*
fitness	el buen estado físico *(ehl bwehn eh-'stah-doh 'fee-see-koh)*
strength	la fuerza *(lah 'fwehr-sah)*
weight loss	la pérdida de peso *(lah 'pehr-dee-dah deh 'peh-soh)*

TIME TO STUDY

La hora de estudiar *(lah 'oh-rah deh eh-stoo-dee-'ahr)*

Help out any student who is lacking those vital study skills. First, get them to the right location, and then explain all the procedures that you can:

We're going to (the)...	Vamos a... *('vah-mohs ah...)*
library	la biblioteca *(lah beeb-lee·oh-'teh-kah)*
resource room	el salón de recursos *(ehl sah-'lohn deh reh-'koor-sohs)*
study hall	el salón de estudio *(ehl sah-'lohn deh eh-'stoo-dee·oh)*

Please finish (the)...	Favor de terminar... *(fah-'vohr deh tehr-'mee-'nahr)*
assignment	la tarea *(lah tah-'reh-ah)*
essay	el ensayo *(ehl ehn-'sah-yoh)*
exam	el examen *(ehl ehk-'sah-mehn)*
project	el proyecto *(ehl proh-'yehk-'toh)*
quiz	el cuestionario *(ehl kweh-stee·oh-'nah-ree·oh)*
report	el reporte *(ehl reh-'pohr-teh)*
research	la investigación *(lah een-veh-stee-gah-see-'ohn)*
summary	el resumen *(ehl reh-'soo-mehn)*
test	la prueba *(lah proo-'eh-bah)*

You need to read (the)...	Necesitas leer... *(neh-seh-'see-tahs leh-'ehr...)*
chapter	el capítulo *(ehl kah-'pee-too-loh)*
section	la sección *(lah sehk-see-'ohn)*
unit	la unidad *(lah oo-nee-'dahd)*

Take out (the)...	Saca... *('sah-kah...)*
copies	las copias *(lahs 'koh-pee·ahs)*
notes	las anotaciones *(lahs ah-noh-tah-see-'oh-nehs)*
outlines	los resúmenes *(lohs reh-'soo-meh-nehs)*

We're looking for...	Buscamos... *(boo-'skah-mohs...)*
appendix	el apéndice *(ehl ah-'pehn-dee-seh)*
archive	el archivo *(ehl ahr-'chee-voh)*
article	el artículo *(ehl ahr-'tee-koo-loh)*
author	el autor *(ehl ow-'tohr)*
bibliography	la bibliografía *(lah bee-blee·oh-grah-'fee·ah)*
biography	la biografía *(lah bee·oh-grah-'fee·ah)*
catalog	el catálogo *(ehl kah-'tah-loh-goh)*
dictionary	el diccionario *(ehl deek-see·oh-'nah-ree·oh)*
encyclopedia	la enciclopedia *(lah ehn-see-kloh-'peh-dee·ah)*
fiction	la ficción *(lah feek-see·'ohn)*
glossary	el glosario *(ehl gloh-'sah-ree·oh)*
librarian	el bibliotecario *(ehl bee-blee·oh-teh-'kah-ree·oh)*
library card	la tarjeta de la biblioteca *(lah tahr-'heh-tah deh lah beeb-lee·oh-'teh-kah)*
magazine	la revista *(lah reh-'vee-stah)*
newspaper	el periódico *(ehl peh-ree·'oh-dee-koh)*
non-fiction	la no ficción *(lah noh feek-see·'ohn)*
records	el registro *(ehl reh-'hee-stroh)*
reference	la referencia *(lah reh-feh-'rehn-see·ah)*
resources	los recursos *(lohs reh-'koor-sohs)*
subject	el tema *(ehl 'teh-mah)*
title	el título *(ehl 'tee-too-loh)*
yearbook	el anuario *(ehl ah-noo-'ah-ree·oh)*

This group will help you explain valuable study skills:

Do you understand (the)..?	¿Entiendes..? *(ehn-tee-'ehn-dehs)*
approach	el enfoque *(ehl ehn-'foh-keh)*
concept	el concepto *(ehl kohn-'sehp-toh)*
content	el contenido *(ehl kohn-teh-'nee-doh)*
data	los datos *(lohs 'dah-tohs)*
evidence	la evidencia *(lah eh-vee-'dehn-see·ah)*
example	el ejemplo *(ehl eh-'hehm-ploh)*
fact	el hecho *(ehl 'eh-choh)*
information	la información *(lah een-fohr-mah-see·'ohn)*

material	**la materia** *(lah mah-'teh-ree·ah)*
method	**el método** *(ehl 'meh-toh-doh)*
model	**el modelo** *(ehl moh-'deh-loh)*
opinion	**la opinión** *(lah oh-pee-nee·'ohn)*
principle	**el principio** *(ehl preen-'see-pee·oh)*
reason	**la razón** *(lah rah-'sohn)*
step	**el paso** *(ehl 'pah-soh)*
strategy	**la estrategia** *(lah eh-strah-'teh-hee·ah)*
technique	**la técnica** *(lah 'tehk-nee-kah)*
theory	**la teoría** *(lah teh-oh-'ree·ah)*
topic	**el tema** *(ehl 'teh-mah)*

 MÁS INFORMACIÓN

➤ During test-taking, teachers need to be sure students understand the instructions. These expressions will come in handy:

You have to...	**Tienes que...** *(tee-'eh-nehs keh...)*
write definitions	**escribir las definiciones** *(eh-skree-'beer lahs deh-fee-nee-see·'oh-nehs)*
listen to dictation	**escuchar el dictado** *(eh-skoo-'chahr ehl deek-'tah-doh)*
say true or false	**decir verdadero o falso** *(deh-'seer vehr-dah-'deh-roh oh 'fahl-soh)*
do multiple choice	**hacer elección múltiple** *(ah-'sehr eh-lehk-see·'ohn 'mool-tee-pleh)*
fill in the blank	**llenar el espacio vacío** *(yeh-'nahr ehl eh-'spah-see·oh vah-'see·oh)*
find the opposite	**encontrar lo opuesto** *(ehn-kohn-'trahr loh oh-'pweh-stoh)*
match the words	**poner en pareja las palabras** *(poh-'nehr ehn pah-'reh-hah lahs pah-'lah-brahs)*
answer the questions	**contestar las preguntas** *(kohn-teh-'stahr lahs preh-'goon-tahs)*

You can use...	Pueden usar... *('pweh-dehn oo-'sahr)*
You cannot use...	No pueden usar... *(noh 'pweh-dehn oo-'sahr)*
online help	ayuda a través de la internet *(ah-'yoo-dah ah trah-'vehs deh lah internet)*
the website	el sitio web *(ehl 'see-tee·oh web)*
your tablet	tu tableta *(too tah-'bleh-tah)*

EXTRACURRICULAR ACTIVITIES
Las actividades extracurriculares
(lahs ahk-tee-vee-'dah-dehs ehks-trah-koo-ree-koo-'lah-rehs)

Not all learning takes place in the classroom. Students have the opportunity to join clubs, teams, or similar youth-oriented organizations. Several terms may be needed as you share information with Spanish-speaking students and their families.

Would you like to join?	¿Quisieras inscribirte? *(kee-see-'eh-rahs een-skree-'beer-teh)*
There's a _____ club.	Hay un club de _____ . *('ah·ee oon kloob deh _____)*

bicycle	ciclismo *(see-'klees-moh)*
business	negocios *(neh-'goh-see·ohs)*
chess	ajedrez *(ah-heh-'drehs)*
computer	computadoras *(kohm-poo-tah-'doh-rahs)*
cooking	cocina *(koh-'see-nah)*
culture	cultura *(kool-'too-rah)*
dance	baile *('bah·ee-leh)*
debate	debate *(deh-'bah-teh)*
drama	drama *('drah-mah)*
ecology	ecología *(eh-koh-loh-'hee·ah)*
film	películas *(peh-'lee-koo-lahs)*
graphic design	el diseño gráfico *(ehl dee-'sehn-yoh 'grah-fee-koh)*
nature	naturaleza *(nah-too-rah-'leh-sah)*
ski	esquí *(eh-'skee)*
travel	viajes *(vee-'ah-hehs)*
yearbook	anuario *(ah-noo-'ah-ree·oh)*

It's a/an...	Es un/una... *(ehs oon / 'oo-nah...)*
club	club *(kloob)*
group	grupo *('groo-poh)*
league	liga *('lee-gah)*
organization	organización *(ohr-gah-nee-sah-see·'ohn)*
team	equipo *(eh-'kee-poh)*
They have (the)...	Tienen... *(tee-'eh-nehn)*
auction	la subasta *(soo-'bah-stah)*
banquet	el banquete *(ehl bahn-'keh-teh)*
carnival	el carnaval *(ehl kahr-nah-'vahl)*
ceremony	la ceremonia *(lah seh-reh-'moh-nee·ah)*
conference	la conferencia *(lah kohn-feh-'rehn-see·ah)*
contest	el concurso *(ehl kohn-'koor-soh)*
dance	el baile *(ehl 'bah·ee-leh)*
event	el evento *(ehl eh-'vehn-toh)*
fair	la feria *(lah 'feh-ree·ah)*
festival	el festival *(ehl feh-stee-'vahl)*
game	el juego *(ehl hoo-'eh-goh)*
meeting	la reunión *(lah reh-oo-nee·'ohn)*
parade	el desfile *(ehl dehs-'fee-leh)*
party	la fiesta *(lah fee-'eh-stah)*
performance	la función *(lah foon-see·'ohn)*
picnic	el picnic *(ehl peek-'neek)*
program	el programa *(ehl proh-'grah-mah)*
raffle	el sorteo *(ehl sohr-'teh-oh)*
show	el espectáculo *(ehl eh-spehk-'tah-koo-loh)*
trip	el viaje *(ehl vee·'ah-heh)*

SPORTS
Los deportes *(lohs deh-'pohr-tehs)*

Throughout the U.S., many extracurricular student events and activities include the world of sports. As you read through the following set of vocabulary items, notice how many Spanish words resemble their equivalents in English.

I really like...	Me gusta mucho... *(meh 'goo-stah 'moo-choh...)*
badminton	el badminton *(ehl bahd-'meen-tohn)*
baseball	el béisbol *(ehl 'beh·ees-bohl)*
basketball	el básquetbol *(ehl 'bah-skeht-bohl)*
boxing	el boxeo *(ehl bohk-'seh-oh)*
cross country	la carrera a campo traviesa *(lah kah-'rreh-rah ah 'kahm-poh trah-vee-'eh-sah)*
football	el fútbol americano *(ehl 'foot-bohl ah-meh-ree-'kah-noh)*
golf	el golf *(ehl gohlf)*
gymnastics	la gimnasia *(lah heem-'nah-see·ah)*
ice hockey	el hockey sobre hielo *(ehl 'hoh-kee 'soh-breh 'yeh-loh)*
lacrosse	el lacrosse *(ehl lah-'kroh-seh)*
ping pong	el pin-pon *(ehl peen-pohn)*
racquetball	el frontón con raqueta *(ehl frohn-'tohn kohn rah-'keh-tah)*
soccer	el fútbol *(ehl 'foot-bohl)*
softball	el sófbol *(ehl 'sohf-bohl)*
tennis	el tenis *(ehl 'teh-nees)*
track and field	el atletismo *(ehl aht-leh-'tees-moh)*
volleyball	el vóleibol *(ehl voh-'leh·ee-bohl)*
water polo	el polo acuático *(ehl 'poh-loh ah-'kwah-tee-koh)*
wrestling	la lucha libre *(lah 'loo-chah 'lee-breh)*

Not all sporting activities are considered competitive athletics. Many groups meet simply for exercise and fun.

Do you like to...?	¿Le gusta...? *(leh 'goo-stah...)*
dance	**bailar** *(bah·ee-'lahr)*
dive	**zambullirse** *(sahm-boo-'yeer-seh)*
fish	**pescar** *(peh-'skahr)*
skate	**patinar** *(pah-tee-'nahr)*
ski	**esquiar** *(eh-skee-'ahr)*
swim	**nadar** *(nah-'dahr)*

Some activities consist of more than one word in Spanish:

Do you want to...?	¿Quieres...? *(kee-'eh-rehs...)*
go camping	**ir a acampar** *(eer ah ah-kahm-'pahr)*
ride bikes	**montar bicicletas** *(mohn-'tahr bee-see-kleh-tahs)*
sail	**navegar a vela** *(nah-veh-'gahr ah 'veh-lah)*
surf	**correr tabla** *(koh-'rrehr tah-'blah)*

And these sports have a special word in Spanish:

bowling	**el boliche** *(ehl boh-lee-cheh)*
hiking	**la caminata** *(lah kah-mee-'nah-tah)*
horseback riding	**la equitación** *(lah eh-kee-tah-see-'ohn)*
jogging	**el trote** *(ehl 'troh-teh)*

➤ If you're into sports, learn those words that relate to what you do:

I go to (the)...	Voy a... *('voh·ee ah...)*
arena	el anfiteatro *(ehl ahn-fee-teh-'ah-troh)*
bowling alley	la bolera *(lah boh-'leh-rah)*
court	la cancha *(lah 'kahn-chah)*
field	el campo *(ehl 'kahm-poh)*
game	el juego *(ehl hoo-'eh-goh)*
golf course	el campo de golf *(ehl 'kahm-poh deh gohlf)*
gym	el gimnasio *(ehl heem-'nah-see·oh)*
match	el partido *(ehl pahr-'tee-doh)*
pool	la piscina *(lah pee-'see-nah)*
practice	la práctica *(lah 'prahk-tee-kah)*
skating rink	el patinadero *(ehl pah-tee-nah-'deh-roh)*
stadium	el estadio *(ehl eh-'stah-dee·oh)*

➤ This selection helps out every high school educator:

I'm a _____   Estoy en el _____ . *(eh-'stoh·ee ehn ehl _____)*

freshman	primer año *(pree-'mehr 'ah-nyoh)*
sophomore	segundo año *(seh-'goon-doh 'ah-nyoh)*
junior	tercer año *(tehr-'sehr 'ah-nyoh)*
senior	cuarto año *('kwahr-toh 'ah-nyoh)*

Translate and then use in a sentence. Notice the sample:

word	la palabra *(lah pah-'lah-brah)*	Estoy estudiando la lista de palabras. *(eh-'stoh·ee eh-stoo-dee-'ahn-doh lah 'lee-stah deh pah-'lah-brahs)*
language	_____	_____

sentence _____ _____

essay _____ _____

Connect the related vocabulary:

el diseño *(ehl dee-'seh-nyoh)*   la banda *(lah 'bahn-dah)*
el balet *(ehl bah-'leh)*   el dibujo *(ehl dee-'boo-hoh)*
el tambor *(ehl tahm-'bohr)*   el baile *(ehl 'bah·ee-leh)*

List three things you can find in a library:

_____ _____ _____

List three different sports facilities:

_____ _____ _____

List three major sports:

_____ _____ _____

THE FIELD TRIP
El paseo educativo *(ehl pah-'seh-oh eh-doo-kah-'tee-voh)*

One of the most effective ways to instruct students is to actually visit those places that are being discussed in the classroom. If you're filling out permission slips for Spanish-speaking students, be sure everyone knows where they are going.

We're going to visit (the)...	Vamos a visitar... *('vah-mohs ah vee-see-'tahr...)*
airport	el aeropuerto *(ehl ah·eh-roh-'pwehr-toh)*
bookstore	la librería *(lah lee-breh-'ree·ah)*
college	la universidad *(lah oo-nee-vehr-see-'dahd)*
factory	la fábrica *(lah 'fah-bree-kah)*
fire department	el departamento de bomberos *(ehl deh-pahr-tah-'mehn-toh deh bohm-'beh-rohs)*
hospital	el hospital *(ehl oh-spee-'tahl)*
library	la biblioteca *(lah bee-blee·oh-'teh-kah)*
mall	el centro comercial *(ehl 'sehn-troh koh-mehr-see-'ahl)*

150

market	el mercado *(ehl mehr-'kah-doh)*
museum	el museo *(ehl moo-'seh-oh)*
office	la oficina *(lah oh-fee-'see-nah)*
park	el parque *(ehl 'pahr-keh)*
police station	la estación de policía *(lah eh-stah-see-'ohn deh poh-lee-'see·ah)*
post office	el correo *(ehl koh-'rreh-oh)*
school	la escuela *(lah eh-'skweh-lah)*
store	la tienda *(lah tee-'ehn-dah)*
theater	el teatro *(ehl teh-'ah-troh)*
university	la universidad *(lah oo-nee-vehr-see-'dahd)*

Keep practicing. Have you ever taken a group to one of these special places?

We will see (the)...	Vamos a ver... *('vah-mohs ah vehr...)*
amusement park	el parque de atracciones *(ehl 'pahr-keh deh ah-trahk-see-'oh-nehs)*
campgrounds	el campamento *(ehl kahm-pah-'mehn-toh)*
cemetery	el cementerio *(ehl seh-mehn-'teh-ree·oh)*
city hall	el municipio *(ehl moo-nee-'see-pee·oh)*
jail	la cárcel *(lah 'kahr-sehl)*
warehouse	el almacén *(ehl ahl-mah-'sehn)*
zoo	el zoológico *(ehl soh-oh-'loh-hee-koh)*

Now, how about those key words needed to share your travel plans with the parents:

It's...	Es... *(ehs...)*
for one night	para una noche *('pah-rah 'oo-nah 'noh-cheh)*
for one day	para un día *('pah-rah oon 'dee·ah)*
for the whole class	para toda la clase *('pah-rah 'toh-dah lah 'klah-seh)*
We need (the)...	Necesitamos... *(neh-seh-see-'tah-mohs...)*
bus	el autobús *(ehl ow-toh-'boos)*
insurance	el seguro *(ehl seh-'goo-roh)*
money	el dinero *(ehl dee-'neh-roh)*
permit	el permiso *(ehl pehr-'mee-soh)*
signature	la firma *(lah 'feer-mah)*
volunteers	los voluntarios *(lohs voh-loon-'tah-ree·ohs)*

You can pick up the students tomorrow in front of the bus.

Usted puede recoger a los estudiantes mañana en frente del autobús.
(oo-'stehd 'pweh-deh reh-koh-'hehr ah lohs eh-stoo-dee-'ahn-tehs mah-'nyah-nah ehn 'frehn-teh dehl ow-toh-'boos)

MÁS INFORMACIÓN

➤ Head to the outdoors las afueras *(lahs ah-'fweh-rahs)*, and your students can learn all kinds of important lessons.

I enjoy (the)...	Me gusta... *(meh 'goo-stah)*
beach	la playa *(lah 'plah-yah)*
cave	la cueva *(lah 'kweh-vah)*
coast	la costa *(lah 'koh-stah)*
desert	el desierto *(ehl deh-see-'ehr-toh)*
forest	el bosque *(ehl 'boh-skeh)*
hill	el cerro *(ehl 'seh-rroh)*
jungle	la selva *(lah 'sehl-vah)*
lagoon	la laguna *(lah lah-'goo-nah)*
lake	el lago *(ehl 'lah-goh)*
mountain	la montaña *(lah mohn-'tah-nyah)*
ocean	el océano *(ehl oh-'seh-ah-noh)*
pond	la charca *(lah 'chahr-kah)*
river	el río *(ehl 'ree·oh)*
sea	el mar *(ehl mahr)*
stream	el arroyo *(ehl ah-'rroh-yoh)*
valley	el valle *(ehl 'vah-yeh)*

Many cultures are somewhat suspicious about after-school activities. If you have new immigrants in school, they may refuse to participate in extracurricular events, or their parents may deny them permission to do so. Not only do many youngsters have responsibilities at home, but many families worry about their children's safety in a foreign land. Be prepared to face parental and student fears and lack of trust.

THE 4-H CLUB
El Club de 4-H *(ehl kloob deh 'kwah-troh 'ah-cheh)*

4-H Clubs and similar community organizations sometimes offer programs or events involving the care and preservation of local domestic animals. Not only do the following words help out club leaders, but they're also valuable to any educator in a science program. Here's a tip—instead of practicing each word you see, first focus on those items that you generally use the most:

They feed (the)...	Alimentan... *(ah-lee-'mehn-tahn...)*
They raise (the)...	Crian... *('kree·ahn)*
They have (the)...	Tienen... *(tee-'eh-nehn)*

bird	el pájaro *(ehl 'pah-hah-roh)*
cat	el gato *(ehl 'gah-toh)*
chicken	la gallina *(lah gah-'yee-nah)*
cow	la vaca *(lah 'vah-kah)*
dog	el perro *(ehl 'peh-rroh)*
duck	el pato *(ehl 'pah-toh)*
fish	el pez *(ehl pehs)*
goat	el chivo *(ehl 'chee-voh)*
hamster	el hámster *(ehl 'ahm-stehr)*
horse	el caballo *(ehl kah-'bah-yoh)*
pig	el cerdo *(ehl 'sehr-doh)*
rabbit	el conejo *(ehl koh-'neh-hoh)*
sheep	la oveja *(lah oh-'veh-hah)*
turtle	la tortuga *(lah tohr-'too-gah)*

➤ Students in rural areas often hold activities at one of these locations:

Let's go to (the)...	Vamos a... *('vah-mohs ah...)*
barn	**el establo** *(ehl eh-'stah-bloh)*
dairy	**la lechería** *(lah leh-cheh-'ree·ah)*
farm	**la granja** *(lah 'grahn-hoh)*
ranch	**el rancho** *(ehl 'rahn-choh)*

➤ Watch out for these animals who live in the wild:

beaver	**el castor** *(ehl kah-'stohr)*
fox	**el zorro** *(ehl 'soh-rroh)*
lizard	**la lagartija** *(lah lah-gahr-'tee-hah)*
raccoon	**el mapache** *(ehl mah-'pah-cheh)*
skunk	**el zorrino** *(ehl soh-'rree-noh)*
snake	**la culebra** *(lah koo-'leh-brah)*
wolf	**el lobo** *(ehl 'loh-boh)*

¡ACCIÓN!

So far we have discovered that in order to converse about educational activities, it was necessary to make changes to the basic verb. Notice the difference in meanings here:

to work	**trabajar** *(trah-bah-'hahr)*
I'm working.	**Estoy trabajando.**
	(eh-'stoh·ee trah-bah-'hahn-doh)
I work.	**Trabajo.** *(trah-'bah-hoh)*
I'm going to work.	**Voy a trabajar.** *('voh·ee ah trah-bah-'hahr)*

Now, check out this new way to refer to future actions. Just add new endings to the infinitive, as shown. Look at this regular -ar verb:

I will work	Trabajaré *(trah-bah-hah-'reh)*
You (informal) will work	Trabajarás *(trah-bah-hah-'rahs)*
You, He, She will work	Trabajará *(trah-bah-hah-'rah)*
You (pl.), They will work	Trabajarán *(trah-bah-hah-'rahn)*
We will work	Trabajaremos *(trah-bah-hah-'reh-mohs)*

The same patterns hold true for the -er and -ir verbs:

to eat (comer) *(koh-'mehr)*	I'll eat.	Comeré *(koh-meh-'reh)*
to live (vivir) *(vee-'veer)*	He'll live.	Vivirá *(vee-vee-'rah)*
to run (correr) *(koh-'rrehr)*	We'll run.	Correremos *(koh-rreh-'reh-mohs)*

MÁS INFORMACIÓN

➤ Beware of those irregular verbs in the future tense! Here are a few examples:

I'll have a job.	Tendré un trabajo. *(tehn-'dreh oon trah-'bah-hoh)*
They'll come soon.	Vendrán luego. *(vehn-'drahn 'lweh-goh)*
She'll leave at two.	Saldrá a las dos. *(sahl-'drah ah lahs dohs)*

➤ Since you already know how to say "going to" in Spanish, there are actually two ways to talk about the future:

to eat	I'm going to eat.	I will eat.
comer	Voy a comer.	Comeré.
(koh-'mehr)	*('voh-ee ah koh-'mehr)*	*(koh-meh-'reh)*
to wait	They're going to wait.	They will wait.
esperar	Van a esperar.	Esperarán.
(eh-speh-'rahr)	*('vahn ah eh-speh-'rahr)*	*(eh-speh-rah-'rahn)*

¡ÓRDENES!

Negative formal commands are easy. Just say no:

Come!	¡Venga! *('vehn-gah)*
Don't come!	¡No venga! *('noh 'vehn-gah)*

Write, you guys!	¡Escriban! *(eh-'skree-bahn)*
Don't write, you guys!	¡No escriban! *(noh eh-'skree-bahn)*

And notice how the verbs with se change in word order:

Get up!	¡Levántese! *(leh-'vahn-teh-seh)*
Don't get up!	¡No se levante! *(noh seh leh-'vahn-teh)*

Sit down, you guys!	¡Siéntense! *(see-'ehn-tehn-seh)*
Don't sit down, you guys!	¡No se sienten! *(noh seh see-'ehn-tehn)*

As for the informal (tú) commands, here's what happens. Both the regular and irregular forms shift to a formal-looking command, but with an -s at the end:

Read!	¡Lee! *('leh-eh)*
Don't read!	¡No leas! *(noh 'leh-ahs)*

Go!	¡Ve! *(veh)*
Don't go!	¡No vayas! *(noh 'vah-yahs)*

Stay!	¡Quédate! *('keh-dah-teh)*
Don't stay!	¡No te quedes! *(noh teh 'keh-dehs)*

Follow this sample set, change the other verbs in the same manner, and add some vocabulary:

llegar *(yeh-'gahr)*

<u>Está llegando ahora.</u>
(eh-'stah yeh-'gahn-doh ah-'oh-rah)
<u>Llega todos los días.</u>
('yeh-gah 'toh-dohs lohs 'dee·ahs)
<u>Llegará mañana.</u>
(yeh-gah-'rah mah-'nyah-nah)

estudiar *(eh-stoo-dee-'ahr)*

Está estudiando ahora. *(eh-'stah eh-stoo-dee-'ahn-doh ah-'oh-rah)*

_____

_____

correr *(koh-'rrehr)*

_____

_____

_____

explicar *(ehks-plee-'kahr)*

_____

_____

_____

Select the word that fits best:

el gato, el caballo, el pollo *(ehl 'gah-toh, ehl kah-'bah-yoh, ehl 'poh-yoh)*

_____ es un pájaro. (_____ ehs oon 'pah-hah-roh)

_____ no le gusta al perro. (_____ noh leh 'goo-stah ahl 'peh-rroh)

_____ está comiendo en el establo. (_____ eh-'stah koh-mee-'ehn-doh ehn ehl eh-'stah-bloh)

Connect the words that relate:

la policía *(lah poh-lee-'see·ah)*   la costa *(lah 'koh-stah)*
la playa *(lah 'plah-yah)*   la cárcel *(lah 'kahr-sehl)*
el almacén *(ehl ahl-mah-'sehn)*   la fábrica *(lah 'fah-bree-kah)*

 DIFERENCIAS CULTURALES

Students from Spanish-speaking countries are often familiar with those extracurricular activities that are offered at schools in their homeland. As a class assignment, ask them to share with other classmates any details about their favorite hobbies, sports, and student organizations.

CHAPTER FIVE
Capítulo Cinco
(kah-'pee-too-loh 'seen-koh)

DISCIPLINE
La disciplina
(lah dee-see-'plee-nah)

SCHOOL RULES

Las reglas de la escuela *(lahs 'reh-glahs deh lah eh-'skweh-lah)*

Regarding student discipline, some settings may require nothing more than personal contracts, while others may demand strictly enforced regulations. For younger students, school rules should be clear and concise, so that they can remember the words more easily. Here are a few general guidelines for conduct that can be presented at the grammar school to Spanish-speaking students and their parents:

Students need to...	**Los estudiantes necesitan...** *(lohs eh-stoo-dee-'ahn-tehs neh-seh-'see-tahn...)*
respect others	**respetar a los otros** *(reh-speh-'tahr ah lohs 'oh-trohs)*
attend school	**asistir a la escuela** *(ah-see-'steer ah lah eh-'skweh-lah)*
arrive on time	**llegar a tiempo** *(yeh-'gahr ah tee-'ehm-poh)*
behave well	**portarse bien** *(pohr-'tahr-seh 'bee·ehn)*
do their assignments	**hacer sus tareas** *(ah-'sehr soos tah-'reh-ahs)*
study for tests	**estudiar para los exámenes** *(eh-stoo-dee-'ahr 'pah-rah lohs ehk-'sah-meh-nehs)*
obey the rules	**obedecer las reglas** *(oh-beh-deh-'sehr lahs 'reh-glahs)*
raise their hands	**levantar las manos** *(leh-vahn-'tahr lahs 'mah-nohs)*
listen to the teacher	**escuchar al maestro** *(eh-skoo-'chahr ahl mah-'eh-stroh)*
participate in class	**participar en la clase** *(pahr-tee-see-'pahr ehn lah 'klah-seh)*
bring supplies	**traer sus útiles** *(trah-'ehr soos 'oo-tee-lehs)*
respect school property	**respetar la propiedad de la escuela** *(reh-speh-'tahr lah proh-pee-eh-'dahd deh lah eh-'skweh-lah)*
wear appropriate clothing	**ponerse ropa apropiada** *(poh-'nehr-seh 'roh-pah ah-proh-pee-'ah-dah)*
clean up their mess	**limpiar su basura** *(leem-pee-'ahr soo bah-'soo-rah)*
take care of their things	**cuidar sus cosas** *(kwee-'dahr soos 'koh-sahs)*
stay seated	**quedarse sentados** *(keh-'dahr-seh sehn-'tah-dohs)*

Now, let everyone know what they're <u>not</u> allowed to do:

___ is not allowed.	No se permite ____ *(noh seh pehr-'mee-teh)*
bothering others	molestar a los demás *(moh-leh-'stahr ah lohs deh-'mahs)*
copying	copiar *(koh-pee-'ahr)*
cursing	decir groserías *(deh-'seer groh-seh-'ree·ahs)*
cutting class	faltar a la clase *(fahl-'tahr ah lah 'klah-seh)*
forgetting pencil and paper	olvidar lápiz y papel *(ohl-vee-'dahr 'lah-pees ee pah-'pehl)*
goofing off	perder el tiempo *(pehr-'dehr ehl tee-'ehm-poh)*
gum chewing	masticar chicle *(mah-stee-'kahr 'chee-kleh)*
littering	tirar basura *(tee-'rahr bah-'soo-rah)*
loitering	holgazanear *(ohl-gah-sah-neh-'ahr)*
losing books	perder los libros *(pehr-'dehr lohs 'lee-brohs)*
making obscene gestures	hacer señales groseras *(ah-'sehr seh-'nyah-lehs groh-'seh-rahs)*
smoking	fumar *(foo-'mahr)*
texting	mandar textos *(mahn-'dahr 'tehks-tohs)*
threatening	amenazar *(ah-meh-nah-'sahr)*
throwing things	tirar cosas *(tee-'rahr 'koh-sahs)*
whistling	silbar *(seel-'bahr)*

 MÁS INFORMACIÓN

➤ Remember these commands from grammar school?

No...	No...
fighting	pelear *(peh-leh-'ahr)*
grabbing	agarrar *(ah-gah-'rrahr)*
hitting	pegar *(peh-'gahr)*
kicking	patear *(pah-teh-'ahr)*
pinching	pellizcar *(peh-yee-'skahr)*
pulling	jalar *(hah-'lahr)*
pushing	empujar *(ehm-poo-'hahr)*
spitting	escupir *(eh-skoo-'peer)*
touching	tocar *(toh-kahr)*
tripping	tropezar *(troh-peh-'sahr)*
wrestling	luchar *(loo-'chahr)*
yelling	gritar *(gree-'tahr)*

DISCIPLINE FOR TEENS
La disciplina para los adolescentes
(lah dee-see-'plee-nah 'pah-rah lohs ah-doh-leh-'sehn-tehs)

For older students, you may want to consider using some of the following terms to explain the rules and regulations:

Let's talk about (the)...	Vamos a hablar de... *('vah-mohs ah ah-'blahr deh...)*
conduct	la conducta *(lah kohn-'dook-tah)*
consequences	las consecuencias *(lahs kohn-seh-'kwehn-see·ahs)*
control	el control *(ehl kohn-'trohl)*
responsibility	la responsabilidad *(lah reh-spohn-sah-bee-lee-'dahd)*
right	el derecho *(ehl deh-'reh-choh)*
maturity	la madurez *(lah mah-doo-'rehs)*
Please do not bring...	Favor de no traer... *(fah-'vohr deh noh trah-'ehr)*
cell phones	los teléfonos celulares *(lohs teh-'leh-foh-nohs seh-loo-'lah-rehs)*
earphones	los auriculares *(lohs ah-oo-ree-koo 'lah-rehs)*
fireworks	los fuegos artificiales *(lohs 'fweh-gohs ahr-tee-fee-see-'ah-lehs)*
laptops	las computadoras portátiles *(lahs kohm-poo-tah-'doh-rahs-por-'tah-tee-lehs)*
lighters	los encendedores *(lohs ehn-sehn-deh-'doh-rehs)*
magazines	las revistas *(lahs reh-'vee-stahs)*
pets	las mascotas *(lahs mah-'skoh-tahs)*
pictures	las fotos *(lahs 'foh-tohs)*
radios	los radios *(lohs 'rah-dee·ohs)*
tobacco	el tabaco *(ehl tah-'bah-koh)*
toys	los juguetes *(lohs hoo-'geh-tehs)*
videogames	los videojuegos *(lohs vee-deh-oh-hoo-'eh-gohs)*

They are...	Son... *(sohn...)*
dangerous	peligrosos *(peh-lee-'groh-sohs)*
disruptive	desordenadores *(deh-'sohr-deh-nah-doh-rehs)*
illegal	ilegales *(ee-leh-'gah-lehs)*

They are not...	No son... *(noh sohn...)*
appropriate	apropiados *(ah-proh-pee-'ah-dohs)*
legal	legales *(leh-'gah-lehs)*
necessary	necesarios *(neh-seh-'sah-ree·ohs)*
permitted	permitidos *(pehr-mee-'tee-dohs)*
safe	seguros *(seh-'goo-rohs)*

For many schools, even these things are considered disruptive:

Give me (the)...	Dame... *('dah-meh...)*
badges	las chapas *(lahs 'chah-pahs)*
hats	los sombreros *(lohs sohm-'breh-rohs)*
jewelry	las joyas *(lahs 'hoh-yahs)*
keys	las llaves *(lahs 'yah-vehs)*
laser	el láser *(ehl 'lah-sehr)*
makeup	el maquillaje *(ehl mah-kee-'yah-heh)*
markers	los marcadores *(lohs mahr-kah-'doh-rehs)*
notes	las notas *(lahs 'noh-tahs)*
skateboards	las patinetas *(lahs pah-tee-'neh-tahs)*
sunglasses	los lentes del sol *(lohs 'lehn-tehs dehl sohl)*

➤ This is what you say when things get out of hand:

We are going to...	**Vamos a...** *('vah-mohs ah...)*
call home	**llamar a tu casa** *(yah-'mahr ah too 'kah-sah)*
call the police	**llamar a la policía** *(yah-'mahr ah lah poh-lee-'see·ah)*
search your locker	**registrar tu armario** *(reh-hee-'strahr too ahr-'mah-ree·oh)*
talk to the witnesses	**hablar con los testigos** *(ah-'blahr kohn lohs teh-'stee-gohs)*

➤ And always give reminders to students who speak only Spanish:

Do not forget (the)...	**No olvidar...** *(noh ohl-vee-'dahr...)*
application	**la solicitud** *(lah soh-lee-see-'tood)*
assignment	**la tarea** *(lah tah-'reh-ah)*
card	**la tarjeta** *(lah tahr-'heh-tah)*
form	**el formulario** *(ehl fohr-moo-'lah-ree·oh)*
lock	**el candado** *(ehl kahn-'dah-doh)*
pass	**el pase** *(ehl 'pah-seh)*
signed note	**la notificación firmada** *(lah noh-tee-fee-kah-see-'ohn feer-'mah-dah)*
ticket	**el boleto** *(ehl boh-'leh-toh)*
written excuse	**la excusa escrita** *(lah ehk-'skoo-sah eh-'skree-tah)*

➤ Pick up on new terms that relate to your concern:

curfew	**el toque de queda** *(ehl 'toh-keh deh 'keh-dah)*
truant	**el estudiante que no va a sus clases** *(ehl eh-stoo-dee-'ahn-teh keh noh vah ah soos 'klah-sehs)*

IT'S A PROBLEM*

Es un problema *(ehs oon proh-'bleh-mah)*

More and more educational institutions face kids with severe behavior problems. Do any of these words sound familiar?

He has (the)...	Tiene... *(tee-'eh-neh...)*
alcohol	el alcohol *(ehl ahl-koh-'ohl)*
drug	la droga *(lah 'droh-gah)*
explosive	el explosivo *(ehl ehk-sploh-'see-voh)*
firearm	el arma de fuego *(ehl 'ahr-mah deh 'fweh-goh)*
illegal substance	la sustancia ilegal *(lah soos-'tahn-see·ah ee-leh-'gahl)*
knife	el cuchillo *(ehl koo-'chee-yoh)*
stolen property	bienes robados *(bee·'eh-nehs roh-'bah-dohs)*

It's...	Es... *(ehs...)*
bullying	la intimidación *(lah een-tee-mee-dah-see·'ohn)*
cheating	el fraude *(ehl 'frow-deh)*
extortion	la extorsión *(lah ehk-stohr-see·'ohn)*
fighting	la pelea *(lah peh-'leh-ah)*
gambling	el juego por dinero *(ehl 'hweh-goh pohr dee-'neh-roh)*
graffiti	el grafiti *(ehl grah-'fee-tee)*
harassment	el acosamiento *(ehl ah-koh-sah-mee-'ehn-toh)*
stealing	el robo *(ehl 'roh-boh)*
trespassing	la intrusión *(lah een-troo-see·'ohn)*

They are...each other!	¡Se están...! *(seh eh-'stahn...)*
hugging	abrazando *(ah-brah-'sahn-doh)*
kissing	besando *(beh-'sahn-doh)*
touching	tocando *(toh-'kahn-doh)*

*See pp. 268–269 for a list of illegal drugs

She is...!	¡Ella está...! *('eh-yah eh-'stah...)*
carrying a dangerous object	**llevando un objeto peligroso** *(yeh-'vahn-doh oon ohb-'heh-toh peh-lee-'groh-soh)*
flashing gang signs	**mostrando las señas de la pandilla** *(moh-'strahn-doh lahs 'seh-nyahs deh lah pahn-'dee-yah)*
threatening the teacher	**amenazando al maestro** *(ah-meh-nah-'sahn-doh ahl mah-'eh-stroh)*

MÁS INFORMACIÓN

➤ You'll need these words as you investigate:

to exaggerate	**exagerar** *(ehk-sah-hehr-'ahr)*
to gossip	**chismear** *(chees-meh-'ahr)*
to lie	**mentir** *(mehn-'teer)*

Speak clearly as you practice:

I've been watching.	**He estado mirando.** *(eh ehs-'tah-doh mee-'rahn-doh)*
I followed you.	**Te seguí.** *(teh seh-'guee)*
I saw you.	**Te ví.** *(teh vee)*

| It was... | **Fue...** *(foo-'eh)* |

a false alarm	**una falsa alarma** *('oo-nah 'fahl-sah ah-'lahr-mah)*
a hoax	**un engaño** *(oon ehn-'gahn-yoh)*
a joke	**una broma** *('oo-nah 'broh-mah)*
a lie	**una mentira** *('oo-nah mehn-'tee-rah)*
a prank	**una travesura** *('oo-nah trah-veh-'soo-rah)*
a threat	**una amenaza** *('oo-nah ah-meh-'nah-sah)*
a trick	**un truco** *(oon 'troo-koh)*
dangerous	**peligroso** *(peh-lee-'groh-soh)*
dumb	**tonto** *('tohn-toh)*
illegal	**ilegal** *(ee-leh-'gahl)*
indecent	**indecente** *(een-deh-'sehn-teh)*
irresponsible	**irresponsable** *(ee-rreh-spohn-'sah-bleh)*
reckless	**temerario** *(teh-meh-'rah-ree·oh)*

CITIZENSHIP GRADES

Las notas de comportamiento *(lahs 'noh-tahs deh kohm-pohr-tah-mee-'ehn-toh)*

Classroom regulations differ from place to place, but these lists deal with the basics:

He/She has a problem with...	**Tiene problema con...** *(tee-'eh-neh proh-'bleh-mah kohn...)*
defiance of authority	**oposición a la autoridad** *(oh-poh-see-see-'ohn ah lah ow-toh-ree-'dahd)*
disruptive behavior	**desorden** *(dehs-'ohr-dehn)*
incomplete assignments	**tareas incompletas** *(tah-'reh-ahs een-kohm-'pleh-tahs)*
poor work habits	**malos hábitos de estudio** *('mah-lohs 'ah-bee-tohs deh eh-'stoo-dee·oh)*
tardiness and attendance	**tardanza y asistencia** *(tahr-'dahn-sah ee ah-see-'stehn-see·ah)*
His/Her behavior is...	**Su comportamiento es...** *(soo kohm-pohr-tah-mee-'ehn-toh ehs...)*
average	**promedio** *(proh-'meh-dee·oh)*
better	**mejor** *(meh-'hohr)*
outstanding	**destacado** *(deh-stah-'kah-doh)*
satisfactory	**satisfactorio** *(sah-tees-fahk-'toh-ree·oh)*
unsatisfactory	**malo** *('mah-loh)*
worse	**peor** *(peh-'ohr)*

Having Spanish-speaking students, rules should be posted in both languages for everyone to see:

No...in class.	**No se permite en la clase.** *(noh seh pehr-'mee-teh ehn lah 'klah-seh)*

chewing gum	**masticar chicle** *(mahs-tee-'kahr 'chee-kleh)*
drinking	**beber** *(beh-'behr)*
eating	**comer** *(koh-'mehr)*
playing	**jugar** *(hoo-'gahr)*
running	**correr** *(koh-'rrehr)*
sleeping	**dormir** *(dohr-'meer)*

Please do not...	**Favor de no...** *(fah-'vohr deh noh...)*

use your cellphone	**usar tu celular** *(oo-'sahr too seh-loo-'lahr)*
leave your desk	**dejar su escritorio** *(deh-'hahr soo eh-skree-'toh-ree·oh)*
pass notes	**pasar notas** *(pah-'sahr 'noh-tahs)*
copy someone else's assignment	**copiar la tarea de otra persona** *(koh-pee-'ahr lah tah-'reh-ah deh 'oh-trah pehr-'soh-nah)*
speak without permission	**hablar sin permiso** *(ah-'blahr seen pehr-'mee-soh)*
write in the textbook	**escribir en el libro de texto** *(eh-skree-'beer ehn ehl 'lee-broh deh 'tehks-toh)*
play with the lights	**jugar con las luces** *(hoo-'gahr kohn lahs 'loo-sehs)*
touch the fire alarm	**tocar la alarma de fuego** *(toh-'kahr lah ah-'lahr-mah deh 'fweh-goh)*

Use the _____, please.	**Por favor, usa _____.** *(pohr fah-'vohr, 'oo-sah_____)*

computer	**la computadora** *(lah kohm-poo-tah-'doh-rah)*
calculator	**la calculadora** *(lah kahl-koo-lah-'doh-rah)*
pencil sharpener	**el sacapuntas** *(ehl sah-kah-'poon-tahs)*
stapler	**la engrapadora** *(lah ehn-grah-pah-'doh-rah)*
trash can	**el bote de basura** *(ehl 'boh-teh deh bah-'soo-rah)*

➤ You need to...   Necesitas... *(neh-seh-'see-tahs...)*

    call your home   llamar a tu casa *(yah-'mahr ah too 'kah-sah)*
    talk to the nurse   hablar con la enfermera *(ah-'blahr kohn lah ehn-fehr-'meh-rah)*

    go to the bathroom   ir al baño *(eer ahl 'bah-nyoh)*
    buy a meal ticket   comprar un boleto de comida *(kohm-'prahr oon boh-'leh-toh deh koh-'mee-dah)*

    wear the uniform   ponerte el uniforme *(poh-'nehr-teh ehl oo-nee-'fohr-meh)*

    use a locker   usar un armario *(oo-'sahr oon ahr-'mah-ree·oh)*

➤ Now ask your students about their homework. Notice the past tense verb form:

    Did you study it?   ¿Lo estudiaste? *(loh eh-stoo-dee-'ahs-teh)*
    Did you turn it in?   ¿Lo entregaste? *(loh ehn-treh-'gah-steh)*
    Did you lose it?   ¿Lo perdiste? *(loh pehr-'dee-steh)*
    Did you finish it?   ¿Lo terminaste? *(loh tehr-mee-'nah-steh)*
    Did you do it?   ¿Lo hiciste? *(loh loh ee-'see-steh)*
    Did you understand it?   ¿Lo entendiste? *(loh ehn-tehn-'dee-steh)*

➤ Speaking of homework, listen closely as the student tries to explain:

    It's...   Está... *(eh-'stah...)*

    lost   perdido *(pehr-'dee-doh)*
    at home   en casa *(ehn 'kah-sah)*
    incomplete   incompleto *(een-kohm-'pleh-toh)*

THE CONTRACT
El contrato *(ehl kohn-'trah-toh)*

It's time to set up disciplinary contracts with some of the students. Parent or guardian signatures are required, so you explain each procedure in Spanish:

This is for the safety of the student.
Esto es para la seguridad del estudiante. *('eh-stoh ehs 'pah-rah lah seh-goo-ree-'dahd dehl eh-stoo-dee-'ahn-teh)*

The student must follow the code of behavior.

El estudiante tiene que cumplir con el código de comportamiento. *(ehl eh-stoo-dee-'ahn-teh tee-'eh-neh keh koom-'pleer kohn ehl 'koh-dee-goh deh kohm-pohr-tah-mee-'ehn-toh)*

They are responsible for their actions.

Son responsables de sus acciones. *(sohn reh-spohn-'sah-blehs deh soos ahk-see-'oh-nehs)*

It is a school-wide progressive discipline plan.

Es un plan de disciplina progresiva para toda la escuela. *(ehs oon plahn deh dee-see-'plee-nah proh-greh-'see-vah 'pah-rah 'toh-dah lah eh-'skweh-lah)*

Please read the contract and sign your name.

Favor de leer el contrato y firmar su nombre. *(fah-'vohr deh leh-'ehr ehl kohn-'trah-toh ee feer-'mahr soo 'nohm-breh)*

Make a comment or two about the agreement:

It's...	**Es...** *(ehs...)*
confidential	**confidencial** *(kohn-fee-dehn-see-'ahl)*
effective now	**efectivo ahora** *(eh-fehk-'tee-voh ah-'oh-rah)*
serious	**serio** *('seh-ree·oh)*

It includes...	**Este incluye...** *('eh-steh een-'kloo-yeh...)*
before and after school activities	**actividades antes y después de la escuela** *(lahs ahk-tee-vee-'dah-dehs 'ahn-tehs ee deh-'spwehs deh lah eh-'skweh-lah)*
all school events	**todos los eventos escolares** *('toh-dohs lohs eh-'vehn-tohs eh-skoh-'lah-rehs)*
the rest of the year	**el resto del año** *(ehl 'reh-stoh dehl 'ah-nyoh)*

➤ Check out this important pattern:

It's a _____ slip.   **Es un formulario de _____ .** *(ehs oon fohr-moo-'lah-ree·oh deh _____)*

attendance	**asistencia** *(ah-see-'stehn-see·ah)*
call	**llamadas** *(yah-'mah-dahs)*
discipline	**disciplina** *(dee-see-'plee-nah)*
health	**salud** *(sah-'lood)*
permission	**permiso** *(pehr-'mee-soh)*
tardiness	**tardanza** *(tahr-'dahn-sah)*
transfer	**transferencia** *(trahns-feh-'rehn-see·ah)*
visitors	**visitantes** *(vee-see-'tahn-tehs)*

➤ Has every concern been addressed?

What do you know about (the) ...?   **¿Qué sabes tú de ...?** *(keh 'sah-behs too deh...)*

insubordination	**la insubordinación** *(lah een-soob-ohr-dee-nah-see·'ohn)*
lack of cooperation	**la falta de cooperación** *(lah 'fahl-tah deh koh-oh-peh-rah-see·'ohn)*
misconduct	**la mala conducta** *(lah 'mah-lah kohn-'dook-tah)*
procrastination	**el incumplimiento a tiempo** *(ehl een-koom-plee-mee-'ehn-toh ah tee-'ehm-poh)*
disturbance	**el tumulto** *(ehl too-'mool-toh)*
confrontation	**la confrontación** *(lah kohn-frohn-tah-see·'ohn)*

¿LISTOS PARA PRACTICAR?

Name in Spanish five student actions that would be considered unacceptable at most high schools:

_____ _____ _____ _____ _____

Name three items that would be considered illegal on a school campus:

_____ _____ _____

Finish the sentences with the best words that fit:

los formularios, los sombreros, las consecuencias *(lohs fohr-moo-'lah-ree·ohs, lohs sohm-'breh-rohs, lahs kohn-seh-'kwehn-see·ahs)*

No traigan _____ *(noh 'trah·ee-gahn _____)*
Escribe en _____ *(eh-skree-beh ehn _____)*
¿Entiendes _____ ? *(ehn-tee-'ehn-dehs _____)*

Translate:

outstanding _____

better _____

worse _____

THE CONSEQUENCES
Las consecuencias *(lahs kohn-seh-'kwehn-see·ahs)*

Along with student rights and responsibilities come well-defined consequences for bad behavior. Each situation varies, so why not make statements using this vocabulary based upon your specific situation. Don't forget to change them to the feminine form if necessary:

He is...   Él es... *(ehl ehs)*

careless   descuidado *(dehs-kwee-'dah-doh)*
critical   crítico *('kree-tee-koh)*
cruel   cruel *(kroo-'ehl)*
dishonest   deshonesto *(dehs-oh-'neh-stoh)*
disrespectful   irrespetuoso *(ee-reh-speh-too-'oh-soh)*
incompetent   incompetente *(een-kohm-peh-'tehn-teh)*
negligent   negligente *(nehg-lee-'hehn-teh)*
rude   grosero *(groh-'seh-roh)*
sarcastic   sarcástico *(sahr-'kah-stee-koh)*

172

He needs...	Necesita... *(neh-seh-'see-tah...)*
detention	la detención *(lah deh-tehn-see-'ohn)*
discipline	la disciplina *(lah dee-see-'plee-nah)*
expulsion	la expulsión *(lah ehk-spool-see-'ohn)*
home phone call	la llamada a la casa *(lah yah-'mah-dah ah lah 'kah-sah)*
juvenile court	el tribunal de menores *(ehl tree-boo-'nahl deh meh-'noh-rehs)*
legal contract	el contrato legal *(ehl kohn-'trah-toh leh-'gahl)*
official transfer	la transferencia oficial *(lah trahns-feh-'rehn-see·ah oh-fee-see-'ahl)*
parent conference	la conferencia con los padres *(lah kohn-feh-'rehn-see·ah kohn lohs 'pah-drehs)*
personal intervention	la intervención personal *(lah een-tehr-vehn-see-'ohn pehr-soh-'nahl)*
punishment	el castigo *(ehl kah-'stee-goh)*
reprimand	la reprensión *(lah reh-prehn-see-'ohn)*
suspension	la suspensión *(lah soo-spehn-see-'ohn)*
warning	la advertencia *(lah ahd-vehr-'tehn-see·ah)*

While you're talking, interject a couple of these terms, also:

It's (the)...	Es... *(ehs...)*
attitude	la actitud *(lah ahk-tee-'tood)*
care	el cuidado *(ehl kwee-'dah-doh)*
change	el cambio *(ehl 'kahm-bee·oh)*
conflict	el conflicto *(ehl kohn-'fleek-toh)*
consent	el consentimiento *(ehl kohn-sehn-tee-mee-'ehn-toh)*
notice	el aviso *(ehl ah-'vee-soh)*
privilege	el privilegio *(ehl pree-vee-'leh-hee·oh)*
second time	la segunda vez *(lah seh-'goon-dah vehs)*
supervision	la supervisión *(lah soo-pehr-vee-see-'ohn)*
violation	la violación *(lah vee·oh-lah-see-'ohn)*
violence	la violencia *(lah vee·oh-'lehn-see·ah)*

➤ Discipline demands action. You may want to learn these verbs soon:

confiscate	confiscar	Confiscamos las drogas. *(kohn-fee-'skah-mohs lahs 'droh-gahs)*
expel	expulsar *(ehks-pool-'sahr)*	_____
assign	asignar *(ah-seeg-'nahr)*	_____
protect	proteger *(proh-teh-'hehr)*	_____
deserve	merecer *(meh-reh-'sehr)*	_____

HOME PHONE CALLS

Las llamadas a la casa *(lahs yah-'mah-dahs ah lah 'kah-sah)*

To maintain discipline, keep in touch with each student's family:

Do you have (the)...?	¿Tienes...? *(tee-'eh-nehs)*
address	la dirección *(lah dee-rehk-see-'ohn)*
area code	el código de área *(ehl 'koh-dee-goh deh 'ah-reh-ah)*
cellular phone	el teléfono celular *(ehl teh-'leh-foh-noh seh-loo-'lahr)*
email	el correo electrónico *(ehl koh-'rreh-oh eh-lehk-'troh-nee-koh)*
extension	la extensión *(lah ehks-tehn-see-'ohn)*
fax	el fax *(ehl fahks)*
voicemail	el contestador telefónico *(ehl kohn-teh-stah-'dohr teh-leh-'foh-nee-koh)*
work number	el número del trabajo *(ehl 'noo-meh-roh dehl trah-'bah-hoh)*

Now, practice the following phrases. Making phone calls in Spanish is a tough task, but with the proper one-liners in hand, you at least will have a chance of getting or giving basic information to parents who only speak Spanish.

Is there someone here who speaks English?
¿Hay alquien aquí que hable inglés?
('ah-ee 'ahl-guee-ehn ah-'kee keh 'ah-bleh een-'glehs)

Hello, is _____ there?
¿Aló, está _____ ?
(ah-'loh, eh-'stah _____)

I'm Mr./Ms. _____, _____'s teacher.
Soy el sr., la sra./srta. _____, el/la maestro/a de su hijo/a _____.
('soh-ee ehl sehn-'yohr/la sehn-'yoh-rah/sehn-yoh-'ree-tah _____, ehl/lah
mah-'ehs-troh/ah deh soo 'ee-hoh/ah _____.)

May I speak to _____ ?
¿Puedo hablar con _____ ?
(pweh-doh ah-'blahr kohn _____)

I'm calling about _____ .
Estoy llamando acerca de _____ .
(eh-'stoh-ee yah-'mahn-doh ah-'sehr-kah deh _____)

I'll transfer you to _____ .
Le voy a transferir a _____ .
(leh 'voh·ee ah trahns-feh-'reer ah _____)

Tell him/her that _____ .
Dígale que _____ .
('dee-gah-leh keh _____)

More slowly, please.
Más despacio, por favor.
(mahs deh-'spah-see·oh, pohr fah-'vohr)

Wait a moment, please.
Espere un momento, por favor.
(eh-'speh-reh oon moh-'mehn-toh, pohr fah-'vohr)

Please, it's very urgent.
Por favor, es muy urgente.
(pohr fah-'vohr, ehs 'moo·ee oor-'hehn-teh)

Your number, please.
Su número, por favor.
(soo 'noo-meh-'roh, pohr fah-'vohr)

Could you please repeat that?
¿Puede repetirlo, por favor?
('pweh-deh reh-peh-'teer-loh, pohr fah-'vohr)

One method is to break your one-liners into vocabulary-specific sets:

Can you call later?
¿Puede llamar más tarde?
('pweh-deh yah-'mahr mahs 'tahr-deh)

He/She will call you later.
El/ella llamará más tarde.
(ehl l'eh-yah yah-mah-'rah mahs 'tahr-deh)

Do you want to leave a message?
¿Quiere dejar un recado?
(kee-'eh-reh deh-'hahr oon reh-'kah-doh)

I'd like to leave a message.
Quisiera dejar un recado.
(kee-see-'eh-rah deh-'hahr oon reh-'kah-doh)

I will give him/her your message.
Le voy a dejar su mensaje.
(leh 'voh·ee ah deh-'hahr soo mehn-'sah-heh)

Is it long distance?
¿Es de larga distancia?
(ehs deh 'lahr-gah dee-'stahn-see·ah)

Is it a local call?
¿Es una llamada local?
(ehs 'oo-nah yah-'mah-dah loh-'kahl)

In any language, using the phone can be frustrating. Here are a few examples:

He isn't here.
No está aquí.
(noh eh-'stah ah-'kee)

She can't come to the phone.
No puede contestar la llamada.
(noh 'pweh-deh kohn-teh-'stahr lah yah-'mah-dah)

He is busy.
Está ocupado.
(eh-'stah oh-koo-'pah-doh)

Is this the correct number?
¿Es el número correcto?
(ehs ehl 'noo-meh-roh koh-'rrehk-toh)

I have the wrong number.
Tengo el número equivocado.
('tehn-goh ehl 'noo-meh-roh eh-kee-voh-'kah-doh)

You have the wrong number.
Tiene el número equivocado.
(tee-'eh-neh ehl 'noo-meh-roh eh-kee-voh-'kah-doh)

The number has been changed.
Se ha cambiado el número.
(seh ah kahm-bee-'ah-doh ehl 'noo-meh-roh)

The line is bad.
La línea está mala.
(lah 'lee-neh-ah eh-'stah 'mah-lah)

The line is busy.
La línea está ocupada.
(lah 'lee-neh-ah eh-'stah oh-koo-'pah-dah)

The line is disconnected.
La línea está desconectada.
(lah 'lee-neh-ah eh-'stah dehs-koh-nehk-'tah-dah)

Now direct others how to handle the calls:

Dial this number.
Marque este número.
('mahr-keh 'eh-steh 'noo-meh-roh)

Press this number.
Oprima este número.
(oh-'pree-mah 'eh-steh 'noo-meh-roh).

Ask for this number.
Pida este número.
('pee-dah 'eh-steh 'noo-meh-roh)

Wait for the tone.
Espere por el tono.
(eh-'speh-reh pohr ehl 'toh-noh)

Hang up the phone.
Cuelgue el teléfono.
('kwehl-geh ehl teh-'leh-foh-noh)

BICYCLE RULES
Las reglas para montar bicicleta
(lahs 'reh-glahs 'pah-rah mohn-'tahr bee-see-'kleh-tah)

Let's read through some of the key Spanish words and phrases needed to discuss bicycle regulations on campus.

Do not ride your bike here.
No montes tu bicicleta aquí. *(noh 'mohn-tehs too bee-see-'kleh-tah ah-'kee)*

Lock your bike in the bike rack.
Asegura tu bicicleta en el sujetador de bicicletas. *(ah-seh-'goo-rah too bee-see-'kleh-tah ehn ehl soo-heh-tah-'dohr deh bee-see-'kleh-tahs)*

Your bike must be registered with the Police Department.
Tu bicicleta tiene que ser registrada en el departamento de policía. *(too bee-see-'kleh-tah tee-'eh-neh keh sehr reh-hee-'strah-dah ehn ehl deh-pahr-tah-'mehn-toh deh poh-lee-'see·ah)*

Bikes are kept in the bicycle area.
Se guardan las bicicletas en la zona de bicicletas. *(seh 'gwahr-dahn lahs bee-see-'kleh-tahs ehn lah 'soh-nah deh bee-see-'kleh-tahs)*

The bike area is not for motorized bicycles.
La zona de bicicletas no es para bicicletas motorizadas. *(lah 'soh-nah deh bee-see-'kleh-tahs noh ehs 'pah-rah bee-see-'kleh-tahs moh-toh-ree-'sah-dahs)*

The school is not responsible for robbery or damage to bikes.
La escuela no es responsable por el robo o daño a las bicicletas. *(lah eh-'skweh-lah noh ehs reh-spohn-'sah-bleh pohr ehl 'roh-boh o 'dah-nyoh ah lahs bee-see-'kleh-tahs)*

You cannot carry passengers on a bike.
No puedes llevar pasajeros en una bicicleta. *(noh 'pweh-dehs yeh-'vahr pah-sah-'heh-rohs ehn 'oo-nah bee-see-'kleh-tah)*

You need to wear a helmet.
Necesitas usar un casco. *(neh-seh-'see-tahs oo-'sahr oon 'kah-skoh)*

You must follow the same rules as automobile drivers.
Tienes que seguir las mismas reglas que los choferes de autos. *(tee-'eh-nehs keh seh-'geer lahs 'mees-mahs 'reh-glahs keh lohs choh-'feh-rehs deh 'ow-tohs)*

Walk your bike!
¡Camina con tu bicicleta! *(kah-'mee-nah kohn too bee-see-'kleh-tah)*

THE PARKING LOT
El lote de estacionamiento *(ehl 'loh-teh deh eh-stah-see·oh-nah-mee-'ehn-toh)*

Knowing how to talk about cars in Spanish will not only help out the teachers in auto shop and driver's education, but it will also assist anyone who needs to explain campus parking procedures.

You need (the/to)...	**Ustedes necesitan...** *(oo-'steh-dehs neh-seh-'see-tahn...)*
handicapped parking	**estacionamiento para incapacitados** *(eh-stah-see·oh-nah-mee-'ehn-toh 'pah-rah een-kah-pah-see-'tah-dohs)*

179

lock your car	**cerrar su carro con llave** *(seh-'rrahr soo 'kay-rroh kohn 'yah-veh)*
permit	**el permiso** *(ehl pehr-'mee-soh)*
stamp	**el sello** *(ehl 'seh-yoh)*
sticker	**la etiqueta** *(lah eh-tee-'keh-tah)*
ticket	**el boleto** *(ehl boh-'leh-toh)*

This is...	**Este está...** *('eh-steh eh-'stah...)*

parked poorly	**mal estacionado** *(mahl eh-stah-see·oh-'nah-doh)*
double parked	**estacionado en doble hilera** *(eh-stah-see·oh-'nah-doh ehn 'doh-bleh ee-'leh-rah)*
parallel parking	**estacionamiento paralelo** *(eh-stah-see·ohn-ah-mee-'ehn-toh pah-rah-'leh-loh)*

Look at (the)...	**Mira...** *('mee-rah...)*

arrow	**la flecha** *(lah 'fleh-chah)*
color	**el color** *(ehl koh-'lohr)*
cone	**el cono** *(ehl 'koh-noh)*
hydrant	**la llave de incendios** *(lah 'yah-veh deh een-'sehn-dee·ohs)*
line	**la línea** *(lah 'lee-neh-ah)*
meter	**el parquímetro** *(ehl pahr-'kee-meh-troh)*
sign	**la señal** *(lah seh-'nyahl)*
space	**el espacio** *(ehl eh-'spah-see·oh)*
zone	**la zona** *(lah 'soh-nah)*

 MÁS INFORMACIÓN

➤ You may have to stop a vehicle and ask these key questions:

Show me your...	**Muéstrame tu...** *('mweh-strah-meh too...)*

insurance	**seguro** *(seh-'goo-roh)*
license	**licencia** *(lee-'sehn-see·ah)*
registration	**registro** *(reh-'hee-stroh)*

➤ It may be a good idea to learn the names in Spanish for various auto parts. They could be useful in an emergency setting.

➤ How about some other ways to travel? Students often get to school by means of one of these:

I come by...   Vengo... ('vehn-gah...)

bus   **por autobús** *(pohr ow-toh-'boos)*
scooter   **en bicicleta motorizada** *(ehn beh-see-'kleh-tah moh-toh-ree-'sah-dah)*
motorcycle   **en motocicleta** *(ehn moh-toh-see-'kleh-tah)*
school bus   **por autobús escolar** *(pohr ow-toh-'boos eh-skoh-'lahr)*
streetcar   **por tranvía** *(pohr trah-'vee·ah)*
subway   **por metro** *(pohr 'meh-troh)*
train   **por tren** *(pohr trehn)*
truck   **en camión** *(ehn kah-mee·'ohn)*

¿LISTOS PARA PRACTICAR?

Name three forms of discipline at a typical public high school:

_____   _____   _____

Practice this phone conversation. It will help get you started:

¿Aló, está el Sr. Sánchez?   No, no está aquí. Está trabajando.
(ah-'loh, eh-'stah ehl seh-'nyohr   *(noh, noh eh-'stah ah-'kee. eh-'stah trah-*
'sahn-chehs)   *bah-'hahn-doh)*

¿Es usted la Sra. Sánchez? *(ehs oo-'stehd lah seh-'nyoh-rah 'sahn-chehs)*

Sí. ¿Quién habla? *(see, kee-'ehn 'ah-blah)*

Soy (your name) *('soh·ee _____)*

de la escuela (your school) *(deh lah eh-'skweh-lah)*

y estoy llamando acerca de *(ee eh-'stoh·ee yah-'mahn-doh ah-'sehr-kah deh)*

su hijo/hija (student's name). *(soo 'hee-hoh)*

How do you say these words in Spanish?

helmet   _____

permit   _____

sign   _____

THE CAFETERIA

La cafetería *(lah kah-feh-teh-'ree·ah)*

School rules also extend into the local dining area, so be sure you know what to say in Spanish when everyone is hungry. Use your hands as you give commands:

Show me the stamp!	¡Enséñame el sello! *(ehn-'seh-nyah-meh ehl 'seh-yoh)*
Get in line!	¡Ponte en fila! *('pohn-teh ehn 'fee-lah)*
Sit over there!	¡Siéntate allí! *(see-'ehn-tah-teh ah-'yee)*
Wait for your turn!	¡Espera tu turno! *(eh-'speh-rah too 'toor-noh)*
Give me your lunch ticket.	Dame tu boleto de almuerzo. *('dah-meh too boh-'leh-toh deh ahl-moo-'ehr-soh)*
Go to (the)...	Ve a... *(veh ah...)*
benches	las bancas *(lahs 'bahn-kahs)*
cafeteria	la cafetería *(lah kah-feh-teh-'ree·ah)*
lunch room	el comedor *(ehl koh-meh-'dohr)*
tables	las mesas *(lahs 'meh-sahs)*
Use (the)...	Usa... *('oo-sah...)*
glass	el vaso *(ehl 'vah-soh)*
machine	la máquina *(lah 'mah-kee-nah)*

napkin	la servilleta *(lah sehr-vee-'yeh-tah)*
plate	el plato *(ehl 'plah-toh)*
silverware	los cubiertos *(lohs koo-bee-'ehr-tohs)*
trash can	el bote para basura *(ehl 'boh-teh 'pah-rah bah-'soo-rah)*
tray	la bandeja *(lah bahn-'deh-hah)*

Continue to use command phrases to control unruly students. These words should look familiar:

| Don't... | No... *(noh...)* |

grab	agarrar *(ah-gah-'rrahr)*
push	empujar *(ehm-poo-'hahr)*
run	correr *(koh-'rrehr)*
shout	gritar *(gree-'tahr)*
throw	tirar *(tee-'rahr)*

Now, let's talk about the food!

| They sell... | Venden... *('vehn-dehn...)* |

breakfast	el desayuno *(ehl deh-sah-'yoo-noh)*
lunch	el almuerzo *(ehl ahl-moo-'ehr-soh)*
dinner	la cena *(lah 'seh-nah)*
snacks	las meriendas *(lahs meh-ree-'ehn-dahs)*

| They serve... | Sirven... *('seer-vehn)* |

bacon	el tocino *(ehl toh-'see-noh)*
cereal	el cereal *(ehl seh-reh-'ahl)*
chicken	el pollo *(ehl 'poh-yoh)*
eggs	los huevos *(lohs 'weh-vohs)*
fish	el pescado *(ehl peh-'skah-doh)*
french fries	las papas fritas *(lahs 'pah-pahs 'free-tahs)*
ham	el jamón *(ehl hah-'mohn)*
hamburgers	las hamburguesas *(lahs ahm-boor-'geh-sahs)*
hot dogs	los perros calientes *(lohs 'peh-rrohs kah-lee-'ehn-tehs)*
meat	la carne *(lah 'kahr-neh)*
noodles	los fideos *(lohs fee-'deh-ohs)*

183

pork	el cerdo *(ehl 'sehr-doh)*
potato chips	las papitas *(lahs pah-'pee-tahs)*
rice	el arroz *(ehl ah-'rrohs)*
roast beef	el rósbif *(ehl rohs-'beef)*
rolls	los panecillos *(lohs pah-neh-'see-yohs)*
salad	la ensalada *(lah ehn-sah-'lah-dah)*
sandwiches	los sandwiches *(lohs 'sahnd-wee-chehs)*
sausage	la salchicha *(lah sahl-'chee-chah)*
seafood	el marisco *(ehl mah-'ree-skoh)*
soup	la sopa *(lah 'soh-pah)*
steak	el bistec *(ehl bee-'stehk)*
toast	el pan tostado *(ehl pahn toh-'stah-doh)*
tuna	el atún *(ehl ah-'toon)*
turkey	el pavo *(ehl 'pah-voh)*

Vegetables — Los vegetales *(lohs veh-heh-'tah-lehs)*

They have... — Tienen... *(tee-'eh-nehn)*

beans	los frijoles *(lohs free-'hoh-lehs)*
beet	la remolacha *(lah reh-moh-'lah-chah)*
cabbage	el repollo *(ehl reh-'poh-yoh)*
carrot	la zanahoria *(lah sah-nah-'oh-ree·ah)*
celery	el apio *(ehl 'ah-pee·oh)*
corn	el maíz *(ehl mah-'ees)*
cucumber	el pepino *(ehl peh-'pee-noh)*
lettuce	la lechuga *(lah leh-'choo-gah)*
mushrooms	los champiñones *(lohs chahm-pee-'nyoh-nehs)*
onion	la cebolla *(lah seh-'boh-yah)*
peas	las arvejitas *(lahs ahr-veh-'hee-tahs)*
potato	la papa *(lah 'pah-pah)*
radish	el rábano *(ehl 'rah-bah-noh)*
spinach	la espinaca *(lah eh-spee-'nah-kah)*
tomato	el tomate *(ehl toh-'mah-teh)*

Fruit	**La fruta** *(lah 'froo-tah)*
Do you like...?	**¿Te gusta...?** *(teh 'goo-stah)*
apple	**la manzana** *(lah mahn-'sah-nah)*
apricot	**el albaricoque** *(ehl ahl-bah-ree-'koh-keh)*
banana	**el plátano** *(ehl 'plah-tah-noh)*
cantaloupe	**el melón** *(ehl meh-'lohn)*
cherry	**la cereza** *(lah seh-'reh-sah)*
coconut	**el coco** *(ehl 'koh-koh)*
grape	**la uva** *(lah 'oo-vah)*
grapefruit	**la toronja** *(lah toh-'rohn-hah)*
lemon	**el limón** *(ehl lee-'mohn)*
orange	**la naranja** *(lah nah-'rahn-hah)*
peach	**el melocotón** *(ehl meh-loh-koh-'tohn)*
pear	**la pera** *(lah 'peh-rah)*
strawberry	**la fresa** *(lah 'freh-sah)*

Dessert and snacks	**El postre y las meriendas** *(ehl 'poh-streh ee lahs meh-ree-'ehn-dahs)*
You can buy (the)...	**Pueden comprar...** *('pweh-dehn kohm-'prahr...)*
cake	**la torta** *(lah 'tohr-tah)*
candy	**los dulces** *(lohs 'dool-sehs)*
cookie/cracker	**la galleta** *(lah gah-'yeh-tah)*
energy bar	**la barra energética** *(lah 'bah-rrah eh-nehr-'heh-tee-kah)*
ice cream	**el helado** *(ehl eh-'lah-doh)*
jello	**la gelatina** *(lah heh-lah-'tee-nah)*
pie	**el pastel** *(ehl pah-'stehl)*
pudding	**el pudín** *(ehl poo-'deen)*
yogurt	**el yogur** *(ehl yoh-'goor)*

How are you doing with the drinks? Quench everyone's thirst with this group of vocabulary:

I'd like...	**Quisiera...** *(kee-see-'eh-rah...)*
coffee	**el café** *(ehl kah-'feh)*
decaffeinated coffee	**el café descafeinado** *(ehl kah-'feh dehs-kah-feh·ee-'nah-doh)*

diet soda	**la soda dietética** *(lah 'soh-dah dee-eh-'teh-tee-kah)*
hot chocolate	**el chocolate caliente** *(ehl choh-koh-'lah-teh kah-lee-'ehn-teh)*
iced tea	**el té helado** *(ehl teh eh-'lah-doh)*
juice	**el jugo** *(ehl 'hoo-goh)*
lemonade	**la limonada** *(lah lee-moh-'nah-dah)*
milk	**la leche** *(lah 'leh-cheh)*
shake	**el batido** *(ehl bah-'tee-doh)*
skim milk	**la leche descremada** *(lah 'leh-cheh dehs-kreh-'mah-dah)*
soft drink	**el refresco** *(ehl reh-'frehs-koh)*
tea	**el té** *(ehl teh)*
vitamin water	**el agua con vitaminas** *(ehl 'ah-gwah kohn vee-tah-'mee-nahs)*
water	**el agua** *(ehl 'ah-gwah)*

 MÁS INFORMACIÓN

➤ How many one-liners can you come up with for use during the lunch hour?

Are you going home for lunch?
¿Vas a tu casa para el almuerzo? *(vahs ah too 'kah-sah 'pah-rah ehl ahl-moo-'ehr-soh)*

Do you have an off-campus pass?
¿Tienes un pase para salir de la escuela? *(tee-'eh-nehs oon 'pah-seh 'pah-rah sah-'leer deh lah eh-'skweh-lah)*

You may sit where you want.
Puedes sentarte dónde quieras.
('pweh-dehs sehn-'tahr-teh 'dohn-deh kee-'eh-rahs)

These are the hours of service.
Estas son las horas de servicio.
('eh-stahs sohn lahs 'oh-rahs deh sehr-'vee-see·oh)

You don't have much time to eat.
No tienes mucho tiempo para comer.
(noh tee-'eh-nehs 'moo-choh tee-'ehm-poh 'pah-rah koh-'mehr)

The food is very good.
La comida es muy buena.
(lah koh-'mee-dah ehs 'moo·ee 'bweh-nah)

You have to pay over there.
Tienes que pagar ahí.
(tee-'eh-nehs keh pah-'gahr ah-'ee)

It's free.
Es gratis. *(ehs 'grah-tees)*

Here's your ticket
Aquí tienes el boleto. *(ah-'kee tee-'eh-nehs ehl boh-'leh-toh)*

You need exact change.
Necesitas el cambio exacto. *(neh-seh-'see-tahs ehl 'kahm-bee·oh ehk-'sahk-toh)*

 DIFERENCIAS CULTURALES

Traditional American foods don't always appeal to a multiethnic student body. Many Hispanics, for example, simply prefer to bring their homemade foods for lunch. To raise campus morale, have an "International Food Day," or consider asking students about the foods they enjoy most, and then add them to the current cafeteria menu.

CLOTHING
La ropa *(lah 'roh-pah)*

One of the toughest areas to control at many schools is the dress code. Open up with a few useful phrases, and then specify which article of clothing is causing the problem. Take as much time as you need—these are important!

You're not supposed to wear that.
No debes ponerte eso. *(noh 'deh-behs poh-'nehr-teh 'eh-soh)*

It's against the regulations.
Es contra los reglamentos. *(ehs 'kohn-trah lohs reh-glah-'mehn-tohs)*

It distracts others from learning.
Distrae la atención de los otros. *(dee-'strah-eh lah ah-tehn-see·'ohn deh lohs 'oh-trohs)*

It isn't appropriate.
No es apropiada. *(noh ehs ah-proh-pee·'ah-dah)*

It's very...   **Es muy...** *(es 'moo-ee)*

loose   **flojo** *('floh-hoh)*
tight   **apretado** *(ah-preh-'tah-doh)*
long   **largo** *('lahr-goh)*
short   **corto** *('kohr-toh)*
offensive   **ofensivo** *(oh-fehn-'see-voh)*

What seems to be the problem? It could be just about anything:

Look at (the)...   **Mira...** *('mee-rah)*

bathing suit   **el traje de baño** *(ehl 'trah-heh deh 'bah-nyoh)*
bathrobe   **la bata de baño** *(lah 'bah-tah deh 'bah-nyoh)*
belt   **el cinturón** *(ehl seen-too-'rohn)*
blouse   **la blusa** *(lah 'bloo-sah)*
boots   **las botas** *(lahs 'boh-tahs)*
brassiere   **el sostén** *(ehl soh-'stehn)*
cap   **la gorra** *(lah 'goh-rrah)*
dress   **el vestido** *(ehl veh-'stee-doh)*
gloves   **los guantes** *(lohs 'gwahn-tehs)*
jacket   **la chaqueta** *(lah chah-'keh-tah)*
mittens   **los mitones** *(lohs mee-'toh-nehs)*
overcoat   **el abrigo** *(ehl ah-'bree-goh)*
panties   **las bragas** *(lahs 'brah-gahs)*
pants   **los pantalones** *(lohs pahn-tah-'loh-nehs)*
raincoat   **el impermeable** *(ehl eem-pehr-meh-'ah-bleh)*
sandals   **las sandalias** *(lahs sahn-'dah-lee·ahs)*
scarf   **la bufanda** *(lah boo-'fahn-dah)*
shirt   **la camisa** *(lah kah-'mee-sah)*
shoes   **los zapatos** *(lohs sah-'pah-tohs)*
shorts   **los calzoncillos** *(lohs kahl-sohn-'see-yohs)*
skirt   **la falda** *(lah 'fahl-dah)*
slippers   **las zapatillas** *(lahs sah-pah-'tee-yahs)*

socks	los calcetines *(lohs kahl-seh-'tee-nehs)*
sportcoat	el saco *(ehl 'sah-koh)*
stockings	las medias *(lahs 'meh-dee·ahs)*
suit	el traje *(ehl 'trah-heh)*
sweater	el suéter *(ehl 'sweh-tehr)*
sweatsuit	la sudadera *(lah soo-dah-'deh-rah)*
T-shirt	la camiseta *(lah kah-mee-'seh-tah)*
tennis shoes	los tenis *(lohs 'teh-nees)*
tie	la corbata *(lah kohr-'bah-tah)*
underwear	la ropa interior *(lah 'roh-pah een-teh-ree-'ohr)*
vest	el chaleco *(ehl chah-'leh-koh)*

 ## MÁS INFORMACIÓN

➤ Keep naming items that disrupt activity in the classroom:

Don't bring (the)...	No traigas... *(noh 'trah·ee-gahs)*

comb	el peine *(ehl 'peh·ee-neh)*
hairbrush	el cepillo *(ehl seh-'pee-yoh)*
handkerchief	el pañuelo *(ehl pah-nyoo-'eh-loh)*
suntan lotion	el bronceador *(ehl brohn-seh-ah-'dohr)*
umbrella	el paraguas *(ehl pah-'rah-gwahs)*

➤ And there's always the jewelry:

Don't wear (the)...	No uses... *(noh 'oo-sehs)*

bracelet	el brazalete *(ehl brah-sah-'leh-teh)*
chain	la cadena *(lah kah-'deh-nah)*
earring	el arete *(ehl ah-'reh-teh)*
jewel	la joya *(lah 'hoh-yah)*
necklace	el collar *(ehl koh-'yahr)*
ring	el anillo *(ehl ah-'nee-yoh)*
watch	el reloj *(ehl reh-'loh)*

List ten popular food items in Spanish:

_____ _____ _____ _____ _____

_____ _____ _____ _____ _____

List ten articles of clothing in Spanish:

_____ _____ _____ _____ _____

_____ _____ _____ _____ _____

GOOD BEHAVIOR!

¡Buen comportamiento! *(bwehn kohm-pohr-tah-mee-'ehn-toh)*

Not all students have discipline problems. One of the chief reasons why students succeed in school is that they feel the support of their educators. Praise and encouragement can be tremendous motivators, even for the most troubled youth. Try out some of these powerful expressions today!

How...!	¡Qué...! *(keh)*
excellent	excelente *(ehk-seh-'lehn-teh)*
exceptional	excepcional *(ehk-sehp-see·oh-'nahl)*
fabulous	fabuloso *(fah-boo-'loh-soh)*
fantastic	fantástico *(fahn-'tah-stee-koh)*
great	bueno *('bweh-noh)*
incredible	increíble *(een-kreh-'ee-bleh)*
marvelous	maravilloso *(mah-rah-vee-'yoh-soh)*
outstanding	destacado *(dehs-tah-'kah-doh)*
remarkable	extraordinario *(ehks-trah-ohr-dee-'nah-ree·oh)*
stupendous	estupendo *(eh-stoo-'pehn-doh)*
tremendous	magnífico *(mahg-'nee-fee-koh)*

Nothing works better than encouraging remarks, so keep it up!

What a great job!	¡Qué buen trabajo! *(keh bweh trah-'bah-hoh)*
Very good!	¡Muy bien! *('moo·ee 'bee·ehn)*
Good work!	¡Bien hecho! *('bee·ehn 'eh-choh)*
You can do it!	¡Puedes hacerlo!
	('pweh-dehs ah-'sehr-loh)
You're important!	¡Tú eres importante!
	(too 'eh-rehs eem-pohr-'tahn-teh)
You learn quickly!	¡Aprendes rápido!
	(ah-'prehn-dehs 'rah-pee-doh)
We need you!	¡Te necesitamos!
	(teh neh-seh-see-'tah-mohs)
We can't do it without you!	¡No podemos hacerlo sin ti!
	(noh poh-'deh-mohs ah-'sehr-loh seen tee)
I trust you!	¡Confío en ti!
	(kohn-'fee·oh ehn tee)
I respect you!	¡Te respeto!
	(teh reh-'speh-toh)
You're valuable!	¡Tú eres valioso!
	(too 'eh-rehs vah-lee-'oh-soh)
I like what you did!	¡Me gusta lo que hiciste!
	(meh 'goo-stah loh keh ee-'sees-teh)

Keep passing out the compliments. Their behavior is improving:

I like the...	Me gusta... *(meh 'goo-stah)*
attitude	la actitud *(lah ahk-tee-'tood)*
mood	el humor *(ehl oo-'mohr)*
spirit	el espíritu *(ehl eh-'spee-ree-'too)*
I have seen...	He visto... *(eh 'vee-stoh)*
appreciation	aprecio *(ah-'preh-see·oh)*
commitment	compromiso *(kohm-proh-'mee-soh)*
confidence	confianza *(kohn-fee-'ahn-sah)*
creativity	creatividad *(kreh-ah-tee-vee-'dahd)*
dialogue	diálogo *(dee-'ah-loh-goh)*
enthusiasm	entusiasmo *(ehn-too-see-'ahs-moh)*
friendship	amistad *(ah-mee-'stahd)*

harmony	armonía *(ahr-moh-'nee·ah)*
honesty	honradez *(ohn-rah-'dehs)*
initiative	iniciativa *(ee-nee-see·ah-'tee-vah)*
patience	paciencia *(pah-see-'ehn-see·ah)*
responsibility	responsabilidad *(reh-spohn-sah-bee-lee-'dahd)*
safety	seguridad *(seh-goo-ree-'dahd)*
value	valor *(vah-'lohr)*

This shows me that you are...
Esto me muestra que tú eres...
('eh-stoh meh 'mweh-strah keh too 'eh-rehs...)

ambitious	ambicioso *(ahm-bee-see·'oh-soh)*
competent	competente *(kohm-peh-'tehn-teh)*
efficient	eficiente *(eh-fee-see-'ehn-teh)*
independent	independiente *(een-deh-pehn-dee-'ehn-teh)*
organized	organizado *(ohr-gah-nee-'sah-doh)*
punctual	puntual *(poon-too-'ahl)*

O.K. Now go back and change all these one-liners so that they refer to your female students!

 ¡ACCIÓN!

Up to now, you've been given the skills to converse about current, everyday, and future activities around the school site.

Now take a look at the past tense in Spanish. You can start by learning the more commonly used form. Read the following examples and, just as you did with present and future actions, make the changes in your verbs. You won't be perfect at first, but Spanish speakers will know what you're trying to say.

-ar Verbs: *To Speak*	hablar *(ah-'blahr)*
I spoke with the child.	**Hablé con el niño.** *(ah-'bleh kohn ehl 'nee-nyoh)*
You (informal) spoke slowly.	**Hablaste lentamente.** *(ah-'blah-steh lehn-tah-'mehn-teh)*
You (formal), He, She spoke a lot.	**Habló mucho.** *(ah-'bloh 'moo-choh)*
You (pl.), They spoke English.	**Hablaron inglés.** *(ah-'blah-rohn een-'glehs)*
We spoke a little.	**Hablamos un poco.** *(ah-'blah-mohs oon 'poh-koh)*

-er/ir Verbs: *To Leave*	salir *(sah-'leer)*
I left at eight	**Salí a las ocho.** *(sah-'lee ah lahs 'oh-choh)*
You (informal) left quickly.	**Saliste rápidamente.** *(sah-'lee-steh 'rah-pee-dah-'mehn-teh)*
You (formal), He, She left late.	**Salió tarde.** *(sah-lee-'oh 'tahr-deh)*
You (pl.), They left.	**Salieron.** *(sah-lee-'eh-rohn)*
We left in a car.	**Salimos en el carro.** *(sah-'lee-mohs ehn ehl 'kah-rroh)*

As usual, some common verbs have irregular past tenses, so be on the lookout for new patterns.

To Go: ir *(eer)*		
I went	**Fui** *(fwee)*	**Fui a la casa.** *(fwee ah lah 'kah-sah)*
You (informal) went	**Fuiste** *('fwee-steh)*	_____
You (formal), He, She went	**Fue** *(fweh)*	_____
You (pl.), They went	**Fueron** *('fweh-rohn)*	_____
We went	**Fuimos** *('fwee-mohs)*	_____

To Have: tener *(teh-'nehr)*

I had	**Tuve** *('too-veh)*	**Tuve la fiesta.** *('too-veh lah fee-'eh-stah)*
You (informal) had	**Tuviste** *('too-vee-steh)*	_____
You (formal), He, She had	**Tuvo** *('too-voh)*	_____
You (pl.), They had	**Tuvieron** *(too-vee-'eh-rohn)*	_____
We had	**Tuvimos** *(too-'vee-mohs)*	_____

To Say: decir *(deh-'seer)*

I said	**Dije** *('dee-heh)*	**Dije la verdad.** *('dee-heh lah vehr-'dahd)*
You (informal) said	**Dijiste** *(dee-'hee-steh)*	_____
You (formal), He, She said	**Dijo** *('dee-hoh)*	_____
You (pl.), They said	**Dijeron** *(dee-'heh-rohn)*	_____
We said	**Dijimos** *(dee-'hee-mohs)*	_____

MÁS INFORMACIÓN

➤ This verb form is called the preterit, and it isn't the only past tense you're going to need. Although these phrases won't be discussed in detail, check out the spellings and meanings of the examples below:

I used to have	**tenía** *(teh-'nee·ah)*
I would have	**tendría** *(tehn-'dree·ah)*
I was having	**estaba teniendo** *(eh-'stah-bah teh-nee-'ehn-doh)*
I have had	**he tenido** *(eh teh-'nee-doh)*

194

➤ The verb **ser** *(sehr)* (to be) has the same preterit forms as the verb **ir** *(eer)* (to go). Take note:

I was	**Fui** *(fwee)*
You (informal) were	**Fuiste** *('fwee-steh)*
You (formal), He, She was	**Fue** *(fweh)*
You (pl.), They were	**Fueron** *('fweh-rohn)*
We were	**Fuimos** *('fwee-mohs)*

¡ÓRDENES!

While learning Spanish commands, you're going to come across the following object pronouns that refer to people. Notice what they can mean in English:

te	you, to you, for you (informal)
le	you, to you, for you, him, to him, for him, her, to her, for her
les	you, to you, for you (plural), them, to them, for them

See how they fit at the end of an affirmative command. Look out for the accent marks:

Talk to him	**Háblale** *('ah-blah-leh)*
Look at them	**Mírales** *('mee-rah-lehs)*
Tell her	**Dile** *('dee-leh)*
Ask them	**Pregúntales** *(preh-'goon-tah-lehs)*

MÁS INFORMACIÓN

➤ Note that, in most sentences, te, le, and les go in front of the verb:

I understand you.	**Te entiendo.** *(teh ehn-tee-'ehn-doh)*
We're going to tell them.	**Les vamos a decir.** *(lehs 'vah-mohs ah deh-'seer)*
She hit him.	**Le pegó.** *(leh peh-'goh)*

➤ Read through the other pronouns that are used to refer to people:

He talks to me.	**Me habla.** *(meh 'ah-blah)*
He talks to you.	**Te habla.** *(teh 'ah-blah)*
He talks to us.	**Nos habla.** *(nohs 'ah-blah)*

¿LISTOS PARA PRACTICAR?

Saying nice things in Spanish is easy, since most of the words are similar to their English equivalents. Guess at the meanings of these:

fantástico *(fahn-'tah-stee-koh)* _____

paciente *(pah-see-'ehn-teh)* _____

creativo *(kreh-ah-'tee-voh)* _____

puntual *(poon-too-'ahl)* _____

fabuloso *(fah-boo-'loh-soh)* _____

Follow the example:

I speak.	**Hablo.** *('ah-bloh)*	I spoke.	**Hablé.** *(ah-'bleh)*
I walk.	_____	_____	_____
I study.	_____	_____	_____
I work.	_____	_____	_____

CHAPTER SIX
Capítulo Seis
(kah-'pee-too-loh 'seh·ees)

THE COUNSELORS
Los consejeros
(lohs kohn-seh-'heh-rohs)

THERE'S A LOT TO DO!

¡Hay mucho que hacer! *('ah·ee 'moo-choh keh ah-'sehr)*

Share these tasks with a Spanish-speaking student or parent. They outline some of the responsibilities of a school counselor:

Talk to me about...	Háblame acerca de... *('ah-blah-meh ah-'sehr-kah deh...)*
application	la solicitud *(lah soh-lee-see-'tood)*
assemblies	las asambleas *(lahs ah-sahm-'bleh-ahs)*
career planning	la planificación de trabajo *(lah plah-nee-fee-kah-see-'ohn deh trah-'bah-hoh)*
counseling	el asesoramiento *(ehl ah-seh-soh-rah-mee-'ehn-toh)*
deadline	la fecha límite *(lah 'feh-chah 'lee-mee-teh)*
discipline	la disciplina *(lah dee-see-'plee-nah)*
enrollment	la matrícula *(lah mah-'tree-koo-lah)*
evaluations	las evaluaciones *(lahs eh-vah-loo-ah-see-'oh-nehs)*
fund-raising	la recolección de fondos *(lah reh-koh-lehk-see-'ohn deh 'fohn-dohs)*
graduation	la graduación *(lah grah-doo-ah-see-'ohn)*
health problems	los problemas de salud *(lohs proh-'bleh-mahs deh sah-'lood)*
personal needs	los requisitos personales *(lohs reh-kee-'see-tohs pehr-soh-'nah-lehs)*
promotion	la promoción *(lah proh-moh-see-'ohn)*
registration	la inscripción *(lah een-skreep-see-'ohn)*
schedules	los horarios *(lohs oh-'rah-ree·ohs)*
special programs	los programas especiales *(lohs proh-'grah-mahs eh-speh-see-'ah-lehs)*
summer school	la escuela del verano *(lah eh-'skweh-lah dehl veh-'rah-noh)*
transfers	las transferencias *(lahs trahns-feh-'rehn-see·ahs)*
transportation	el transporte *(ehl trahns-'pohr-teh)*
transcript	la transcripción *(lah trahn-skreep-see-'ohn)*

I have meetings with...	Tengo reuniones con... *('tehn-goh reh-oo-nee-'oh-nehs kohn...)*
administrators	los administradores *(lohs ahd-mee-nee-strah-'doh-rehs)*
other counselors	los otros consejeros *(lohs 'oh-trohs kohn-seh-'heh-rohs)*
parents	los padres *(lohs 'pah-drehs)*
students	los estudiantes *(lohs eh-stoo-dee-'ahn-tehs)*
teachers	los maestros *(lohs mah-'eh-strohs)*

Before you help anyone, make sure you have the correct general information:

I need to know (the)...	Necesito saber... *(neh-seh-'see-toh sah-'behr...)*
average	el promedio *(ehl proh-'meh-dee·oh)*
class	la clase *(lah 'klah-seh)*
grade in class	la nota *(lah 'noh-tah)*
grade in school	el grado *(ehl 'grah-doh)*
level	el nivel *(ehl nee-'vehl)*
name	el nombre *(ehl 'nohm-breh)*
number	el número *(ehl 'noo-meh-roh)*
requirements	los requisitos *(lohs reh-kee-'see-tohs)*
score	la calificación *(lah kah-lee-fee-kah-see-'ohn)*
title	el título *(ehl 'tee-too-loh)*
year	el año *(ehl 'ah-nyoh)*

 DIFERENCIAS CULTURALES

As you have learned, a number of high school events simply don't exist in Spanish-speaking countries. Get an interpreter to help you explain these activities to non-English speakers:

Grad night	Cap and gown
Homecoming	Class photos
Prom	Class rings
Yearbooks	Commencement

ATTENDANCE

La asistencia *(lah ah-see-'stehn-see·ah)*

Counselors can't do their job if the students don't attend school, so you may use these examples to get your message across:

Why are you late?	¿Por qué llegas tarde? *(pohr keh 'yeh-gahs 'tahr-deh)*
Why were you absent?	¿Por qué estabas ausente? *(pohr keh eh-'stah-bahs ow-'sehn-teh)*
Why didn't you go to class?	¿Por qué no fuiste a la clase? *(pohr keh noh 'fwee-steh ah lah'klah-seh)*
Why didn't you come?	¿Por qué no viniste? *(pohr keh noh vee-'nee-steh)*
Where is (the)...?	¿Dónde está...? *('dohn-deh eh-'stah...)*
doctor's note	la nota del médico *(lah 'noh-tah dehl 'meh-dee-koh)*
e-mail	el correo electrónico *(ehl koh-rreh-oh eh-lehk-tron-'ee-koh)*
excuse permit	el permiso *(ehl pehr-'mee-soh)*
letter from home	la carta de tu casa *(lah 'kahr-tah deh too'kah-sah)*
parent signature	la firma de los padres *(lah 'feer-mah deh lohs'pah-drehs)*
tardy slip	la nota de tardanzas *(lah 'noh-tah deh tahr-'dahn-sahs)*
work phone number	el número de teléfono del trabajo *(ehl 'noo-meh-roh deh teh-'leh-foh-noh dehl trah-'bah-hoh)*
What...?	¿Qué...? *(keh...)*
class	clase *('klah-seh)*
day	día *('dee·ah)*
hour/period	hora *('oh-rah)*
month	mes *(mehs)*
quarter	trimestre *(tree-'meh-streh)*
semester	semestre *(seh-'meh-streh)*
term	período de estudios *(peh-'ree·oh-doh deh eh-'stoo-dee·ohs)*
week	semana *(seh-'mah-nah)*
year	año *('ah-nyoh)*

You may have to pull the student aside, and discuss your concern in detail:

You are missing school a lot.
Faltas mucho a la escuela. *('fahl-tahs 'moo-choh ah lah eh-'skweh-lah)*

It's affecting your grade.
Está afectando tu nota. *(eh-'stah ah-fehk-'tahn-doh too 'noh-tah)*

You may not graduate.
Quizás no te graduarás. *(kee-'sahs noh teh grah-doo-ah-'rahs)*

You always arrive late.
Siempre llegas tarde. *(see-'ehm-preh 'yeh-gahs 'tahr-deh)*

You can't learn if you're not here.
No puedes aprender si no estás aquí. *(noh 'pweh-dehs ah-prehn-'dehr see noh eh-'stahs ah-'kee)*

Now, explain the situation in simple terms:

This is your last chance. **Esta es tu última oportunidad.** *('eh-stah ehs too 'ool-tee-mah oh-pohr-too-nee-'dahd)*

This is a serious problem. **Este problema es muy serio.** *('eh-steh proh-'bleh-mah ehs 'moo·ee 'seh-ree·oh)*

This is the rule. **Esta es la regla.** *('eh-stah ehs lah 'reh-glah)*

If things get worse, lay down the law:

You will stay after school. **Te quedarás después de clases.** *(teh keh-dah-'rahs deh-'spwehs deh 'klah-sehs)*

We'll suspend you. **Te vamos a suspender.** *(teh 'vah-mohs ah soo-spehn-'dehr)*

I'll call your parents. **Voy a llamar a tus padres.** *('voh·ee ah yah-'mahr ah toos 'pah-drehs)*

 MÁS INFORMACIÓN

➤ Again, remember that some English phrases such as "call slip" and "hall pass" can't be translated exactly the same into Spanish.

➤ Find out why the student has trouble getting to school:

Do you live...?	¿Vives...? *('vee-vehs)*
in this city	en esta ciudad *(ehn 'eh-stah see-oo-'dahd)*
near the school	cerca de la escuela *('sehr-kah deh lah eh-'skweh-lah)*
far from here	lejos de aquí *('leh-hohs deh ah-'kee)*
outside the district	fuera del distrito *('fweh-rah dehl dee-'stree-toh)*
Is/Are there...?	¿Hay...? *('ah·ee...)*
a major illness	una enfermedad grave *('oo-nah ehn-fehr-meh-'dahd 'grah-veh)*
family problems	problemas familiares *(proh-'bleh-mahs fah-mee-lee·'ah-rehs)*
transportation to school	transporte a la escuela *(trahns-'pohr-teh ah lah eh-'skweh-lah)*

➤ Keep acquiring questions related to student attendance:

Are you going to miss school?
¿Vas a faltar a la escuela?
(vahs ah fahl-'tahr ah lah ehs-'kweh-lah)

Are you going to be late?
¿Vas a llegar tarde?
(vahs ah yeh-'gahr 'tahr-deh)

Did you call the office?
¿Llamaste a la oficina?
(yah-'mah-steh ah lah oh-fee-'see-nah)

Do you have an excuse?
¿Tienes una excusa?
(tee-'eh-nehs 'oo-nah ehk-'skoo-sah)

What's the reason?
¿Cuál es la razón?
(kwahl ehs lah rah-'sohn)

Did you talk to your parents?
¿Hablaste con tus padres?
(ah-'blahs-teh kohn toos 'pah-drehs)

And, here's what you can say about their make-up work:

The work is late.
La tarea está atrasada. *(lah tah-'reh-ah eh-'stah ah-trah-'sah-dah)*

You have to make up the work.
Tiene que completar el trabajo. *(tee-'eh-neh keh kohm-pleh-'tahr ehl trah-'bah-hoh)*

You will get a lower grade.
Recibirás una nota más baja. *(reh-see-bee-'rahs 'oo-nah 'noh-tah mahs 'bah-hah)*

DIFERENCIAS CULTURALES

Absences are often due to family-related events that require the attendance of all family members. Here's a brief list of common excuses for missing class:

anniversary	**el aniversario** *(ehl ah-nee-vehr-'sah-ree·oh)*
birth	**el nacimiento** *(ehl nah-see-mee-'ehn-toh)*
birthday	**el cumpleaños** *(ehl koom-pleh-'ah-nyohs)*
emergency	**la emergencia** *(lah eh-mehr-'hehn-see·ah)*
engagement	**el compromiso** *(ehl kohm-proh-'mee-soh)*
family activity	**la actividad familiar** *(lah ahk-tee-vee-'dahd fah-mee-lee-'ahr)*
funeral	**el funeral** *(ehl foo-neh-'rahl)*
shower	**el shower** *(ehl 'shah-wehr)*
15-year-old daughter's "coming out" party	**la quinceañera** *(lah keen-seh-ah-'nyeh-rah)*
wedding	**el casamiento** *(ehl kah-sah-mee-'ehn-toh)*

¿LISTOS PARA PRACTICAR?

Practice this dialog about school attendance:

¿Por qué estabas ausente?
(pohr keh eh-'stah-bahs ow-'sehn-teh)

Porque estaba enfermo. *('pohr-keh eh-'stah-bah ehn-'fehr-moh)*

¿Dónde está la nota del doctor?   No la tengo. *(noh lah'tehn-goh)*
('dohn-deh eh-'stah lah'noh-tah
dehl dohk-'tohr)

Muy bien. Voy a llamar a tus padres. *('moo·ee 'bee·ehn. 'voh·ee ah yah-'mahr*
ah toos'pah-drehs)

PERSONAL PROBLEMS

Los problemes personales *(lohs proh-'bleh-mahs pehr-soh-'nah-lehs)*

Students often talk to counselors, teachers, and administrators about issues related to their personal lives. Pay attention to some of the topics listed below—you'll probably need an interpreter to handle these discussions in detail:

I need (the)...	Necesito... *(neh-seh-'see-toh...)*
clothing	la ropa *(lah'roh-pah)*
food	la comida *(lah koh-'mee-dah)*
help	la ayuda *(lah ah-'yoo-dah)*
medicine	la medicina *(lah meh-dee-'see-nah)*
money	el dinero *(ehl dee-'neh-roh)*
transportation	el transporte *(ehl trahn-'spohr-teh)*

Someone is.... me.	Alguien me está.... *('ahl-gee·ehn meh eh-'stah...)*
beating	golpeando *(gohl-peh-'ahn-doh)*
grabbing	agarrando *(ah-gah-'rrahn-doh)*
hitting	pegando *(peh-'gahn-doh)*
looking at	mirando *(mee-'rahn-doh)*
threatening	amenazando *(ah-meh-nah-'sahn-doh)*

Stay with simple patterns. Some of these words you've seen before:

Let's talk about (the)...	Vamos a hablar de... *('vah-mohs ah ah-'blahr deh...)*
absences	las ausencias *(lahs ow-'sehn-see·ahs)*
alcohol	el alcohol *(ehl ahl-koh-'ohl)*
attitude	la actitud *(lah ahk-tee-'tood)*
cigarettes	los cigarrillos *(lohs see-gah-'rree-yohs)*

conflict	**el conflicto** *(ehl kohn-'fleek-toh)*
drugs	**las drogas** *(lahs 'droh-gahs)*
grades	**las notas** *(lahs 'noh-tahs)*
harassment	**el acosamiento** *(ehl ah-koh-sah-mee-'ehn-toh)*
illness	**la enfermedad** *(lah ehn-fehr-meh-'dahd)*
injury	**la lesión** *(lah leh-see-'ohn)*
Internet	**la internet** *(lah een-'tehr-net)*
tardiness	**las tardanzas** *(lahs tahr-'dahn-sahs)*
I heard about (the)...	**Escuché de...** *(eh-skoo-'cheh deh...)*
accident	**el accidente** *(ehl ahk-see-'dehn-teh)*
altercation	**la disputa** *(lah dee-'spoo-tah)*
argument	**la discusión** *(lah dees-koo-see-'ohn)*
confrontation	**la confrontación** *(lah kohn-frohn-tah-see-'ohn)*
crime	**el crimen** *(ehl 'kree-mehn)*
disturbance	**el tumulto** *(ehl too-'mool-toh)*
fight	**la pelea** *(lah peh-'leh-ah)*
interruption	**la interrupción** *(lah een-teh-roop-see-'ohn)*
threat	**la amenaza** *(lah ah-meh-'nah-sah)*

Create more clusters for each concern:

There's a problem with (the)...	**Hay un problema con...** *('ah·ee oon proh-'bleh-mah kohn...)*
lack of support	**la falta de apoyo** *(lah 'fahl-tah deh ah-'poh-yoh)*
language proficiency	**la competencia en el lenguaje** *(lah kohm-peh-'tehn-see·ah ehn ehl lehn-'gwah-heh)*
personality differences	**las diferencias de personalidad** *(lahs dee-feh-'rehn-see·ahs deh pehr-soh-nah-lee-'dahd)*
personal hygiene	**la higiene personal** *(lah ee-hee-'eh-neh pehr-soh-'nahl)*
style of clothing	**el estilo de ropa** *(ehl eh-'stee-loh deh'roh-pah)*

➤ Personal concerns often involve serious matters, so learn the following terms:

abuse	**el abuso** *(ehl ah-'boo-soh)*
addiction	**la adicción** *(lah ah-deek-see-'ohn)*
alcoholism	**el alcoholismo** *(ehl ahl-koh·ohl-ees-moh)*
discrimination	**la discriminación** *(lah dee-skree-mee-nah-see-'ohn)*
pregnancy	**el embarazo** *(ehl ehm-bah-'rah-soh)*
sex relations	**las relaciones sexuales** *(lahs reh-lah-see-'oh-nehs sehk-soo-'ah-lehs)*
violence	**la violencia** *(lah vee·oh-'lehn-see·ah)*

TELL ME EVERYTHING!
¡Dime todo! *('dee-meh'toh-doh)*

When there's trouble, make sure the student speaks to the proper authorities. Do any of these words look familiar?

Tell (the)...	Dígale a... *('dee-gah-leh ah...)*
administrator	**el administrador** *(ehl ahd-mee-nee-strah-'dohr)*
counselor	**el consejero** *(ehl kohn-seh-'heh-roh)*
doctor	**el médico** *(ehl'meh-dee-koh)*
family	**la familia** *(lah fah-'mee-lee·ah)*
nurse	**la enfermera** *(lah ehn-fehr-'meh-rah)*
officer	**el oficial** *(ehl oh-fee-see-'ahl)*
police	**la policía** *(lah poh-lee-'see·ah)*
principal	**el director** *(ehl dee-rehk-'tohr)*
psychiatrist	**el psiquiatra** *(ehl see-kee·'ah-trah)*
psychologist	**el psicólogo** *(ehl see-'koh-loh-goh)*
secretary	**el secretario** *(ehl seh-kreh-'tah-ree·oh)*
social worker	**el trabajador social** *(ehl trah-bah-hah-'dohr soh-see-'ahl)*
specialist	**el especialista** *(ehl eh-speh-see·ah-'lee-stah)*
supervisor	**el supervisor** *(ehl soo-pehr-vee-'sohr)*
teacher	**el maestro** *(ehl mah-'eh-stroh)*
therapist	**el terapeuta** *(ehl teh-rah-peh-'oo-tah)*

Now, ask the right questions. Keep things brief:

Are you OK?	¿Estás bien? *(eh-'stahs 'bee·ehn)*
Are you sick?	¿Estás enfermo? *(eh-'stahs ehn-'fehr-moh)*
Are you injured?	¿Estás lastimado? *(eh-'stahs lah-stee-'mah-doh)*
What's the trouble?	¿Cuál es el problema? *(kwahl ehs ehl proh-'bleh-mah)*
Do you need help?	¿Necesitas ayuda? *(neh-seh-'see-tahs ah-'yoo-dah)*
Do you wish to talk to me?	¿Deseas hablarme? *(deh-'seh-ahs ah-'blahr-meh)*
Can you tell me?	¿Puedes decirme? *('pweh-dehs deh-'seer-meh)*
Do you have information?	¿Tienes información? *(tee-'eh-nehs een-fohr-mah-see·'ohn)*
Who is the person?	¿Quién es la persona? *(kee-'ehn ehs lah pehr-'soh-nah)*
How can I help you?	¿Cómo puedo ayudarte? *('koh-moh 'pweh-doh ah-yoo-'dahr-teh)*
What do you want to do?	¿Qué quieres hacer? *(keh kee-'eh-rehs ah-'sehr)*
Do you know the procedure?	¿Sabes el procedimiento? *('sah-behs ehl proh-seh-dee-mee-'ehn-toh)*

MÁS INFORMACIÓN

➤ Notice how these new verb forms below refer to past actions. We'll talk more about this verb tense later on in this chapter:

What happened?
¿Qué pasó? *(keh pah·'soh)*

Where did it happen?
¿Dónde pasó eso? *('dohn-deh pah-'soh 'eh-soh)*

Who saw what happened?
¿Quién vio lo que pasó? *(kee-'ehn vee-'oh loh keh pah-'soh)*

When did it happen?
¿Cuándo pasó eso? *('kwahn-doh pah-'soh 'eh-soh)*

How did it happen?
¿Cómo pasó eso? *('koh-moh pah-'soh 'eh-soh)*

➤ And why was the student sent to the office? Memorize this pattern:

Did you argue?
¿Discutiste? *(dees-koo-'tee-steh)*
Did you refuse?
¿Te negaste? *(teh neh-'gahs-teh)*
Did you disobey?
¿Desobedeciste? *(des-oh-beh-deh-'see-steh)*
Did you steal?
¿Robaste? *(roh-'bah-steh)*
Did you break it?
¿Lo quebraste? *(loh keh-'brah-steh)*
Did you lie?
¿Mentiste? *(men-'tee-steh)*
Did you lose it?
¿Lo perdiste? *(loh pehr-'dee-steh)*
Did you forget it?
¿Lo olvidaste? *(loh ohl-vee-'dah-steh)*

HOW DO YOU FEEL?
¿Cómo te sientes? *('koh-moh teh see-'ehn-tehs)*

A good part of counseling involves getting the other person to talk. This is especially true in an educational setting. Even though you'll probably end up asking for an interpreter, there's still a lot you can say all by yourself. Remember to change the o endings to a if you are addressing a female:

It seems you are...	**Parece que estás...** *(pah-'reh-seh keh eh-'stahs)*
afraid	**asustado** *(ah-soo-'stah-doh)*
angry	**enojado** *(eh-noh-'hah-doh)*
apathetic	**apático** *(ah-'pah-tee-koh)*
bitter	**amargado** *(ah-mahr-'gah-doh)*
distracted	**distraído** *(dee-strah-'ee-doh)*
frustrated	**frustrado** *(froo-'strah-doh)*
hostile	**hostil** *(oh-'steel)*
in mourning	**de luto** *(deh 'loo-toh)*
nervous	**nervioso** *(nehr-vee-'oh-soh)*
sad	**triste** *('tree-steh)*
tense	**tenso** *('tehn-soh)*

Don't stop talking about how the person feels. One method is to hold up a list of feelings in Spanish, and then ask the student to point to the word that best describes his or her emotions:

| Do you feel...? | ¿Te sientes..? *(teh see-'ehn-tehs)* |
| I feel... | Me siento... *(meh see-'ehn-toh)* |

abused	abusado *(ah-boo-'sah-doh)*
anxious	ansioso *(ahn-see-'oh-soh)*
ashamed	avergonzado *(ah-vehr-gohn-'sah-doh)*
bored	aburrido *(ah-boo-'rree-doh)*
bothered	molesto *(moh-'leh-stoh)*
burned out	agotado *(ah-goh-'tah-doh)*
confused	confundido *(kohn-foon-'dee-doh)*
depressed	deprimido *(deh-pree-'mee-doh)*
desperate	desesperado *(dehs-eh-speh-'rah-doh)*
embarrassed	turbado *(toor-'bah-doh)*
fed up	harto *('ahr-toh)*
furious	furioso *(foo-ree-'oh-soh)*
guilty	culpable *(kool-'pah-bleh)*
hated	odiado *(oh-dee-'ah-doh)*
impatient	impaciente *(eem-pah-see-'ehn-teh)*
inferior	inferior *(een-feh-ree-'ohr)*
insecure	inseguro *(een-seh-'goo-roh)*
jealous	celoso *(seh-'loh-soh)*
resentful	resentido *(reh-sehn-'tee-doh)*
restless	inquieto *(een-kee-'eh-toh)*

sensitive	sensible *(sehn-'see-bleh)*
strange	raro *('rah-roh)*
trapped	atrapado *(ah-trah-'pah-doh)*
uncomfortable	incómodo *(een-'koh-moh-doh)*
unhappy	descontento *(dehs-kohn-'tehn-toh)*
worried	preocupado *(preh-oh-koo-'pah-doh)*

MÁS INFORMACIÓN

➤ Keep altering your descriptive words to reflect the feelings of female students:

La muchacha está <u>preocupada</u> y <u>confundida</u>. *(lah moo-'chah-chah eh-'stah pre-oh-koo-'pah-dah ee kohn-foon-'dee-dah)*

➤ Deeper emotions are a little tougher to describe:

suicidal tendencies	tendencias suicidas *(teh-'dehn-see·ahs soo-ee-'see-dahs)*
emotional instability	inestabilidad emocional *(een-eh-stah-bee-lee-'dahd eh-moh-see·oh-'nahl)*
violent behavior	comportamiento violento *(kohm-pohr-tah-mee-'ehn-toh vee·oh-'lehn-toh)*

¿LISTOS PARA PRACTICAR?

Connect the words that have similar meanings:

triste *('tree-steh)*	relajado *(reh-lah-'hah-doh)*
enojado *(eh-noh-'hah-doh)*	ansioso *(ahn-see·'oh-soh)*
nervioso *(nehr-vee·'oh-soh)*	descontento *(dehs-kohn-'tehn-toh)*
cómodo *('koh-moh-doh)*	furioso *(foo-ree·'oh-soh)*

Are you able to name three professionals who help out when students are in trouble?

_____ _____ _____

EMOTIONAL PROBLEMS

Los problemas emocionales *(lohs proh-'bleh-mahs eh-moh-see·oh-'nah-lehs)*

There's no need to elaborate on body parts and health problems since they were covered in an earlier chapter. However, some emotions may be health-related. Here are a few more phrases you may be exposed to during a counseling session:

I feel...	**Me siento...** *(meh see-'ehn-toh...)*
dizzy	**mareado** *(mah-reh-'ah-doh)*
faint	**débil** *('deh-beel)*
poorly	**mal** *(mahl)*
sleepy	**soñoliento** *(soh-nyoh-lee-'ehn-toh)*
sore	**dolorido** *(doh-loh-'ree-doh)*

I have problems with (the)...	**Tengo problemas con...** *('tehn-goh proh-'bleh-mahs kohn...)*
balance	**el equilibrio** *(ehl eh-kee-'lee-bree·oh)*
breathing	**la respiración** *(lah reh-spee-rah-see-'ohn)*
hearing	**el oído** *(ehl oh-'ee-doh)*
nerves	**los nervios** *(lohs 'nehr-vee·ohs)*
sight	**la vista** *(lah 'vee-stah)*
speech	**el habla** *(ehl 'ah-blah)*

There is/are...	**Hay...** *('ah·ee...)*
bad dreams	**sueños malos** *('sweh-nyohs 'mah-lohs)*
convulsions	**convulsiones** *(kohn-vool-see-'oh-nehs)*
headaches	**dolores de cabeza** *(doh-'loh-rehs deh kah-'beh-sah)*
insomnia	**insomnio** *(een-'sohm-nee·oh)*
loss of memory	**falta de memoria** *('fahl-tah deh meh-'moh-ree·ah)*
numbness	**adormecimiento** *(ah-dohr-meh-see-mee-'ehn-toh)*
seizures	**ataques** *(ah-'tah-kehs)*

Check the medical file on the student. Are there any causes for special attention or alarm?

It's (the)...	Es... *(ehs...)*
abnormality	la anormalidad *(lah ah-nohr-mah-lee-'dahd)*
disability	la discapacidad *(lah dees-cah-pah-'see-dahd)*
disease	la enfermedad *(lah ehn-fehr-meh-'dahd)*
disorder	el desorden *(ehl dehs-'ohr-dehn)*
handicap	la incapacidad *(lah een-kah-pah-see-'dahd)*
syndrome	el síndrome *(ehl 'seen-droh-meh)*

MÁS INFORMACIÓN

➤ When it comes to concerns about emotional health, make an effort to ask questions carefully. Practice with these:

Are you eating and sleeping OK?
¿Estás comiendo y durmiendo bien?
(eh-'stahs koh-mee-'ehn-doh ee door-mee-'ehn-doh'bee·ehn)

Are you worried about anything?
¿Estás preocupado por algo?
(eh-'stahs preh-oh-koo-'pah-doh pohr'ahl-goh)

Did you have problems when you were a child?
¿Tuviste problemas de niño?
(too-'vees-teh proh-'bleh-mahs deh'nee-nyoh)

Do you have good relations with your relatives and friends?
¿Tienes buenas relaciones con sus parientes y amigos?
(tee-'eh-nehs 'bweh-nahs reh-lah-see-'oh-nehs kohn soos pah-ree-'ehn-tehs ee ah-'mee-gohs)

Do you have many responsibilities?
¿Tienes muchas responsabilidades?
(tee-'eh-nehs 'moo-chahs reh-spohn-sah-bee-lee-'dah-dehs)

What illnesses and operations have you had?

¿Qué enfermedades y operaciones has tenido?

('keh ehn-fehr-meh-'dah-dehs ee oh-peh-rah-see·'oh-nehs ahs teh-'nee-doh)

When did the problem start?

¿Cuándo empezó el problema?

('kwahn-doh ehm-peh-'soh ehl proh-'bleh-mah)

SENSITIVE ISSUES

Los temas delicados *(lohs'teh-mahs deh-lee-'kah-dohs)*

Learn to discuss any sensitive issue, but be sure that a fluent Spanish-speaking professional is there to assist you:

Would you like to talk about (the)...?

¿Quisieras hablar sobre...?

(kee-see-'eh-rahs ah-'blahr 'soh-breh)

abandonment	el abandono *(ehl ah-bahn-'doh-noh)*
abortion	el aborto *(ehl ah-'bohr-toh)*
abuse	el abuso *(ehl ah-'boo-soh)*
death	la muerte *(lah 'mwehr-teh)*
depression	la depresión *(lah deh-preh-see·'ohn)*
divorce	el divorcio *(ehl dee-'vohr-see·oh)*
failure	el fracaso *(ehl frah-'kah-soh)*
loneliness	la soledad *(lah soh-leh-'dahd)*
molestation	el acoso sexual *(ehl ah-'koh-soh sehk-soo-'ahl)*
obesity	la obesidad *(lah oh-beh-see-'dahd)*
phobia	la fobia *(lah 'foh-bee·ah)*
rape	la violación *(lah vee·oh-lah-see-'ohn)*
tragedy	la tragedia *(lah trah-'heh-dee·ah)*
trauma	el trauma *(ehl 'trah-ooh-mah)*

It's (the)...	Es... *(ehs)*

belief	la creencia *(lah kreh-'ehn-see·ah)*
dream	el sueño *(ehl 'sweh-nyoh)*

feeling	**el sentimiento** *(ehl sehn-tee-mee-'ehn-toh)*
personality	**la personalidad** *(lah pehr-soh-nah-lee-'dahd)*
thought	**el pensamiento** *(ehl-pehn-sah-mee-'ehn-toh)*

To provide a few words of support:

There's no...	**No hay...** *(noh'ah·ee...)*
danger	**peligro** *(peh-'lee-groh)*
harm	**daño** *('dah-nyoh)*
obstacle	**obstáculo** *(ohb-'stah-koo-loh)*
pain	**dolor** *(doh-'lohr)*
risk	**riesgo** *(ree-'ehs-goh)*

MÁS INFORMACIÓN

➤ The topic of sex can get delicate, but don't hesitate to probe if there's a concern. Here are some words you may hear:

birth control	**la anticoncepción** *(lah ahn-tee-kohn-sehp-see-'ohn)*
breasts and bras	**los senos y sostenes** *(lohs 'seh-nohr ee sohs-'teh-nehs)*
condom	**el condón** *(ehl kohn-'dohn)*
family planning	**la planificación familiar** *(lah plah-nee-fee-kah-see-'ohn fah-mee-lee-'ahr)*
homosexuality	**la homosexualidad** *(lah oh-moh-sehk-soo-ah-lee-'dahd)*
hormones	**las hormonas** *(lahs ohr-'moh-nahs)*
intercourse	**el coito** *(ehl koh-'ee-toh)*
masturbation	**la masturbación** *(lah mah-stoor-bah-see-'ohn)*
menstrual period	**la regla** *(lah'reh-glah)*
pornography	**la pornografía** *(lah pohr-noh-grah-'fee·ah)*
pregnancy test	**el examen de embarazo** *(ehl ehk-'sah-mehn deh ehm-bah-'rah-soh)*
puberty	**la pubertad** *(lah poo-behr-'tahd)*
sexual relations	**las relaciones sexuales** *(lahs reh-lah-see·'oh-nehs sehk-soo-'ah-lehs)*

THE STUDENT WITH DISABILITIES
El estudiante con discapacidad
(ehl eh-stoo-dee-'ahn-teh cohn dees-cah-pah-'see-dad)

As the young people wander in and out for assistance, be sure that all who speak Spanish receive the attention they need. In some cases, students with very special needs are mainstreamed into regular programs, which puts unique demands on the counseling staff. Begin with these medical conditions:

It's a case of...	**Es un caso de...** *(ehs oon 'kah-soh deh...)*
ADHD	**ADHD** *(ah deh hache deh)*
autism	**autismo** *(ow-'tees-moh)*
cerebral palsy	**parálisis cerebral** *(pah-'rah-lee-sees seh-reh-'brahl)*
cystic fibrosis	**fibrosis quística** *(fee-'broh-sees 'kee-stee-kah)*
Down's syndrome	**síndrome de Down** *('seen-droh-meh deh 'dowhn)*
epilepsy	**epilepsia** *(eh-pee-'lehp-see·ah)*
multiple sclerosis	**esclerosis múltiple** *(eh-skleh-'roh-sees 'mool-tee-pleh)*
muscular dystrophy	**distrofia muscular** *(dees-'troh-fee·ah moo-skoo-'lahr)*
paralysis	**parálisis** *pah-'rah-lee-sees)*
It's...	**Es...** *(ehs...)*
heart disease	**enfermedad de corazón** *(ehn-fehr-meh-'dahd deh koh-rah-'sohn)*
cancer	**cáncer** *('kahn-sehr)*
leukemia	**leucemia** *(leh-oo-'seh-mee·ah)*

MORE CHALLENGES
Más retos *(mahs 'reh-tos)*

The reasons why a student struggles often vary:

Do you have...	**¿Tienes...?** *(tee-'eh-nehs...)*
allergies	**alergias** *(ah-'lehr-hee·ahs)*
asthma	**asma** *('ahs-mah)*

astigmatism	astigmatismo *(ah-steeg-mah-'tees-moh)*
attention deficit disorder	dificultades a prestar atención *(dee-fee-kool-'tah-dehs ah preh-'stahr ah-tehn-see-'ohn)*
diabetes	diabetes *(dee·ah-'beh-tehs)*
hay fever	fiebre del heno *(fee-'eh-breh dehl'eh-noh)*
high blood pressure	presión de sangre alta *(preh-see-'ohn deh'sahn-greh'ahl-tah)*
limp	cojera *(koh-'heh-rah)*
myopia	miopía *(mee·oh-'pee·ah)*
stutter	tartamudeo *(tahr-tah-moo-'deh-oh)*
weight loss	pérdida de peso *('pehr-dee-dah deh-'peh-soh)*
He is...	Es... *(ehs...)*
hyperactive	hiperactivo *(ee-pehr-ahk-'tee-voh)*
impaired	debilitado *(deh-bee-lee-'tah-doh)*

MÁS INFORMACIÓN

➤ You may also hear about items that students with disabilities bring to school. Utilize the phrases below:

He needs (the)...	Necesita... *(neh-seh-'see-tah...)*
She uses (the)...	Usa... *('oo-sah...)*
braces	las abrazaderas *(lahs ah-brah-sah-'deh-rahs)*
cane	el bastón *(ehl bah-'stohn)*
contact lenses	los lentes de contacto *(lohs 'lehn-tehs deh kohn-'tahk-toh)*
crutches	las muletas *(lahs moo-'leh-tahs)*
glasses	los lentes *(lohs'lehn-tehs)*
guide dog	el perro lazarillo *(ehl'peh-rroh lah-sah-'ree-yoh)*
hearing aids	los audífonos *(lohs ow-'dee-foh-nohs)*
wheelchair	la silla de ruedas *(lah 'see-yah deh roo-'eh-dahs)*

➤ Don't forget surgery. Notice this key phrase:

He had _____ surgery.   **Tuvo cirugía en** _____ . *('too-voh see-roo-'hee·ah ehn _____)*

arm	**el brazo** *(ehl 'brah-soh)*
brain	**el cerebro** *(ehl seh-'reh-broh)*
heart	**el corazón** *(ehl koh-rah-'sohn)*
leg	**la pierna** *(lah pee-'ehr-nah)*
lungs	**los pulmones** *(lohs pool-'moh-nehs)*
stomach	**el estómago** *(ehl eh-'stoh-mah-goh)*

It's not difficult to guess the meanings of these Spanish words:

anemia *(ah-'neh-mee·ah)*
anorexia *(ah-noh-'rehk-see·ah)*
bulimia *(boo-'lee-mee·ah)*

SOME ADVICE
Unos consejos *('oo-nohs kohn-'seh-hohs)*

Now that you've heard what's troubling the student, how about offering a little advice. Of course, if the problem is serious, contact the family along with anyone else who can help. Next, request an interpreter. Open with one-liners that get everyone to settle down.

You should...	Debe... *('deh-beh...)*
calm down	calmarse *(kahl-'mahr-seh)*
relax	relajarse *(reh-lah-'hahr-seh)*
rest	descansar *(deh-skahn-'sahr)*
breathe deeply	respirar profundamente *(reh-spee-'rahr proh-foon-dah-'mehn-teh)*
leave this office	salir de esta oficina *(sah-'leer deh 'eh-stah oh-fee-'see-nah)*
lower your voice	bajar la voz *(bah-'hahr lah vohs)*
come back later	regresar más tarde *(reh-greh-'sahr mahs 'tahr-deh)*
pay attention	prestar atención *(preh-'stahr ah-tehn-see-'ohn)*

Are you all set to counsel? Keep your comments short as you create the phrases that you'll need:

You need to...	Necesitas... *(neh-seh-'see-tahs...)*
call your doctor	llamar a tu doctor *(yah-'mahr ah too dohk-'tohr)*
get more sleep	dormir más *(dohr-'meer mahs)*
see a specialist	ver a un especialista *(vehr ah oon eh-speh-see·ah-'lee-stah)*
take your medication	tomar tu medicamento *(toh-'mahr too meh-dee-kah-'mehn-toh)*
tell your family	decirle a tu familia *(deh-'seer-leh ah too fah-'mee-lee·ah)*
go to class	ir a tu clase *(eer ah too 'klah-seh)*
stay away from them	apartarte de ellos *(ah-pahr-'tahr-teh deh 'eh-yohs)*
change your class schedule	cambiar tu horario de clases *(kahm-bee-'ahr too oh-'rah-ree·oh deh 'klah-sehs)*

You shouldn't...	No debes... *(noh 'deh-behs...)*
antagonize	antagonizar *(ahn-tah-goh-nee-'sahr)*
argue	discutir *(dees-koo-'teer)*
bother	molestar *(moh-leh-'stahr)*
bully	intimidar *(een-tee-mee-'dahr)*
curse	maldecir *(mahl-deh-'seer)*
gossip	chismear *(chees-meh-'ahr)*

humiliate	humillar *(oo-mee-'yahr)*
joke	bromear *(broh-meh-'ahr)*
lie	mentir *(mehn-'teer)*
tease	burlar *(boor-'lahr-teh)*
threaten	amenazar *(ah-meh-nah-'sahr)*

Keep mentioning solutions or suggestions:

We offer (the)...	Ofrecemos... *(oh-freh-'seh-mohs...)*
different classes	diferentes clases *(dee-feh-'rehn-tehs 'klah-sehs)*
individualized plans	planes individualizados *('plah-nehs een-dee-vee-doo-ah-lee-'sah-dohs)*
intensive therapy	terapia intensiva *(teh-'rah-pee·ah een-tehn-'see-vah)*
personal contracts	contratos personales *(kohn-'trah-tohs pehr-soh-'nah-lehs)*
personality tests	pruebas de personalidad *(proo-'eh-bahs deh pehr-soh-nah-lee-'dahd)*
recovery groups	grupos de recuperación *('groo-pohs deh reh-koo-peh-rah-see-'ohn)*
rehabilitation	rehabilitación *(reh-ah-bee-lee-tah-see-'ohn)*
sign language	lenguaje de sordomudos *(lehn-'gwah-heh deh sohr-doh-'moo-dohs)*
special programs	programas especiales *(proh-'grah-mahs eh-speh-see-'ah-lehs)*
tutoring	tutores *(too-'toh-rehs)*
The program is...	El programa es... *(ehl proh-'grah-mah ehs...)*
adaptive	adaptivo *(ah-dahp-'tee-voh)*
educational	educativo *(eh-doo-kah-'tee-voh)*
for home study	para estudiar en casa *('pah-rah eh-stoo-dee-'ahr ehn 'kah-sah)*
online	en línea *(ehn 'lee-neh-ah)*
private	privado *(pree-'vah-doh)*
vocational	vocacional *(voh-kah-see·oh-'nahl)*

➤ Get help from these professionals:

Talk to (the)...	Habla con... *('ah-blah kohn...)*
allergist	el alergista *(ehl ah-lehr-'hee-stah)*
chiropractor	el quiropráctico *(ehl kee-roh-'prahk-tee-koh)*
dentist	el dentista *(ehl dehn-'tee-stah)*
gynecologist	el ginecólogo *(ehl hee-neh-'koh-loh-goh)*
ophthalmologist	el oftalmólogo *(ehl ohf-tahl-'moh-loh-goh)*
optometrist	el optometrista *(ehl ohp-toh-meh-'tree-stah)*
orthodontist	el ortodontista *(ehl ohr-toh-dohn-'tee-stah)*
pediatrician	el pediatra *(ehl peh-dee-'ah-trah)*
physician	el médico *(ehl 'meh-dee-koh)*

I'll teach you to deal with:	Te enseñaré a tratar con: *(teh ehn-sehn-yah-'reh ah trah-'tahr kohn)*
bullies	los matones *(lohs mah-'toh-nehs)*
peer pressure	la presión de grupo *(lah preh-see·'ohn deh 'groo-poh)*
stress	el estrés *(ehl ehs-'tres)*

¿LISTOS PARA PRACTICAR?

Translate, and then connect the related vocabulary:

la vista *(lah 'vee-stah)*   la silla de ruedas *(lah 'see-yah deh roo-'eh-dahs)*

el oído *(ehl oh-'ee-doh)*   los lentes *(lohs 'lehn-tehs)*

el equilibrio *(ehl eh-kee-'lee-bree·oh)*   los audífonos *(lohs ow-'dee-foh-nohs)*

Name in Spanish three internal organs:

_____   _____   _____

Name in Spanish three traumatic events that often result in emotional problems:

_____   _____   _____

Complete each sentence with words you've just learned:

terapia, calmarse, bastón, polio, dolorido *(teh-'rah-pee·ah, kahl-'mahr-seh, bah-'stohn, 'poh-lee·oh, doh-loh-'ree-doh)*

Debes _____ *('deh-behs _____)*

Me siento _____ *(meh see-'ehn-toh _____)*

Es un caso de _____ *(ehs oon 'kah-soh deh _____)*

Ofrecemos _____ *(oh-freh-'seh-mohs _____)*

Usa _____ *('oo-sah _____)*

WORDS OF ENCOURAGEMENT
Palabras de ánimo *(pah-'lah-brahs deh 'ah-nee-moh)*

Personal problems can be helped once the comment focuses on the positive. The following list of questions ask the student to come up with a solution. Have an interpreter at your side.

I'd like to hear your ideas.
Quisiera escuchar tus ideas.
(kee-see-'eh-rah eh-skoo-'chahr toos ee-'deh-ahs)

What other possibilities do you see?
¿Cuáles son las otras posibilidades que ves?
('kwah-lehs sohn lahs 'oh-trahs poh-see-bee-lee-'dah-dehs keh vehs)

What steps would you take to correct the problem?
¿Qué medidas tomarías para corregir el problema?
(keh meh-'dee-dahs toh-mah-'ree·ahs 'pah-rah koh-rreh-'heer ehl proh-'bleh-mah)

Are you convinced that this is the best solution?
¿Estás seguro de que ésta es la mejor solución?
(eh-'stahs seh-'goo-roh deh keh 'eh-stah ehs lah meh-'hohr soh-loo-see·'ohn)

How do you feel about it?
¿Cómo te sientes acerca de eso?
('koh-moh teh see-'ehn-tehs ah-'sehr-kah deh 'eh-soh)

Let's analyze and resolve the problem.
Vamos a analizar y resolver el problema.
(vah-mohs ah ah-nah-lee-'sahr ee reh-sohl-'vehr ehl proh-'bleh-mah)

| I'd like to hear your... | **Quisiera escuchar tu...** |
| | *(kee-see-'eh-rah eh-skoo-'chahr too...)* |

comment	**comentario** *(koh-mehn-'tah-ree·oh)*
idea	**idea** *(ee-'deh-ah)*
interpretation	**interpretación** *(een-tehr-preh-tah-see-'ohn)*
opinion	**opinión** *(oh-pee-nee-'ohn)*
response	**respuesta** *(reh-'spweh-stah)*

This time, add a smile as you motivate others around you:

You have...	**Tú tienes...** *(too tee-'eh-nehs...)*
I see...	**Yo veo...** *(yoh 'veh-oh...)*
This is/These are...	**Hay...** *('ah·ee...)*

excellent achievements
logros excelentes
('loh-grohs eks-seh-'lehn-tehs)

fast development
desarrollo rápido
(dehs-ah-'rroh-yoh 'rah-pee-doh)

good effort
buen esfuerzo
(bwehn ehs-'fwehr-soh)

great potential
gran potencial
(grahn poh-tehn-see-'ahl)

lots of desire
mucho deseo
('moo-choh deh-'seh-oh)

more success
más éxito
(mahs 'ehk-see-toh)

obvious progress
progreso obvio
(proh-'greh-soh 'ohb-vee·oh)

outstanding conduct
conducta destacada
(kohn-'dook-tah deh-stah-'kah-dah)

self-motivation
motivación personal
(moh-tee-vah-see·'ohn pehr-soh-'nahl)

sense of accomplishment
sentido de logro
(sehn-'tee-doh deh 'loh-groh)

tremendous growth
crecimiento tremendo
(kreh-see-mee-'ehn-toh treh-'mehn-doh)

wise choices
decisiones inteligentes
(deh-see-see-'oh-nehs een-teh-lee-'hehn-tehs)

Now, say something to the students that will motivate them: Are you still making changes if they are females?

You are...   Tú eres... *(too 'eh-rehs...)*

attentive   **atento** *(ah-'tehn-toh)*
bright   **brillante** *(bree-'yahn-teh)*
capable   **capaz** *(kah-'pahs)*
clever   **listo** *('lee-stoh)*
compassionate   **compasivo** *(kohm-pah-'see-voh)*
confident   **seguro** *(seh-'goo-roh)*
cooperative   **dispuesto** *(dee-'spweh-stoh)*
courageous   **valiente** *(vah-lee-'ehn-teh)*

223

decent	decente *(deh-'sehn-teh)*
ethical	ético *('eh-tee-koh)*
fair	justo *('hoo-stoh)*
friendly	amistoso *(ah-mee-'stoh-soh)*
healthy	sano *('sah-noh)*
helpful	servicial *(sehr-vee-see-'ahl)*
honest	honesto *(oh-'neh-stoh)*
intelligent	inteligente *(een-teh-lee-'hehn-teh)*
kind	amable *(ah-'mah-bleh)*
loved	querido *(keh-'ree-doh)*
nice	simpático *(seem-'pah-tee-koh)*
patient	paciente *(pah-see-'ehn-teh)*
polite	cortés *(kohr-'tehs)*
respectful	respetuoso *(reh-speh-too-'oh-soh)*
responsible	responsable *(reh-spohn-'sah-bleh)*
thoughtful	considerado *(kohn-see-deh-'rah-doh)*

MÁS INFORMACIÓN

➤ Let the family know how you feel about their child:

He has...	Tiene... *(tee-'eh-neh...)*
self-respect	amor propio *(ah-'mohr 'proh-pee·oh)*
self-control	control de sí mismo *(kohn-'trohl deh see 'mees-moh)*
nice manners	buenos modales *('bweh-nohs moh-'dah-lehs)*
strong values	valores fuertes *(vah-'loh-rehs 'fwehr-tehs)*
personal convictions	convicciones personales *(kohn-veek-see-'oh-nehs pehr-soh-'nah-lehs)*

CAN YOU GIVE A DESCRIPTION?

¿Puedes dar una descripción? *('pweh-dehs dahr'oo-nah deh-skreep-see-'ohn)*

How well do you know your students? While practicing the next series of words, picture a person who fits the descriptive word. As usual, some of these need to be changed when you refer to a female:

The student is...	El estudiante es... *(ehl eh-stoo-dee-'ahn-teh ehs...)*
beautiful	bella *('beh-yah)*
blonde	rubio *('roo-bee·oh)*
brunette	moreno *(moh-'reh-noh)*
fat	gordo *('gohr-doh)*
funny	chistoso *(chee-'stoh-soh)*
handsome	guapo *('gwah-poh)*
immature	inmaduro *(een-mah-'doo-roh)*
left-handed	zurdo *('soor-doh)*
loud	ruidoso *(roo-ee-'doh-soh)*
mature	maduro *(mah-'doo-roh)*
older	mayor *(mah-'yohr)*
poor	pobre *('poh-breh)*
quiet	quieto *(kee-'eh-toh)*
red-headed	pelirrojo *(peh-lee-'rroh-hoh)*
rich	rico *('ree-koh)*
right-handed	diestro *(dee-'eh-stroh)*
short	bajo *('bah-hoh)*
shy	tímido *('tee-mee-doh)*
sloppy	descuidado *(dehs-kwee-'dah-doh)*
strong	fuerte *('fwehr-teh)*
tall	alto *('ahl-toh)*
thin	delgado *(dehl-'gah-doh)*
weak	débil *('deh-beel)*
young	joven *('hoh-vehn)*
younger	menor *(meh-'nohr)*

➤ Look a little closer at your student. Did you mention everything?

I see (the)...   Veo... *('veh-oh...)*

body piercing	la perforación *(lah pehr-foh-rah-see-'ohn)*
goatee	la perita *(lah peh-'ree-tah)*
ponytail	la coleta *(lah koh-'leh-tah)*
sideburns	las patillas *(lahs pah-'tee-yahs)*
tattoo	el tatuaje *(ehl tah-too-'ah-heh)*

THE FAMILY CONFERENCE
La reunión con la familia *(lah reh-oo-nee-'ohn kohn lah fah-'mee-lee·ah)*

Working on issues with students is one thing, but sharing that information with their families is something else. Why not start at the beginning. By email, phone, or in person, let the family know why you need to meet. And be sure to use the formal usted form:

Could you come to the office?
¿Puede usted venir a la oficina? *('pweh-deh oo-'stehd veh-'neer ah lah oh-fee-'see-nah)*

I would like to talk to you.
Quisiera hablar con usted. *(kee-see-'eh-rah ah-'blahr kohn oo-'stehd)*

It's about _____ .
Tiene que ver con _____ . *(tee-'eh-neh keh vehr kohn _____)*

It's important that you come.
Es importante que venga usted. *(ehs eem-pohr-'tahn-teh keh 'vehn-gah oo-'stehd)*

Be here at _____ .
Venga a _____ . *('vehn-gah ah _____)*

It's...	Es... *(ehs...)*
necessary	**necesario** *(neh-seh-'sah-ree·oh)*
serious	**serio** *('seh-ree·oh)*
urgent	**urgente** *(oor-'hehn-teh)*

Invite the appropriate person. Use this pattern to clarify who everyone is.

Are you the...?	**¿Es usted...?** *(ehs oo-'stehd...)*
aunt	**la tía** *(lah 'tee·ah)*
brother	**el hermano** *(ehl ehr-'mah-noh)*
cousin	**el primo** *(ehl 'pree-moh)*
daughter	**la hija** *(lah 'ee-hah)*
father	**el padre** *(ehl 'pah-dreh)*
granddaughter	**la nieta** *(lah nee-'eh-tah)*
grandfather	**el abuelo** *(ehl ah-'bweh-loh)*
grandmother	**la abuela** *(lah ah-'bweh-lah)*
grandson	**el nieto** *(ehl nee-'eh-toh)*
husband	**el esposo** *(ehl eh-spoh-soh)*
mother	**la madre** *(lah 'mah-dreh)*
nephew	**el sobrino** *(ehl soh-'bree-noh)*
niece	**la sobrina** *(lah soh-'bree-nah)*
sister	**la hermana** *(lah ehr-'mah-nah)*
son	**el hijo** *(ehl 'ee-hoh)*
uncle	**el tío** *(ehl 'tee·oh)*
wife	**la esposa** *(lah eh-'spoh-sah)*

 DIFERENCIAS CULTURALES

Because the traditional Hispanic family includes more than just its immediate members, you may want to consider learning the names for relatives outside the immediate family:

acquaintance	**el compañero** *(ehl kohm-pah-'nyeh-roh)*
boyfriend	**el novio** *(ehl 'noh-vee·oh)*
brother-in-law	**el cuñado** *(ehl koo-'nyah-doh)*
close friend	**el amigo** *(ehl ah-'mee-goh)*
daughter-in-law	**la nuera** *(lah noo-'eh-rah)*
father-in-law	**el suegro** *(ehl 'sweh-groh)*

foster family	los padres adoptivos *(lohs 'pah-drehs ah-dohp-'tee-vohs)*
goddaughter	la ahijada *(lah ah-ee-'hah-dah)*
godson	el ahijado *(ehl ah-ee-'hah-doh)*
godfather	el compadre *(ehl kohm-'pah-dreh)*
godmother	la comadre *(lah koh-'mah-dreh)*
godparents	los padrinos *(lohs pah-'dree-nohs)*
girlfriend	la novia *(lah 'noh-vee·ah)*
legal guardian	el tutor legal *(ehl too-'tohr leh-'gahl)*
mother-in-law	la suegra *(lah 'sweh-grah)*
relative	el pariente *(ehl pah-ree-'ehn-teh)*
sister-in-law	la cuñada *(lah koo-'nyah-dah)*
son-in-law	el yerno *(ehl 'yehr-noh)*
stepfather	el padrastro *(ehl pah-'drah-stroh)*
stepmother	la madrastra *(lah mah-'drah-strah)*
stepdaughter	la hijastra *(lah ee-'hahs-trah)*
stepson	el hijastro *(ehl ee-'hahs-troh)*

HOW ARE THEY DOING IN SCHOOL?

¿Cómo van en la escuela? *('koh-moh vahn ehn lah eh-'skweh-lah)*

In most cases, educators invite the parents to visit in order to discuss student progress. Let's begin with the positive.

The student is very...	El estudiante es muy... *(ehl eh-stoo-dee-'ahn-teh ehs 'moo·ee...)*
artistic	artístico *(ahr-'tee-stee-koh)*
athletic	atlético *(aht-'leh-tee-koh)*

industrious	aplicado *(ah-plee-'kah-doh)*
neat	limpio *('leem-pee·oh)*
obedient	obediente *(oh-beh-dee-'ehn-teh)*
organized	organizado *(ohr-gah-nee-'sah-doh)*
punctual	puntual *(poon-too-'ahl)*
respectful	respetuoso *(reh-speh-too-'oh-soh)*
studious	aplicado *(ah-plee-'kah-doh)*

He/She...	El/Ella... *(ehl/'eh-yah)*
retains information	retiene la información *(reh-tee-'eh-neh lah een-fohr-mah-see-'ohn)*
is good at it	tiene facilidad para eso *(tee-'eh-neh fah-see-lee-'dahd 'pah-rah 'eh-soh)*
takes the time	toma su tiempo *('toh-mah soo tee-'ehm-poh)*
behaves well	se porta bien *(seh 'pohr-tah 'bee·ehn)*
follows directions	sigue instrucciones *('see-geh een-strook-see-'oh-nehs)*
obeys the rules	obedece las reglas *(oh-beh-'deh-seh lahs 'reh-glahs)*
does the homework	hace la tarea *('ah-seh lah tah-'reh-ah)*
pays attention	presta atención *('preh-stah ah-tehn-see-'ohn)*
is very advanced	es muy adelantado(a) *(ehs 'moo·ee ah-deh-lahn-'tah-doh/ah)*

You're welcome to add phrases to the lists above. Also remember that in order to create a negative statement in Spanish, all you need to do is add **no** in front of the verb:

| She doesn't behave well. | Ella no se porta bien. *('eh-yah noh seh'pohr-tah 'bee·ehn)* |

Speaking of negative statements, here are a few more words you might want to know:

He/she is...	Es... *(ehs...)*
antisocial	antisocial *(ahn-tee-soh-see-'ahl)*
cruel	cruel *(kroo-'ehl)*
forgetful	olvidadizo/a *(ohl-vee-dah-'dee-soh/ah)*
lazy	perezoso/a *(peh-reh-'soh-soh/ah)*
restless	inquieto/a *(een-kee-'eh-toh/ah)*

rude	grosero/a *(groh-'seh-roh/ah)*
sassy	fresco/a *('freh-skoh/ah)*
selfish	egoísta *(eh-goh-'ee-stah)*

Close out the conference by asking a few questions or sharing your opinion. If you studied hard and feel brave, make any recommendations that you feel may be necessary:

Why do you think he/she...?
¿Por qué piensa usted que...? *(pohr keh pee-'ehn-sah oo-'stehd keh...)*

isn't interested	no está interesado/a *(noh eh-'stah een-teh-reh-'sah-doh/ah)*
doesn't study	no estudia *(noh eh-'stoo-dee·ah)*
stays quiet	se queda quieto/a *(seh 'keh-dah kee-'eh-toh/ah)*
always arrives late	siempre llega tarde *(see-'ehm-preh 'yeh-gah 'tahr-deh)*
misses school	falta a la escuela *('fahl-tah ah lah eh-'skweh-lah)*
likes to fight	le gusta pelear *(leh 'goo-stah peh-leh-'ahr)*
is failing classes	está fallando en sus clases *(eh-'stah fah-'yahn-doh ehn soos 'klah-sehs)*

Ask your son/daughter what he/she learned.
Pregúnte le a su hijo/a qué aprendió. *(preh-'goon-teh leh ah soo 'ee-hoh/ah keh ah-prehn-dee·'oh)*

Come to the parent meetings.
Venga a las reuniones de los padres. *('vehn-gah ah lahs reh-oo-nee·'oh-nehs deh lohs 'pah-drehs)*

Call us if there is a problem.
Llámenos si hay un problema. *('yah-meh-nohs see 'ah·ee oon proh-'bleh-mah)*

Students need...	Los estudiantes necesitan... *(lohs eh-stoo-dee-'ahn-tehs neh-seh-'see-tahn...)*
counseling	consejos *(kohn-'seh-hohs)*
discipline	disciplina *(dee-see-'plee-nah)*
independence	independencia *(een-deh-pehn-'dehn-see·ah)*
praise	alabanzas *(ah-lah-'bahn-sahs)*
support	apoyo *(ah-'poh-yoh)*

➤ Continue questioning the family members:

Do you help him/her?	¿Lo/la ayuda? *(loh / lah ah-'yoo-dah)*
Do you praise him/her?	¿Lo/la alaba? *(loh / lah ah-'lah-bah)*
Do you punish him/her?	¿Lo/la castiga? *(loh / lah kah-'stee-gah)*

➤ Sometimes meetings with counselors don't go exactly as planned:

It's cancelled.	Está cancelado. *(eh-'stah kahn-seh-'lah-doh)*
I'm going to postpone it.	Voy a posponerlo. *('voh·ee ah pohs-poh-'nehr-loh)*
They changed it.	Lo han cambiado. *(loh ahn kahm-bee-'ah-doh)*
I have to go to a meeting.	Tengo que ir a una reunión. *('tehn-goh keh eer ah 'oo-nah reh-oo-nee·'ohn)*
I'm with another student.	Estoy con otro estudiante. *(eh-'stoh·ee kohn 'oh-troh eh-stoo-dee-'ahn-teh)*
Talk to me after school.	Hábleme después de horas de escuela. *('ah-bleh-meh deh-'spwehs deh 'oh-rahs deh eh-'skweh-lah)*
Please come back later.	Regrese más tarde, por favor. *(reh-'greh-seh mahs 'tahr-deh, pohr fah-'vohr)*
I can't meet right now.	No puedo reunirme ahora. *(noh 'pweh-doh reh-oo-neer-me ah-'oh-rah)*
Go to the website.	Vaya al sitio web. *('vah-yah ahl 'see-tee·oh web)*

¿LISTOS PARA PRACTICAR?

Make five positive comments about your favorite student:

_____ _____ _____ _____ _____

Match these opposites:

rubio *('roo-bee·oh)*	delgado *(dehl-'gah-doh)*
gordo *('gohr-doh)*	alto *('ahl-toh)*
fuerte *('fwehr-teh)*	rico *('ree-koh)*
bajo *('bah-hoh)*	moreno *(moh-'reh-noh)*
pobre *('poh-breh)*	débil *('deh-beel)*

Translate into English:

Ella no se porta bien. *('eh-yah noh seh 'pohr-tah 'bee·ehn)*
Ella falta a la escuela. *('eh-yah 'fahl-tah ah lah eh-'skweh-lah)*
Ella es fresca y ruda. *('eh-yah ehs 'freh-skah ee 'roo-dah)*

Complete these sets:

tío:tía *('tee·oh,'tee·ah)*
sobrino:sobrina *(soh-'bree-noh, soh-'bree-nah)*

yerno: _____ *('yehr-noh)*

nieto: _____ *(nee-'eh-toh)*

padrino: _____ *(pah-'dree-noh)*

novia: _____ *('noh-vee·ah)*

madrastra: _____ *(mah-'drah-strah)*

PLANNING FOR THE FUTURE
La planificación para el futuro
(lah plah-nee-fee-kah-see·'ohn 'pah-rah ehl foo-'too-roh)

Guidance and career counselors take on special duties as they deal with older students. These sample phrases should help:

There are...	**Hay...** *('ah·ee...)*
job opportunities	**oportunidades para trabajar** *(oh-pohr-too-nee-'dah-dehs 'pah-rah trah-bah-'hahr)*
job placement	**asignación de trabajo** *(ah-seeg-nah-see·'ohn deh trah-'bah-hoh)*
job requirements	**requisitos para el trabajo** *(reh-kee-'see-tohs 'pah-rah ehl trah-'bah-hoh)*
It's (the)...	**Es...** *(ehs...)*
career planning	**la planificación de carreras** *(lah plah-nee-fee-kah-see·'ohn deh kah-'rreh-rahs)*
summer school	**la escuela de verano** *(lah eh-'skweh-lah deh veh-'rah-noh)*

232

technical training	**el entrenamiento técnico** *(ehl ehn-treh-nah-mee-'ehn-toh 'tehk-nee-koh)*
volunteer program	**el programa voluntario** *(ehl proh-'grah-mah voh-loon-'tah-ree·oh)*
work experience	**la experiencia en el trabajo** *(lah ehk-speh-ree-'ehn-see·ah ehn ehl trah-'bah-hoh)*

Here's information about (the)...
Aquí tiene información acerca de... *(ah-'kee tee-'eh-neh een-fohr-mah-see-'ohn ah-'sehr-kah deh...)*

application	**la solicitud** *(lah soh-lee-see-'tood)*
armed forces	**las fuerzas armadas** *(lahs 'fwehr-sahs ahr-'mah-dahs)*
degree	**la licenciatura** *(lah lee-sehn-see·ah-'too-rah)*
electives	**la materia optativa** *(lah mah-'teh-ree·ah ohp-tah-'tee-vah)*
entrance exams	**los exámenes de entrada** *(lohs ehk-'sah-meh-nehs deh ehn-'trah-dah)*
financial aid	**la ayuda financiera** *(lah ah-'yoo-dah fee-nahn-see-'eh-rah)*
funding	**la obtención de fondos** *(lah ohb-tehn-see-'ohn deh 'fohn-dohs)*
letters of recommendation	**las cartas de recomendación** *(lahs 'kahr-tahs deh reh-koh-mehn-dah-see-'ohn)*
loan	**el préstamo** *(ehl 'preh-stah-moh)*
prerequisites	**los prerrequisitos** *(lohs preh-rreh-kee-'see-tohs)*
registration	**la inscripción** *(lah een-skreep-see-'ohn)*
scholarship	**la beca** *(lah 'beh-kah)*
testing	**los exámenes** *(lohs ehk-'sah-meh-nehs)*
transcripts	**la copia de los certificados de estudio** *(lah 'koh-pee·ah deh lohs sehr-tee-fee-'kah-dohs deh eh-'stoo-dee·oh)*

MÁS INFORMACIÓN

➤ How about summer employment:

There's work at (the)...   Hay trabajo en... *('ah·ee trah-'bah-hoh ehn...)*

camp	el campamento *(ehl kahm-pah-'mehn-toh)*
club	el club *(ehl kloob)*
hotel	el hotel *(ehl oh-'tehl)*
lodge	la logia *(lah 'loh-hee·ah)*
ranch	el rancho *(ehl 'rahn-choh)*
resort	el lugar de vacaciones *(ehl loo-'gahr deh vah-kah-see·'oh-nehs)*

➤ These terms should be familiar to most educators:

Bachelor of Arts	la licenciatura de letras *(lah lee-sehn-see·ah-'too-rah deh 'leh-trahs)*
Bachelor of Science	la licenciatura de ciencias *(lah lee-sehn-see·ah-'too-rah deh see-'ehn-see·ahs)*
Doctorate degree	el doctorado *(ehl dohk-toh-'rah-doh)*
Master of Arts	la maestría en letras *(lah mah-eh-'stree·ah ehn 'leh-trahs)*
Master of Science	la maestría en ciencias *(lah mah-eh-'stree·ah ehn see-'ehn-see·ahs)*
Ph.D.	el doctorado en el campo de las humanidades *(ehl dohk-toh-'rah-doh ehn ehl 'kahm-poh deh lahs oo-mah-nee-'dah-dehs)*

DIFERENCIAS CULTURALES

Many of the words here can be used to assist educators at schools of higher learning. The only difference might be in the way you talk to students. Instead of using the "tú" form, try sending messages formally with "usted."

Here's still another way to talk about past actions. The past progressive tense has two parts, so pay attention:

First, give your **-ar** verbs the **-ando** endings and the **-er** or **-ir** verbs the **-iendo** endings. You've done this before:

hablar *(ah-'blahr)*	hablando *(ah-'blahn-doh)*
comer *(koh-'mehr)*	comiendo *(koh-mee-'ehn-doh)*
escribir *(eh-skree-'beer)*	escribiendo *(eh-skree-bee-'ehn-doh)*

Second, change the verb estar *(eh-'stahr)* to the following past tense form:

I was	estaba *(eh-'stah-bah)*
You were (informal)	estabas *(eh-'stah-bahs)*
You (formal) were; He, She was	estaba *(eh-'stah-bah)*
You (pl.), They were	estaban *(eh-'stah-bahn)*
We were	estábamos *(eh-'stah-bah-mohs)*

Now, put them together. This past progressive is like the present progressive because it gets easier the more you practice:

I was studying.	Estaba estudiando. *(eh-'stah-bah eh-stoo-dee-'ahn-doh)*
She was reading.	Estaba leyendo. *(eh-'stah-bah leh-'yehn-doh)*
They were leaving.	Estaban saliendo. *(eh-'stah-bah sah-lee-'ehn-doh)*
We were calling.	Estábamos llamando. *(eh-'stah-bah-mohs yah-'mahn-doh)*

¡ÓRDENES!

Generally speaking, the words lo *(loh)* or la *(lah)* refer to "it" in Spanish (lo for masculine, la for feminine). They can be very useful when they are added to your formal or informal commands:

Bring	Traiga *('trah·ee-gah)*
Bring it.	Tráigala. *('trah·ee-gah-lah)*
Do	Haz *(ahs)*
Do it.	Hazlo. *('ahs-loh)*

All set to put a few together? Try talking to several students at once:

Everyone, pick it up and put it in the trash!
¡Todos, recójanlo y métanlo en la basura!
('toh-dohs, reh-'koh-hahn-loh ee 'meh-tahn-loh ehn lah bah-'soo-rah)

MÁS INFORMACIÓN

➤ Check the pattern in these negative commands:

Don't do it!	¡No lo hagas! *(noh loh 'ah-gahs)*
Don't throw it!	¡No la tires! *(noh lah 'tee-rehs)*
Don't move it!	¡No lo muevas! *(noh loh 'mweh-vahs)*

➤ Obviously, when you refer to more than one object in a command phrase, the pronouns are in the plural:

Don't throw them!	¡No las tires! *(noh lahs 'tee-rehs)*
Don't move them!	¡No los muevas! *(noh lohs 'mweh-vahs)*

➤ And just like the other pronouns, these little words go before your actions in a standard sentence:

I'm writing it.	Lo estoy escribiendo. *(loh eh-'stoh·ee eh-skree-bee-'ehn-doh)*
She studies them.	Los estudia. *(lohs eh-'stoo-dee·ah)*
We have it.	La tenemos. *(lah teh-'neh-mohs)*

236

Practice this dialog with a Spanish speaker:

—Necesito información acerca de la universidad. *(neh-seh-'see-toh een-fohr-mah-see-'ohn ah-'sehr-kah deh lah oo-nee-vehr-see-'dahd)*

—¡Muy bien! ¿Cómo puedo ayudarle? *('moo·ee bee·'ehn.'koh-moh 'pweh-doh ah-yoo-'dahr-leh)*

—¿Hay becas? *('ah·ee 'beh-kahs)*

—Sí, y hay préstamos, también. *(see, ee'ah·ee 'preh-stah-mohs, tahm-bee-'ehn)*

Follow the examples and fill in the blanks:

I'm studying.	I was studying.
Estoy estudiando.	*(eh-'stoh·ee eh-stoo-dee-'ahn-doh)*
Estaba estudiando.	*(eh-'stah-bah eh-stoo-dee-'ahn-doh)*

Estoy leyendo.
(eh-'stoh·ee leh-'yehn-doh)   _____

Estoy escribiendo.
(eh-'stoh·ee eh-skree-bee-'ehn-doh)   _____

Estoy comiendo.
(eh-'stoh·ee koh-mee-'ehn-doh)   _____

Watch out for **le** and **lo**. Translate!

Don't talk to <u>him</u>.   _____

Don't throw <u>it</u>.   _____

Don't hit <u>her</u>.   _____

237

CHAPTER SEVEN
Capítulo Siete
(kah-'pee-too-loh see-'eh-teh)

THE ADMINISTRATORS
Los administradores
(lohs ahd-mee-nee-strah-'doh-rehs)

ADMINISTRATION

La administración *(lah ahd-mee-nees-trah-see·'ohn)*

Some professionals are the administrators. Perhaps as you introduce yourself to a Spanish speaker, you will remember to say one of these. Make changes if you are a female:

I'm (the)...	Soy... *('soh·ee)*
assistant principal	el subdirector *(ehl soob-dee-rehk-'tohr)*
assistant superintendent	el subsuperintendente *(ehl soob-soo-pehr-een-tehn-'dehn-teh)*
principal	el director *(ehl dee-rehk-'tohr)*
superintendent	el superintendente *(ehl soo-pehr-een-tehn-'dehn-teh)*

Fill in the blanks with English, and see if you can translate them.

I'm (the)...	Soy... *('soh·ee...)*
_____ administrator	el administrador _____ *(ehl ahd-mee-nee-strah-'dohr ____)*
_____ coordinator	el coordinador de _____ *(ehl koh-ohr-dee-nah-'dohr deh ____)*
_____ dean	el decano de _____ *(ehl deh-'kah-noh deh ____)*
_____ director	el director de _____ *(ehl dee-rehk-'tohr deh ____)*
_____ manager	el gerente de _____ *(ehl heh-'rehn-teh deh ____)*
_____ specialist	el especialista de _____ *(ehl eh-speh-see·ah-'lee-stah deh)*
_____ supervisor	el supervisor de _____ *(ehl soo-pehr-vee-'sohr deh ____)*
_____ trainer	el entrenador de _____ *(ehl ehn-treh-nah-'dohr deh ____)*

➤ The word *board* is used all the time in education:

Board of Education	la junta de educadores *(lah 'hoon-tah deh eh-doo-kah-'doh-rehs)*
Board of Supervisors	la junta de supervisores *(lah 'hoon-tah deh soo-pehr-vee-'soh-rehs)*
Board of Trustees	la junta de fideicomisarios *(lah 'hoon-tah deh fee-deh-ee-koh-mee-'sah-ree·ohs)*

➤ Schools vary, so fill in the blanks with words of your choice:

It's the director of _____   Es el director del _____ *(ehs ehl dee-rehk-'tohr dehl ___)*

finance   las finanzas *(lahs fee-'nahn-sahs)*
personnel   el personal *(ehl pehr-soh-'nahl)*
special services   los servicios especiales *(lohs sehr-'vee-see·ohs eh-speh-see-'ah-lehs)*

➤ As you are aware, many words in Spanish are very close to their English equivalents. Do you see any patterns?

aide   el ayudante *(ehl ah-yoo-'dahn-teh)*
assistant   el asistente *(ehl ah-see-'stehn-teh)*
associate   el asociado *(ehl ah-soh-see-'ah-doh)*
clerk   el dependiente *(ehl deh-pehn-dee-'ehn-teh)*
consultant   el consultor *(ehl kohn-sool-'tohr)*
facilitator   el facilitador *(ehl fah-see-lee-tah-'dohr)*
leader   el líder *(ehl 'lee-dehr)*
official   el funcionario *(ehl foon-see·oh-'nah-ree·oh)*
operator   el operador *(ehl oh-peh-rah-'dohr)*
secretary   el secretario *(ehl seh-kreh-'tah-ree·oh)*
technician   el técnico *(ehl 'tehk-nee-koh)*

LOTS OF RESPONSIBILITY
Mucha responsabilidad *('moo-chah reh-spohn-sah-bee-lee-'dahd)*

Can you name some of the common duties of a school or district administrator? This is only a sample, so feel free to add to the list:

I'm in charge of (the)...   Estoy encargado/a de... *(eh-'stoh·ee ehn-kahr-'gah-doh / ah deh...)*

announcements   los anuncios *(lohs ah-'noon-see·ohs)*
attendance   la asistencia *(lah ah-see-'stehn-see·ah)*
budget   el presupuesto *(ehl preh-soo-'pweh-stoh)*
contracts   los contratos *(lohs kohn-'trah-tohs)*

curriculum	el plan de estudios *(ehl plahn deh eh-'stoo-dee·ohs)*
discipline	la disciplina *(lah dee-see-'plee-nah)*
food service	la alimentación *(lah ah-lee-mehn-tah-see-'ohn)*
grades	las notas *(lahs 'noh-tahs)*
graduation	la graduación *(lah grah-doo-ah-see-'ohn)*
health care	el cuidado de la salud *(ehl kwee-'dah-doh deh lah sah-'lood)*
maintenance	el mantenimiento *(ehl mahn-teh-nee-mee-'ehn-toh)*
orientation	la orientación *(lah oh-ree-ehn-tah-see-'ohn)*
promotion	la promoción *(lah proh-moh-see-'ohn)*
public relations	las relaciones públicas *(lahs reh-lah-see-'oh-nehs 'poo-blee-kahs)*
registration	la inscripción *(lah een-skreep-see-'ohn)*
security	la seguridad *(lah seh-goo-ree-'dahd)*
supplies	los materiales *(lohs mah-teh-ree-'ah-lehs)*
tech support	el apoyo técnico *(ehl ah-'poh-yoh 'tehk-nee-koh)*
training	el entrenamiento *(ehl ehn-treh-nah-mee-'ehn-toh)*
I work in (the)...	Trabajo en... *(trah-'bah-hoh ehn...)*
city	la ciudad *(lah see-oo-'dahd)*
county	el condado *(ehl kohn-'dah-doh)*
department	el departamento *(ehl deh-pahr-tah-'mehn-toh)*
district	el distrito *(ehl dee-'stree-toh)*
main office	la sede *(lah 'seh-deh)*
region	la región *(lah reh-hee-'ohn)*
I teach at (the)...	Enseño en... *(ehn-'seh-nyoh ehn...)*
conference	la conferencia *(lah kohn-feh-'rehn-see·ah)*
convention	la convención *(lah kohn-vehn-see-'ohn)*
inservice	la práctica *(lah 'prahk-tee-kah)*
seminar	el seminario *(ehl seh-mee-'nah-ree·oh)*
workshop	el entrenamiento *(ehl ehn-treh-nah-mee-'ehn-toh)*
I speak with my...	Hablo con mi/mis... *('ah-bloh kohn mee / mees...)*
employees	empleados *(ehm-pleh-'ah-dohs)*
faculty	facultad *(fah-kool-'tahd)*
staff	personal *(pehr-soh-'nahl)*

➤ Learn everyone's title as introductions are made. Again, make changes if they are females:

He's (the)...   Es... *(ehs...)*

advisor   el consejero *(ehl kohn-seh-'heh-roh)*
mentor   el mentor *(ehl mehn-'tohr)*
neighbor   el vecino *(ehl veh-'see-noh)*
partner   el socio *(ehl 'soh-see·oh)*
sponsor   el patrocinador *(ehl pah-troh-see-nah-'dohr)*

➤ You might be asked to discuss your affiliation:

I'm a member of (the)...   Soy miembro de... *('soh·ee mee-'ehm-broh deh...)*

association   la asociación *(lah ah-soh-see·ah-see-'ohn)*
coalition   la coalición *(lah koh-ah-lee-see-'ohn)*
commission   la comisión *(lah koh-mee-see-'ohn)*
council   el consejo *(ehl kohn-'seh-hoh)*
organization   la organización *(lah ohr-gah-nee-sah-see-'ohn)*

¿LISTOS PARA PRACTICAR?

What do these words mean? Write it down!

La escuela necesita más materiales y el dinero no está en el presupuesto.
(lah eh-'skweh-lah neh-seh-'see-tah mahs mah-teh-ree-'ah-lehs ee ehl dee-'neh-roh noh eh-'stah ehn ehl preh-soo-'pweh-stoh)

_____

Tenemos problemas con la asistencia y disciplina de los estudiantes.
(teh-'neh-mohs proh-'bleh-mahs kohn lah ah-see-'stehn-see·ah ee dee-see-'plee-nah deh lohs eh-stoo-dee-'ahn-tehs)

_____

Me gusta mucho nuestro plan de estudio para el próximo año.
(meh 'goo-stah 'moo-choh 'nweh-stroh plahn deh eh-'stoo-dee·oh 'pah-rah ehl 'prohk-see-moh 'ah-nyoh)

_____

LET'S EVALUATE!

¡Vamos a evaluar! *('vah-mohs ah eh-vah-loo-'ahr)*

One of the primary jobs of the school administrator is to help assess student success. Numerous tools are used for testing, so the Spanish that you'll need may vary. The sample sentences that follow should be useful to anyone who evaluates student progress in school:

We are using (the)...	Estamos usando... *(eh-'stah-mohs oo-'sahn-doh...)*
analysis	el análisis *(ehl ah-'nah-lee-sees)*
check-up	la comprobación *(lah kohm-proh-bah-see·'ohn)*
diagnosis	el diagnóstico *(ehl dee·ahg-'noh-stee-koh)*
evaluation	la evaluación *(lah eh-vah-loo-ah-see·'ohn)*
exam	el examen *(ehl ehk-'sah-mehn)*
follow-up	la continuación *(lah kohn-tee-noo-ah-see·'ohn)*
instrument	el instrumento *(ehl een-stroo-'mehn-toh)*
test	la prueba *(lah proo-'eh-bah)*

It's from the...	Es de... *(ehs deh...)*
college	la universidad *(lah oo-nee-vehr-see-'dahd)*
company	la compañía *(lah kohm-pah-'nyee·ah)*
county	el condado *(ehl kohn-'dah-doh)*
district	el distrito *(ehl dee-'stree-toh)*
government	el gobierno *(ehl goh-bee-'ehr-noh)*
school	la escuela *(lah eh-'skweh-lah)*
state	el estado *(ehl eh-'stah-doh)*

The level is...	El nivel es... *(ehl nee-'vehl ehs...)*
advanced	avanzado *(ah-vahn-'sah-doh)*
average	promedio *(proh-'meh-dee·oh)*
beginning	inicial *(ee-nee-see-'ahl)*
high	alto *('ahl-toh)*
intermediate	intermedio *(een-tehr-'meh-dee·oh)*
low	bajo *('bah-hoh)*

Stay on a roll. All of these words are important:

The purpose is to evaluate...
El propósito es evaluar...
(ehl proh-'poh-see-toh ehs eh-vah-loo-'ahr)

intelligence	la inteligencia *(lah een-teh-lee-'hehn-see·ah)*
knowledge	el conocimiento *(ehl koh-noh-see-mee-'ehn-toh)*
language	el lenguaje *(ehl lehn-'gwah-heh)*
performance	el rendimiento *(ehl rehn-dee-mee-'ehn-toh)*
personality	la personalidad *(lah pehr-soh-nah-lee-'dahd)*
potential	el potencial *(ehl poh-tehn-see-'ahl)*
skill	la habilidad *(lah ah-bee-lee-'dahd)*
strengths	los puntos fuertes *(lohs 'poon-tohs 'fwehr-tehs)*
talent	el talento *(ehl tah-'lehn-toh)*
weaknesses	las debilidades *(lahs deh-bee-lee-'dah-dehs)*

We count (the)...	Contamos... *(kohn-'tah-mohs...)*
credits	los créditos *(lohs 'kreh-dee-tohs)*
grades	las notas *(lahs 'noh-tahs)*
hours	las horas *(lahs 'oh-rahs)*
points	los puntos *(lohs 'poon-tohs)*
units	las unidades *(lahs oo-nee-'dah-dehs)*

I have (the)...	Tengo... *('tehn-goh...)*
answers	las respuestas *(lahs reh-'spweh-stahs)*
data	los datos *(lohs 'dah-tohs)*
information	la información *(lah een-fohr-mah-see·'ohn)*
report card	el boletín de evaluación *(ehl boh-leh-'teen deh eh-vah-loo-ah-see·'ohn)*
results	los resultados *(lohs reh-sool-'tah-dohs)*
scores	las calificaciones *(lahs kah-lee-fee-kah-see·'oh-nehs)*
summary	el resumen *(ehl reh-'soo-mehn)*

Now use these one-liners as you explain the evaluation process to the students and their families:

These are the times and dates.
Estas son las horas y fechas.
('eh-stahs sohn lahs 'on-rahs ee 'feh-chahs)

You have time to prepare.
Tienes tiempo para prepararte.
(tee-'eh-nehs tee-'ehm-poh'pah-rah preh-pah-'rahr-teh)

The evaluation will last...
La evaluación durará...
(lah eh-vah-loo-ah-see-'ohn doo-rah-'rah...)

Let me explain the procedure.
Déjame explicar el procedimiento.
('deh-hah-meh ehks-plee-'kahr ehl proh-seh-dee-mee-'ehn-toh)

It will help the school.
Ayudará a la escuela.
(ah-yoo-dah-'rah ah lah ehs-'kweh-lah)

 MÁS INFORMACIÓN

➤ If you're asked to describe the evaluation, these words will get the message across:

It is...   Es... *(ehs...)*

acceptable	aceptable *(ah-sehp-'tah-bleh)*
cognitive	cognitivo *(kohg-nee-'tee-voh)*
constructive	constructivo *(kohn-strook-'tee-voh)*
convenient	conveniente *(kohn-veh-nee-'ehn-teh)*
critical	crítico *('kree-tee-koh)*
customized	personalizado *(pehr-soh-nah-lee-'sah-doh)*
diagnostic	diagnóstico *(dee·ahg-'noh-stee-koh)*
effective	eficaz *(eh-fee-'kahs)*
fair	justo *('hoo-stoh)*

functional	funcional *(foon-see·oh-'nahl)*
generalized	generalizado *(heh-neh-rah-lee-'sah-doh)*
objective	objetivo *(ohb-heh-'tee-voh)*
optional	opcional *(ohp-see·oh-'nahl)*
positive	positivo *(poh-see-'tee-voh)*
significant	significativo *(seeg-nee-fee-kah-'tee-voh)*
subjective	subjetivo *(soob-heh-'tee-voh)*
transitional	transicional *(trahn-see-see·ohn-'nahl)*

➤ Do you have students who always seem to excel?

They are...	Son... *(sohn...)*

accelerated	avanzados *(ah-vahn-'sah-dohs)*
gifted	talentosos *(tah-lehn-'toh-sohs)*
high-achievers	acelerados *(ah-seh-leh-'rah-dohs)*

➤ Use English when referring to most technology: el software, la internet, la app, etc.

THE TEST
El examen *(ehl ehk-'sah-mehn)*

If some form of testing is part of the evaluation, guide the students carefully through each phase. Try these lines:

Come on this date.	Vengan en esta fecha. *('vehn-gahn ehn'eh-stah 'feh-chah)*
Don't be nervous.	No se pongan nerviosos. *(noh seh 'pohn-gahn nehr-vee-'oh-sohs)*
Don't take too long.	No se demoren mucho. *(noh seh deh-'moh-rehn 'moo-choh)*
Download the program.	Descargue el programa. *(deh-'skahr-geh ehl proh-'grah-mah)*

Just do the best you can. **Háganlo lo mejor que puedan.**
('ah-gahn-loh loh meh-'hohr keh 'pweh-dahn)

You'll receive the results soon. **Recibirán los resultados pronto.**
(reh-see-bee-'rahn lohs reh-sool-'tah-dohs 'prohn-toh)

Now, be helpful, using this vocabulary from previous lessons:

Use (the)...	**Usen...** *('oo-sehn...)*
approach	**el enfoque** *(ehl ehn-'foh-keh)*
method	**el método** *(ehl 'meh-toh-doh)*
model	**el modelo** *(ehl moh-'deh-loh)*
module	**el módulo** *(ehl 'moh-doo-loh)*
principle	**el principio** *(ehl preen-'see-pee·oh)*
strategy	**la estrategia** *(lah eh-strah-'teh-hee·ah)*
technique	**la técnica** *(lah 'tehk-nee-kah)*

Look at (the)...	**Miren...** *('mee-rehn...)*
examples	**los ejemplos** *(lohs eh-'hehm-plohs)*
instructions	**las instrucciones** *(lahs een-strook-see-'oh-nehs)*
questions	**las preguntas** *(lahs preh-'goon-tahs)*

Esta es una evaluación diagnóstica crítica con el objetivo funcional de tener información constructiva, eficaz y justa.

Continue to explain, but this time get some feedback from everyone about the evaluation. Keep it simple with the patterns shown:

Are you...?	**¿Estás...?** *(eh-'stahs...)*
capable	**capacitado/a** *(kah-pah-see-'tah-doh / ah)*
interested	**interesado/a** *(een-teh-reh-'sah-doh / ah)*

motivated	motivado/a *(moh-tee-'vah-doh / ah)*
optimistic	optimista *(ohp-tee-'mee-stah)*
prepared	preparado/a *(preh-pah-'rah-doh / ah)*
satisfied	satisfecho/a *(sah-tees-'feh-choh / ah)*

 MÁS INFORMACIÓN

➤ Very technical words will be required, so keep a few nearby:

data collection	el banco de datos *(ehl 'bahn-koh deh 'dah-tohs)*
learning curve	la curva de aprendizaje *(lah 'koor-vah deh ah-prehn-dee-'sah-heh)*
pre-test	el pre-examen *(ehl preh-ehk-'sah-mehn)*
post-test	el post-examen *(ehl pohst-ehk-'sah-mehn)*
time frame	el lapso de tiempo *(ehl 'lahp-soh deh tee-'ehm-poh)*
top priority	la prioridad máxima *(lah pree·oh-ree-'dahd 'makh-see-mah)*
track record	el récord de trabajo *(ehl 'reh-kohrd deh trah-'bah-hoh)*
workload	la cantidad de trabajo *(lah kahn-tee-'dahd deh trah-'bah-hoh)*

➤ Watch for word patterns.

cooperation	la cooperación *(lah koh-oh-peh-rah-see·'ohn)*
correction	la corrección *(lah koh-rrehk-see·'ohn)*
implementation	la implementación *(lah eem-pleh-mehn-tah-see·'ohn)*
initiation	la iniciación *(lah ee-nee-see·ah-see·'ohn)*
integration	la integración *(lah een-teh-grah-see·'ohn)*
limitation	la limitación *(lah lee-mee-tah-see·'ohn)*

observation	la observación
	(lah ohb-sehr-vah-see-'ohn)
preparation	la preparación
	(lah preh-pah-rah-see-'ohn)
satisfaction	la satisfacción
	(lah sah-tees-fahk-see-'ohn)
specification	la especificación
	(lah eh-speh-see-fee-kah-see-'ohn)

➤ But stay alert—not every word follows the rule

competition	la competencia *(lah kohm-peh-'tehn-see·ah)*
examination	el examen *(ehl ehk-'sah-mehn)*
expectation	la esperanza *(lah eh-speh-'rahn-sah)*

TELL US THE RESULTS!
¡Díganos los resultados! *('dee-gah-nohs lohs reh-sool-'tah-dohs)*

In many cases, the administrator must share the evaluation with students and their families. When you speak Spanish, sometimes only a few brief comments are all that's required to get your messages across. Here are the patterns.

Begin with a group of positive action words. Notice how the word le *(leh)* can refer to "you":

I would like to _____you.	Quisiera ____. *(kee-see-'eh-rah)*
assure	asegurarle *(ah-seh-goo-'rahr-leh)*
commend	alabarle *(ah-lah-'bahr-leh)*
compliment	felicitarle *(feh-lee-see-'tahr-leh)*
encourage	animarle *(ah-nee-'mahr-leh)*
motivate	motivarle *(moh-tee-'vahr-leh)*
persuade	persuadirle *(pehr-swah-'deer-leh)*
reward	recompensarle *(reh-kohm-pehn-'sahr-leh)*
support	apoyarle *(ah-poh-'yahr-leh)*
thank	agradecerle *(ah-grah-deh-'sehr-leh)*

Your post-evaluation meeting could last awhile, so don't run out of things to say:

I'm going to...	**Voy a...** *('voh·ee ah)*

clarify	**clarificar** *(klah-ree-fee-'kahr)*
confirm	**confirmar** *(kohn-feer-'mahr)*
explain	**explicar** *(ehk-splee-'kahr)*
identify	**identificar** *(ee-dehn-tee-fee-'kahr)*
suggest	**sugerir** *(soo-heh-'reer)*

If you need to reveal specific test results, try out the following key terms:

It's acceptable	**Es aceptable** *(ehs ah-sehp-'tah-bleh)*
It's adequate	**Es adecuado** *(ehs ah-deh-'kwah-doh)*
It's appropriate	**Es apropiado** *(ehs ah-proh-pee-'ah-doh)*
It's approved	**Está aprobado** *(eh-'stah ah-proh-'bah-doh)*
It's better	**Está mejor** *(eh-'stah meh-'hohr)*
It's correct	**Está correcto** *(eh-'stah koh-'rrehk-toh)*
It's excellent	**Es excelente** *(ehs ehk-seh-'lehn-teh)*
It's good	**Es bueno** *(ehs 'bweh-noh)*
It's high	**Es alto** *(ehs 'ahl-toh)*
It's more	**Es más** *(ehs mahs)*
It's outstanding	**Es fantástico** *(ehs fahn-'tah-stee-koh)*
It's satisfactory	**Está satisfactorio** *(eh-'stah sah-tees-fahk-'toh-ree·oh)*

It's (the)...	**Es...** *(ehs...)*

average	**el promedio** *(ehl proh-'meh-dee·oh)*
maximum	**el máximo** *(ehl 'mahk-see-moh)*
minimum	**el mínimo** *(ehl 'mee-nee-moh)*

Unfortunately, the results aren't always positive:

It's less than expected.	**Es menos de lo esperado.** *(ehs 'meh-nohs deh loh eh-speh-'rah-doh)*
It's a low result.	**Es un resultado bajo.** *(ehs oon reh-sool-'tah-doh 'bah-hoh)*

It's unacceptable.	**Es inaceptable.**
	(ehs een-ah-sehp-'tah-bleh)
It's incorrect.	**Está incorrecto.**
	(eh-'stah een-koh-'rrehk-toh)
poor	**Está mal.**
	(eh-'stah mahl)
worse	**Está peor.**
	(eh-'stah peh-'ohr)

MÁS INFORMACIÓN

➤ The verb, "to make a mistake" is **equivocarse** *(eh-kee-voh-'kahr-seh)*:

You make mistakes sometimes.
A veces te equivocas.
(ah 'veh-sehs teh eh-kee-'voh-kahs)

➤ Here are more words and phrases that deal with assessments:

I agree.	**Estoy de acuerdo.**
	(eh-'stoh·ee deh ah-'kwehr-doh)
I disagree.	**No estoy de acuerdo.** *(noh eh-'stoh·ee deh*
	ah-'kwehr-doh)
It needs improvement.	**Necesita mejorar.**
	(neh-seh-'see-tah meh-hoh-'rahr)
There were a lot of mistakes.	**Había muchos errores.**
	(ah-'bee·ah 'moo-chohs eh-'rroh-rehs)

¿LISTOS PARA PRACTICAR?

Connect the words that are similar in meaning:

el examen *(ehl ehk-'sah-mehn)*   **la universidad**   *(lah oo-nee-vehr-see-'dahd)*

la habilidad *(lah ah-bee-lee-'dahd)*   **el técnico** *(ehl 'tehk-nee-koh)*

el método *(ehl 'meh-toh-doh)*   **la respuesta** *(lah reh-'spweh-stah)*

el crédito *(ehl 'kreh-dee-toh)*
la escuela *(lah eh-'skweh-lah)*
el resultado *(ehl reh-sool-'tah-doh)*

la unidad *(lah oo-nee-'dahd)*
la prueba *(lah proo-'eh-bah)*
el talento *(ehl tah-'lehn-toh)*

You know what to do here. Simply follow the example:

encourage	Quisiera animarte. *(kee-see-'eh-rah ah-nee-'mahr-teh)*
thank	_____
commend	_____
tell	_____

TO BE ON DUTY

Estar de servicio *(eh-'stahr deh sehr-'vee-see·oh)*

Many administrators also are responsible for campus control. Let's break our new Spanish phrases into areas where students generally tend to congregate. See if you can find any familiar patterns that can be used just about anywhere:

In the Halls	En los corredores *(ehn lohs koh-rreh-'doh-rehs)*
Stay in line.	Quédense en fila. *('keh-dehn-seh ehn 'fee-lah)*
Keep to the right.	Quédense a la derecha. *('keh-dehn-seh ah lah deh-'reh-chah)*
Remain quiet.	Quédense quietos. *('keh-dehn-seh kee-'eh-tohs)*
Don't push.	No empujen. *(noh ehm-'poo-hehn)*
Don't run.	No corran. *(noh 'koh-rrahn)*
Don't yell.	No griten. *(noh 'gree-tehn)*
Please put those away.	Favor de guardar las cosas. *(fah-'vohr deh gwahr-'dahr lahs 'koh-sahs)*
Please don't touch the doors.	Favor de no tocar las puertas. *(fah-'vohr deh noh toh-'kahr lahs 'pwehr-tahs)*
Please hurry up.	Favor de apurarse. *(fah-'vohr deh ah-poo-'rahr-seh)*

Where are you going?	¿Adónde van? *(ah-'dohn-deh vahn)*
Where is your teacher?	¿Dónde está su maestro? *('dohn-deh eh-'stah soo mah-'eh-stroh)*
Where are you coming from?	¿De dónde vienen? *(deh 'dohn-deh vee-'eh-nehn)*

In the Restrooms

En los cuartos de baño
(ehn lohs 'kwahr-tohs deh 'bah-nyoh)

Go before class.	Vayan antes de la clase. *('vah-yahn 'ahn-tehs deh lah 'klah-seh)*
Go to your classes.	Vayan a sus clases. *('vah-yahn ah soos 'klah-sehs)*
Go quickly.	Vayan rápido. *('vah-yahn 'rah-pee-doh)*
Put the paper in the toilet.	Pongan el papel en el excusado. *('pohn-gahn ehl pah-'pehl ehn ehl ehk-skoo-'sah-doh)*
Put the soap on the sink.	Pongan el jabón en el lavabo. *('pohn-gahn ehl hah-'bohn ehn ehl lah-'vah-boh)*
Put the trash in the can.	Pongan la basura en el bote. *('pohn-gahn lah bah-'soo-rah ehn ehl 'boh-teh)*
Flush the toilet, please.	Descarguen el agua, por favor. *(dehs-'kahr-gehn ehl 'ah-gwah, pohr fah-'vohr)*
Turn off the water, please.	Cierren el agua, por favor. *(see-'eh-rrehn ehl 'ah-gwah pohr fah-'vohr)*
Close the door, please.	Cierren la puerta, por favor. *(see-'eh-rehn lah 'pwehr-tah, pohr fah-'vohr)*
Who is inside?	¿Quién está dentro? *(kee-'ehn eh-'stah 'dehn-troh)*
Who did this?	¿Quién hizo esto? *(kee-'ehn 'ee-soh 'eh-stoh)*
Who turned off the light?	¿Quién apagó la luz? *(kee-'ehn ah-pah-'goh lah loos)*

In the Lunch Area

En el comedor *(ehn ehl koh-meh-'dohr)*

You need to line up.	Necesitan hacer fila. *(neh-seh-'see-tahn ah-'sehr 'fee-lah)*

You need to have tickets.	Necesitan tener boletos. (*neh-seh-'see-tahn teh-'nehr boh-'leh-tohs*)
You need to pay.	Necesitan pagar. (*neh-seh-'see-tahn pah-'gahr*)
Wait for your turn.	Esperen su turno. (*eh-'speh-rehn soo 'toor-noh*)
Wait for the bell.	Esperen hasta que suene el timbre. (*eh-'speh-rehn 'ah-stah keh 'sweh-neh ehl 'teem-breh*)
Wait for your class.	Esperen su clase. (*eh-'speh-rehn soo 'klah-seh*)
You are dismissed.	Pueden irse. (*'pweh-dehn 'eer-seh*)
You can clear the table.	Pueden limpiar la mesa. (*'pweh-dehn leem-pee-'ahr lah 'meh-sah*)
You can bring your lunch.	Pueden traer su almuerzo. (*'pweh-dehn trah-'ehr soo ahl-moo-'ehr-soh*)
Pick up the food.	Recojan la comida. (*reh-'koh-hahn lah koh-'mee-dah*)
Pick up the trash.	Recojan la basura. (*reh-'koh-hahn lah bah-'soo-rah*)
Pick up the drinks.	Recojan las bebidas. (*reh-'koh-hahn lahs beh-'bee-dahs*)
There is a lunch pass.	Hay un pase para almorzar afuera. (*ah·ee oon 'pah-seh 'pah-rah ahl-mohr-'sahr ah-'fweh-rah*)
There is a free lunch.	Hay un almuerzo gratis. (*ah·ee oon ahl-moo-'ehr-soh 'grah-tees*)
There is a sack lunch.	Hay un almuerzo en bolsa. (*ah·ee oon ahl-moo-'ehr-soh ehn 'bohl-sah*)
On the Playground	**En el campo de recreo** (*ehn ehl 'kahm-poh deh reh-'kreh-oh*)
Talk to the team captain.	Hablen con el capitán del equipo. (*'ah-blehn kohn ehl kah-pee-'tahn dehl eh-'kee-poh*)
Talk to the teacher.	Hablen con el maestro. (*'ah-blehn kohn ehl mah-'eh-stroh*)
Talk to the coach.	Hablen con el entrenador. (*'ah-blehn kohn ehl ehn-treh-nah-'dohr*)
Why aren't you playing?	¿Por qué no están jugando? (*pohr keh noh eh-'stahn hoo-'gahn-doh*)

Why are you fighting?	¿Por qué están peleando? *(pohr keh eh-'stahn peh-leh-'ahn-doh)*
Why are you crying?	¿Por qué están llorando? *(pohr keh eh-'stahn yoh-'rahn-doh)*
They're going to choose teams.	Van a escoger miembros del equipo. *(vahn ah ehs-koh-'hehr mee-'ehm-brohs dehl eh-'kee-poh)*
They're going to win.	Van a ganar. *(vahn ah gah-'nahr)*
They're going to play there.	Van a jugar ahí. *(vahn ah hoo-'gahr ah-'ee)*
You should go to the office.	Deben ir a la oficina. *('deh-behn eer ah lah oh-fee-'see-nah)*
You should go to the nurse.	Deben ir a la enfermera. *('deh-behn eer ah lah ehn-fehr-'meh-rah)*
You should go to the class.	Deben ir a la clase. *('deh-behn eer ah lah 'klah-seh)*

MÁS INFORMACIÓN

➤ Use brief phrases to give informal commands:

Stop it!	¡No hagas eso! *(noh 'ah-gahs 'eh-soh)*
Don't be late!	¡No llegues tarde! *(noh 'yeh-gehs 'tahr-deh)*
Come here!	¡Ven aquí! *(vehn ah-'kee)*

➤ Notice this pattern:

Keep moving.	Sigan caminando. *('see-gahn kah-mee-'nahn-doh)*
Keep studying.	Sigan estudiando. *('see-gahn eh-stoo-dee-'ahn-doh)*
Keep working.	Sigan trabajando. *('see-gahn trah-bah-'hahn-doh)*

➤ Refer to your English in an emergency:

Give me your ____	Dame tu ____

iPad, laptop, cell phone, etc.

➤ Do you know what to say when suspicious characters wander onto school property?

Are you visiting?	¿Está visitando? *(eh-'stah vee-see-'tahn-doh)*
Do you have an appointment?	¿Tiene una cita? *(tee-'eh-neh 'oo-nah 'see-tah)*
Who are you waiting for?	¿Por quién está esperando? *(pohr kee-'ehn eh-'stah eh-speh-'rahn-doh)*

You cannot stay on school property.
No puedes quedarte en el terreno de la escuela. *(noh 'pweh-dehs keh-'dahr-teh ehn ehl teh-'rreh-noh deh lah eh-'skweh-lah)*

You have to leave now.
Tienes que irte ahora. *(tee-'eh-nehs keh 'eer-teh ah-'oh-rah)*

You need to show me identification.
Necesitas mostrarme identificación. *(neh-seh-'see-tahs mohs-'trahr-meh ee-dehn-tee-fee-kah-see-'ohn)*

 ## ¿LISTOS PARA PRACTICAR?

Try out your new Spanish skills all around the campus!

Give three commands to children who are moving through a school hallway:

_____ _____ _____

Give three commands to children who are crowded in a school bathroom:

_____ _____ _____

Give three commands to children who are having lunch in a school cafeteria:

_____ _____ _____

SERIOUS PROBLEMS
Los problemas serios *(lohs proh-'bleh-mahs 'seh-ree·ohs)*

Perhaps the toughest job for school officials is dealing with on-site emergencies and disasters. Not only is a lot of preparation required, but there's no guarantee that everything will run smoothly. Here's a list of events that demands an immediate response:

We had a/an...	Tuvimos un/una... *(too-'vee-mohs oon / 'oo-nah...)*
blackout	apagón *(ah-pah-'gohn)*
bomb	bomba *('bohm-bah)*
car accident	accidente de carro *(ahk-see-'dehn-teh deh 'kah-rroh)*
chemical spill	derrame de sustancia química *(deh-'rrah-meh deh soo-'stahn-see·ah 'kee-mee-kah)*
explosion	explosión *(ehk-sploh-see-'ohn)*
fire	incendio *(een-'sehn-dee·oh)*
overdose	sobredosis *(soh-breh-'doh-sees)*
raid	incursión *(een-koor-see-'ohn)*
rape	violación *(vee·oh-lah-see-'ohn)*
riot	disturbio *(dee-'stoor-bee·oh)*
robbery	robo *('roh-boh)*
shooting	disparo *(dee-'spah-roh)*
stabbing	puñalada *(poo-nyah-'lah-dah)*
strike	huelga *('wehl-gah)*
suicide	suicidio *(soo-ee-'see-dee·oh)*
threat	amenaza *(ah-meh-'nah-sah)*

There is/are...	Hay... *('ah·ee...)*
a strange package	un paquete raro *(oon pah-'keh-teh 'rah-roh)*
flames	llamas *('yah-mahs)*
fumes	vapores *(vah-'poh-rehs)*
gas	gas *(gahs)*
poison	veneno *(veh-'neh-noh)*
smoke	humo *('oo-moh)*
toxic materials	materiales tóxicos *(mah-teh-ree-'ah-lehs 'tohk-see-kohs)*

Is everything secured? For safety purposes, these things should be memorized also:

Always use (the)...	Siempre usa... *(see-'ehm-preh 'oo-sah)*
alarm	la alarma *(lah ah-'lahr-mah)*
chain	la cadena *(lah kah-'deh-nah)*
deadbolt	el pestillo *(ehl peh-'stee-yoh)*
key	la llave *(lah 'yah-veh)*
latch	el cerrojo *(ehl seh-'rroh-hoh)*
lock	la cerradura *(lah seh-rrah-'doo-rah)*
padlock	el candado *(ehl kahn-'dah-doh)*
safe	la caja fuerte *(lah 'kah-hah 'fwehr-teh)*
shelter	el refugio *(ehl reh-'foo-hee·oh)*

Now post labels in both languages on each piece of emergency equipment in your building. Check out the examples:

Use (the)...	Usa... *('oo-sah...)*
binoculars	los binoculares *(lohs bee-noh-koo-'lah-rehs)*
candle	la vela *(la 'veh-lah)*
cone	el cono *(ehl 'koh-noh)*
fire extinguisher	el extintor *(ehl ehks-teen-'tohr)*
first aid kit	el botiquín de primeros auxilios *(ehl boh-tee-'keen deh pree-'meh-rohs owk-'see-lee·ohs)*
flare	la luz de bengala *(lah loos deh behn-'gah-lah)*
flashlight	la linterna *(lah leen-'tehr-nah)*
gloves	los guantes *(lohs 'gwahn-tehs)*
hand radio	el radio de mano *(ehl 'rah-dee·oh deh 'mah-noh)*
helmet	el casco *(ehl 'kahs-koh)*
hose	la manguera *(lah mahn-'geh-rah)*
hydrant	la llave de agua *(lah 'yah-veh deh 'ah-gwah)*
masks	las máscaras *(lahs 'mah-skah-rahs)*
matches	los fósforos *(lohs 'fohs-foh-rohs)*
vest	el chaleco *(ehl chah-'leh-koh)*

Let's talk about (the)...	**Vamos a hablar de...** *('vah-mohs ah ah-'blahr deh...)*
exercise	**el ejercicio** *(ehl eh-hehr-'see-see·oh)*
instructions	**las instrucciones** *(lahs een-strook-see-'oh-nehs)*
phases	**las etapas** *(lahs eh-'tah-pahs)*
plan	**el plan** *(ehl plahn)*
procedures	**los procedimientos** *(lohs proh-seh-dee-mee-'ehn-tohs)*
steps	**los pasos** *(lohs 'pah-sohs)*
system	**el sistema** *(ehl see-'steh-mah)*
Listen to (the)...	**Escucha a...** *(eh-'skoo-chah ah...)*
alarm	**la alarma** *(lah ah-'lahr-mah)*
bell	**la campana** *(lah kahm-'pah-nah)*
bulletin	**el anuncio** *(ehl ah-'noon-see·oh)*
buzzer	**el timbre** *(ehl 'teem-breh)*
code	**el código** *(ehl 'koh-dee-goh)*
drill	**el simulacro** *(ehl see-moo-'lah-kroh)*
horn	**la bocina** *(lah boh-'see-nah)*
report	**el reporte** *(ehl reh-'pohr-teh)*
signal	**la señal** *(lah seh-'nyahl)*
siren	**la sirena** *(lah see-'reh-nah)*
warning	**la advertencia** *(lah ahd-vehr-'tehn-see·ah)*
whistle	**el silbato** *(ehl seel-'bah-toh)*

 MÁS INFORMACIÓN

➤ Emergency vocabulary could be used to save lives, so don't treat this list lightly:

capacity	**la capacidad** *(lah kah-pah-see-'dahd)*
caution	**la advertencia** *(lah ahd-vehr-'tehn-see·ah)*
danger	**el peligro** *(ehl peh-'lee-groh)*
emergency	**la emergencia** *(lah eh-mehr-'hehn-see·ah)*
rescue	**el rescate** *(ehl reh-'skah-teh)*

safety	**la seguridad** *(lah seh-goo-ree-'dahd)*
threat	**la amenaza** *(lah ah-meh-'nah-sah)*
There is...	**Hay...***('ah ee)*
a broken elevator	**un ascensor quebrado** *(oon ah-sehn-'sohr keh-'brah-doh)*
a gang fight	**una pelea entre pandillas** *('oo-nah pe-'leh-ah 'ehn-treh pahn-'dee-yahs)*
a family dispute	**una disputa de familia** *('oo-nah dees-'poo-tah deh fah-'mee-lee·ah)*
a lost child	**un niño perdido** *(oon 'neen-yoh pehr-'dee-doh)*
someone in a parked car	**alguien en un carro estacionado** *('ahl-ghee-ehn ehn oon 'kahr-roh ehs-tah-see·oh-'nah-doh)*
someone hiding on campus	**alguien escondiéndose en la escuela** *('ahl-ghee-ehn ehs-kohn-dee-'ehn-doh-she ehn lah ehs-koo-'eh-lah)*
someone selling drugs	**alguien vendiendo drogas** *('ahl-ghee-ehn vehn-dee-'ehn-doh 'droh-gahs)*

Neighborhood pets establish a unique set of problems for school officials:

It needs a leash.	**Necesita una correa.** *(neh-she-'see-tah oo-nah kohr-'reh-ah)*
You have to clean up its mess.	**Tiene que limpiar el excremento.** *(tee-'eh-neh keh leem-pee-'ahr ehl ehks-kreh-'mehn-toh)*
It's lost.	**Está perdido.** *(ehs-'tah pehr-'dee-doh)*
It is ferocious and dangerous.	**Es feroz y peligroso.** *(ehs feh-'rohs ee peh-lee-'groh-soh)*
Dogs are not allowed.	**Los perros están prohibidos.** *(lohs 'pehr-rohs ehs-'tahn pro-hee-'bee-dohs)*

➤ Stick with an easy pattern:

evacuation	**la evacuación** *(lah eh-vah-koo-ah-see·'ohn)*
precaution	**la precaución** *(lah preh-kow-see·'ohn)*
preparation	**la preparación** *(lah preh-pah-rah-see·'ohn)*
prevention	**la prevención** *(lah preh-vehn-see·'ohn)*
protection	**la protección** *(lah proh-tehk-see·'ohn)*

➤ Try to put your new words together. All of these expressions will be useful:

emergency exit	**la salida de emergencia** *(lah sah-'lee-dah deh eh-mehr-'hehn-see·ah)*
evacuation procedure	**el plan de evacuación** *(ehl plahn deh eh-vah-koo-ah-see·'ohn)*
rescue team	**el equipo de rescate** *(ehl eh-'kee-poh deh reh-'skah-teh)*
room capacity	**la capacidad del salón** *(lah kah-pah-see-'dahd dehl sah-'lohn)*
safety manual	**el manual de seguridad** *(ehl mah-noo-'ahl deh seh-goo-ree-'dahd)*

DIFERENCIAS CULTURALES

Did your student just move to this country? Is he or she confused about our language and culture? When you find the time, share a few insights on U.S. customs toward campus life, dress, dining, holidays, and social skills. Make them feel welcome by respecting their perspective and watch your relationship grow!

NATURAL DISASTERS
Los desastres naturales *(lohs deh-'sah-strehs nah-too-'rah-lehs)*

Instruction is often disrupted by Mother Nature. When you have to battle the elements, talk about the situation **en español** *(ehn eh-spah-'nyohl)*:

The school is closed today.	**La escuela está cerrada hoy.** *(lah eh-'skweh-lah eh-'stah seh-'rrah-dah-oh·ee)*
It was (the)...	**Fue...** *(fweh...)*

earthquake	**el terremoto** *(ehl teh-rreh-'moh-toh)*
flood	**la inundación** *(lah een-oon-dah-see·'ohn)*
frost	**la escarcha** *(lah eh-'skahr-chah)*
hail	**el granizo** *(ehl grah-'nee-soh)*
hurricane	**el huracán** *(ehl oo-rah-'kahn)*
ice	**el hielo** *(ehl 'yeh-loh)*

landslide	**el desprendimiento de tierra** *(ehl dehs-prehn-dee-mee-'ehn-toh deh tee-'eh-rrah)*
rain	**la lluvia** *(lah 'yoo-vee·ah)*
sleet	**el aguanieve** *(ehl ah-gwah-nee-'eh-veh)*
snow	**la nieve** *(lah nee-'eh-veh)*
storm	**la tormenta** *(lah tohr-'mehn-tah)*
tornado	**el tornado** *(ehl tohr-'nah-doh)*
wind	**el viento** *(ehl vee-'ehn-toh)*

When foul weather strikes, you may have to mention a few medical concerns:

It's...	**Es...** *(ehs...)*
a heart attack	**un ataque cardíaco** *(oon ah-'tah-keh kahr-'dee·ah-koh)*
dehydration	**deshidratación** *(lah dehs-ee-drah-tah-see-'ohn)*
frostbite	**congelamiento** *(kohn-heh-lah-mee-'ehn-toh)*
heatstroke	**postración** *(poh-strah-see-'ohn)*
sunstroke	**insolación** *(een-soh-lah-see-'ohn)*

HELP ME!
¡Ayúdeme! *(ah-'yoo-deh-meh)*

If the emergency situation persists, chances are someone is going to get hurt. Do you know enough Spanish to lend a hand?

He/She is...	**Está...** *(eh-'stah...)*
bleeding	**sangrando** *(sahn-'grahn-doh)*
choking	**asfixiándose** *(ahs-feek-see-'ahn-doh-seh)*

drowning	ahogándose *(ah-oh-'gahn-doh-seh)*
dying	muriéndose *(moo-ree-'ehn-doh-seh)*
inebriated	ebrio/a *('eh-bree·oh / ah)*
intoxicated	intoxicado/a *(eeu-toks-ee-'kah-doh / ah)*
unconscious	inconsciente *(een-kohn-see-'ehn-teh)*
Call (the)...	Llame a... *('ya-meh ah)*
911	el nueve-uno-uno *(ehl noo-'eh-veh 'oo-noh 'oo-noh)*
ambulance	la ambulancia *(lah ahm-boo-'lahn-see·ah)*
clinic	la clínica *(lah 'klee-nee-kah)*
dentist	el dentista *(ehl dehn-'tee-stah)*
doctor	el doctor *(ehl dohk-'tohr)*
fire department	el departamento de bomberos *(ehl deh-pahr-tah-'mehn-toh deh bohm-'beh-rohs)*
home	la casa *(lah 'kah-sah)*
hospital	el hospital *(ehl oh-spee-'tahl)*
neighbor	el vecino *(ehl veh-'see-noh)*
office	la oficina *(lah oh-fee-'see-nah)*
operator	la operadora *(lah oh-'peh-rah-'doh-rah)*
paramedic	el paramédico *(ehl pah-rah-'meh-dee-koh)*
pharmacy	la farmacia *(lah fahr-'mah-see·ah)*
police	la policía *(lah poh-lee-'see·ah)*
relative	el pariente *(ehl pah-ree-'ehn-teh)*
tow truck	la grúa *(lah 'groo-ah)*

MÁS INFORMACIÓN

➤ In extreme circumstances, use these command phrases:

Cover yourselves!	¡Cúbranse! *('koo-brahn-seh)*
Danger!	¡Peligro! *(peh-'lee-groh)*
Fire!	¡Fuego! *('fweh-goh)*
Get under the table!	¡Pónganse debajo de la mesa! *('pohn-gahn-seh deh-'bah-hoh deh lah'meh-sah)*
Help!	¡Socorro! *(soh-'koh-rroh)*
Run outside!	¡Corran hacia afuera! *('koh-rrahn 'ah-see·ah ah-'fweh-rah)*
Be careful!	¡Tengan cuidado! *('tehn-gahn kwee-'dah-doh)*

| Stay away from the windows! | ¡Quédense lejos de las ventanas! *('keh-dehn-seh 'leh-hohs deh lahs vehn-'tah-nahs)* |
| Watch out! | ¡Ojo! *('oh-hoh)* |

➤ Local rescue organizations may need to be contacted. Tell the community who's coming to help:

Civil Defense	la Milicia Civil *(lah mee-'lee-see·ah see-'veel)*
National Guard	la Guardia Nacional *(lah 'gwahr-dee·ah nah-see·oh-'nahl)*
Red Cross	la Cruz Roja *(lah kroos 'roh-hah)*

¿LISTOS PARA PRACTICAR?

Choose the *best* word to complete each sentence below:

plan, paramédico, lluvia, campana, cadena, humo *(plahn, pah-rah-'meh-dee-koh, 'yoo-vee·ah, kahm-'pah-nah, kah-'deh-nah, 'oo-moh)*

El incendio tiene _____. *(ehl een-'sehn-dee·oh tee-'eh-neh ____)*

El candado tiene _____. *(ehl kahn-'dah-doh tee-'eh-neh ____)*

El ejercicio tiene _____. *(ehl eh-hehr-'see-see·oh tee-'eh-neh ____)*

La tormenta tiene _____. *(lah tohr-'mehn-tah tee-'eh-neh ____)*

La ambulancia tiene _____. *(lah ahm-boo-'lahn-see·ah tee-'eh-neh ____)*

La clase tiene _____. *(lah 'klah-seh tee-'eh-neh ____)*

What would you shout in Spanish if there were a fire?

¡_____!

IT'S A CRIME!

¡Es un crimen! *(ehs oon 'kree-mehn)*

At some schools, administrators are in a battle with campus crime. For the protection of all students and their families, let the Spanish-speaking public know exactly what the situation is:

He was arrested for (the)...	Fue arrestado por... *(fweh ah-rreh-'stah-doh pohr)*
abuse	el abuso *(ehl ah-'boo-soh)*
arson	el incendio premeditado *(ehl een-'sehn-dee·oh preh-meh-dee-'tah-doh)*
assault	el asalto *(ehl ah-'sahl-toh)*
battery	la agresión *(lah ah-greh-see·'ohn)*
counterfeiting	la falsificación *(lah fahl-see-fee-kah-see·'ohn)*
drugs	las drogas *(lahs 'droh-gahs)*
drunkenness	la embriaguez *(lah ehm-bree·ah-'gehs)*
embezzling	el desfalco *(ehl dehs-'fahl-koh)*
extortion	la extorsión *(lah ehks-tohr-see·'ohn)*
firearm	la arma de fuego *(lah 'ahr-mah deh foo-'eh-goh)*
fraud	el fraude *(ehl 'frow-deh)*
gambling	los juegos de apuestas *(ehl 'hweh-gohs deh ah-'pweh-stahs)*
hacking	la piratería *(lah pee-rah-teh-'ree·ah)*
harassment	el acoso *(ehl ah-'koh-soh)*
hate crime	el crimen de odio *(ehl 'kree-mehn deh 'oh-dee·oh)*
hijacking	el robo en tránsito *(lohs 'roh-boh ehn 'trahn-see-toh)*
kidnapping	el secuestro *(ehl seh-'kweh-stroh)*
larceny	el hurto *(ehl 'oor-toh)*
manslaughter	el homicidio involuntario *(ehl oh-mee-'see-dee·oh een-voh-loon-'tah-ree·oh)*
possession of	la posesión de *(lah poh-seh-see·'ohn deh)*
robbery	el robo *(ehl 'roh-boh)*
vandalism	el vandalismo *(ehl vahn-dah-'lees-moh)*

These crimes are related to sex:

It was...	Fue... *(fweh...)*
incest	el incesto *(ehl een-'seh-stoh)*
lewd behavior	el comportamiento indecente *(ehl kohm-pohr-tah-mee-'ehn-toh een-deh-'sehn-teh)*
molestation	el abuso sexual *(ehl ah-'boo-soh sehk-soo-'ahl)*
obscene phone calls	las llamadas obscenas *(lahs yah-'mah-dahs ohb-'seh-nahs)*
pornography	la pornografía *(lah pohr-noh-grah-'fee·ah)*
prostitution	la prostitución *(lah proh-stee-too-see-'ohn)*
rape	la violación *(lah vee·oh-lah-see-'ohn)*
solicitation	la incitación *(lah een-see-tah-see-'ohn)*
stalking	el acecho *(ehl ah-'seh-choh)*

If you have the legal authority, you should now have enough language to make the arrest:

I am going to...	Voy a... *('voh·ee ah...)*
arrest you	arrestarlo *(ah-rreh-'stahr-loh)*
frisk you	registrarlo *(reh-hee-'strahr-loh)*
handcuff you	esposarlo *(eh-spoh-'sahr-loh)*
use a police dog	usar un perro policía *(oo-'sahr oon 'peh-rroh poh-lee-'see·ah)*

When a child's behavior is headed in the wrong direction, some of these words and phrases surface in conversation. Take the ones you need:

We talked about (the)...	Hablamos de... *(ah-'blah-mohs deh...)*
community service	el servicio para la comunidad *(ehl sehr-'vee-see·oh 'pah-rah lah koh-moo-nee-'dahd)*

continuation school	la escuela secundaria especial *(lah eh-'skweh-lah seh-koon-'dah-ree·ah eh-speh-see- 'ahl)*
county jail	la cárcel del condado *(lah 'kahr-sehl dehl kohn-'dah-doh)*
federal prison	la prisión federal *(lah pree-see·'ohn feh-deh-'rahl)*
felony	el delito mayor *(ehl deh-'lee-toh mah-'yohr)*
juvenile court	la corte de menores *(lah 'kohr-teh deh meh-'noh-rehs)*
lawsuit	el pleito *(ehl 'pleh·ee-toh)*
legal aid	la ayuda legal *(lah ah-'yoo-dah leh-'gahl)*
misdemeanor	el delito menor *(ehl deh-'lee-toh meh-'nohr)*
parole	la libertad bajo palabra *(lah lee-behr-'tahd 'bah-hoh pah-'lah-brah)*
penitentiary	la penitenciaría *(lah peh-nee-tehn-see·ah-'ree·ah)*
probation officer	el agente encargado de la libertad provisional *(ehl ah-'hehn-teh ehn-kahr-'gah-doh deh lah lee- behr-'tahd proh-vee-see·oh-'nahl)*
reformatory	el reformatorio *(ehl reh-fohr-mah-'toh-ree·oh)*
rehabilitation	la rehabilitación *(lah reh-ah-bee-lee-tah-see·'ohn)*
state prison	la prisión del estado *(lah pree-see·'ohn dehl eh-'stah-doh)*

MÁS INFORMACIÓN

➤ Kids may be drinking these on school property:

beer	la cerveza *(lah sehr-'veh-sah)*
liquor	el licor *(ehl lee-'kohr)*
wine	el vino *(ehl 'vee-noh)*

DRUG ABUSE
El abuso de las drogas *(ehl ah-'boo-soh deh lahs 'droh-gahs)*

Does the crime involve drugs? Here are a few that you may hear about. Most look a lot like English:

He/She had (the)   Tenía... *(teh-'nee·ah...)*

acid   el ácido *(ehl 'ah-see-doh)*
amphetamine   la anfetamina *(lah ahn-feh-tah-'mee-nah)*
angel dust   el polvo de ángel *(ehl 'pohl-voh deh 'ahn-hel)*
barbiturate   el barbitúrico *(ehl bahr-bee-'too-ree-koh)*
benzedrine   la bencedrina *(lah behn-seh-'dree-nah)*
cocaine   la cocaína *(lah koh-kah-'ee-nah)*
crack   el crack *(ehl krahk)*
crystal   el cristal *(ehl krees-'tahl)*
ecstasy (MDMA)   la éxtasis *(lah 'ehks-tah-sees)*
hashish   el hashish *(ehl ah-'sheesh)*
heroin   la heroína *(lah eh-roh-'ee-nah)*
inhalant   el inhalante *(ehl een-ah-'lahn-teh)*
marijuana   la marijuana *(lah mah-ree-'wah-nah)*
mescaline   la mescalina *(lah meh-skah-'lee-nah)*
methanphetamine   la metanfetamina *(lah meh-tahn-feh-tah-'mee-nah)*
morphine   la morfina *(lah mohr-'fee-nah)*
mushrooms   los hongos *(lohs 'ohn-gohs)*
opium   el opio *(ehl 'oh-pee·oh)*
pain reliever   el analgésico *(ehl ah-nahl-'heh-see-koh)*
peyote   el peyote *(ehl peh-'yoh-teh)*
seconal   el seconal *(ehl seh-koh-'nahl)*
sedative   el sedante *(ehl seh-'ahn-teh)*
sleeping pill   la píldora para dormir *(lah 'peel-doh-rah 'pah-rah dohr-'meer)*
steroid   el esteroide *(ehl ehs-teh-'roh-ee-deh)*
tranquilizer   el tranquilizante *(ehl trahn-kee-lee-'sahn-teh)*
valium   el valium *(ehl 'vahl-ee-oom)*

Use the Spanish alphabet when referring to these:

La droga: PCP, DXM, GHB, LSD, PSE, etc.

There's no need to elaborate on this topic of concern. Stop the student, and get a few questions answered:

What do you know about...?	¿Qué sabes de...? *(keh 'sah-behs deh)*

depressants	los depresores *(lohs deh-preh-'sores)*
illicit drugs	las drogas ilícitas *(lahs 'droh-gahs ee-'lee-see-tahs)*
narcotics	los narcóticos *(lohs nahr-'koh-tee-kohs)*
prescription drugs	las drogas de receta *(lahs 'droh-gahs deh reh-'seh tah)*
stimulants	los estimulantes *(lohs ehs-tee-moo-'lahn-tehs)*

Most words related to narcotics and drug paraphernalia can easily be translated into Spanish:

We found... (the)	Encontramos... *(ehn-kohn-'trah-mohs)*

cigarette	el cigarrillo *(ehl see-gahr-'ree-yoh)*
cube	el cubito *(ehl koo-'bee-toh)*
e-cigarette	el cigarrillo de vapor *(ehl see-gah-'rree-yoh deh 'bah-pohr)*
liquid	el líquido *(ehl 'lee-kee-doh)*
needle	la aguja *(lah ah-'goo-hah)*
outfit	el estuche *(ehl ehs-'too-cheh)*
papers	los papelitos *(lohs pah-peh-'lee-tohs)*
pipe	la pipa *(lah 'pee-pah)*
powder	el polvo *(ehl 'pohl-voh)*
razor	la navaja *(lah nah-'vah-hah)*
syringe	la jeringa *(lah heh-'reen-gah)*
vial	el frasco *(ehl 'frahs-koh)*

Don't forget to mention the inhalants:

We found...	Encontramos... *(ehn-kohn-'trah-mohs)*

aerosol can	el aerosol *(ehl ah·eh-roh-'sohl)*
cleaning fluid	el líquido para limpiar *(ehl 'lee-kee-doh' pah-rah leem-pee-'ahr)*
ether	el éter *(ehl 'eh-tehr)*
freon	el freón *(ehl freh-'ohn)*
gasoline	la gasolina *(lah gah-soh-'lee-nah)*
hydrocarbons	los hidrocarbonos *(lohs ee-droh-kahr-'boh-nohs)*

lighter fluid	el líquido de encendedor
	(ehl 'lee-kee-doh deh ehn-sehn-deh-'dohr)
model glue	el pegamento de modelos
	(ehl peh-gah-'mehn-toh deh moh-'deh-lohs)

Drug conversations could also require this important terminology:

dealer	el droguero *(ehl droh-'geh-roh)*
drug addict	el drogadicto *(ehl drohg-ah-'deek-toh)*
habit	el hábito *(ehl 'ah-bee-toh)*
illegal possession	la posesión ilegal
	(lah poh-seh-see-'ohn ee-leh-'gahl)
overdose	la sobredosis *(lah soh-breh-'doh-sees)*

Formulate more quesions using the language you know:

Where did you get that?
¿Dónde conseguiste eso?
('dohn-deh kohn-seh-'gee-steh 'eh-soh)

Do you have a prescription?
¿Tiene una receta?
(tee-'eh-neh 'oo-nah reh-'seh-tah)

Have you been arrested before?
¿Has estado arrestado antes?
(ahs eh-'stah-doh ah-rreh-'stah-doh 'ahn-tehs)

How long have you been using...?
¿Por cuánto tiempo has estado usando?
(pohr 'kwahn-toh tee-'ehm-poh ahs eh-'stah-doh oo-'sahn-doh...)

What's the name of your contact?
¿Cuál es el nombre de tu conexión?
(kwahl ehs ehl 'nohm-breh deh too koh-nehk-see-'ohn)

When did you buy it?
¿Cuándo lo compraste?
('kwahn-doh loh kohm-'prah-steh)

Where did you buy it?
¿Dónde lo compraste?
('dohn-deh loh kohm-'prah-steh)

When did you start using drugs?

¿Cuándo comenzaste a tomar drogas?

('kwahn-doh koh-mehn-'sah-steh ah 'toh-'mahr 'droh-gahs)

What kind have you taken?

¿Qué clase has tomado?

(keh'klah-seh ahs toh-'mah-doh)

 MÁS INFORMACIÓN

If the crime is robbery:

They stole (the)...	**Robaron...** *(roh-'bah-rohn...)*
backpack	**la mochila** *(lah moh-'chee-lah)*
bicycle	**la bicicleta** *(lah bee-see-'kleh-tah)*
cell phone	**el celular** *(ehl seh-loo-'lahr)*
clothing	**la ropa** *(lah 'roh-pah)*
equipment	**el equipo** *(ehl eh-'kee-poh)*
jewelry	**las joyas** *(lahs 'hoh-yahs)*
laptop	**el portátil** *(ehl pohr-'tah-teel)*
machine	**la máquina** *(lah 'mah-kee-nah)*
money	**el dinero** *(ehl dee-'neh-roh)*

➤ Assure the families that things are back to normal:

The students are safe.	**Los estudiantes están seguros.** *(lohs eh-stoo-dee-'ahn-tehs eh-'stahn seh-'goo-rohs)*
Everything is under control.	**Todo está bajo nuestro control.** *('toh-doh eh-'stah 'bah-hoh 'nweh-stroh kohn-'trohl)*
We have called the police.	**Hemos llamado a la policía.** *('eh-mohs yah-'mah-doh ah lah poh-lee-'see·ah)*
There is proof.	**Hay evidencia.** *('ah·ee eh-vee-'dehn-see·ah)*
There will be an investigation.	**Habrá una investigación.** *(ah-'brah 'oo-nah een-veh-stee-gah-see-'ohn)*

271

We know (the)...	**Conocemos a...** *(koh-noh-'seh-mohs ah...)*
suspect	**el sospechoso** *(ehl soh-speh-'choh-soh)*
victim	**la víctima** *(lah 'veek-tee-mah)*
witness	**el testigo** *(ehl teh-'stee-goh)*

➤ Stay alert as you confront the suspects with the following command words:

Come here!	**¡Vengan aquí !** *('vehn-gahn ah-'kee)*
Raise your hands!	**¡Levanten las manos!** *(leh-'vahn-tehn lahs 'mah-nohs)*
Sit down!	**¡Siéntense!** *(see-'ehn-tehn-seh)*
Turn around!	**¡Dénse vuelta!** *('dehn-seh 'vwehl-tah)*
Empty your pockets!	**¡Vacíen los bolsillos!** *(vah-'see-ehn lohs bohl-'see-yohs)*
Give it to me!	**¡Dénmelo!** *('dehn-meh-loh)*
Show me your hands!	**¡Muéstrenme las manos!** *('mweh-strehn-meh lahs 'mah-nohs)*

 DIFERENCIAS CULTURALES

One of the most difficult things to discuss in a foreign language concerns social ethics and values. Your personal feelings, attitudes, and beliefs cannot be communicated in a few short sentences. Therefore, the best way to express any serious matter such as criminal behavior is either through an interpreter or by preparing a written note. Be sure that your students know exactly what is right and what is wrong in your institution.

TELL THEM, PLEASE

Dígales, por favor *('dee-gah-lehs, pohr fah-'vohr)*

Don't try to handle every situation all by yourself. Ask the nearest Spanish speaker to assist you when valuable information needs to be shared. This pattern works well with the words and phrases below:

Tell them that...	Dígales que... *('dee-gah-lehs keh...)*
they have to calm down	tienen que calmarse *(tee-'eh-nehn keh kahl-'mahr-seh)*
they should obey the rules	deben obedecer las reglas *('deh-behn oh-beh-deh-'sehr lahs 'reh-glahs)*
they need to be careful	necesitan tener cuidado *(neh-seh-'see-tahn teh-'nehr kwee-'dah-doh)*
they cannot do that	no pueden hacer eso *(noh 'pweh-dehn ah-'sehr 'eh-soh)*
it is an emergency	es una emergencia *(ehs 'oo-nah eh-mehr-'hehn-see·ah)*
I need to call their parents	necesito hablar con sus padres *(neh-seh-'see-toh ah-'blahr kohn soos 'pah-drehs)*

Now, tell one student to advise another. Use this pattern to make an administrative decision:

Tell him/her that...	Dígale que... *('dee-gah-leh keh...)*
this is a warning	ésta es una advertencia *('eh-stah ehs 'oo-nah ahd-vehr-'tehn-see·ah)*
this is going in his file	ésto va en su archivo personal *('eh-stoh vah ehn soo ahr-'chee-voh pehr-soh-'nahl)*
we are going to make some changes	vamos a hacer algunos cambios *('vah-mohs ah ah-'sehr ahl-'goo-nohs 'kahm-bee·ohs)*
this is the last time	ésta es la última vez *('eh-stah ehs lah 'ool-tee-mah vehs)*
I'm calling security	estoy llamando a los guardias *(eh-'stoh·ee yah-'mahn-doh ah lohs 'gwahr-dee·ahs)*

273

➤ Continue to discuss the situation in detail:

If it happens again...   Si pasa de nuevo...
                            (see 'pah-sah deh noo-'eh-voh)

you will be expelled   serás expulsado
                            (seh-'rahs eks-pool-'sah-doh)
you will be transferred   serás transferido
                            (seh-'rahs trahns-feh-'ree-doh)
you will be suspended   serás suspendido
                            (seh-'rahs soo-spehn-'dee-doh)

➤ Copy these down. They make good opening phrases:

I told you that...
Te dije que... *(teh 'dee-heh keh)*

Remember that...
Recuerda que... *(reh-'kwehr-dah keh)*

It's important that...
Es importante que... *(ehs eem-pohr-'tahn-teh keh)*

When you finish...
Cuando termina... *('kwahn-doh tehr-'mee-nah)*

If it's possible...
Si es posible... *(see ehs poh-'see-bleh)*

Before you go...
Antes de irse... *('ahn-tehs deh 'eer-seh)*

Translate:
Cuando termines, apaga la luz.
('kwahn-doh tehr-'mee-nehs, ah-'pah-gah lah loos)

Si es posible, ven temprano.
(see ehs poh-'see-bleh,'vehn tehm-'prah-noh)

_____

Antes de irse, cierre la puerta.
('ahn-tehs deh 'eer-seh, see-'eh-reh lah 'pwehr-tah)

_____

➤ And here's a pattern that requires more verb infinitives:

Make sure that you guys...   Asegúrense de... *(ah-seh-'goo-rehn-seh deh...)*

ask me   preguntarme *(preh-goon-'tahr-meh)*
call them   llamarles *(yah-'mahr-lehs)*
read it   leerlo *(leh-'ehr-loh)*

¿LISTOS PARA PRACTICAR?

In Spanish, name three serious crimes:

_____   _____   _____

Connect the related terms:

la cárcel *(lah 'kahr-sehl)*   la cicatriz *(lah see-kah-'trees)*
la droga *(lah 'droh-gah)*   la prisión *(lah pree-see-'ohn)*
el tatuaje *(ehl tah-too-'ah-heh)*   la medicina *(lah meh-dee-'see-nah)*

Follow these commands:

¡Dése vuelta y levante las manos!
('deh-seh 'vwehl-tah ee leh-'vahn-teh las 'mah-nohs)

Translate into Spanish:

Remember that it is an emergency. _____

If it happens again, you will be expelled. _____

Tell them that they can't do that. _____

TO TALK TO THE PUBLIC!

¡Hablar al público! *(ah-'blahr ahl 'poo-blee-koh)*

Educators in administrative positions are often overloaded with duties and responsibilities on campus, as well as public gatherings. Maybe they're headed to one of these:

He/She went to (the)...	Fue a... *(fweh ah...)*
assembly	la asamblea *(lah ah-sahm-'bleh-ah)*
committee	el comité *(ehl koh-mee-'teh)*
conference	la conferencia *(lah kohn-feh-'rehn-see·ah)*
council	la junta *(lah 'hoon-tah)*
meeting	la reunión *(lah reh-oo-nee-'ohn)*
seminar	el seminario *(ehl seh-mee-'nah-ree·oh)*

He/She is...	Está... *(eh-'stah...)*
discussing	conversando *(kohn-vehr-'sahn-doh)*
hiring	contratando *(kohn-trah-'tahn-doh)*
organizing	organizando *(ohr-gah-nee-'sahn-doh)*
planning	planeando *(plah-neh-'ahn-doh)*
presenting	presentando *(preh-sehn-'tahn-doh)*
speaking	hablando *(ah-'blahn-doh)*
teaching	enseñando *(ehn-seh-'nyahn-doh)*
training	entrenando *(ehn-treh-'nahn-doh)*
traveling	viajando *(vee·ah-'hahn-doh)*
visiting	visitando *(vee-see-'tahn-doh)*

And, what's the topic for discussion? At your next public gathering, step up to the microphone and refer to any important issue:

I'd like to talk about (the)...	Quisiera discutir... *(kee-see-'eh-rah dee-skoo-'teer...)*
community support	el apoyo de la comunidad *(ehl ah-'poh-yoh deh lah koh-moo-nee-'dahd)*
course of study	el curso de estudio *(ehl 'koor-soh deh eh-'stoo-dee·oh)*
district boundaries	las fronteras del distrito *(lahs frohn-'teh-rahs dehl dee-'stree-toh)*
drop out rate	la proporción de estudiantes que dejan sus estudios *(lah proh-pohr-see-'ohn deh eh-stoo-dee-'ahn-tehs keh 'deh-hahn soos eh-'stoo-dee·ohs)*
emergency preparedness	el plan de emergencia *(ehl plahn deh eh-mehr-'hehn-see·ah)*
graduation requirements	los requisitos para la graduación *(lohs reh-kee-'see-tohs 'pah-rah lah grah-doo-ah-see-'ohn)*
new construction	la nueva construcción *(lah noo-'eh-vah kohn-strook-see-'ohn)*
new technology	la nueva tecnología *(lah noo·'eh-vah tehk-noh-loh-'hee·ah)*
proficiency testing	los exámenes de competencia *(lohs ehk-'sah-meh-nehs deh kohm-peh-'tehn-see·ah)*
PTA	la asociación de los padres de alumnos *(lah ah-soh-see·ah-see-'ohn deh lohs 'pah-drehs deh ah-'loom-nohs)*
remedial programs	los programas de refuerzo *(lohs proh-'grah-mahs deh reh-'fwehr-soh)*
sanitary conditions	las condiciones sanitarias *(lahs kohn-dee-see-'oh-nehs sah-nee-'tah-ree·ahs)*
school budget	el presupuesto de la escuela *(ehl preh-soo-'pweh-stoh deh lah eh-'skweh-lah)*
special services	los servicios especiales *(lohs sehr-'vee-see·ohs eh-speh-see-'ah-lehs)*
substitute teachers	los profesores suplentes *(lohs proh-feh-'soh-rehs soo-'plehn-tehs)*

Insert a key word once in a while. Make sure your pronunciation is clear:

We have (the)...   Tenemos... *(teh-'neh-mohs...)*

alternatives   las alternativas *(lahs ahl-tehr-nah-'tee-vahs)*
goals   las metas *(lahs 'meh-tahs)*
instructions   las instrucciones *(lahs een-strook-see-'ohn-ehs)*
needs   los requisitos *(lohs reh-kee-'see-tohs)*
objectives   los objetivos *(lohs ohb-heh-'tee-vohs)*
recommendations   las recomendaciones *(lahs reh-koh-mehn-dah-
                                see-'oh-nehs)*
solutions   las soluciones *(lahs soh-loo-see-'oh-nehs)*
studies   las investigaciones *(las een-veh-stee-gah-see-'oh-
                                nehs)*
suggestions   las sugerencias *(lahs soo-heh-'rehn-see·ahs)*

Stress each point using descriptive words. Do any of the following look like English?

It's...   Es/Está... *(ehs/eh-'stah...)*

flexible   (Es) flexible *(ehs flehk-'see-bleh)*
formal   (Es) formal *(ehs fohr-'mahl)*
individualized   (Está) individualizado *(eh-'stah een-dee-vee-doo-
                                ah-lee-'sah-doh)*
modified   (Está) modificado *(eh-'stah moh-dee-fee-'kah-doh)*
modular   (Es) modular *(ehs moh-doo-'lahr)*
online   (Está) en línea *(eh-'stah ehn 'lee-neh-ah)*
programmed   (Está) programado *(eh-'stah proh-grah-'mah-doh)*
recorded   (Está) documentado *(eh-'stah doh-koo-mehn-'tah-
                                doh)*
supplementary   (Es) suplementario *(ehs soo-pleh-mehn-'tah-ree·oh)*
tracked   (Está) seguido *(eh-'stah seh-'gee-doh)*

Let the audience know that you are there to help. Eagerly mention what you are willing to do:

We offer (the)...   Ofrecemos... *(oh-freh-'seh-mohs)*

clothing   la ropa *(lah 'roh-pah)*
day care center   la guardería infantil *(lah gwahr-deh-'ree·ah een-
                                fahn-'teel)*

food stamps	los cupones de alimentos *(lohs koo-'poh-nehs deh ah-lee-'mehn-tohs)*
free meals	las comidas gratis *(lahs koh-'mee-dahs 'grah-tees)*
housing	la vivienda *(lah vee-vee-'ehn-dah)*
insurance	el seguro *(ehl seh-'goo-roh)*
legal service	el servicio legal *(ehl sehr-'vee-see·oh leh-'gahl)*
medical care	el cuidado médico *(ehl kwee-'dah-doh'meh-dee-koh)*
vaccination	la vacunación *(lah vah-koo-nah-see-'ohn)*
welfare	el bienestar social *(ehl bee-ehn-eh-'stahr soh-see-'ahl)*

 MÁS INFORMACIÓN

➤ Keep student family needs on target:

assistance	la ayuda *(lah ah-'yoo-dah)*
resource	el recurso *(ehl reh-'koor-soh)*
shelter	el amparo *(ehl ahm-'pah-roh)*
support	el apoyo *(ehl ah-'poh-yoh)*
therapy	la terapia *(lah teh-'rah-pee·ah)*

➤ Nobody can survive without the following expressions:

Above all...	Sobre todo... *('soh-breh 'toh-doh...)*
At first...	Al principio... *(ahl preen-'see-pee·oh...)*
At last...	Por fin... *(pohr feen...)*
At least...	Por lo menos... *(pohr loh 'meh-nohs...)*
By the way...	A propósito... *(ah proh-'poh-see-toh...)*
For example...	Por ejemplo... *(pohr eh-'hehm-ploh)*
In general...	En general... *(ehn heh-neh-'rahl...)*
In other words...	Es decir... *(ehs deh-'seer...)*
On the other hand...	En cambio... *(ehn 'kahm-bee·oh...)*

➤ Don't forget your English: el Common Core, No Child Left Behind, etc.

Try some:

En general, estoy bien.
(ehn heh-neh-'rahl, eh-'stoh·ee bee·ehn)

A propósito, mañana no hay escuela.
(a proh-'poh-see-toh, mah-'nyah-nah noh 'ah-ee eh-'skweh-lah)

Al principio, vengan a la clase.
(ahl preen-'see-pee·oh 'vehn-gahn ah lah 'klah-seh)

DIFERENCIAS CULTURALES

Spanish-speaking people are identical to us in that they use slang or idiomatic expressions to talk about routine activities. Many also use Spanglish, that is, English words adapted for Spanish use (la troca *[lah 'troh-kah]* for "the truck" and el rufo *[ehl 'roo-foh]* for "the roof.)" If you're having trouble understanding certain words or expressions, use the phrase ¿Qué significa eso? *[keh seeg-nee-'fee-kah 'eh-soh]*, which translates, "What does that mean?" Chances are they'll come up with the Spanish words that are more familiar to you. Just be patient and take note of what they're saying for future reference.

POLITICS
La política *(lah poh-'lee-tee·kah)*

Make references to what's going on in the political arena. Decisions at the top affect educational policies:

It has to do with (the)...	Tiene que ver con... *(tee-'eh-neh keh'vehr kohn...)*
affirmative action	la acción afirmativa *(lah ahk-see·'ohn ah-feer-mah-'tee-vah)*
bilingual education	la educación bilingüe *(lah eh-doo-kah-see·'ohn bee-'leen-gweh)*
civil rights	los derechos civiles *(lohs deh-'reh-chohs see-'vee-'lehs)*
election	la elección *(lah eh-lehk-see·'ohn)*
government	el gobierno *(ehl goh-bee-'ehr-noh)*
immigration	la inmigración *(lah een-mee-grah-'see·ohn)*
law	la ley *(lah 'leh·ee)*

media	los medios de comunicación *(lohs 'meh-dee·ohs deh koh-moo-nee-kah-see·'ohn)*
population	la población *(lah poh-blah-see·'ohn)*

Negative themes are bound to surface, so prepare yourself for trouble:

There is/are...	Hay... *('ah·ee...)*

alcoholism	el alcoholismo *(ehl ahl-koh-oh-'lees-moh)*
crime rate	el índice de crimen *(ehl 'een-dee-seh deh 'kree-mehn)*
disease	las enfermedades *(lahs ehn-fehr-meh-'dah-dehs)*
domestic violence	la violencia doméstica *(lah vee·oh-'lehn-see·ah doh-'meh-stee-kah)*
drug abuse	el abuso de drogas *(ehl ah-'boo-soh deh 'droh-gahs)*
drug addiction	la drogadicción *(lah drohg-ah-deek-see·'ohn)*
drug traffic	el narcotráfico *(ehl nahr-koh-'trah-fee-koh)*
gangs	las pandillas *(lahs pahn-'dee-yahs)*
homelessness	la gente desamparada *(lah 'hehn-teh dehs-ahm-pah-'rah-dah)*
hunger	el hambre *(ehl 'ahm-breh)*
juvenile delinquency	la delincuencia juvenil *(lah deh-leen-'kwehn-see·ah hoo-veh-'neel)*
poverty	la pobreza *(lah poh-'breh-sah)*
racism	el racismo *(ehl rah-'sees-moh)*
runaway children	los niños fugitivos *(lohs 'nee-nyohs foo-hee-'tee-vohs)*
segregation	la segregación *(lah seh-greh-gah-see·'ohn)*
teen suicide	el suicidio de adolescentes *(ehl soo-ee-'see-dee·oh deh ah-doh-leh-'sehn-tehs)*
terrorism	el terrorismo *(ehl teh-rroh-'rees-moh)*
unemployment	el desempleo *(ehl dehs-ehm-'pleh-oh)*
violence	la violencia *(lah vee·oh-'lehn-see·ah)*

➤ Group all your vocabulary according to patterns:

It's...	Es... *(ehs...)*
bicultural	bicultural *(bee-kool-too-'rahl)*
cross-cultural	intercultural *(een-tehr-kool-too-'rahl)*
multicultural	multicultural *(mool-tee-kool-too-'rahl)*

Take (the)...	Toma... *('toh-mah...)*
brochure	el folleto *(ehl foh-'yeh-toh)*
flyer	la hoja informativa *(lah 'oh-hah een-fohr-mah-'tee-vah)*
syllabus	el programa de estudio *(ehl proh-'grah-mah deh eh-'stoo-dee·oh)*

We have (the)...	Tenemos... *(teh-'neh-mohs...)*
home school	la escuela en casa *(lah eh-'skweh-lah ehn 'kah-sah)*
night school	la escuela de noche *(lah eh-'skweh-lah deh 'noh-cheh)*
summer school	la escuela de verano *(lah eh-'skweh-lah deh veh-'rah-noh)*

There's...	Hay... *('ah·ee...)*
teacher shortage	falta de maestros *('fahl-tah deh mah-'eh-strohs)*
teacher recruitment	contratación de maestros *(kohn-trah-tah-see·'ohn deh mah-'eh-strohs)*
teacher certification	certificación de maestros *(sehr-tee-fee-kah-see·'ohn deh mah-'eh-strohs)*

There's no...	No hay... *(noh 'ah·ee...)*
interest	interés *(een-teh-'rehs)*
money	dinero *(dee-'neh-roh)*
time	tiempo *(tee-'ehm-poh)*

It isn't...	No es... *(noh ehs...)*
co-ed	colegio mixto *(koh-'leh-hee·oh 'meek-stoh)*
nonprofit	sin fines de lucro *(seen 'fee-nehs deh 'loo-kroh)*
year-round	para todo el año *('pah-rah 'toh-doh ehl 'ah-nyoh)*

➤ End your presentation with a kind word or two.

Thank you very much for coming.
Muchas gracias por venir. *('moo-chahs 'grah-see·ahs pohr veh-'neer)*

The students will receive...	Los estudiantes van a recibir... *(lohs eh-stoo-dee-'ahn-tehs vahn ah reh-see-'beer...)*
awards	galardones *(gah-lahr-'doh-nehs)*
certificates	certificados *(sehr-tee-fee-'kah-dohs)*
gifts	regalos *(reh-'gah-lohs)*
medals	medallas *(meh-'dah-yahs)*
prizes	premios *('preh-mee·ohs)*
rewards	recompensas *(reh-kohm-'pehn-sahs)*
ribbons	cintas meritorias *('seen-tahs meh-ree-'toh-ree·ahs)*
trophies	trofeos *(troh-'feh-ohs)*

TO CONVERSE WITH EMPLOYEES
Conversar con los empleados *(kohn-vehr-'sahr kohn lohs ehm-pleh-'ah-dohs)*

Besides using Spanish with students, families, and the community, there's also an occasional opportunity to chat with fellow employees. If a Spanish speaker works for you, you may have to discuss the following topics:

Let's talk about (the)....	Hablamos de... *(ah-'blah-mohs deh)*
benefits	los beneficios *(lohs beh-neh-'fee-see·ohs)*
contracts	los contratos *(lohs kohn-'trah-tohs)*
credit union	el banco cooperativo *(ehl 'bahn-koh koh-oh-peh-rah-'tee-voh)*

employee party	la fiesta para los empleados *(lah fee-'eh-stah 'pah-rah lohs ehm-pleh-'ah-dohs)*
holidays	los días feriados *(lohs 'dee·ahs feh-ree-'ah-dohs)*
insurance	el seguro *(ehl seh-'goo-roh)*
interviews	las entrevistas *(lahs ehn-treh-'vee-stahs)*
job description	la descripción del trabajo *(lah deh-skreep-see-'ohn dehl trah-'bah-hoh)*
overtime	el sobretiempo *(ehl soh-breh-tee-'ehm-poh)*
raise	el aumento de sueldo *(ehl ow-'mehn-toh deh 'swehl-doh)*
retirement	la jubilación *(lah hoo-bee-lah-see-'ohn)*
staff development	el entrenamiento del personal *(ehl ehn-treh-nah-mee-'ehn-toh dehl pehr-soh-'nahl)*
trade union	el sindicato *(ehl seen-dee-'kah-toh)*
vacations	las vacaciones *(lahs vah-kah-see-'oh-nehs)*
wages	el sueldo *(ehl 'swehl-doh)*

This time give a schedule to anyone who asks:

Be here at _____.	Esté aquí a _____.
	(eh-'steh ah-'kee·ah _____)
You may leave at _____.	Se puede ir a _____.
	(seh 'pweh-deh eer ah _____)
Take a break at _____.	Tome un descanso a _____.
	('toh-meh oon deh-'skahn-soh ah _____)
Return at _____.	Regrese a _____.
	(reh-'greh-seh ah _____)
You will work on _____.	Va a trabajar en _____.
	(vah ah trah-bah-'hahr ehn _____)

And do the Spanish-speaking employees know all the regulations around the worksite?

| Use (the)... | Use... *('oo-seh)* |
| authorized area | la zona autorizada *(lah 'soh-nah ow-toh-ree-'sah-dah)* |

password	**la contraseña** *(lah kohn-trah-'seh-nyah)*
personal identification	**la identificación personal** *(lah ee-dehn-tee-fee-kah-see·'ohn pehr-soh-'nahl)*
security code	**el código de seguridad** *(ehl 'koh-dee-goh deh seh-goo-ree-'dahd)*
sign-in sheet	**la lista de registro** *(lah 'lee-stah deh reh-'hee-stroh)*
time card	**la tarjeta de trabajo** *(lah tahr-'heh-tah deh trah-'bah-hoh)*
time clock	**el reloj de trabajo** *(ehl reh-'loh deh trah-'bah-hoh)*

Use the employee _____.	**Use _____ para los empleados.** *('oo-seh _____ 'pah-rah lohs ehm-pleh-'ah-dohs)*

cafeteria	**la cafetería** *(lah kah-feh-teh-'ree·ah)*
entrance	**la entrada** *(lah ehn-'trah-dah)*
lounge	**el salón de espera** *(ehl sah-'lohn deh eh-'speh-rah)*
parking area	**la zona de estacionamiento** *(lah 'soh-nah deh eh-stah-see·oh-nah-mee·'ehn-toh)*
restroom	**el baño** *(ehl 'bah-nyoh)*
telephone	**el teléfono** *(ehl teh-'leh-foh-noh)*
website	**el sitio web** *(ehl 'see-tee·oh web)*

MÁS INFORMACIÓN

➤ These words are used for special occasions:

Let's...	**Vamos a...** *('vah-mohs ah...)*

contribute	**contribuir** *(kohn-tree-boo-'eer)*
donate	**donar** *(doh-'nahr)*
volunteer	**ser voluntarios** *(sehr voh-loon-'tah-ree·ohs)*

DIFERENCIAS CULTURALES

Once Hispanics establish friendly relationships, they often use nicknames when referring to each other. It is meant to show intimacy, and not disrespect. Besides, it might be fun to look up the translations for any terms of endearment that you hear.

¿LISTOS PARA PRACTICAR?

Pick the *best* word to fill in the blank:

los premios, la junta, el presupuesto *(lohs 'preh-mee·ohs, lah 'hoon-tah, ehl preh-soo-'pweh-stoh)*

El director fue a _____ . *(ehl dee-rehk-'tohr fweh ah _____)*

Los niños reciben _____ . *(lohs 'nee-nyohs reh-'see-behn _____)*

Quiero discutir _____ . *(kee-'eh-roh dees-koo-'teer _____)*

Connect the terms that seem to relate best:

la ley *(lah 'leh·ee)*   la conferencia *(lah kohn-feh-'rehn-see·ah)*

las metas *(lahs 'meh-tahs)*   la pobreza *(lah poh-'breh-sah)*

el sobretiempo *(ehl soh-breh-tee-'ehm-poh)*   los objetivos *(lohs ohb-heh-'tee-vohs)*

el hambre *(ehl 'ahm-breh)*

la reunión *(lah reh-oo-nee·'ohn)*   el sueldo *(ehl 'swehl-doh)*

                                           el gobierno *(ehl goh-bee-'ehr-noh)*

Review the verb forms we've studied so far in this guidebook. Note the spelling and pronunciation changes that take place when you shift from one time reference to the next:

I'm working now.	**Estoy trabajando ahora.**
	(eh-'stoh·ee trah-bah-'hahn-doh ah-oh-rah)
I work every day.	**Trabajo todos los días.**
	(trah-'bah-hoh 'toh-dohs lohs 'dee·ahs)
I will work tomorrow.	**Trabajaré mañana.**
	(trah-bah-hah-'reh mah-'nyah-nah)
I worked yesterday.	**Trabajé ayer.**
	(trah-bah-'heh ah-'yehr)

Now, study the following two-part verb pattern. It's extremely important in school-related conversations because it refers to actions that have already taken place. It's a past action pattern that is used frequently in everyday communication, so pay close attention to each example. Here's how the words go together.

The first part consists of forms of the verb "to have" **haber** *(ah-'behr)*.

The second part consists of the past participle of the action word. Both parts must be used together.

I've	He	left	salido (sah-'lee-doh)
		eaten	comido (koh-'mee-doh)
You've (informal)	Has	studied	estudiado (ehs-too-dee·'ah-doh)
		written	escrito (ehs-'kree-toh)
You've (formal), She's, He's	Ha	closed	cerrado (seh-'rrah-doh)
		cleaned	limpiado (leem-pee-'ah-doh)
You've (pl.), They've	Han	worked	trabajado (trah-bah-'hah-doh)
		arrived	llegado (yeh-'gah-doh)
We've	Hemos	learned	aprendido (ah-prehn-'dee-doh)

To learn more about these past participle verb forms, consider taking a beginning Spanish class. It's worth the effort, because in education this two-part verb tense can be very useful. Watch:

I've arrived late many times.
He llegado tarde muchas veces.
(eh yeh-'gah-doh 'tahr-deh 'moo-chahs 'veh-sehs)

She's passed the test.
Ella ha pasado el examen.
('eh-yah ah pah-'sah-doh ehl ek-'sah-mehn)

We've cleaned the desks.
Hemos limpiado los escritorios.
('eh-mohs leem-pee·'ah-doh lohs eh-skree-'toh-ree·ohs)

MÁS INFORMACIÓN

➤ Some past participles can be used as descriptive words:

They are parked cars.	**Son carros <u>estacionados</u>.** *(sohn 'kah-rrohs eh-stah-see·oh-'nah-dohs)*
They are painted doors.	**Son puertas <u>pintadas</u>.** *(sohn 'pwehr-tahs peen-'tah-dahs)*
They are washed floors.	**Son pisos <u>lavados</u>.** *(sohn 'pee-sohs lah-'vah-dohs)*

➤ A handful of past participles are considered irregular. Memorize these examples:

I've broken the pencil.	**He <u>roto</u> el lápiz.** *(eh 'roh-toh ehl 'lah-pees)*
We've written the report.	**Hemos <u>escrito</u> el reporte.** *('eh-mohs eh-'skree-toh ehl reh-'pohr-teh)*
He's seen the program.	**Ha <u>visto</u> el programa.** *(ah 'vee-stoh ehl proh-'grah-mah)*

¡ÓRDENES!

Now that we can add pronouns to our command words, let's attempt to create a few one-word expressions for everyday use.

Tell it to me	**Dímelo** *('dee-meh-loh)*
Show it to me	**Enséñamela** *(ehn-'seh-nyah-meh-lah)*
Give it to me	**Dámelo** *('dah-meh-loh)*
Turn it in to me	**Entrégamela** *(ehn-'treh-gah-meh-lah)*
Bring it to me	**Tráemelo** *('trah-eh-meh-loh)*
Throw it to me	**Tíramela** *('tee-rah-meh-lah)*

Watch what happens when the same commands are in the formal mode:

Tell it to me	**Dígamelo** *('dee-gah-meh-loh)*
Show it to me	**Enséñemela** *(ehn-'seh-nyeh-meh-lah)*
Give it to me	**Démelo** *('deh-meh-loh)*

Turn it in to me	Entréguemela *(ehn-'treh-geh-meh-lah)*
Bring it to me	Tráigamelo *('trah·ee-gah-meh-loh)*
Throw it to me	Tíremela *('tee-reh-meh-lah)*

¿LISTOS PARA PRACTICAR?

Study the examples, and then write in the missing verb forms:

enseñar *(ehn-seh-'nyahr)*   **trabajar** *(trah-bah-'hahr)*   **hablar** *(ah-'blahr)*

Estoy enseñando.
(eh-'stoh·ee ehn-seh-
'nyahn-doh)
Enseño.
(ehn-'seh-'nyoh)
Enseñaré.
(ehn-seh-nyah-'reh)
Enseñé.
(ehn-seh-'nyeh)
Estaba enseñando.
(eh-'stah-bah ehn-seh-
'nyahn-doh)
He enseñado.
(eh ehn-seh-'nyah-doh)

aprender *(ah-prehn-'dehr)*   **comer** *(koh-'mehr)*   **escribir** *(eh-skree-'beer)*

Estoy aprendiendo.
(eh-'stoh·ee ah-prehn-dee-
'ehn-doh)
Aprendo. *(ah-'prehn-doh)*
Aprenderé.
(ah-prehn-deh-'reh)
Aprendí. *(ah-prehn-'dee)*
Estaba aprendiendo.
(eh-'stah-bah ah-prehn-dee-
'ehn-doh)
He aprendido.
(eh ah-prehn-'dee-doh)

290

CHAPTER EIGHT
Capítulo Ocho
(kah-'pee-too-loh 'oh-choh)

SUPPORT STAFF
El personal auxiliar
(ehl pehr-soh-'nahl owk-see-lee-'ahr)

OFFICE ASSISTANCE
Ayuda en la oficina *(ah-'yoo-dah ehn lah oh-fee-'see-nah)*

At educational facilities everywhere, nothing gets done without the help of skilled office professionals. Spend time with this series of words and phrases designed specifically for clerical staff who need to use Spanish:

May I help you?
¿Puedo ayudarle? *('pweh-doh ah-yoo-'dahr-leh)*

You need to talk to _____ .
Necesita hablar con _____ .*(neh-seh-'see-tah ah-'blahr kohn _____)*

Do you know where it is?
¿Sabe dónde está? *('sah-beh 'dohn-deh eh-'stah)*

Someone will help you in a few minutes.
Alguien le atenderá en algunos minutos. *('ahl-gee·ehn·leh ah-tehn-deh-'rah ehn ahl-'goo-nohs mee-'noo-tohs)*

Please have a seat.
Por favor, tome asiento. *(pohr fah-'vohr, 'toh-meh ah-see-'ehn-toh)*

These are the office hours.
Estas son las horas de oficina. *('eh-stahs sohn lahs 'oh-rahs deh oh-fee-'see-nah)*

Go to our website.
Vaya a nuestro sitio web. *('vah-yah ah noo·'eh-stroh 'see-tee·oh web)*

I NEED INFORMATION, PLEASE
Necesito información, por favor
(neh-seh-'see-toh een-fohr-mah-see-'ohn, pohr fah-'vohr)

For those situations involving orientation, registration, or minor emergencies, utilize the one-liners below. Start off by talking to the student:

Where do you go to school?
¿Adónde vas a la escuela? *(ah-'dohn-deh vahs ah lah eh-'skweh-lah)*

292

You need to go back to class.
Necesitas regresar a tu clase. *(neh-seh-'see-tahs reh-greh-'sahr ah too 'klah-seh)*

What grade are you in?
¿En qué grado estás? *(ehn keh 'grah-doh eh-'stahs)*

Are your parents at home?
¿Están tus padres en casa? *(eh-'stahn toos 'pah-drehs ehn 'kah-sah)*

Do any of your brothers or sisters attend this school?
¿Asiste algún hermano o hermana a esta escuela? *(ah-'see-steh ahl-'goon ehr-'mah-noh oh ehr-'mah-nah ah 'eh-stah eh-'skweh-lah)*

Who would you like to talk to?
¿Con quién te gustaría hablar? *(kohn kee-'ehn teh goo-stah-'ree·ah ah-'blahr)*

What is your student ID number?
¿Cuál es tu número de estudiante? *(kwahl ehs too 'noo-meh-roh deh eh-stoo-dee-'ahn-teh)*

Who sent you here?
¿Quién te mandó aquí? *(kee-'ehn teh mahn-'doh ah-'kee)*

Now, say a few things to the parents, families, and friends:

Read all of the information.
Lea toda la información. *('leh-ah 'toh-dah lah een-fohr-mah-see·'ohn)*

Do you have all the forms?
¿Tiene todos los formularios? *(tee-'eh-neh 'toh-dohs lohs fohr-moo-'lah-ree·ohs)*

Who is the legal parent or guardian?
¿Quién es el padre o guardián legal? *(kee-'ehn ehs ehl 'pah-dreh oh gwahr-dee-'ahn leh-'gahl)*

These are the instructions.
Estas son las instrucciones. *('eh-stahs sohn lahs een-strook-see·'oh-nehs)*

Is there someone in the home who speaks English?
¿Hay alguien en la casa que hable inglés? *('ah·ee 'ahl-gee·ehn ehn lah 'kah-sah keh 'ah-bleh een-'glehs)*

Please fill out everything and sign here.

Llene todo y firme aquí, por favor. *('yeh-neh 'toh-doh ee 'feer-meh ah-'kee, pohr fah-'vohr)*

Who can we call in case of emergency?

¿A quién podemos llamar en caso de emergencia? *(ah kee-'ehn poh-'deh-mohs yah-'mahr ehn 'kah-soh deh eh-mehr-'hehn-see·ah)*

What is your email?

¿Cuál es tu correo electrónico? *(kwahl ehs too koh-'rreh-oh eh-lehk-'troh-nee-koh)*

 ## MÁS INFORMACIÓN

➤ At the front counter, employees discuss various costs, fees, and charges with students and their families, and these phrases are used all the time:

How much does it cost?	**¿Cuánto cuesta?** *('kwahn-toh 'kweh-stah)*
When do I have to pay?	**¿Cuándo tengo que pagar?** *('kwahn-doh 'tehn-goh keh pah-'gahr)*
Who do I give the money to?	**¿A quién doy el dinero?** *(ah kee-'ehn 'doh·ee ehl dee-'neh-roh)*
Please give me (the)...	**Por favor, deme...** *(pohr fah-'vohr, 'deh-meh...)*
bill	**la cuenta** *(lah 'kwehn-tah)*
bills	**los billetes** *(lohs bee-'yeh-tehs)*
change	**el cambio** *(ehl 'kahm-bee·oh)*
check	**el cheque** *(ehl 'cheh-keh)*
coins	**las monedas** *(lahs moh-'neh-dahs)*
credit card	**la tarjeta de crédito** *(lah tahr-'heh-tah deh 'kreh-dee-toh)*
invoice	**la factura** *(lah fahk-'too-rah)*
money	**el dinero** *(ehl dee-'neh-roh)*
order	**la orden** *(lah 'ohr-dehn)*
payment	**el pago** *(ehl 'pah-goh)*
receipt	**el recibo** *(ehl reh-'see-boh)*
dollar	**el dólar** *(ehl 'doh-lahr)*
cent	**el centavo** *(ehl sehn-'tah-voh)*

THE COMPLAINTS
Las quejas *(lahs 'keh-hahs)*

No doubt you'll get a few complaints from parents about legal procedures, or perhaps the behavior of certain staff members. Respond with tact:

It's our responsibility.	**Es nuestra responsabilidad.** *(ehs noo-'ehs-trah rehs-pohn-sah-bee-lee-'dahd)*
We are very sorry.	**Lo sentimos mucho.** *(loh sehn-'tee-mohs 'moo-choh)*
We will do everything possible.	**Haremos todo lo posible.** *(ah-'reh-mohs 'toh-doh loh poh-'see-bleh)*
We're going to check it out.	**Vamos a averiguarlo.** *('vah-mohs ah ah-veh-ree-goo-'ahr-loh)*
It's going to be corrected.	**Va a ser corregido.** *(vah ah sehr kohr-reh-'hee-doh)*
It won't happen again.	**No volverá a pasar.** *(noh vohl-veh-'rah ah pah-'sahr)*
It's our obligation.	**Es nuestra obligación.** *(ehs noo-'ehs-trah oh-blee-gah-see-'ohn)*
The police will be notified.	**Notificaremos a la policía.** *(noh-tee-fee-kah-'reh-mohs ah lah poh-lee-'see·ah)*
Write down everything that happened.	**Escriba todo lo que pasó.** *(ehs-'kree-bah 'toh-doh loh keh pah-'soh)*
We want to resolve it.	**Queremos resolverlo.** *(keh-'reh-mohs reh-sohl-'vehr-loh 'prohn-toh)*
We will notify you soon.	**Le notificaremos pronto.** *(leh noh-tee-fee-kah-'reh-mohs 'prohn-toh)*

DIFERENCIAS CULTURALES

Many front office employees work with new immigrant families who are unfamiliar with local, state, or federal laws and regulations. If you plan to establish a long-term relationship, you can prevent potential problems by giving them as much legal information as possible. By contacting a variety of service agencies, one can pick up literature in Spanish concerning citizenship, taxes, health care, housing, employment, transportation, and residence, as well as personal rights and privileges.

THE SCHOOL NURSE

La enfermera en la escuela *(lah ehn-fehr-'meh-rah ehn lah eh-'skweh-lah)*

Right up the hallway from the main office, a school nurse prepares for the day's activities. These questions only require a **sí** or **no** for an answer. Start with those words that you already know:

Do you have...?	¿Tienes...? *(tee-'eh-nehs)*
a lot of pain	mucho dolor *('moo-choh doh-'lohr)*
backaches	los dolores de espalda *(lohs doh-'loh rehs deh eh-'spahl-dah)*
blister	la ampolla *(lah ahm-'poh-yah)*
bruise	la contusión *(lah kohn-too-see-'ohn)*
cavities	las caries *(lahs 'kah-ree-ehs)*
chills	los escalofríos *(lohs eh-skah-loh-'free·ohs)*
cold	el resfriado *(ehl rehs-free·'ah-doh)*
constipation	el estreñimiento *(ehl eh-streh-nyee-mee-'ehn-toh)*
convulsions	las convulsiones *(lahs kohn-vool-see-'oh-nehs)*
cramps	los calambres *(lohs kah-'lahm-brehs)*
cut	la cortadura *(lah kohr-tah-'doo-rah)*
diarrhea	la diarrea *(lah dee·ah-'rreh-ah)*
dizziness	los mareos *(lohs mah-'reh-ohs)*
fever	la fiebre *(lah fee-'eh-breh)*
flu	la influenza *(lah een-floo-'ehn-sah)*
gas	el gas *(ehl gahs)*
hay fever	la fiebre del heno *(lah-fee-'eh-breh dehl 'eh-noh)*
headaches	los dolores de cabeza *(lohs doh-'loh-rehs deh kah-'beh-sah)*
hiccups	el hipo *(ehl 'ee-poh)*
insomnia	el insomnio *(ehl een-'sohm-nee·oh)*
itching	la picazón *(lah pee-kah-'sohn)*
menstruation	la menstruación *(lah mehn-stroo-ah-see-'ohn)*
nausea	la náusea *(lah 'now-seh-ah)*
numbness	el adormecimiento *(ehl ah-dohr-meh-see-mee-'ehn-toh)*
phlegm	la flema *(lah 'fleh-mah)*
rashes	las erupciones *(lahs eh-roop-see-'oh-nehs)*
scratch	el rasguño *(ehl rahs-'goo-nyoh)*
seizures	los ataques *(lohs ah-'tah-kehs)*

stomachaches	los dolores de estómago *(lohs doh-'loh-rehs deh eh-'stoh-mah-goh)*
swelling	la hinchazón *(lah een-chah-'sohn)*
toothache	el dolor de muelas *(ehl doh-'lohr deh 'mweh-lahs)*
vomiting	los vómitos *(lohs 'voh-mee-tohs)*

Keep mentioning your concerns about their health:

It could be (the)...	Podría ser... *(poh-'dree·ah sehr...)*
allergies	las alergias *(ah-'lehr-hee·ahs)*
appendicitis	la apendicitis *(lah ah-pehn-dee-'see-tees)*
contagious disease	la enfermedad contagiosa *(lah ehn-fehr-meh-'dahd kohn-tah-hee·'oh-sah)*
dog bite	la mordedura de perro *(lah mohr-deh-'doo-rah deh 'peh-rroh)*
high blood pressure	la presión alta *(lah preh-see·'ohn 'ahl-tah)*
illness	la enfermedad *(lah ehn-fehr-meh-'dahd)*
infection	la infección *(lah een-fehk-see·'ohn)*
injury	la herida *(lah eh-'ree-dah)*
insect bite	la picadura de insecto *(lah pee-kah-'doo-rah deh een-'sehk-toh)*
poisoning	el envenenamiento *(ehl ehn-veh-neh-nah-mee-'ehn-toh)*
shock	la prostración nerviosa *(lah proh-strah-see·'ohn nehr-vee·'oh-sah)*
virus	el virus *(ehl 'vee-roos)*

MORE EMERGENCIES

Más emergencias *(mahs eh-mehr-'hehn-see·ahs)*

While everyone around you is trying to explain what happened, listen carefully for the words appearing below. Repeat what you hear to make sure that there's absolutely no misunderstanding:

a coma	una coma *('oo-nah 'coh-mah)*
a concussion	una conmoción cerebral *('oo-nah kohn-moh-see·'ohn seh-reh-'brahl)*
fatigue	fatiga *(fah-'tee-gah)*
intoxication	intoxicación *(een-tohk-see-kah-see·'ohn)*
an overdose	una sobredosis *('oo-nah soh-breh-'doh-sees)*
a stroke	una apoplejía *('oo-nah ah-poh-pleh-'hee·ah)*
a trauma	un traumatismo *(oon trah-oo-mah-'tees-moh)*

Now move right in and calm the student's fears:

I will help you.	Te ayudaré. *(teh ah-you-dah-'reh)*
You will be OK.	Estarás bien. *(ehs-tah-'rahs bee-'ehn)*
This will hurt a little.	Esto te dolerá un poco. *('ehs-toh the doh-leh-'rah oon 'poh-koh)*

Before you go on, check up on their medical background:

Does this happen a lot?	¿Te pasa mucho esto? *(teh 'pah-sah 'moo-choh 'ehs-toh)*
Are you under a doctor's care?	¿Estás bajo el cuidado de un doctor? *(ehs-'tahs 'bah-hoh ehl koo-ee-'dah-doh deh oon dohk-'tohr)*
Did you lose consciousness?	¿Perdiste el conocimiento? *(pehr-'dees-teh ehl koh-noh-see-mee-'ehn-toh)*
Are you allergic?	¿Eres alérgico/a? *('eh-rehs ah-'lehr-hee-koh / ah)*
Are you taking medication?	¿Tomas medicina? *('toh-mahs meh-dee-'see-nah)*

Now, use the Internet to find lists of common concerns:

It's...	Es...
an ear infection	una infección del oído *('oon-ah een-fehk-see-'ohn dehl oh-'ee-doh)*
cold sores	herpes labial *('ehr-pehs lah-bee-'ahl)*
croup	faringitis *(fah-reen-'hee-tees)*

pink eye	conjuntivitis *(kohn-hoon-tee-'vee-tees)*
strep throat	amigdalitis *(ah-meeg-dah-'lee-tees)*
whooping cough	tos ferina *(tohs feh-'ree-nah)*

When drugs or alcohol are the cause for emergency assistance, interject some of these terms to communicate your messages:

He's/She's...	Está... *(ehs-'tah)*

asleep	dormido *(dohr-'mee-doh)*
awake	despierto *(dehs-pee-'ehr-toh)*
disoriented	desorientado *(deh-soh-ree-ehn-'tah-doh)*
dizzy	mareado *(mah-reh-'ah-doh)*
drugged	drogado *(droh-'gah-doh)*
unconscious	inconsciente *(een-kohns-see-'ehn-teh)*

If the student consumed something he or she shouldn't have, ask around:

What did he/she swallow?	¿Qué tragó? *(keh trah-'goh)*
What did he/she eat?	¿Qué comió? *(keh koh-mee-'oh)*
What did he/she drink?	¿Qué bebió? *(keh beh-bee-'oh)*
What did he/she do?	¿Qué hizo? *(keh 'ee-soh)*
What did he/she take?	¿Qué tomó? *(keh toh-'moh)*

 MÁS INFORMACIÓN

Notice how many medical words are spelled the same in both languages:

anorexia   mononucleosis   bulimia

➤ Isolate the problem:

There are...	Hay... *('ah·ee...)*

physical problems	problemas físicos *(proh-'bleh-mahs 'fee-see-kohs)*
respiratory problems	problemas respiratorios *(proh-'bleh-mahs reh-spee-rah-'toh-ree·ohs)*
visual problems	problemas de visión *(proh-'bleh-mahs deh vee-see-'ohn)*

➤ There should be something on file about the child's health history. This can work as a checklist:

chicken pox	varicela *(vah-ree-'seh-lah)*
diabetes	diabetes *(dee·ah-'beh-tehs)*
measles	sarampión *(sah-rahm-pee-'ohn)*
mumps	paperas *(pah-'peh-rahs)*
West Nile virus	virus del Nilo Occidental *('vee-roos dehl 'nee-loh ok-see-dehn-'tahl)*

➤ All set to make a suggestion?

You need a _____ test. Necesitas un examen de _____. *(neh-seh-'see-tahs oon ehk-'sah-mehn deh _____)*

blood	sangre *('sahn-greh)*
Pap smear	Papinicolaou *(pah-pee-nee-koh-'lah·oh-oo)*
saliva	saliva *(sah-'lee-vah)*
urine	orina *(oh-'ree-nah)*

➤ Can you figure out what these words mean?

difteria	cáncer	leucemia
(deef-'teh-ree·ah)	*('kahn-sehr)*	*(leh·oo-'seh-mee·ah)*
tétano	tuberculosis	hepatitis
('teh-tah-noh)	*(too-behr-koo-'loh-sees)*	*(eh-pah-'tee-tees)*
epilepsia	meningitis	influenza
(eh-pee-'lehp-see·ah)	*(meh-neen-'hee-tees)*	*(een-floo-'ehn-sah)*

TREATMENT
El tratamiento *(ehl trah-tah-mee-'ehn-toh)*

Anyone responsible for student health care should learn the medical terms below. Do you recall these terms from an earlier lesson?

We have (the)... Tenemos... *(teh-'neh-mohs...)*

aspirin	la aspirina *(lah ah-spee-'ree-nah)*
bandage	el vendaje *(ehl vehn-'dah-heh)*
cream	la crema *(lah 'kreh-mah)*

lotion	la loción *(lah loh-see·'ohn)*
medicine	la medicina *(lah meh-deh-'see-nah)*
powder	el talco *(ehl 'tahl-koh)*

Now, use this pattern to explain the situation in greater detail:

He/She needs (the)...	Necesita... *(neh-seh-'see-tah...)*
antibiotic	el antibiótico *(ehl ahn-tee-bee·'oh-tee-koh)*
alcohol	el alcohol *(ehl ahl-koh-'ohl)*
Band-Aid®	la curita *(lah koo-'ree-tah)*
calamine lotion	la loción de calamina *(lah loh-see·'ohn deh kah-lah-'mee-nah)*
capsules	las cápsulas *(lahs 'kahp-soo-lahs)*
cast	la armadura de yeso *(lah ahr-mah-'doo-rah deh 'yeh-soh)*
cough syrup	el jarabe para la tos *(ehl hah-'rah-beh 'pah-rah lah tohs)*
CPR	la respiración artificial *(lah reh-spee-rah-see·'ohn ahr-tee-fee-see-'ahl)*
disinfectant	el desinfectante *(ehl dehs-een-fehk-'tahn-teh)*
drops	las gotas *(lahs 'goh-tahs)*
iodine	el yodo *(ehl 'yoh-doh)*
liniment	el linimento *(ehl lee-nee-'mehn-toh)*
lozenges	las pastillas *(lahs pah-'stee-yahs)*
pills	las píldoras *(lahs 'peel-doh-rahs)*
prescription	la receta *(lah reh-'seh-tah)*
shot	la inyección *(lah een-yehk-see·'ohn)*
stitches	las puntadas *(lahs poon-'tah-dahs)*
tablets	las tabletas *(lahs tah-'bleh-tahs)*
thermometer	el termómetro *(ehl tehr-'moh-meh-troh)*
vaseline	la vaselina *(lah vah-seh-'lee-nah)*
vitamins	las vitaminas *(lahs vee-tah-'mee-nahs)*
X rays	los rayos equis *(lohs 'rah-yohs 'eh-kees)*

➤ While treating the child, keep an eye out for these little critters:

bacteria	las bacterias *(lahs bahk-'teh-ree·ahs)*
germs	los gérmenes *(lohs 'hehr-meh-nehs)*
fleas	las pulgas *(lahs 'pool-gahs)*
lice	los piojos *(lohs pee·'oh-hohs)*
ticks	las garrapatas *(lahs gah-rrah-'pah-tahs)*
worms	los gusanos *(lohs goo-'sah-nohs)*

SCHOOL MAINTENANCE
El mantenimiento de la escuela
(ehl mah-teh-nee-mee-'ehn-toh deh lah eh-'skweh-lah)

Look at all the employees around the campus. Perhaps one of the most noticeable staff members is the janitor or maintenance professional. When they use Spanish, here's their favorite set of vocabulary words:

I need (the)...	Necesito... *(neh-seh-'see-toh...)*
Give me (the)...	Dame... *('dah-meh...)*
Where's (the) ...	¿Dónde está ...? *('dohn-deh eh-'stah...)*

ammonia	el amoníaco *(ehl ah-moh-'nee·ah-koh)*
bleach	el blanqueador *(ehl blahn-keh-ah-'dohr)*
cleaner	el limpiador *(ehl leem-pee·ah-'dohr)*
polish	el lustrador *(ehl loo-strah-'dohr)*
powder	el polvo *(ehl 'pohl-voh)*
soap	el jabón *(ehl hah-'bohn)*
spray gun	el rociador *(ehl roh-see·ah-'dohr)*
wax	la cera *(lah 'seh-rah)*

Can you guess what these words mean?

el detergente *(ehl deh-tehr-'hehn-teh)*

---

el desinfectante *(ehl dehs-een-fehk-'tahn-teh)*

---

la solución *(lah soh-loo-see·'ohn)*

When there's cleaning to do, be sure that the mess is clearly defined:

There is/are...	Hay... *('ah ee)*
crumbs	las migas *(lahs 'mee-gahs)*
dirt	la tierra *(lah tee-'eh-rrah)*
dust	el polvo *(ehl 'pohl-voh)*
fungi	los hongos *(lohs 'ohn-gohs)*
grime	la mugre *(lah 'moo-greh)*
mold	el moho *(ehl 'moh-oh)*
mud	el lodo *(ehl 'loh-doh)*
rust	la herrumbre *(lah eh-'rroom-breh)*
sewage	el desagüe *(ehl dehs-'ah-gweh)*
trash	la basura *(lah bah-'soo-rah)*
waste	los desperdicios *(lohs dehs-pehr-'dee-see·ohs)*

And be aware of any tools that are being used on campus:

Bring (the)...	Trae... *('trah-eh)*
broom	la escoba *(lah eh-'skoh-bah)*
brush	el cepillo *(ehl seh-'pee-yoh)*
bucket	el balde *(ehl 'bahl-deh)*
feather duster	el plumero *(ehl ploo-'meh-roh)*
hose	la manguera *(lah mahn-'geh-rah)*
mask	la máscara *(lah 'mah-skah-rah)*
mop	el trapeador *(ehl trah-peh-ah-'dohr)*
rag	el trapo *(ehl 'trah-poh)*
scraper	el raspador *(ehl rah-spah-'dohr)*
sponge	la esponja *(lah eh-'spohn-hah)*
stepladder	la escalera *(lah eh-skah-'leh-rah)*
towel	la toalla *(lah toh-'ah-yah)*
trashbag	la bolsa para basura *(lah 'bohl-sah 'pah-rah bah-'soo-rah)*
vacuum cleaner	la aspiradora *(lah ah-spee-rah-'doh-rah)*

If students gather around, keep them away from dangerous items. Follow the patterns:

Don't touch (the) ...   No toques ... *(noh 'toh-kehs...)*

cart	la carreta *(lah kah-'rreh-tah)*
equipment	el equipo *(ehl eh-'kee-poh)*
extension cord	el cable de extensión *(ehl 'kah-bleh deh ehk-stehn-see·'ohn)*
glass	el vidrio *(ehl 'vee-dree·oh)*
machinery	la maquinaria *(lah mah-kee-'nah-ree·ah)*
pipe	la tubería *(lah too-beh-'ree·ah)*
rope	la soga *(lah 'soh-gah)*
switch	el interruptor *(ehl een-teh-rroop-'tohr)*
tool	la herramienta *(lah eh-rrah-mee-'ehn-tah)*
wire	el alambre *(ehl ah-'lahm-breh)*

Continue making phrases, but this time, only mention the tools:

drill	el taladro *(ehl tah-'lah-droh)*
file	la lima *(lah 'lee-mah)*
hammer	el martillo *(ehl mahr-'tee-yoh)*
paintbrush	la brocha *(lah 'broh-chah)*
pliers	el alicate *(ehl ah-lee-'kah-teh)*
saw	el serrucho *(ehl seh-'rroo-choh)*
screwdriver	el atornillador *(ehl ah-tohr-nee-yah-'dohr)*
tape measure	la cinta para medir *(lah 'seen-tah 'pah-rah meh-'deer)*
wrench	la llave inglesa *(lah 'yah-veh een-'gleh-sah)*

 MÁS INFORMACIÓN

When children are near, these one-liners should help:

Don't press (the)...   No oprimas... *(noh oh-'pree-mahs...)*

button	el botón *(ehl boh-'tohn)*
dial	el marcador *(ehl mahr-kah-'dohr)*

key	la tecla *(lah 'teh-klah)*
knob	el tirador *(ehl tee-rah-'dohr)*
timer	el reloj *(ehl reh-'loh)*

| Don't touch (the)... | No toques... *(noh 'toh-kehs...)* |

fuse box	la caja de fusibles
	(lah 'kah-hah deh foo-'see-blehs)
gas meter	el medidor de gas
	(ehl meh-dee-'dohr deh gahs)
smoke alarm	el detector de humo
	(ehl deh-tehk-'tohr deh 'oo-moh)
thermostat	el termostato *(ehl tehr-moh-'stah-toh)*
water valve	la válvula de agua
	(lah 'vahl-voo-lah deh 'ah-gwah)

¿LISTOS PARA PRACTICAR?

Name three common physical ailments in Spanish:

_____ _____ _____

Name three things in Spanish that belong in a first-aid kit:

_____ _____ _____

Put in the word that best completes each series:

el dinero, la cápsula, la basura, el detergente, el equipo *(ehl dee-'neh-roh, lah 'kahp-soo-lah, lah bah-'soo-rah, ehl deh-tehr-'hehn-teh, ehl eh-'kee-poh)*

el jabón, el limpiador, _____ *(ehl hah-'bohn, ehl leem-pee·ah-'dohr)*

la tableta, la píldora, _____ *(lah tah-'bleh-tah, lah 'peel-doh-rah)*

el billete, la moneda, _____ *(ehl bee-'yeh-teh, lah moh-'neh-dah)*

la herramienta, la maquinaria, _____ *(lah eh-rrah-'mee-*
'ehn-tah, lah mah-kee-'nah-ree·ah)

la tierra, el desagüe, _____ *(lah tee-'eh-rrah, ehl dehs-'ah-*
gweh)

Name three tools in Spanish that are used by a school janitor:

_____ _____ _____

THE GARDENER
El jardinero *(ehl hahr-dee-'neh-roh)*

The landscapers also need language skills if they consistently meet people who speak Spanish. Don't hesitate to practice saying the following terms:

We're working with the...	Estamos trabajando con... *(eh-'stah-mohs trah-bah-'hahn-doh kohn)*
branches	las ramas *(lahs 'rah-mahs)*
bushes	los arbustos *(lohs ahr-'boo-stohs)*
flowers	las flores *(lahs 'floh-rehs)*
foliage	el follaje *(ehl foh-'yah-heh)*
grass	el pasto *(ehl 'pah-stoh)*
gravel	la grava *(lah 'grah-vah)*
land	el terreno *(ehl teh-'rreh-noh)*
lawn	el césped *(ehl sehs-'pehd)*
leaves	las hojas *(lahs 'oh-hahs)*
plants	las plantas *(lahs 'plahn-tahs)*
rocks	las piedras *(lahs pee·'eh-drahs)*
roots	las raíces *(lah rah-'ee-sehs)*
sand	la arena *(lah ah-'reh-nah)*
seeds	las semillas *(lahs seh-'mee-yahs)*
tree	el árbol *(ehl 'ahr-bohl)*
weeds	las malas hierbas *(lahs 'mah-lahs 'yehr-bahs)*

Look at (the) ...	Mire... *('mee-reh)*
flower bed	el arriate *(ehl ah-rree-'ah-teh)*
greenhouse	el invernadero
	(ehl een-vehr-nah-'deh-roh)
grove	la arboleda *(lah arh-boh-'leh-dah)*
nursery	el criadero *(ehl kree·ah-'deh-roh)*
orchard	la huerta *(lah 'wehr-tah)*

Tell the kids to stay away from hazardous areas:

Do not go near (the)...	No acercarse a... *(noh ah-sehr-'kahr-seh ah...)*
channel	el canal *(ehl kah-'nahl)*
ditch	la zanja *(lah 'sahn-hah)*
drainage	el drenaje *(ehl dreh-'nah-heh)*
hole	el hoyo *(ehl 'oh-yoh)*
irrigation	la irrigación *(lah ee-rree-gah-see-'ohn)*
slope	el declive *(ehl deh-'klee-veh)*
sprinklers	las rociadoras
	(lahs roh-see·ah-'doh-rahs)

MÁS INFORMACIÓN

➤ Although you've learned a few tools and materials already, there are some that are generally used by employees who do most of their work outdoors:

Move (the)...	Mueve... *('mweh-veh)*
ax	el hacha *(ehl 'ah-chah)*
blower	el soplador *(ehl soh-plah-'dohr)*
chain saw	la motosierra *(lah 'moh-toh-see-'eh-rrah)*
fertilizer	el abono *(ehl ah-'boh-noh)*
hoe	el azadón *(ehl ah-sah-'dohn)*
insecticide	el insecticida *(ehl een-sehk-tee-'see-dah)*
lawn mower	la cortadora de césped
	(lah kohr-tah-'doh-rah deh 'sehs-pehd)
pick	el pico *(ehl 'pee-koh)*

pitchfork	la horquilla *(lah ohr-'kee-yah)*
rake	el rastrillo *(ehl rah-'stree-yoh)*
shovel	la pala *(lah 'pah-lah)*
tractor	el tractor *(ehl trahk-'tohr)*
wheelbarrow	la carretilla *(lah kah-rreh-'tee-yah)*

ALL AROUND TOWN

Por toda la ciudad *(pohr 'toh-dah lah see-oo-'dahd)*

Several staff members conduct their business off-site, and therefore communicate at different locations throughout the city. Check over the following list, which identifies parts of your local community. We learned some of these already:

I went to (the)...	Fui a... *(fwee ah...)*
airport	el aeropuerto *(ehl ah-eh-roh-'pwehr-toh)*
bank	el banco *(ehl 'bahn-koh)*
church	la iglesia *(lah ee-'gleh-see·ah)*
city hall	el municipio *(ehl moo-nee-'see-pee·oh)*
courthouse	la corte *(lah 'kohr-teh)*
warehouse	el almacén *(ehl ahl-mah-'sehn)*
factory	la fábrica *(lah 'fah-bree-kah)*
gas station	la gasolinera *(lah gah-soh-lee-'neh-rah)*
hospital	el hospital *(ehl oh-spee-'tahl)*
library	la biblioteca *(lah beeb-lee·oh-'teh-kah)*
movie theater	el cine *(ehl 'see-neh)*
office	la oficina *(lah oh-fee-'see-nah)*
pharmacy	la farmacia *(lah fahr-'mah-see·ah)*
police station	la estación de policía *(lah eh-stah-see-'ohn deh poh-lee-'see·ah)*
post office	el correo *(ehl koh-'rreh-oh)*
restaurant	el restaurante *(ehl reh-stah-oo-'rahn-teh)*
store	la tienda *(lah tee-'ehn-dah)*
supermarket	el supermercado *(ehl soo-pehr-mehr-'kah-doh)*

This new vocabulary will assist anyone who travels, delivers, or visits educational facilities around town:

It's near (the)...   Está cerca de... *(eh-'stah 'sehr-kah deh...)*

alley	el callejón *(ehl kah-yeh-'hohn)*
apartment building	el edificio de departamentos *(ehl eh-dee-'fee-see·oh deh deh-pahr-tah-'mehn-tohs)*
avenue	la avenida *(lah ah-veh-'nee-dah)*
billboard	el letrero *(ehl leh-'treh-roh)*
bridge	el puente *(ehl 'pwehn-teh)*
bus stop	la parada de autobús *(lah pah-'rah-dah deh ow-toh-'boos)*
car lot	el lote de carros *(ehl 'loh-teh deh 'kah-rrohs)*
corner	la esquina *(lah eh-'skee-nah)*
crosswalk	el cruce de peatones *(ehl 'kroo-seh deh peh-ah-'toh-nehs)*
downtown	el centro *(ehl 'sehn-troh)*
fountain	la fuente *(lah 'fwehn-teh)*
highway	la carretera *(lah kah-rreh-'teh-rah)*
neighborhood	el barrio *(ehl 'bah-rree·oh)*
outskirts	las afueras *(lahs ah-'fweh-rahs)*
railroad track	la vía del ferrocarril *(lah 'vee·ah dehl feh-rroh-kah-'rreel)*
road	el camino *(ehl kah-'mee-noh)*
sidewalk	la acera *(lah ah-'seh-rah)*
statue	la estatua *(lah eh-'stah-too-ah)*
stop sign	el señal de parada *(ehl seh-'nyahl deh pah-'rah-dah)*
street	la calle *(lah 'kah-yeh)*
telephone pole	el poste de teléfono *(ehl 'poh-steh deh teh-'leh-foh-noh)*
tower	la torre *(lah 'toh-rreh)*
traffic signal	el semáforo *(ehl seh-'mah-foh-roh)*
tunnel	el túnel *(ehl 'too-nehl)*

➤ The names for some businesses follow a similar pattern in the Spanish language. They end in the letters -ería. This is just a sample:

bakery	la panadería *(lah pah-nah-deh-'ree·ah)*
barber shop	la peluquería *(lah peh-loo-keh-'ree·ah)*
bookstore	la librería *(lah lee-breh-'ree·ah)*
butcher shop	la carnicería *(lah kahr-nee-seh-'ree·ah)*
laundromat	la lavandería *(lah lah-vahn-deh-'ree·ah)*
shoe store	la zapatería *(lah sah-pah-teh-'ree·ah)*

➤ Can you relate to any of these places of worship?

They go to (the) ...	Van a ... *(vahn ah...)*
cathedral	la catedral *(lah kah-teh-'drahl)*
chapel	la capilla *(lah kah-'pee-yah)*
church	la iglesia *(lah ee-'gleh-see·ah)*
mosque	la mezquita *(lah mehs-'kee-tah)*
synagogue	la sinagoga *(lah see-nah-'goh-gah)*
temple	el templo *(ehl 'tehm-ploh)*

Translate into English:

Tráigame la pala, el rastrillo y el azadón.
('trah ee-gah-meh lah 'pah-lah, ehl rah-'stree-yoh ee ehl ah-sah-'dohn)

Cortaré el arbusto, el césped y el árbol.
(kohr-tah-'reh ehl ahr-'boo-stoh, ehl 'sehs-pehd ee ehl 'ahr-bohl)

Fui a la tienda, el correo y el banco.
(fwee ah lah tee-'ehn-dah, ehl koh-'rreh-oh, ee ehl 'bahn-koh)

Mire la fuente, el puente y la estatua.
('mee-reh lah 'fwehn-teh, ehl 'pwehn-teh ee lah eh-'stah-too-ah)

He hablado con el jardinero, la enfermera y el bedel.
(eh ah-'blah-doh kohn ehl hahr-dee-'neh-roh, lah ehn-fehr-'meh-rah ee ehl beh-'dehl)

READ THE SIGN!

¡Lee el letrero! *('leh-eh ehl leh-'treh-roh)*

Do all the students and their families know what these words mean?

Curve	CURVA *('koor-vah)*
Detour	DESVIACION *(dehs-vee·ah-see·'ohn)*
Do Not Cross	NO CRUZAR *(noh kroo-'sahr)*
Do Not Litter	NO TIRE BASURA *(noh 'tee-reh bah-'soo-rah)*
Emergency	EMERGENCIA *(eh-mehr-'hehn-see·ah)*
Entrance	ENTRADA *(ehn-'trah-dah)*
Exit	SALIDA *(sah-'lee-dah)*
Handicapped	DISCAPACIDAD *(dees-cah-pah-'see-dad)*
Narrow Road	CAMINO ESTRECHO
	(kah-'mee-noh eh-'streh-choh)
No Entrance	PASO PROHIBIDO *('pah-soh proh-ee-'bee-doh)*
No Passing	NO PASAR *(noh pah-'sahr)*
No U Turn	PROHIBIDA LA VUELTA EN U
	(proh-ee-'bee-dah lah 'vwehl-tah ehn oo)
One Way	CIRCULACION *(seer-koo-lah-see·'ohn)*
Parking	ESTACIONAMIENTO
	(eh-stah-see·oh-nah-mee-'ehn-toh)
Pedestrian Crossing	PASO DE PEATONES
	('pah-soh deh peh-ah-'toh-nehs)
Railroad Crossing	CRUCE DE VIAS *('kroo-seh deh 'vee·ahs)*
Slow	DESPACIO *(deh-'spah-see·oh)*
Speed Limit	LIMITE DE VELOCIDAD
	('lee-mee-teh deh veh-loh-see-'dahd)
Stop	ALTO *('ahl-toh)*
Tow Away Zone	SE USARA GRUA *(seh oo-sah-'rah 'groo-ah)*
Traffic Circle	GLORIETA *(gloh-ree-'eh-tah)*
Wait	ESPERE *(eh-'speh-reh)*
Walk	CAMINE *(kah-'mee-neh)*
Wrong Way	VIA EQUIVOCADA
	('vee·ah eh-kee-voh-'kah-dah)
Yield	CEDA EL PASO *('seh-dah ehl 'pah-soh)*

Speaking of written signs, what about those around the school grounds? Post these words in two languages today!

Closed	CERRADO *(seh-'rrah-doh)*
Danger	PELIGRO *(peh-'lee-groh)*
For Rent	SE ALQUILA *(seh ahl-'kee-lah)*
For Sale	SE VENDE *(seh 'vehn-deh)*
No Smoking	NO FUMAR *(noh foo-'mahr)*
Open	ABIERTO *(ah-bee-'ehr-toh)*
Out of Order	DESCOMPUESTO *(dehs-kohm-'pweh-stoh)*
Pull	JALE *('hah-leh)*
Push	EMPUJE *(ehm-'poo-heh)*
Red Cross	CRUZ ROJA *(kroos 'roh-hah)*
Restrooms	BAÑOS *('bah-nyohs)*

Keep going:

Authorized Personnel Only	SÓLO PARA PERSONAL AUTORIZADO *('soh-loh 'pah-rah pehr-soh-'nahl ow-toh-ree-'sah-doh)*
Change Machine	MÁQUINA DE CAMBIO *('mah-kee-nah deh 'kahm-bee·oh)*
Do Not Block Entrance	NO OBSTRUIR LA ENTRADA *(noh ohb-stroo-'eer lah ehn-'trah-dah)*
Emergency Exit	SALIDA DE EMERGENCIA *(sah-'lee-dah deh eh-mehr-'hehn-see·ah)*
Employee Parking	ESTACIONAMIENTO PARA EMPLEADOS *(eh-stah-see·oh-nah-mee-'ehn-toh 'pah-rah ehm-pleh-'ah-dohs)*
Next Window Please	PASAR A LA SIGUIENTE VENTANILLA *(pah-'sahr ah lah see-gee-'ehn-teh vehn-tah-'nee-yah)*

 DIFERENCIAS CULTURALES

Do not translate names of businesses, brands, streets. All over the world, most formal titles in English remain the same.

KITCHEN EMPLOYEES

Los empleados de la cocina *(lohs ehm-pleh-'ah-dohs deh lah koh-'see-nah)*

When the bell rings, and everyone fills the cafeteria or lunch area, numerous conversations begin. Here are the names for a few condiments:

We need more of (the) ... Necesitamos más de ... *(neh-seh-see-'tah-mohs mahs deh...)*

chocolate	el chocolate *(ehl choh-koh-'lah-teh)*
cinnamon	la canela *(lah kah-'neh-lah)*
garlic	el ajo *(ehl 'ah-hoh)*
honey	la miel *(lah mee-'ehl)*
hot pepper	el chile *(ehl 'chee-leh)*
marmalade	la mermelada *(lah mehr-meh-'lah-dah)*
mayonnaise	la mayonesa *(lah mah-yoh-'neh-sah)*
mustard	la mostaza *(lah moh-'stah-sah)*
nuts	las nueces *(lahs noo-'eh-sehs)*
oil	el aceite *(ehl ah-'seh ee-teh)*
olive	la aceituna *(lah ah-seh ee-'too-nah)*
peanut butter	la crema de maní *(lah 'kreh-mah deh mah-'nee)*
pepper	la pimienta *(lah pee-mee-'ehn-tah)*
pickle	el encurtido *(ehl ehn-koor-'tee-doh)*
salad dressing	la salsa para la ensalada *(lah 'sahl-sah 'pah-rah lah ehn-sah-'lah-dah)*
salt	la sal *(lah sahl)*
sauce	la salsa *(lah 'sahl-sah)*
sugar	el azúcar *(ehl ah-'soo-kahr)*
tomato sauce	la salsa de tomate *(lah 'sahl-sah deh toh-'mah-teh)*
vanilla	la vainilla *(lah vah·ee-'nee-yah)*
vinegar	el vinagre *(ehl vee-'nah-greh)*

Think about labeling some of these kitchen objects with removable stickers:

Bring (the)... Traiga... *('trah ee-gah...)* or Trae... *('trah-eh)*

apron	el delantal *(ehl deh-lahn-'tahl)*
bowl	el plato hondo *(ehl 'plah-toh 'ohn-doh)*
butter dish	la mantequillera *(lah mahn-teh-kee-'yeh-rah)*

coffeepot	la cafetera *(lah kah-feh-'teh-rah)*
creamer	la cremera *(lah kreh-'meh-rah)*
cup	la taza *(lah 'tah-sah)*
fork	el tenedor *(ehl teh-neh-'dohr)*
glass	el vaso *(ehl 'vah-soh)*
grill	la parrilla *(lah pah-'rree-yah)*
knife	el cuchillo *(ehl koo-'chee-yoh)*
matches	los fósforos *(lohs 'fohs-foh-rohs)*
napkin	la servilleta *(lah sehr-vee-'yeh-tah)*
pan	el sartén *(ehl sahr-'tehn)*
pepper shaker	el pimentero *(ehl pee-mehn-'teh-roh)*
pitcher	el cántaro *(ehl 'kahn-tah-roh)*
plate	el plato *(ehl 'plah-toh)*
platter	la fuente *(lah 'fwehn-teh)*
pot	la olla *(lah 'oh-yah)*
rack	el estilador *(ehl eh-stee-lah-'dohr)*
salad bowl	la ensaladera *(lah ehn-sah-lah-'deh-rah)*
salt shaker	el salero *(ehl sah-'leh-roh)*
saucepan	la cacerola *(lah kah-seh-'roh-lah)*
saucer	el platillo *(ehl plah-'tee-yoh)*
spoon	la cuchara *(lah koo-'chah-rah)*
sugar bowl	la azucarera *(lah ah-soo-kah-'reh-rah)*
tablecloth	el mantel *(ehl mahn-'tehl)*
thermos	el termo *(ehl 'tehr-moh)*
towel	la toalla *(lah toh-'ah-yah)*
tray	la bandeja *(lah bahn-'deh-hah)*

Everyone has something to say about their meal. Listen to these comments in Spanish:

It's...	Está... *(eh-'stah)*

bitter	amargo *(ah-'mahr-goh)*
burned	quemado *(keh-'mah-doh)*
cooked	cocido *(koh-'see-doh)*
delicious	delicioso *(deh-lee-see-'oh-soh)*
dry	seco *('seh-koh)*
fresh	fresco *('frehs-koh)*
fried	frito *('free-toh)*
frozen	congelado *(kohn-heh-'lah-doh)*
hard	duro *('doo-roh)*

moist	**húmedo** *('oo-meh-doh)*
raw	**crudo** *('kroo-doh)*
rotten	**podrido** *(poh-'dree-doh)*
salty	**salado** *(sah-'lah-doh)*
soft	**suave** *('swah-veh)*
sour	**agrio** *('ah-gree·oh)*
spicy	**picante** *(pee-'kahn-teh)*
sweet	**dulce** *('dool-seh)*
tasty	**sabroso** *(sah-'broh-soh)*
warm	**tibio** *('tee-bee·oh)*

Keep it up, but with these words, talk to the students about good health. Bear in mind that descriptions must change according to gender and number:

It's...	**Es...** *(ehs)*
dietary	**dietético** *(dee-eh-'teh-tee-koh)*
fat-free	**desgrasado** *(dehs-grah-'sah-doh)*
kosher	**preparado conforme a la ley judía** *(preh-pah-'rah-doh kohn-'fohr-meh ah lah 'leh eehoo-'dee·ah)*
natural	**natural** *(nah-too-'rahl)*
organic	**orgánico** *(ohr-'gah-nee-koh)*
sugar-free	**sin azúcar** *(seen ah-'soo-kahr)*
vegetarian/vegan	**vegetariano/vegano** *(veh-heh-tah-ree·'ah-noh / veh-'gahn-o)*

315

SECURITY PERSONNEL

El personal de seguridad *(ehl pehr-soh-'nahl deh seh-goo-ree-'dahd)*

Yet another key figure at school sites today is the campus security guard. When they address people in Spanish, their first question is to find out who everyone is. Change these to the feminine form if necessary:

Who is (the)...?	¿Quién es...? *(kee-'ehn ehs...)*
bystander	el espectador *(ehl eh-spehk-tah-'dohr)*
companion	el compañero *(ehl kohm-pah-'nyeh-roh)*
cyclist	el ciclista *(ehl see-'klee-stah)*
driver	el chofer *(ehl choh-'fehr)*
employee	el empleado *(ehl ehm-pleh-'ah-doh)*
friend	el amigo *(ehl ah-'mee-goh)*
minor	el menor de edad *(ehl meh-'nohr deh eh-'dahd)*
neighbor	el vecino *(ehl veh-'see-noh)*
passenger	el pasajero *(ehl pah-sah-'heh-roh)*
pedestrian	el peatón *(ehl peh-ah-'tohn)*
stranger	el desconocido *(ehl dehs-koh-noh-'see-doh)*
visitor	el visitante *(ehl vee-see-'tahn-teh)*

Now mention some of the folks who may create a problem. Do you recall any of these words from before?

I saw (the)...	Yo ví... *(yoh vee...)*
beggar	el limosnero *(ehl lee-mohs-'neh-roh)*
criminal	el criminal *(ehl kree-mee-'nahl)*
delinquent	el delincuente *(ehl deh-leen-'kwehn-teh)*
drug dealer	el droguero *(ehl droh-'geh-roh)*
drunkard	el borracho *(ehl boh-'rrah-choh)*
gang member	el pandillero *(ehl pahn-dee-'yeh-roh)*
loiterer	el holgazán *(ehl ohl-gah-'sahn)*
pickpocket	el carterista *(ehl kahr-teh-'ree-stah)*
prostitute	la prostituta *(lah proh-stee-'too-tah)*
thief	el ladrón *(ehl lah-'drohn)*
vagrant	el vagabundo *(ehl vah-gah-'boon-doh)*

When you confront and question all suspicious characters, combine your question words to collect the data you need. Write down a few of these phrases so that you won't forget. Fortunately, the answers to these questions are often brief and to the point:

Whose is it?	¿De quién es? *(deh kee-'ehn ehs)*
What's that?	¿Qué es eso? *(keh ehs 'eh-soh)*
Where are you from?	¿De dónde es? *(deh 'dohn-deh ehs)*
Where do you live?	¿Dónde vive? *('dohn-deh 'vee-veh)*
For what reason?	¿Por qué razón? *(pohr keh rah-'sohn)*
What kind?	¿Qué clase? *(keh 'klah-seh)*

This next Spanish action form is helpful in any conversation. Remember to use the formal **usted** form:

Have you been in jail?	¿Ha estado en la cárcel? *(ah eh-'stah-doh ehn lah 'kahr-sehl)*
Have you been drinking?	¿Ha estado tomando alcohol? *(ah eh-'stah-doh toh-'mahn-doh ahl-koh-'ohl)*
Have you been taking drugs?	¿Ha estado tomando drogas? *(ah eh-'stah-doh toh-'mahn-doh 'droh-gahs)*
Have you ever been arrested?	¿Ha sido arrestado alguna vez? *(ah 'see-doh ah-rreh-'stah-doh ahl-'goo-nah vehs)*

ON PATROL
Patrullando *(pah-troo-'yahn-doh)*

Practice these one-liners as you help out drivers in trouble:

Can you drive it?	¿Puede manejarlo? *(poo-'eh-deh mah-neh-'hahr-loh)*
Did you leave your keys inside?	¿Dejó las llaves adentro? *(deh-'hoh lahs 'yah-vehs ah-'dehn-troh)*
Was something stolen?	¿Le robaron algo? *(leh roh-'bah-rohn 'ahl-goh)*
Did someone hit you?	¿Le chocaron su carro? *(leh choh-'kah-rohn soo 'kahr-roh)*
Do you need to charge the battery?	¿Necesita cargar la bateria? *(neh-seh-'see-tah kahr-'gahr lah bah-teh-'ree·ah)*

317

Now address the car trouble:

You're out of gas.	Le falta gasolina. *(leh 'fahl-tah gah-soh-'lee-nah)*
Your tires are flat.	Sus neumáticos están desinflados. *(soos neh-oo-'mah-tee-kohs ehs-'tahn deh-seen-'flah-dohs)*
There's lots of exhaust.	Hay mucho escape de humo. *('ah-ee 'moo-choh ehs-'kah-peh deh 'oo-moh)*
There's a leak.	Hay una gotera. *('ah-ee 'oo-nah goh-'teh-rah)*
It's not working.	No está funcionando. *(noh ehs-'tah foon-see·oh-'nahn-doh)*

Continue to use the formal **usted** form as you offer assistance:

How can I help you?	¿Cómo puedo ayudarle? *('koh-moh poo-'eh-doh ah-you-'dahr-leh)*
Do you want a push?	¿Quiere una empujada? *(kee-'eh-reh 'oo-nah ehm-poo-'hah-dah)*
I'm calling...(the)	Estoy llamando a... *(ehs-'toh-ee yah-'mahn-doh ah)*
garage	el garaje *(ehl gah-'rah-heh)*
police	la policía *(lah poh-lee-'see·ah)*
locksmith	el cerrajero *(ehl sehr-rah-'heh-roh)*
gas station	la gasolinera *(lah gah-soh-lee-'neh-rah)*
towing company	la compañía de remolque *(lah kohm-pah-'nee·ah deh reh-'mohl-keh)*

Whenever you depart, always send folks away with a friendly expression:

Drive with care!	¡Maneje con cuidado! *(mah-'neh-heh kohn koo-ee-'dah-doh)*
Have a nice day!	¡Que tenga un buen día! *(keh 'tehn-gah oon boo-'ehn 'dee·ah)*
See you later!	¡Hasta luego! *('ahs-tah loo-'eh-goh)*

If you're a crossing guard, tell the students what they're doing wrong:

You crossed when the *Don't Walk* sign was on.	Cruzaste cuando la señal decía *No Caminar*. *(kroo-'sahs-teh koo-'ahn-doh lah sehn-'yahl deh-'see·ah noh kah-mee-'nahr)*
You didn't use the crosswalk.	No usaste el cruce de peatones. *(noh oo-'sahs-teh ehl 'kroo-seh deh peh-ah-'toh-nehs)*

You were walking in the street.	Caminabas por la calle. *(kah-mee-'nah-bahs pohr lah 'kah-yeh)*
You crossed when there was a lot of traffic.	Cruzaste cuando había mucho tráfico. *(kroo-'sahs-teh koo-'ahn-doh a-'bee·ah 'moo-choh 'trah-fee-koh)*
You didn't wait for the green light.	No esperaste por la luz verde. *(noh ehs-peh-'rahs-teh pohr lah loos 'vehr-deh)*

And be sure to warn both drivers and pedestrians that there are hazards on school grounds or in the area:

Be careful with (the) ...	Tengan cuidado con... *('tehn-gahn koo-ee-'dah-doh kohn)*
bump	el rompemuelle *(ehl rohm-peh-moo-'eh-yeh)*
construction	la construcción *(lah kohn-strook-see-'ohn)*
detour	el desvío *(ehl dehs-'vee·oh)*
glass	los vidrios *(lohs 'veed-ree·ohs)*
hole	el hoyo *(ehl 'oh-yoh)*
pothole	el bache *(ehl 'bah-cheh)*
It's...	Está... *(ehs-'tah)*
blocked off	obstruída *(ohbs-troo-'ee-dah)*
slippery	resbaladiza *(rehs-bah-lah-'dee-sah)*
flooded	inundada *(ee-noon-'dah-dah)*

MÁS INFORMACIÓN

➤ To know the Spanish names of your uniform and equipment will be useful, and it will boost your self-confidence.

This is (the)...	Esto es... *('eh-stoh ehs...)*
badge	el emblema *(ehl ehm-'bleh-mah)*
bullhorn	el altavoz *(ehl ahl-tah-'vohs)*
equipment belt	la correa de equipaje *(lah koh-'rreh-ah deh eh-kee-'pah-heh)*
flashlight	la linterna *(lah leen-'tehr-nah)*
handcuff	las esposas *(lahs eh-'spoh-sahs)*

radio transmitter	el radiotransmisor
	(ehl rah-dee·oh-trahns-mee-sohr)
uniform	el uniforme *(ehl oo-nee-'fohr-meh)*
whistle	el silbato *(ehl seel-'bah-toh)*

¿LISTOS PARA PRACTICAR?

Connect the opposites:

sal *(sahl)*	suave *('swah-veh)*
duro *('doo-roh)*	tenedor *(teh-neh-'dohr)*
cuchara *(koo-'chah-rah)*	pimienta *(pee-mee-'ehn-tah)*

Select the word that should go next:

sartén, mostaza, delicuente, amigo, dulce *(sahr-'tehn, moh-'stah-sah, deh-leen-'kwehn-teh, ah-'mee-goh, 'dool-seh)*

agrio, picante, _____ *('ah-gree oh, pee-'kahn-teh)*

mayonesa, salsa de tomate, _____ *(mah-yoh-'neh-sah, 'sahl-sah deh toh-'mah-teh)*

cacerola, olla, _____ *(kah-seh-'roh-lah, 'oh-yah)*

compañero, vecino, _____ *(kohm-pah-'nyeh-roh, veh-'see-noh)*

ladrón, pandillero, _____ *(lah-'drohn, pahn-dee-'yeh-roh)*

¡ACCIÓN!

Let's close out this guidebook with a quick review of the grammar material that was presented earlier. Instruction on verb usage can be found at the end of each chapter. Closely study this next example and then fill in the blanks below with the correct verb forms:

to buy   comprar (*kohm-'prahr*)

I'm buying   Estoy comprando (*eh-'stoh·ee kohm-'prahn-doh*)
I buy   Compro (*'kohm-proh*)
I will buy   Compraré (*kohm-prahr-'reh*)
I bought   Compré (*kohm-'preh*)
I have bought   He comprado (*eh kohm-'prah-doh*)

to walk   caminar (*kah-mee-'nahr*)

I'm walking   _____

I walk   _____

I will walk   _____

I walked   _____

I have walked   _____

to try   tratar (*trah-'tahr*)

I'm trying   _____

I try   _____

I will try   _____

I tried   _____

I have tried   _____

Again, one of the best methods for practicing verbs is to insert them into short, practical phrases. Here are some shortcuts that were presented earlier. Translate, and then choose one of the verb phrases below to complete a sentence:

No... *(noh)* _____

Puedo... *('pweh-doh)* _____

Me gusta... *(meh 'goo-stah)* _____

Voy a... *('voh·ee ah)* _____

Quiero... *(kee-'eh-roh)* _____

Quisiera... *(kee-see-'eh-rah)* _____

Favor de... *(fah-'vohr deh)* _____

Tienes que... *(tee-'eh-nehs keh)* _____

Necesitas... *(neh-seh-'see-tahs)* _____

Debes... *('deh-behs)* _____

> **estudiar la lección** *(eh-stoo-dee-'ahr lah lehk-see·'ohn)*
> **trabajar en el libro** *(trah-bah-'hahr ehn ehl 'lee-broh)*
> **leer el papel** *(leh-'ehr ehl pah-'pehl)*
> **escribir con el lápiz** *(eh-skree-'beer kohn ehl 'lah-pees)*
> **hablar inglés** *(ah-'blahr een-'glehs)*

 ¿LISTOS PARA PRACTICAR?

Create real-life scenarios every chance you get! Make up a situation, choose characters, and role-play the scene over and over again. Obviously, the more you practice, the easier it will become. The key is to select a dialog that you know will take place soon; practicing unreal or irrelevant scenarios will only slow down the process. And remember, if you worry too much about your grammar and pronunciation errors, you'll never get started at all!

➤ Take note of this new shortcut to using Spanish verbs. If you are struggling with the past tense, stick this one-liner in front of any infinitive:

I just finished...   Acabo de... *(ah-'kah-boh deh...)*

I just finished eating.   Acabo de comer. *(ah-'kah-boh deh koh-'mehr)*
I just finished reading.   Acabo de leer. *(ah-'kah-boh deh leh-'ehr)*
I just finished playing.   Acabo de jugar. *(ah-'kah-boh deh hoo-'gahr)*

To practice the past tense, follow the pattern in the example. Don't forget to translate:

Acabo de hablar   Hablé *(ah-'bleh)*
(ah-'kah-boh deh ah-'blahr)   _____

Acabo de aconsejar
(ah-'kah-boh deh ah-kohn-seh-'hahr)   _____

Acabo de consultar
(ah-'kah-boh deh kohn-sool-'tahr)   _____

Acabo de gritar
(ah-'kah-boh deh gree-'tahr)   _____

Acabo de discutir
(ah-'kah-boh deh dee-skoo-'teer)   _____

Acabo de dormir
(ah-'kah-boh deh dohr-'meer)   _____

Acabo de escribir
(ah-'kah-boh deh eh-skree-'beer)   _____

¡ÓRDENES!

No educator who needs Spanish can last long without the command words. Let's review some of the key phrases. Translate as you read through these popular informal commands, and then create some expressions of your own:

Contesta *(kohn-'teh-stah)*
Contesta en inglés. *(kohn-'teh-stah ehn eeh-'glehs)*

Trae *('trah-eh)*
Trae el formulario. *('trah-eh ehl fohr-moo-'lah-ree·oh)*

Llama *('yah-mah)*
Llama a tus padres. *('yah-mah ah toos pah-'drehs)*

Escucha *(eh-'skoo-chah)*
Escucha la pregunta. *(eh-'skoo-chah lah preh-'goon-tah)*

Lee *('leh-eh)*
Lee el papel. *('leh-eh ehl pah-'pehl)*

Regresa *(reh-'greh-sah)*
Regresa mañana. *(reh-'greh-sah mah-'nyah-nah)*

Firma *('feer-mah)*
Firma aquí. *('feer-mah ah-'kee)*

Habla *('ah-blah)*
Habla más despacio. *('ah-blah mahs deh-'spah-see·oh)*

Toma *('toh-mah)*
Toma asiento. *('toh-mah ah-see-'ehn-toh)*

Keep it up; however, this time say things using the *formal* command form:

Try	Trate *('trah-teh)*	_____
Study	Estudie *(eh-'stoo-dee-eh)*	_____
Ask for	Pida *('pee-dah)*	_____
Explain	Explique *(ehks-'plee-keh)*	_____
Measure	Mida *('mee-dah)*	_____
Check	Verifique *(veh-ree-'fee-keh)*	_____
Let	Deje *('deh-heh)*	_____
Touch	Toque *('toh-keh)*	_____
Cut	Corte *('kohr-teh)*	_____
Pass	Pase *('pah-seh)*	_____
Learn	Aprenda *(ah-'prehn-dah)*	_____

MÁS INFORMACIÓN

➤ Since we're talking about formal commands, do you recall the le, lo, and la words? Follow the model as you review:

Bring it	Tráigalo *('trah ee-gah-loh)*
Choose it	_____
Deliver it	_____
Do it	_____
Change it	_____
Talk to him	Háblele *('ah-bleh-leh)*
Look for him	_____

Pay him	_____
Look at him	_____
Give it to him	_____

These phrases are a bit more complicated:

Send it to me	Mándemelo *('mahn-deh-meh-loh)*
Lift it up	_____
Tell it to me	_____

 ## DIFERENCIAS CULTURALES

To get a true feel for communication in Spanish, find time to observe a group of Hispanics in public or at a social gathering. Facial expressions, touch, changes in tone, and hand signals are a few of the many nonverbal differences between the Latin American and U.S. cultures.

THAT'S IT, FELLOW EDUCATORS!
¡Eso es todo, colegas! *('eh-soh ehs 'toh-doh, koh-'leh-gahs)*

Now that you have learned all the important vocabulary and phrases needed to converse in Spanish, are you ready to use them in public? No matter what you do in the field of education, the skills that are required to communicate have been presented somewhere in this guidebook. So, what's the delay? The Spanish-speaking world is waiting for you, so get out there and go for it! Trust me—once you get started, your life as an educator will never be the same!

Buena suerte, amigos, y Dios les bendiga,
('bweh-nah 'swehr-teh, ah-'mee-gohs, ee 'dee·ohs lehs behn-'dee-gah)

Bill

Bill

TOP 10 SPANISH FOR EDUCATORS PRACTICE TIPS

Obviously, the best way to practice Spanish is with the assistance of a fluent Spanish speaker. If that's not possible, then seriously commit to some, if not all, of the following practice activities. And do it regularly!

I. Listen to any:

- Audio files or music CDs
- DVDs, online clips, or video downloads
- Radio, TV, or online programming
- Language learning audio-visual products
- Foreign language interactive websites

II. Experiment with the language where you can also have some fun:

- Have real-life conversations with local folks, family, or trusted friends
- Participate in activities where you can learn Spanish lyrics and sing along
- Take a class in Latin dance where you'll be exposed to both language and cultural interaction
- Consider attending any event or activity where Spanish will be spoken in a social setting

III. Use the *label and command* method, especially around the home, by placing removable labels on objects with their names in Spanish clearly in sight. Then have someone command you to touch, lift, look at, or move whatever it is you've labeled.

IV. Interview other Spanish students by listing a variety of simple questions in Spanish, using different verb tenses. Then meet regularly, and fill in their responses to your homemade questionnaire.

V. Create online flashcards in order to remember the meanings and conjugations of Spanish verbs. Start off with one set of cards for "regular" verbs. Then create other cards for those pesky "irregular" ones.

VI. Gather all the Spanish reading materials that you can and see if you can guess what they are trying to say. Online notices, advertisements, and brochures are readily available, and many Spanish language websites have a home page that is easy to understand.

VII. No matter what your age, games are incredible teaching tools. So shop around or search the internet for any language learning games in Spanish. Concentration,

Bingo, crosswords, and word search puzzles are the easiest kinds to begin with. Start with those designed for kids.

VIII. It also might be a good idea to know the most common mistakes that Spanish beginners make. Consider the following as common areas of concern:

A. LISTENING AND SPEAKING SKILLS

- Confusing the vowel sounds, such as hearing the "*i*" and thinking it's an "*e*".
- Confusing the consonant sounds, such as hearing the "*j*" sound and thinking it's an "*h*".
- Pronouncing words with "*rr*" without rolling the "r", such as saying "*caro*" (expensive) instead of "*carro*" (car).
- Confusing the "*r*" and "*d*" in Spanish, such as hearing "*todo*" (all) and thinking "*toro*" (bull).
- Mispronouncing "*que*" and "*qui*" in Spanish, forgetting that "*qu*" makes the "k" sound.
- Mispronouncing "*gui*" and "*gue*" in Spanish, forgetting that the "*g*" is hard and the "*u*" is silent.
- Pronouncing words with "*ll*" as if it were "*l*", such as saying "*polo*" (shirt) instead of "*pollo*" (chicken).
- Putting the wrong intonation on words in a sentence, such as stressing the last word of every question.
- Pronouncing words with "ñ" as if they were "*n*", such as saying "*ano*" (anus) instead of "*año*" (year).
- Mispronouncing words due to not understanding accentuation, such as saying "*esta*" instead of "*está*".
- Mixing up the gender of nouns, such as incorrectly saying "*la problema*" instead of "*el problema*".
- Remembering that the "*z*" is pronounced as an "*s*" in Latin American Spanish.
- Remembering that the "*v*" is pronounced more like a "*b*" in Spanish.
- Translating literally, such as saying "*Estoy frío.*" instead of "*Tengo frío.*" (I'm cold.)
- Distinguishing between the informal "*tú*" and the formal "*usted*" forms, such as addressing a stranger with "*¿Cómo estás tú?*" instead of "*¿Cómo está usted?*" (How are you?).
- Using Spanish slang, street language, or curse words without knowing what the words really mean.

B. READING AND WRITING SKILLS

- Forgetting to write accent marks on words that require them, such as with "*sí*" and "*cómo*".
- Spelling words as if they were in English, such as writing "*impossible*" instead of "*imposible*".
- Forgetting to apply a double negative, such as writing "*Hay nadie*" instead of "*No hay nadie*" to express "There is no one."

- Forgetting to reverse the usual order of adjectives and nouns in a sentence, such as writing *"grande casa"* instead of *"casa grande."*
- Inserting *"por"* instead of *"para"* to always mean "for", such as writing *"Es por usted."* instead of *"Es para usted."* (It's for you.)
- Guessing incorrectly at cognate word translations, such as reading *"sopa"* (soup) and thinking it means "soap."
- Overusing the subject pronouns, such as constantly adding *"yo"* (I) before verbs in a sentence even when it's already understood who's doing the talking.
- Mixing up the verbs, *ser* and *estar*, such as writing *"Estoy estudiante."* instead of *"Soy estudiante."* (I am a student.)
- Forgetting proper use of prepositions, such as writing *"en la mañana"* instead of *"de la mañana"* for "in the morning."
- Making capitalization errors, such as putting capitals on the days of the week.
- Dropping the article on the days of the week, such as writing *"Trabajo lunes"* instead of *"Trabajo el lunes."*
- Forgetting that in Spanish strings of words have to be in "agreement." Not only must articles agree with nouns in gender and number, but so must all modifiers (ie: *Hay cinco estudiantes altos.*)
- Using *"se"* and the reflexive verbs incorrectly, such as writing *"Se fue al banco."* instead of *"Fue al banco."* (He went to the bank.)
- Applying regular verb conjugations upon irregular verbs, such as writing *"sabo"* instead of *"sé"* (I know).
- Forgetting to use indirect object pronouns, such as *"le"* in *"Le dí el dinero al Juan"* (I gave the money to John.)
- Getting the Preterite and Imperfect tenses confused, such as writing *"Trabajé toda la noche"* instead of *"Trabajaba toda la noche."* (I was working all night.)

IX. Focus on the positive! By now, you should realize that Spanish can be learned if one has the proper mindset. Dwell on the following as often as you can:

- *Learning Spanish is painless!* Unlike most other languages, thousands of Spanish words are spelled the same in English or are very similar!
- *Learning Spanish is simple!* Most Spanish-speakers use simple vocabulary and verb forms to communicate, and they also tend to repeat the same basic words over and over again!
- *Learning Spanish is practical!* Millions of Latinos in the U.S. and Mexico speak some "Spanglish", a mixture of English and Spanish, so now hundreds of new words are easier to understand!
- *Learning Spanish is valuable!* Don't forget that bilingual employees are in high demand and the pay is generally higher!
- *Learning Spanish is beneficial!* Research suggests that people who know two languages are basically "smarter" than those with only one!
- *Learning Spanish is fun!* Knowing a foreign language can lead to new friend-ships and exciting cultural experiences!

X. Practice without fear! According to experts, learning Spanish is not supposed to be an experience rocked by fear! Evidently, when adults pick it up naturally, like children do with their first language, all the fears and pressures seem to fade away. Kids in a sandbox can learn no matter how many languages there are, simply because they tend to "play' with their communication skills until they get it right. Surprisingly, that's also the way older students like you are designed to learn—by having a good time—naturally. So the truth is there's no reason to fear learning Spanish at all. Here are the facts:

- Personal communication is always more important than conjugation. The fact that you are even trying to speak Spanish will motivate Latinos to kindly help you along.
- If Spanish speakers try to respond back to you in English instead of Spanish, they are not being critical. They just want to try out their new English skills.
- People with a light-hearted, outgoing, childlike approach seem to pick up Spanish faster than others. They appear to overcome shyness, forget about their pride, and just go for it.
- When Latinos giggle as you speak, they're enjoying themselves and the experience. Your mistakes may sound funny to them, so feel free to join in the laughter.
- Humiliation or embarrassment in public is never fun, but it's not that serious when caused by common language errors! Simply embrace the fact that you'll need plenty of healthy self-esteem if you want to learn Spanish well.

ENGLISH-SPANISH VERBS

act, to	actuar	*ahk-too-'ahr*
add, to	sumar	*soo-'mahr*
advise, to	avisar	*ah-vee-'sahr*
allow, to	dejar	*deh-'hahr*
analyze, to	analizar	*ah-nah-lee-'sahr*
answer, to	contestar	*kohn-teh-'stahr*
apply, to	aplicar	*ah-plee-'kahr*
argue, to	discutir	*dee-skoo-'teer*
arrange, to	arreglar	*ah-rreh-'glahr*
arrest, to	arrestar	*ah-rreh-'stahr*
arrive, to	llegar	*yeh-'gahr*
ask for, to	pedir	*peh-'deer*
ask, to	preguntar	*preh-goon-'tahr*
assign, to	asignar	*ah-seeg-'nahr*
assure, to	asegurar	*ah-seh-goo-'rahr*
attend, to	asistir	*ah-see-'steer*
bathe, to	bañarse	*bah-'nyahr-seh*
be able, to	poder	*poh-'dehr*
be in charge, to	encargar	*ehn-kahr-'gahr*
be, to	estar, ser	*eh-'stahr, sehr*
beat up, to	golpear	*gohl-peh-'ahr*
begin, to	comenzar, empezar	*koh-mehn-'sahr, ehm-peh-'sahr*
behave, to	portarse	*pohr-'tahr-seh*
bite, to	morder	*mohr-'dehr*
bother, to	molestar	*moh-leh-'stahr*
bounce, to	rebotar	*reh-boh-'tahr*
break, to	quebrar, romper	*keh-'brahr, rohm-'pehr*
breathe, to	respirar	*reh-spee-'rahr*
bring, to	traer	*trah-'ehr*
build, to	construir	*kohn-stroo-'eer*
buy, to	comprar	*kohm-'prahr*
bullying	la intimidación	*lah een-tee-mee-dah-see-'ohn*
calculate, to	calcular	*kahl-koo-'lahr*
call, to	llamar	*yah-'mahr*
calm down, to	calmarse	*kahl-'mahr-seh*
cancel, to	cancelar	*kahn-seh-'lahr*
carry, to	llevar	*yeh-'vahr*
catch, to	agarrar	*ah-gah-'rrahr*
change, to	cambiar	*kahm-bee-'ahr*
chase, to	perseguir	*pehr-seh-'geer*
check, to	revisar	*reh-vee-'sahr*
chew, to	masticar	*mah-stee-'kahr*
choose, to	escoger	*eh-skoh-'hehr*
clarify, to	clarificar	*klah-ree-fee-'kahr*

clean, to	limpiar	*leem-pee-'ahr*
click, to	pulsar	*pool-'sahr*
climb, to	subir	*soo-'beer*
close, to	cerrar	*seh-'rrahr*
comb one's hair, to	peinarse	*peh·ee-'nahr-seh*
come, to	venir	*veh-'neer*
commend, to	alabar	*ah-lah-'bahr*
communicate, to	comunicar	*koh-moo-nee-'kahr*
compare, to	comparar	*kohm-pah-'rahr*
compete, to	competir	*kohm-peh-'teer*
complain, to	quejarse	*keh-'hahr-seh*
complete, to	completar	*kohm-pleh-'tahr*
compliment, to	felicitar	*feh-lee-see-'tahr*
confirm, to	confirmar	*kohn-feer-'mahr*
confiscate, to	confiscar	*kohn-fee-'skahr*
connect, to	conectar	*koh-nehk-'tahr*
consult, to	consultar	*kohn-sool-'tahr*
converse, to	conversar	*kohn-vehr-'sahr*
copy, to	copiar	*koh-pee-'ahr*
correct, to	corregir	*koh-rreh-'heer*
counsel, to	aconsejar	*ah-kohn-seh-'hahr*
count, to	contar	*kohn-'tahr*
cover, to	cubrir	*koo-'breer*
cry, to	llorar	*yoh-'rahr*
curse, to	decir groserías, maldecir	*deh-'seer groh-seh-'ree·ahs, mahl-deh-'seer*
cut, to	cortar	*kohr-'tahr*
cut and paste, to	cortar y pegar	*kohr-'tahr ee peh-'gahr*
dance, to	bailar	*'bah·ee-'lahr*
debate, to	debatir	*deh-bah-'teer*
defecate, to	defecar	*deh-feh-'kahr*
define, to	definir	*deh-fee-'neer*
delete, to	eliminar	*eh-lee-mee-'nahr*
deliver, to	entregar	*ehn-treh-'gahr*
deny, to	negarse	*neh-'gahr-seh*
deserve, to	merecer	*meh-reh-'sehr*
dial, to	marcar	*mahr-'kahr*
die, to	morir	*moh-'reer*
dissect it	disecarlo	*dee-seh-'kahr-loh*
distract, to	distraer	*dee-strah-'ehr*
dive, to	zambullirse	*sahm-boo-'yeer-seh*
divide, to	dividir	*dee-vee-'deer*
do, to	hacer	*ah-'sehr*
download, to	descargar	*dehs-kahr-'gahr*
drag, to	arrastrar	*ah-rrahs-'trahr*
draw, to	dibujar	*dee-boo-'hahr*
drink, to	beber	*beh-'behr*

drive, to	manejar	*mah-neh-'hahr*
eat, to	comer	*koh-'mehr*
empty, to	vaciar	*vah-see-'ahr*
encourage, to	animar	*ah-nee-'mahr*
end, to	terminar	*tehr-mee-'nahr*
enroll, to	inscribirse, matricularse	*een-skree-'beer-seh, mah-tree-koo-'lahr-seh*
enter, to	entrar	*ehn-'trahr*
erase, to	borrar	*boh-'rrahr*
evaluate, to	evaluar	*eh-vah-loo-'ahr*
examine, to	examinar	*ehk-sah-mee-'nahr*
expel, to	expulsar	*ehk-spool-'sahr*
explain, to	explicar	*ehk-splee-'kahr*
factor, to	factorar	*fahk-toh-'rahr*
fall, to	caerse	*kah-'ehr-seh*
feel, to	sentirse	*sehn-'teer-seh*
fight, to	pelear	*peh-leh-'ahr*
fill out, to	llenar	*yeh-'nahr*
find, to	encontrar	*ehn-kohn-'trahr*
fish, to	pescar	*peh-'skahr*
fold, to	doblar	*doh-'blahr*
follow, to	seguir	*seh-'geer*
forget, to	olvidar	*ohl-vee-'dahr*
forward, to	reenviar	*reh-ehn-vee-'ahr*
get dressed, to	vestirse	*veh-'steer-seh*
get lost, to	perderse	*pehr-'dehr-seh*
get, to	conseguir	*kohn-seh-'geer*
give, to	dar	*dahr*
go, to	ir	*eer*
gossip, to	chismear	*chees-meh-'ahr*
grab, to	agarrar	*ah-gah-'rrahr*
graduate, to	graduarse	*grah-doo-'ahr-seh*
guess, to	adivinar	*ah-dee-vee-'nahr*
hacking	la piratería	*lah pee-rah-teh-'ree·ah*
hang up, to	colgar	*kohl-'gahr*
hate, to	odiar	*oh-dee-'ahr*
have, to	tener	*teh-'nehr*
hear, to	oír	*oh-'eer*
help, to	ayudar	*ah-yoo-'dahr*
hide, to	esconder	*eh-skohn-'dehr*
hire, to	contratar	*kohn-trah-'tahr*
hit, to	pegar	*peh-'gahr*
hug, to	abrazar	*ah-brah-'sahr*
hurry, to	apurarse	*ah-poo-'rahr-seh*
hurt, to	herir	*eh-'reer*
identify, to	identificar	*ee-dehn-tee-fee-'kahr*
improve, to	mejorar	*meh-hoh-'rahr*

include, to	incluir	een-kloo-'eer
inform, to	informar	een-fohr-'mahr
invest, to	invertir	een-vehr-'teer
joke, to	bromear	broh-meh-'ahr
jump, to	saltar	sahl-'tahr
kick, to	patear	pah-teh-'ahr
know someone, to	conocer	koh-noh-'sehr
know something, to	saber	sah-'behr
learn, to	aprender	ah-prehn-'dehr
leave, to	irse, salir	'eer-seh, sah-'leer
lie down, to	acostarse	ah-koh-'stahr-seh
lie, to	mentir	mehn-'teer
listen, to	escuchar	eh-skoo-'chahr
loan, to	prestar	preh-'stahr
loiter, to	holgazanear	ohl-gah-sah-neh-'ahr
look for, to	buscar	boo-'skahr
look, to	mirar	mee-'rahr
lose, to	perder	pehr-'dehr
love, to	amar	ah-'mahr
make a mistake, to	equivocarse	eh-kee-voh-'kahr-seh
measure, to	medir	meh-'deer
miss, to	faltar	fahl-'tahr
motivate, to	motivar	moh-tee-'vahr
move, to	mover	moh-'vehr
multiply, to	multiplicar	mool-tee-plee-'kahr
obey, to	obedecer	oh-beh-deh-'sehr
observe, to	observar	ohb-sehr-'vahr
offer, to	ofrecer	oh-freh-'sehr
omit, to	eliminar	eh-lee-mee-'nahr
open, to	abrir	ah-'breer
organize, to	organizar	ohr-gah-nee-'sahr
owe, to	deber	deh-'behr
paint, to	pintar	peen-'tahr
park, to	estacionar	eh-stah-see·oh-'nahr
participate, to	participar	pahr-tee-see-'pahr
pass out, to	repartir	reh-pahr-'teer
pass, to	pasar	pah-'sahr
persuade, to	persuadir	pehr-swah-'deer
pitch, to	lanzar	lahn-'sahr
plan, to	planear	plah-neh-'ahr
play, to	jugar	hoo-'gahr
point, to	señalar	seh-nyah-'lahr
practice, to	practicar	prahk-tee-'kahr
present, to	presentar	preh-sehn-'tahr
press, to	oprimir	oh-pree-'meer
print, to	imprimir	een-pree-'meer
pronounce, to	pronunciar	proh-noon-see-'ahr

protect, to	proteger	*proh-teh-'hehr*
pull, to	jalar	*hah-'lahr*
push, to	empujar	*ehm-poo-'hahr*
put in, to	meter	*meh-'tehr*
put, to	poner	*poh-'nehr*
read, to	leer	*leh-'ehr*
receive, to	recibir	*reh-see-'beer*
reduce, to	reducir	*reh-doo-'seer*
relax, to	relajarse	*reh-lah-'hahr-seh*
remember, to	recordar	*reh-kohr-'dahr*
repeat, to	repetir	*reh-peh-'teer*
reply, to	responder	*rehs-pohn-'dehr*
respect, to	respetar	*reh-speh-'tahr*
rest, to	descansar	*deh-skahn-'sahr*
retain, to	retener	*reh-teh-'nehr*
return, to	regresar	*reh-greh-'sahr*
reward, to	recompensar	*reh-kohm-pehn-'sahr*
ride, to	montar	*mohn-'tahr*
roll, to	rodar	*roh-'dahr*
run, to	correr	*koh-'rrehr*
sail, to	navegar	*nah-veh-'gahr*
save, to	ahorrar	*ah-ohr-'rahr*
say, to	decir	*deh-'seer*
search, to	buscar	*boos-'kahr*
see, to	ver	*vehr*
seem, to	parecer	*pah-reh-'sehr*
select, to	escoger	*ehs-koh-'hehr*
sell, to	vender	*vehn-'dehr*
send, to	enviar	*ehn-vee-'vahr*
separate, to	separar	*seh-pah-'rahr*
serve, to	servir	*sehr-'veer*
sew, to	coser	*koh-'sehr*
shake, to	sacudir	*sah-koo-'deer*
shoot, to	disparar	*dee-spah-'rahr*
show, to	mostrar	*moh-'strahr*
sign, to	firmar	*feer-'mahr*
simplify, to	simplificar	*seem-plee-fee-'kahr*
sing, to	cantar	*kahn-'tahr*
skate, to	patinar	*pah-tee-'nahr*
ski, to	esquiar	*eh-skee-'ahr*
sleep, to	dormir	*dohr-'meer*
smoke, to	fumar	*foo-'mahr*
solve, to	resolver	*reh-sohl-'vehr*
speak, to	hablar	*ah-'blahr*
spell, to	deletrear	*deh-leh-treh-'ahr*
spit, to	escupir	*eh-skoo-'peer*
stack, to	amontonar	*ah-mohn-toh-'nahr*

stalking	acecho, el	*ehl ah-'seh-choh*
steal, to	robar	*roh-'bahr*
stroll, to	pasear	*pah-seh-'ahr*
study, to	estudiar	*eh-stoo-dee-'ahr*
subtract, to	restar	*reh-'stahr*
suggest, to	sugerir	*soo-heh-'reer*
support, to	apoyar	*ah-poh-'yahr*
suspend, to	suspender	*soo-spehn-'dehr*
swallow, to	tragar	*trah-'gahr*
swim, to	nadar	*nah-'dahr*
take care of oneself, to	cuidarse	*kwee-'dahr-seh*
take out, to	sacar	*sah-'kahr*
take, to	tomar	*toh-'mahr*
teach, to	enseñar	*ehn-seh-'nyahr*
tease, to	burlarse	*boor-'lahr-seh*
tell, to	decir	*deh-'seer*
text, to	mandar texto	*mahn-'dahr 'tehks-toh*
thank, to	agradecer	*ah-grah-deh-'sehr*
think, to	pensar	*pehn-'sahr*
threaten, to	amenazar	*ah-meh-nah-'sahr*
throw, to	tirar	*tee-'rahr*
tie, to	amarrar	*ah-mah-'rrahr*
touch, to	tocar	*toh-'kahr*
train, to	entrenar	*ehn-treh-'nahr*
travel, to	viajar	*vee·ah-'hahr*
trip, to	tropezar	*troh-peh-'sahr*
try, to	tratar	*trah-'tahr*
turn around, to	darse vuelta	*'dahr-seh 'vwehl-tah*
understand, to	entender	*ehn-tehn-'dehr*
urinate, to	orinar	*oh-ree-'nahr*
use, to	usar	*oo-'sahr*
verify, to	verificar	*veh-ree-fee-'kahr*
visit, to	visitar	*vee-see-'tahr*
vomit, to	vomitar	*voh-mee-'tahr*
wait, to	esperar	*eh-speh-'rahr*
want, to	querer	*keh-'rehr*
wash, to	lavar	*lah-'vahr*
win, to	ganar	*gah-'nahr*
work, to	trabajar	*trah-bah-'hahr*
worry, to	preocuparse	*preh-oh-koo-'pahr-seh*
wrestle, to	luchar	*loo-'chahr*
write, to	escribir	*eh-skree-'beer*
yell, to	gritar	*gree-'tahr*

SPANISH-ENGLISH VERBS

abrazar	hug, to	*ah-brah-'sahr*
abrir	open, to	*ah-'breer*
acecho, el	stalking	*ehl ah-'seh-choh*
aconsejar	counsel, to	*ah-kohn-seh-'hahr*
acostarse	lie down, to	*ah-koh-'stahr-seh*
actuar	act, to	*ahk-too-'ahr*
adivinar	guess, to	*ah-dee-vee-'nahr*
agarrar	catch, to; to grab	*ah-gah-'rrahr*
agradecer	thank, to	*ah-grah-deh-'sehr*
ahorrar	save, to	*ah-ohr-'rahr*
alabar	commend, to	*ah-lah-'bahr*
amar	love, to	*ah-'mahr*
amarrar	tie, to	*ah-mah-'rrahr*
amenazar	threaten, to	*ah-meh-nah-'sahr*
amontonar	stack, to	*ah-mohn-toh-'nahr*
analizar	analyze, to	*ah-nah-lee-'sahr*
animar	encourage, to	*ah-nee-'mahr*
aplicar	apply, to	*ah-plee-'kahr*
apoyar	support, to	*ah-poh-'yahr*
aprender	learn, to	*ah-prehn-'dehr*
apurarse	hurry, to	*ah-poo-'rahr-she*
arrastrar	drag, to	*ah-rrahs-'trahr*
arreglar	arrange, to	*ah-rreh-'glahr*
arrestar	arrest, to	*ah-rreh-'stahr*
asegurar	assure, to	*ah-seh-goo-'rahr*
asignar	assign, to	*ah-seeg-'nahr*
asistir	attend, to	*ah-see-'steer*
avisar	advise, to	*ah-vee-'sahr*
ayudar	help, to	*ah-yoo-'dahr*
bailar	dance, to	*'bah·ee-'lahr*
bañarse	bathe, to	*bah-'nyahr-seh*
beber	drink, to	*beh-'behr*
borrar	erase, to	*boh-'rrahr*
bromear	joke, to	*broh-meh-'ahr*
burlarse	tease, to	*boor-'lahr-seh*
buscar	look for, to/search, to	*boo-'skahr*
caerse	fall, to	*kah-'ehr-seh*
calcular	calculate, to	*kahl-koo-'lahr*
calmarse	calm down, to	*kahl-'mahr-seh*
cambiar	change, to	*kahm-bee-'ahr*
cancelar	cancel, to	*kahn-seh-'lahr*
cantar	sing, to	*kahn-'tahr*
cerrar	close, to	*seh-'rrahr*
chismear	gossip, to	*chees-meh-'ahr*

clarificar	clarify, to	*klah-ree-fee-'kahr*
colgar	hang up, to	*kohl-'gahr*
comenzar	begin, to	*koh-mehn-'sahr*
comer	eat, to	*koh-'mehr*
comparar	compare, to	*kohm-pah-'rahr*
competir	compete, to	*kohm-peh-'teer*
completar	complete, to	*kohm-pleh-'tahr*
comprar	buy, to	*kohm-'prahr*
comunicar	communicate, to	*koh-moo-nee-'kahr*
conectar	connect, to	*koh-nehk-'tahr*
confirmar	confirm, to	*kohn-feer-'mahr*
confiscar	confiscate, to	*kohn-fee-'skahr*
conocer	know someone, to	*koh-noh-'sehr*
conseguir	get, to	*kohn-seh-'geer*
construir	build, to	*kohn-stroo-'eer*
consultar	consult, to	*kohn-sool-'tahr*
contar	count, to	*kohn-'tahr*
contestar	answer, to	*kohn-teh-'stahr*
contratar	hire, to	*kohn-trah-'tahr*
conversar	converse, to	*kohn-vehr-'sahr*
copiar	copy, to	*koh-pee-'ahr*
corregir	correct, to	*koh-rreh-'heer*
correr	run, to	*koh-'rrehr*
cortar	cut, to	*kohr-'tahr*
cortar y pegar	cut and paste, to	*kohr-'tahr ee peh-'gahr*
coser	sew, to	*koh-'sehr*
cubrir	cover, to	*koo-'breer*
cuidarse	take care of oneself, to	*kwee-'dahr-seh*
dar	give, to	*dahr*
darse vuelta	turn around, to	*'dahr-seh 'vwehl-tah*
debatir	debate, to	*deh-bah-'teer*
deber	owe, to	*deh-'behr*
decir	say, to; to tell	*deh-'seer*
decir groserías	curse, to	*deh-'seer groh-seh-'ree·ahs*
defecar	defecate, to	*deh-feh-'kahr*
definer	define, to	*deh-fee-'neer*
dejar	allow, to	*deh-'hahr*
deletrear	spell, to	*deh-leh-treh-'ahr*
descansar	rest, to	*deh-skahn-'sahr*
descargar	download, to	*dehs-kahr-'gahr*
dibujar	draw, to	*dee-boo-'hahr*
discutir	argue, to	*dee-skoo-'teer*
disecarlo	dissect it	*dee-seh-'kahr-loh*
disparar	shoot, to	*dee-spah-'rahr*
distraer	distract, to	*dee-strah-'ehr*
divider	divide, to	*dee-vee-'deer*

doblar	fold, to	doh-'blahr
dormer	sleep, to	dohr-'meer
eliminar	omit, to/to delete	eh-lee-mee-'nahr
empezar	begin, to	ehm-peh-'sahr
empujar	push, to	ehm-poo-'hahr
encargar	be in charge, to	ehn-kahr-'gahr
encontrar	find, to	ehn-kohn-'trahr
enseñar	teach, to	ehn-seh-'nyahr
entender	understand, to	ehn-tehn-'dehr
entrar	enter, to	ehn-'trahr
entregar	deliver, to	ehn-treh-'gahr
entrenar	train, to	ehn-treh-'nahr
enviar	send, to	ehn-vee-'ahr
equivocarse	make a mistake, to	eh-kee-voh-'kahr-seh
escoger	choose, to/select, to	eh-skoh-'hehr
esconder	hide, to	eh-skohn-'dehr
escribir	write, to	eh-skree-'beer
escuchar	listen, to	eh-skoo-'chahr
escupir	spit, to	eh-skoo-'peer
esperar	wait, to	eh-speh-'rahr
esquiar	ski, to	eh-skee-'ahr
estacionar	park, to	eh-stah-see·oh-'nahr
estar	be, to	eh-'stahr
estudiar	study, to	eh-stoo-dee-'ahr
evaluar	evaluate, to	eh-vah-loo-'ahr
examinar	examine, to	ehk-sah-mee-'nahr
explicar	explain, to	ehk-splee-'kahr
expulsar	expel, to	ehk-spool-'sahr
factorar	factor, to	fahk-toh-'rahr
faltar	miss, to	fahl-'tahr
felicitar	compliment, to	feh-lee-see-'tahr
firmar	sign, to	feer-'mahr
fumar	smoke, to	foo-'mahr
ganar	win, to	gah-'nahr
golpear	beat up, to	gohl-peh-'ahr
graduarse	graduate, to	grah-doo-'ahr-seh
gritar	yell, to	gree-'tahr
hablar	speak, to	ah-'blahr
hacer	do, to	ah-'sehr
herir	hurt, to	eh-'reer
holgazanear	loiter, to	ohl-gah-sah-neh-'ahr
identificar	identify, to	ee-dehn-tee-fee-'kahr
imprimir	print, to	een-pree-'meer
incluir	include, to	een-kloo-'eer
informar	inform, to	een-fohr-'mahr
inscribirse	enroll, to	een-skree-'beer-she
la intimidación	bullying	lah een-tee-mee-dah-see-'ohn

invertir	invest, to	*een-vehr-'teer*
ir	go, to	*eer*
irse	leave, to	*'eer-seh*
jalar	pull, to	*hah-'lahr*
jugar	play, to	*hoo-'gahr*
lanzar	pitch, to	*lahn-'sahr*
lavar	wash, to	*lah-'vahr*
leer	read, to	*leh-'ehr*
limpiar	clean, to	*leem-pee-'ahr*
llamar	call, to	*yah-'mahr*
llegar	arrive, to	*yeh-'gahr*
llenar	fill out, to	*yeh-'nahr*
llevar	carry, to	*yeh-'vahr*
llorar	cry, to	*yoh-'rahr*
luchar	wrestle, to	*loo-'chahr*
maldecir	curse, to	*mahl-deh-'seer*
manejar	drive, to	*mah-neh-'hahr*
marcar	dial, to	*mahr-'kahr*
masticar	chew, to	*mah-stee-'kahr*
matricularse	enroll, to	*mah-tree-koo-'lahr-seh*
medir	measure, to	*meh-'deer*
mejorar	improve, to	*meh-hoh-'rahr*
mentir	lie, to	*mehn-'teer*
merecer	deserve, to	*meh-reh-'sehr*
meter	put in, to	*meh-'tehr*
mirar	look, to	*mee-'rahr*
molestar	bother, to	*moh-leh-'stahr*
mandar texto	text, to	*mahn-'dahr 'tehks-toh*
montar	ride, to	*mohn-'tahr*
morder	bite, to	*mohr-'dehr*
morir	die, to	*moh-'reer*
mostrar	show, to	*moh-'strahr*
motivar	motivate, to	*moh-tee-'vahr*
mover	move, to	*moh-'vehr*
multiplicar	multiply, to	*mool-tee-plee-'kahr*
nadar	swim, to	*nah-'dahr*
navegar	sail, to	*nah-veh-'gahr*
negarse	deny, to	*neh-'gahr-seh*
obedecer	obey, to	*oh-beh-deh-'sehr*
observar	observe, to	*ohb-sehr-'vahr*
odiar	hate, to	*oh-dee-'ahr*
ofrecer	offer, to	*oh-freh-'sehr*
oír	hear, to	*oh-'eer*
olvidar	forget, to	*ohl-vee-'dahr*
oprimir	press, to	*oh-pree-'meer*
organizar	organize, to	*ohr-gah-nee-'sahr*
orinar	urinate, to	*oh-ree-'nahr*

parecer	seem, to	*pah-reh-'sehr*
participar	participate, to	*pahr-tee-see-'pahr*
pasar	pass, to	*pah-'sahr*
pasear	stroll, to	*pah-seh-'ahr*
patear	kick, to	*pah-teh-'ahr*
patinar	skate, to	*pah-tee-'nahr*
pedir	ask for, to	*peh-'deer*
pegar	hit, to	*peh-'gahr*
peinarse	comb one's hair, to	*peh·ee-'nahr-seh*
pelear	fight, to	*peh-leh-'ahr-seh*
pensar	think, to	*pehn-'sahr*
perder	lose, to	*pehr-'dehr*
perderse	get lost, to	*pehr-'dehr-seh*
perseguir	chase, to	*pehr-seh-'geer*
persuadir	persuade, to	*pehr-swah-'deer*
pescar	fish, to	*peh-'skahr*
pintar	paint, to	*peen-'tahr*
piratería	hacking	*lah pee-rah-teh-'ree·ah*
planear	plan, to	*plah-neh-'ahr*
poder	be able, to	*poh-'dehr*
poner	put, to	*poh-'nehr*
portarse	behave, to	*pohr-'tahr-seh*
practicar	practice, to	*prahk-tee-'kahr*
preguntar	ask, to	*preh-goon-'tahr*
preocuparse	worry, to	*preh-oh-koo-'pahr-seh*
presentar	present, to	*preh-sehn-'tahr*
prestar	loan, to	*preh-'stahr*
pronunciar	pronounce, to	*proh-noon-see-'ahr*
proteger	protect, to	*proh-teh-'hehr*
pulsar	click, to	*pool-'sahr*
quebrar	break, to	*keh-'brahr*
quejarse	complain, to	*keh-'hahr-seh*
querer	want, to	*keh-'rehr*
rebotar	bounce, to	*reh-boh-'tahr*
recibir	receive, to	*reh-see-'beer*
recompensar	reward, to	*reh-kohm-pehn-'sahr*
recordar	remember, to	*reh-kohr-'dahr*
reducir	reduce, to	*reh-doo-'seer*
reenviar	forward, to	*reh-ehn-vee-'ahr*
registrar	search, to	*reh-hee-'strahr*
regresar	return, to	*reh-greh-'sahr*
relajarse	relax, to	*reh-lah-'hahr-seh*
repartir	pass out, to	*reh-pahr-'teer*
repetir	repeat, to	*reh-peh-'teer*
resolver	resolve, to; to solve	*reh-sohl-'vehr*
respetar	respect, to	*reh-speh-'tahr*
respirar	breathe, to	*reh-spee-'rahr*

restar	subtract, to	*reh-'stahr*
responder	reply, to	*rehs-pohn-'dehr*
retener	retain, to	*reh-teh-'nehr*
revisar	check, to	*reh-vee-'sahr*
robar	steal, to	*roh-'bahr*
rodar	roll, to	*roh-'dahr*
romper	break, to	*rohm-'pehr*
saber	know something, to	*sah-'behr*
sacar	take out, to	*sah-'kahr*
sacudir	shake, to	*sah-koo-'deer*
salir	leave, to	*sah-'leer*
saltar	jump, to	*sahl-'tahr*
seguir	follow, to	*seh-'geer*
señalar	point, to	*seh-nyah-'lahr*
sentirse	feel, to	*sehn-'teer-seh*
separar	separate, to	*seh-pah-'rahr*
ser	be, to	*sehr*
servir	serve, to	*sehr-'veer*
simplificar	simplify, to	*seem-plee-fee-'kahr*
subir	climb, to	*soo-'beer*
sugerir	suggest, to	*soo-heh-'reer*
sumar	add, to	*soo-'mahr*
suspender	suspend, to	*soo-spehn-'dehr*
tener	have, to	*teh-'nehr*
terminar	end, to	*tehr-mee-'nahr*
tirar	throw, to	*tee-'rahr*
tocar	touch, to	*toh-'kahr*
tomar	take, to	*toh-'mahr*
trabajar	work, to	*trah-bah-'hahr*
traer	bring, to	*trah-'ehr*
tragar	swallow, to	*trah-'gahr*
tratar	try, to	*trah-'tahr*
tropezar	trip, to	*troh-peh-'sahr*
usar	use, to	*oo-'sahr*
vaciar	empty, to	*vah-see-'ahr*
vender	sell, to	*vehn-'dehr*
venir	come, to	*veh-'neer*
ver	see, to	*vehr*
verificar	verify, to	*veh-ree-fee-'kahr*
vestirse	get dressed, to	*veh-'steer-seh*
viajar	travel, to	*vee·ah-'hahr*
visitar	visit, to	*vee-see-'tahr*
vomitar	vomit, to	*voh-mee-'tahr*
zambullirse	dive, to	*sahm-boo-'yeer-she*

ENGLISH-SPANISH DICTIONARY

➤ The gender of Spanish nouns is indicated by the article (el or la).

➤ When a noun can be either masculine or feminine, it is shown in the masculine form and then in the feminine form: adulto, el (la adulta).

➤ All adjectives are shown in the masculine form. An (a) is added to remind you of the feminine ending.

abortion	el aborto	*ehl ah-'bohr-toh*
above	encima	*ehn-'see-mah*
absences	ausencias, las	*lahs ow-'sehn-see·ah*
abuse	abuso, el	*ehl ah-'boo-soh*
academy	academia, la	*lah ah-kah-'deh-mee·ah*
accident	accidente, el	*ehl ahk-see-'dehn-teh*
acne	acné, el	*ehl ahk-'neh*
action	acción, la	*lah ahk-see-'ohn*
activity	actividad, la	*lah ahk-tee-vee-'dahd*
addiction	adicción, la	*lah ah-deek-see-'ohn*
address	dirección, la	*lah dee-rehk-see-'ohn*
ADHD	ADHD	*ah deh a-cheh deh*
administration	administración, la	*lah ahd-mee-nee-strah-see·'ohn*
administrator	administrador, el (la administradora)	*ehl ahd-mee-nee-strah-'dohr (lah ahd-mee-nee-strah-'doh-rah)*
admissions	admisiones, las	*lahs ahd-mee-see·'oh-nehs*
adult	adulto, el (la adulta)	*ehl ah-'dool-toh (lah ah-'dool-tah)*
advanced	avanzado(a)	*ah-vahn-'sah-doh(ah)*
advisor	consejero, el (la consejera)	*ehl kohn-seh-'heh-roh (lah kohn-seh-'heh-rah)*
afraid	asustado(a)	*ah-soo-'stah-doh(ah)*
African-American	afroamericano(a), el *or* la	*ehl / lah ah-froh-ah-meh-ree-'kah-noh(ah)*
afterward	después	*deh-'spwehs*
against	contra	*'kohn-trah*
age	edad, la	*lah eh-'dahd*
agency	agencia, la	*lah ah-'hehn-see·ah*
ahead	adelante	*ah-deh-'lahn-teh*
aide	ayudante, el (la ayudanta)	*ehl ah-yoo-'dahn-teh, (lah ah-yoo-'dahn-tah)*
air conditioner	acondicionador de aire, el	*ehl ah-kohn-dee-see·oh-nah-'dohr deh 'ah·ee-reh*
airplane	avión, el	*ehl ah-vee-'ohn*
airport	aeropuerto, el	*ehl ah-eh-roh-'pwehr-toh*

aisle	pasillo, el	*ehl pah-'see-yoh*
alarm	alarma, la	*lah ah-'lahr-mah*
alcohol	alcohol, el	*ehl ahl-koh-'ohl*
algebra	álgebra, el	*ehl 'ahl-heh-'brah*
all	todo(a)(os)(as)	*'toh-doh (ah) (ohs) (ahs)*
allergies	alergias, las	*lahs ah-'lehr-hee·ahs*
alley	callejón, el	*ehl kah-yeh-'hohn*
alphabet	alfabeto, el	*ehl ahl-fah-'beh-toh*
already	ya	*yah*
altercation	disputa, la	*lah dee-'spoo-'tah*
alternative	alternativa, la	*lah ahl-tehr-nah-'tee-vah*
always	siempre	*see-'ehm-preh*
ambulance	ambulancia, la	*lah ahm-boo-'lahn-see·ah*
amusement park	parque de atracciones, el	*ehl 'pahr-keh deh ah-trahk-see-'oh-nehs*
and	y	*ee*
angry	enojado(a)	*eh-noh-'hah-doh(ah)*
animal	animal, el	*ehl ah-nee-'mahl*
ankle	tobillo, el	*ehl toh-'bee-yoh*
announcement	anuncio, el	*ehl ah-'noon-see·oh*
answer	respuesta, la	*lah reh-'spweh-stah*
apartment	apartamento, el	*ehl ah-pahr-tah-'mehn-toh*
apple	manzana, la	*lah mahn-'sah-nah*
appliance	electrodoméstico, el	*ehl eh-lehk-troh-doh-'meh-stee-koh*
application (computer)	aplicación, la	*lah ah-plee-kah-see-'ohn*
application	solicitud, la	*lah soh-lee-see-'tood*
appointment	cita, la	*lah 'see-tah*
approach	enfoque, el	*ehl ehn-'foh-keh*
April	abril	*ah-'breel*
apron	delantal, el	*ehl deh-lahn-'tahl*
aquarium	acuario, el	*ehl ah-'kwah-ree·oh*
architect	arquitecto, el *or* la	*ehl / lah ahr-kee-'tehk-toh*
archive	archivo, el	*ehl ahr-'chee-voh*
area	área, el	*ehl 'ah-reh-ah*
area code	código telefonico	*'koh-dee-goh teh-leh-'foh-nee-koh*
arena	anfiteatro, el	*ehl ah-fee-teh-'ah-troh*
argument	argumento, el	*ehl ahr-goo-'mehn-toh*
arm	brazo, el	*ehl 'brah-soh*
armchair	sillón, el	*ehl see-'yohn*
armed forces	fuerzas armadas, las	*lahs 'fwehr-sahs ahr-'mah-dahs*
arrow	flecha, la	*lah 'fleh-chah*

art	arte, el	*ehl 'ahr-teh*
article	artículo, el	*ehl ahr-'tee-koo-loh*
aspirin	aspirina, la	*lah ah-spee-'ree-nah*
assembly	asamblea, la	*lah ah-sahm-'bleh-ah*
assessment	evaluación, la	*lah eh-vah-loo-ah-see-'ohn*
assignment	tarea, la	*lah tah-'reh-ah*
assistance	ayuda, la	*lah ah-'yoo-dah*
assistant	asistente, el (la asistenta)	*ehl ah-see-'stehn-teh (lah ah-see-'stehn-tah)*
associate	asociado, el (la asociada)	*ehl ah-soh-see-'ah-doh (lah ah-soh-see-'ah-dah)*
astronomy	astronomía, la	*lah ah-stroh-noh-'mee·ah*
at	en	
atlas	atlas, el	*ehl 'aht-lahs*
attachment	adjunto, el	*ehl ahd-'hoon-toh*
attendance	asistencia, la	*lah ah-see-'stehn-see·ah*
attitude	actitud, la	*lah ahk-tee-'tood*
audience	audiencia, la	*lah ow-dee-'ehn-see·ah*
auditorium	auditorio, el	*ehl ow-dee-'toh-ree·oh*
August	agosto	*ah-'goh-stoh*
aunt	tía, la	*lah 'tee·ah*
autism	autismo	*ow-'tees-moh*
author	autor, el (la autora)	*ehl ow-'tohr (lah ow-'toh-rah)*
available	disponible	*dee-spoh-'nee-bleh*
avenue	avenida, la	*lah ah-veh-'nee-dah*
average	promedio, el	*ehl proh-'meh-dee·oh*
award	galardón, el	*ehl gah-lahr-'dohn*
ax	hacha, el	*ehl 'ah-chah*
baby	bebé, el *or* la	*ehl / lah beh-'beh*
back	espalda, la	*lah eh-'spahl-dah*
backache	dolor de espalda, el	*ehl doh-'lohr deh eh-'spahl-dah*
backpack	mochila, la	*lah moh-'chee-yah*
backwards	revés, al	*ahl reh-'vehs*
bad	malo(a)	*'mah-loh(ah)*
badge	emblema, el	*ehl ehm-'bleh-mah*
badminton	bádminton, el	*ehl 'bahd-meen-tohn*
bag	bolsa, la	*lah 'bohl-sah*
balance	equilibrio, el	*ehl eh-kee-'lee-bree·oh*
balcony	balcón, el	*ehl bahl-'kohn*
bald	calvo(a)	*'kahl-voh(ah)*
ball	pelota, la	*lah peh-'loh-tah*
balloon	globo, el	*ehl 'gloh-boh*
banana	plátano, el	*ehl 'plah-tah-noh*

band	banda, la	*lah 'bahn-da*
bandage	vendaje, el	*ehl vehn-'dah-heh*
Band Aid®	curita, la	*lah koo-'ree-tah*
bank	banco, el	*ehl 'bahn-koh*
banquet	banquete, el	*ehl bahn-'keh-teh*
baseball	béisbol, el	*ehl 'beh·ees-bohl*
basket	canasta, la	*lah kah-'nah-stah*
basketball	básquetbol, el	*ehl 'bah-skeht-bohl*
bassinet	bacinete, el	*ehl bah-see-'neh-teh*
bat	bate, el	*ehl 'bah-teh*
bathing suit	traje de baño, el	*ehl 'trah-heh deh 'bahn-yoh*
bathrobe	bata de baño, la	*lah 'bah-tah deh 'bah-nyoh*
battery	pila, la	*lah 'pee-lah*
battle	batalla, la	*lah bah-'tah-yah*
beach	playa, la	*lah 'plah-yah*
beaker	tazón, el	*ehl tah-'sohn*
beans	frijoles, los	*lohs free-'hoh-lehs*
beautiful	bello(a)	*'beh-yoh(ah)*
bed	cama, la	*lah 'kah-mah*
beef	carne, la	*lah 'kahr-neh*
before	antes	*'ahn-tehs*
beggar	mendigo, el	*ehl mehn-'dee-goh*
behavior	comportamiento, el	*ehl kohm-pohr-tah-mee-'ehn-toh*
behind	detrás	*deh-'trahs*
belief	creencia, la	*lah kreh-'ehn-see·ah*
bell	campana, la	*lah kahm-'pah-nah*
belt	cinturón, el	*ehl seen-too-'rohn*
benches	bancas, las	*lahs 'bahn-kahs*
benefits	beneficios, los	*lohs beh-neh-'fee-see·ohs*
better	mejor	*meh-'hohr*
bib	babero, el	*ehl bah-'beh-roh*
bicycle	bicicleta, la	*lah bee-see-'kleh-tah*
big	grande	*'grahn-de*
bilingual	bilingüe	*bee-'leen-gweh*
bill	cuenta, la	*lah 'kwehn-tah*
billboard	letrero, el	*ehl leh-'treh-roh*
bin	depósito, el	*ehl deh-'poh-see-toh*
binder	encuadernador, el	*ehl ehn-kwah-dehr-nah-'dohr*
biography	biografía, la	*lah bee·oh-grah-'fee·ah*
biology	biología, la	*lah bee·oh-loh-'hee·ah*
bird	pájaro, el	*ehl 'pah-hah-roh*
birth	nacimiento, el	*ehl nah-see-mee-'ehn-toh*
black	negro(a)	*'neh-groh(ah)*

blanket	cobija, la	*lah koh-'bee-hah*
blender	licuadora, la	*lah lee-kwah-'doh-rah*
blind	ciego(a)	*see-'eh-goh(ah)*
blister	ampolla, la	*lah ahm-'poh-yah*
block	cubito, el	*ehl koo-'bee-toh*
blond	rubio(a)	*'roo-bee·oh(ah)*
blood	sangre, la	*lah 'sahn-greh*
blouse	blusa, la	*lah 'bloo-sa*
blue	azul	*ah-'sool*
Board of Education	junta de educación	*lah 'hoon-tah deh eh-doo-kah-see-'ohn*
boat	barco, el	*ehl 'bahr-koh*
body	cuerpo, el	*ehl 'kwehr-poh*
bomb	bomba, la	*lah 'bohm-bah*
book	libro, el	*ehl 'lee-broh*
bookstore	librería, la	*lah lee-breh-'ree·ah*
boot	bota, la	*lah 'boh-tah*
bored	aburrido(a)	*ah-boo-rree-doh(ah)*
bowl	plato hondo, el	*ehl 'plah-toh 'ohn-doh*
box	caja, la	*lah 'kah-hah*
boxing	boxeo, el	*ehl bohk-'seh-oh*
boy	niño, el	*ehl 'nee-nyoh*
boyfriend	novio, el	*ehl 'noh-vee·oh*
bracelet	brazalete, el	*ehl brah-sah-'leh-teh*
brain	cerebro, el	*ehl seh-'reh-broh*
branch	rama, la	*lah 'rah-mah*
brassiere	sostén, el	*ehl soh-'stehn*
break	descanso, el	*ehl deh-'skahn-soh*
breakfast	desayuno, el	*ehl deh-sah-'yoo-noh*
breath	aliento, el	*ehl ah-lee-'ehn-toh*
bridge	puente, el	*ehl 'pwehn-teh*
brochure	folleto, el	*ehl foh-'yeh-toh*
broom	escoba, la	*lah eh-'skoh-bah*
brother	hermano, el	*ehl ehr-'mah-noh*
brown	café	*kah-'feh*
browser	navegador, el	*ehl nah-veh-gah-dohr*
bruise	contusión, la	*lah kohn-too-see-'ohn*
brunette	moreno(a)	*moh-'reh-noh(ah)*
brush	pincel, el	*ehl peen-'sel*
bucket	balde, el	*ehl 'bahl-deh*
budget	presupuesto, el	*ehl preh-soo-'pweh-stoh*
building	edificio, el	*ehl eh-dee-'fee-see·oh*
bulletin	anuncio, el	*ehl ah-'noon-see·oh*

bulletin board	tablero de anuncios, el	*ehl tah-'bleh-roh deh ah-'noon-see·ohs*
bullhorn	altavoz, el	*ehl ahl-tah-'vohs*
burn	quemadura, la	*lah keh-mah-'doo-rah*
burp	eructo, el	*ehl eh-'rook-toh*
bus	autobús, el	*ehl ow-toh-'boos*
bus driver	chofer de autobús, el *or* la	*ehl / lah choh-'fehr deh ow-toh-'boos*
bus stop	parada de autobús, la	*lah pah-'rah-dah deh ow-toh-'boos*
busy	ocupado(a)	*oh-koo-'pah-doh(ah)*
but	pero	*'peh-roh*
buzzer	timbre, el	*ehl 'teem-breh*
cabinet	gabinete, el	*ehl gah-bee-'neh-teh*
cable	cable, el	*ehl 'kah-bleh*
cafeteria	cafetería, la	*lah kah-feh-teh-'ree·ah*
cake	torta, la	*lah 'tohr-tah*
calculator	calculadora, la	*lah kahl-koo-lah-'doh-rah*
calculus	cálculo, el	*ehl 'kahl-koo-loh*
calendar	calendario, el	*ehl kah-lehn-'dah-ree·oh*
camp	campamento, el	*ehl kahm-pah-'mehn-toh*
campus	campo, el	*ehl 'kahm-poh*
candle	vela, la	*lah 'veh-lah*
candy	dulces, los	*lohs 'dool-sehs*
cap	gorra, la	*lah 'goh-rrah*
capacity	capacidad, la	*lah kah-pah-see-'dahd*
captain	capitán, el (la capitana)	*ehl kah-pee-'tahn (lah kah-pee-'tah-nah)*
car	carro, el	*ehl 'kah-rroh*
card	tarjeta, la	*lah tahr-'heh-tah*
cardboard	cartón, el	*ehl kahr-'tohn*
care	cuidado, el	*ehl kwee-'dah-doh*
careless	descuidado(a)	*dehs-kwee-'dah-doh(ah)*
carnival	carnaval, el	*ehl kahr-nah-'vahl*
carpenter	carpintero, el (la carpintera)	*ehl kahr-peen-'teh-roh (lah kahr-peen-'teh-rah)*
carrot	zanahoria, la	*lah sah-nah-'oh-ree·ah*
cart	carreta, la	*lah kah-'rreh-tah*
cartoons	dibujos animados, los	*lohs dee-'boo-hohs ah-nee-'mah-dohs*
cashier	cajero, el (la cajera)	*ehl kah-'heh-roh (lah kah-'heh-rah)*
cat	gato, el (la gata)	*ehl 'gah-toh (lah 'gah-tah)*
cave	cueva, la	*lah 'kweh-vah*

CDs	discos compactos, los	lohs 'dee-skohs kohm-'pahk-tohs
cell phone	celular, el	ehl seh-loo-'lahr
cemetery	cementerio, el	ehl seh-mehn-'teh-ree·oh
cent	centavo, el	ehl sehn-'tah-voh
center	centro, el	ehl 'sehn-troh
ceremony	ceremonia, la	lah seh-reh-'moh-nee·ah
certificate	certificado, el	ehl sehr-tee-fee-'kah-doh
chain	cadena, la	lah kah-'deh-nah
chair	silla, la	lah 'see-yah
chairperson	director (la directora) del departamento, el	ehl dee-rehk-'tohr dehl deh-pahr-tah-'mehn-toh (lah dee-rehk-'toh-rah)
chalk	tiza, la	lah 'tee-sah
chalkboard	pizarrón, el	ehl pee-sah-'rrohn
change	cambio, el	ehl 'kahm-bee·oh
chapter	capítulo, el	ehl kah-'pee-too-loh
charger	cargador, el	ehl kahr-gah-'dohr
chart	diagrama, el	ehl dee·ah-'grah-mah
cheap	barato(a)	bah-'rah-toh(ah)
cheating	fraude, el	ehl 'frow-deh
check	cheque, el	ehl 'cheh-keh
checkers	juego de damas, el	ehl 'hoo·ee-goh deh 'dah-mahs
cheek	mejilla, la	lah meh-'hee-yah
chemical	producto químico, el	ehl proh-'dook-toh 'kee-mee-koh
chemistry	química, la	lah 'kee-mee-kah
chess	ajedrez, el	ehl ah-heh-'drehs
chest (body)	pecho, el	ehl 'peh-choh
chest (trunk)	baúl, el	ehl bah-'ool
chicken	pollo, el	ehl 'poh-yoh
chin	barbilla, la	lah bahr-'bee-yah
chocolate	chocolate, el	ehl choh-koh-'lah-teh
choir	coro, el	ehl 'koh-roh
Christmas	Navidad, la	lah nah-vee-'dahd
church	iglesia, la	lah ee-'gleh-see·ah
cigarettes	cigarrillos, los	lohs see-gah-'rree-yohs
city	ciudad, la	lah see-oo-'dahd
city hall	municipio, el	ehl moo-nee-'see-pee·oh
civil rights	derechos civiles, los	lohs deh-'reh-chohs see-'vee-lehs
class	clase, la	lah 'klah-seh
classroom	sala de clase, la	lah 'sah-lah deh 'klah-seh

clean	limpio(a)	'*leem-pee·oh(ah)*
clerk	dependiente, el (la dependienta)	*ehl deh-pehn-dee-'ehn-teh (lah deh-pehn-dee-'ehn-tah)*
clever	listo(a)	'*lee-stoh(ah)*
climate	clima, el	*ehl 'klee-mah*
clinic	clínica, la	*lah 'klee-nee-kah*
clock	reloj, el	*ehl reh-'hoh*
cloth	tela, la	*lah 'teh-lah*
clothing	ropa, la	*lah 'roh-pah*
club	club, el	*ehl kloob*
coach	entrenador, el (la entrenadora)	*ehl ehn-treh-nah-'dohr (lah ehn-treh-nah-'doh-rah)*
coast	costa, la	*lah 'koh-stah*
code	código, el	*ehl 'koh-dee-goh*
coffee	café, el	*ehl kah-'feh*
cold	frío(a)	'*free·oh(ah)*
college	universidad, la	*lah oo-nee-vehr-see-'dahd*
color	color, el	*ehl koh-'lohr*
colors	colores, los	*lohs koh-'loh-rehs*
comb	peine, el	*ehl 'peh·ee-neh*
comfortable	cómodo(a)	'*koh-moh-doh(ah)*
comment	comentario, el	*ehl koh-mehn-'tah-ree·oh*
committee	comité, el	*ehl koh-mee-'teh*
communication	comunicación, la	*lah koh-moo-nee-kah-see-'ohn*
companion, acquaintance	compañero, el (la compañera)	*ehl kohm-pah-'nyeh-roh (lah kohm-pah-'nyeh-rah)*
competitive athletics	deportes competitivos, los	*lohs deh-'pohr-tehs kohm-peh-tee-'tee-vohs*
computer	computadora, la	*lah kohm-poo-tah-'doh-rah*
concept	concepto, el	*ehl kohn-'sehp-toh*
conduct	comportamiento, el	*ehl kohm-pohr-tah-'mee-'ehn toh*
cone	cono, el	*ehl 'koh-noh*
conference	conferencia, la	*lah kohn-feh-'rehn-see·ah*
conflict	conflicto, el	*ehl kohn-'fleek-toh*
confused	confundido(a)	*kohn-foon-'dee-doh(ah)*
congratulations	felicitaciones, las	*lahs feh-lee-see-tah-see-'oh-nehs*
consent	consentimiento, el	*ehl kohn-sehn-tee-mee-'ehn-toh*
consultant	consultor, el (la consultora)	*ehl kohn-sool-'tohr (lah kohn-sool-'toh-rah)*
contact	contacto, el	*ehl kohn-'tahk-toh*
content	contenido, el	*ehl kohn-teh-'nee-doh*
contest	concurso, el	*ehl kohn-'koor-soh*

contract	contrato, el	*ehl kohn-'trah-toh*
convention	convención, la	*lah kohn-vehn-see-'ohn*
cook	cocinero, el (la cocinera)	*ehl koh-see-'neh-roh (lah koh-see-'neh-rah)*
cookie	galleta, la	*lah gah-'yeh-tah*
cool	fresco	*'freh-koh*
cooperative	dispuesto	*dee-'spweh-stoh*
copier	copiadora, la	*lah koh-pee·ah-'doh-rah*
corn	maíz, el	*ehl mah-'ees*
corner	esquina, la	*lah eh-'skee-nah*
corporal punishment	castigo corporal, el	*ehl kah-'stee-goh kohr-poh-'rahl*
correct	correcto(a)	*koh-'rrehk-toh(ah)*
cost	costo, el	*ehl 'koh-stoh*
costume	disfraz, el	*ehl dees-'frahs*
cotton	algodón, el	*ehl ahl-goh-'dohn*
cough	tos, la	*lah tohs*
council	junta, la	*lah 'hoon-tah*
counseling	consejo, el	*ehl koh-'seh-hoh*
counselor	consejero, el (la consejera)	*ehl kohn-seh-'heh-roh (lah kohn-seh-'heh-rah)*
country	país, el	*ehl pah-'ees*
county	condado, el	*ehl kohn-'dah-doh*
coupon	cupón, el	*ehl koo-'pohn*
course	curso, el	*ehl 'koor-soh*
court (law)	corte, la	*lah 'kohr-teh*
court (tennis)	cancha, la	*lah 'kahn-chah*
courthouse	corte, la	*lah 'kohr-teh*
courtyard	plaza, la	*lah 'plah-sah*
cousin	primo, el (la prima)	*ehl 'pree-moh (lah 'pree-mah)*
cow	vaca, la	*lah 'vah-kah*
cradle	cuna mecedora, la	*lah 'ko-onah meh-seh-'doh-rah*
crayon	gis, el	*ehl hees*
cream	crema, la	*lah 'kreh-mah*
creative	creativo(a)	*kreh-ah-'tee-voh(ah)*
credit	crédito, el	*ehl 'kreh-dee-toh*
crib	cuna, la	*lah 'koo-nah*
crime	crimen, el	*ehl 'kree-mehn*
criminal	criminal, el *or* la	*ehl/lah kree-mee-'nahl*
cross country	correr a campo traviesa, el	*ehl koh-'rrehr ah 'kahm-poh trah-vee-'eh-sah*
crossing guard	guardia del tráfico, el or la	*ehl/lah 'gwahr-dee·ah dehl 'trah-fee-koh*

crosswalk	cruce de peatones, el	*ehl 'kroo-seh deh peh-ah-'toh-nehs*
crutches	muletas, las	*lahs moo-'leh-tahs*
culture	cultura, la	*lah kool-'too-rah*
cup	taza, la	*lah 'tah-sah*
cupboard	armario, el	*ehl ahr-'mah-ree·oh*
curriculum	plan de estudios, el	*ehl plahn deh eh-'stoo-dee·ohs*
custom	costumbre, la	*lah koh-'stoom-breh*
cut	cortadura, la	*lah kohr-tah-'doo-rah*
dance	baile, el	*ehl 'bah·ee-leh*
danger	peligro, el	*ehl peh-'lee-groh*
dangerous	peligroso(a)	*peh-lee-'groh-soh(ah)*
dark-haired	moreno(a)	*moh-'reh-noh(ah)*
data	datos, los	*lohs 'dah-tohs*
date	fecha, la	*lah 'feh-chah*
daughter	hija, la	*lah 'ee-ha*
day	día, el	*ehl 'dee·ah*
deadbolt	pestillo, el	*ehl peh-'stee-yoh*
deadline	fecha límite, la	*lah 'feh-chah 'lee-mee-teh*
deaf	sordo(a)	*'sohr-doh(ah)*
death	muerte, la	*lah 'mwehr-teh*
December	diciembre	*dee-see-'ehm-bre*
deck	terraza, la	*lah teh-'rrah-sah*
deep	profundo(a)	*proh-'foon-doh(ah)*
degree (college)	licenciatura, la	*lah lee-sehn-see·ah-'too-rah*
degree (measurement)	grado, el	*ehl 'grah-doh*
delicious	delicioso(a)	*deh-lee-see-'oh-soh(ah)*
delinquent	delicuente, el *or* la	*ehl / lah deh-leen-'kwehn-teh*
dentist	dentista, el *or* la	*ehl / lah den-'tee-stah*
department	departamento, el	*ehl deh-pahr-tah-'mehn-toh*
description	descripción, la	*lah deh-skreep-see-'ohn*
desert	desierto, el	*ehl deh-see-'ehr-toh*
desk	pupitre, el; escritorio, el	*ehl poo-'pee-treh, ehl eh-skree-'toh-ree·oh*
dessert	postre, el	*ehl 'poh-streh*
detention	detención, la	*lah deh-tehn-see-'ohn*
diaper	pañal, el	*ehl pah-'nyahl*
dictionary	diccionario, el	*ehl deek-see·oh-'nah-ree·oh*
difference	diferencia, la	*lah dee-feh-'rehn-see·ah*
difficult	difícil	*dee-'fee-seel*
digital camera	cámara digital, la	*lah 'kah-mah-rah dee-gee-'tahl*
dinner	cena, la	*lah 'seh-nah*

director	director, el (la directora)	*ehl dee-rehk-'tohr (lah dee-rehk-'toh-rah)*
dirt	tierra, la	*lah tee-'eh-rrah*
dirty	sucio(a)	*'soo-see·oh(ah)*
disability	discapacidad, la	*lah dees-cah-pah-'see-dad*
disaster	desastre, el	*ehl deh-'sah-streh*
discipline	disciplina, la	*lah dee-see-'plee-nah*
discovery	descubrimiento, el	*ehl deh-skoo-bree-mee-'ehn-toh*
discrimination	discriminación, la	*lah dee-skree-mee-nah-see-'ohn*
dish	traste, el	*ehl 'trah-steh*
dishwasher	lavaplatos, el	*ehl lah-vah-'plah-tohs*
disk	disco, el	*ehl 'dee-skoh*
dispenser	distribuidor, el (la distribuidora)	*ehl dee-stree-boo-ee-'dohr (lah dee-stree-boo-ee-'doh-rah)*
disrespectful	irrespetuoso(a)	*ee-reh-speh-too-'oh-soh(ah)*
distance	distancia, la	*lah dee-'stahn-see·ah*
district	distrito, el	*ehl dee-'stree-toh*
disturbance	tumulto, el	*ehl too-'mool-toh*
ditch	zanja, la	*lah' sahn-hah*
division	división, la	*lah dee-vee-see-'ohn*
divorce	divorcio, el	*ehl dee-'vohr-see·oh*
dizziness	mareos, los	*lohs mah-'reh-ohs*
doctor	doctor, el (la doctora)	*ehl dohk-'tohr (lah dohk-'toh-rah)*
dog	perro, el (la perra)	*ehl 'peh-rroh (lah 'peh-rrah)*
doll	muñeca, la	*lah moo-'nyeh-kah*
dollar	dólar, el	*ehl 'doh-lahr*
dollhouse	casa de muñecas, la	*lah 'kah-sah deh moo-'nyeh-kahs*
door	puerta, la	*lah 'pwehr-tah*
dormitory	dormitorio, el	*ehl dohr-mee-'toh-ree·oh*
double	doble, el	*ehl 'doh-bleh*
down	abajo	*ah-'bah-hoh*
downtown	centro, el	*ehl 'sehn-troh*
dozen	docena, la	*lah doh-'seh-nah*
drama	drama, el	*ehl 'drah-mah*
drawer	cajón, el	*ehl kah-'hohn*
dream	sueño, el	*ehl 'sweh-nyoh*
dress	vestido, el	*ehl veh-'stee-doh*
drill (exercise)	simulacro, el	*ehl see-moo-'lah-kroh*
drill (tool)	taladro, el	*ehl tah-'lah-droh*
driver	chofer, el *or* la	*ehl / lah choh-'fehr*

driver's education	enseñanza de conducir, la	*lah ehn-seh-'nyahn-sah deh kohn-doo-'seer*
driveway	entrada para carros, la	*lah ehn-'trah-dah 'pah-rah 'kah-rrohs*
drug	droga, la	*lah 'droh-gah*
drug addict	drogadicto, el (la drogadicta)	*ehl drohg-ah-'deek-toh (lah drohg-ah-'deek-tah)*
drug dealer	vendedor (la vendedora) de drogas, el	*ehl vehn-deh-'dohr (lah vehn-deh-'doh-rah) deh 'droh-gahs*
drum	tambor, el	*ehl tahm-'bohr*
drunkard	borracho, el (la borracha)	*ehl boh-'rrah-choh (lah boh-'rrah-chah)*
dry	seco(a)	*'seh-koh(ah)*
dryer	secadora, la	*lah seh-kah-'doh-rah*
duck	pato, el (la pata)	*ehl 'pah-toh (lah 'pah-tah)*
duster	limpiador, el	*ehl leem-pee·ah-'dohr*
dustpan	recogedor de basura, el	*ehl reh-koh-heh-'dohr deh bah-'soo-rah*
DVD player	tocador de DVD, el	*ehl toh-kah-'dohr deh DVD*
email	correo electrónico, el	*ehl koh-'rreh-oh eh-lehk-'troh-nee-koh*
ear	oreja, la	*lah oh-'reh-hah*
early	temprano(a)	*tehm-'prah-noh(ah)*
earphones	auriculares, los	*lohs ah-oo-ree-koo-'lah-rehs*
earring	arete, el	*ehl ah-'reh-teh*
earth science	ciencia del mundo, la	*lah see-'ehn-see·ah dehl 'moon-doh*
earthquake	temblor, el	*ehl tehm-'blohr*
easel	caballete, el	*ehl kah-bah-'yeh-teh*
east	este	*'eh-steh*
easy	fácil	*'fah-seel*
economics	economía, la	*lah eh-koh-noh-'mee·ah*
educator	educador, el (la educadora)	*ehl eh-doo-kah-'dohr (lah eh-doo-kah-'doh-rah)*
egg	huevo, el	*ehl 'weh-voh*
eighth	octavo(a)	*ohk-'tah-voh(ah)*
elbow	codo, el	*ehl 'koh-doh*
election	elección, la	*lah eh-lehk-see-'ohn*
electrical outlet	enchufe, el	*ehl ehn-'choo-feh*
electricity	electricidad, la	*lah eh-lehk-tree-see-'dahd*
elevator	ascensor, el	*ehl ah-sehn-'sohr*
email	correo electrónico, el	*ehl kohr-'reh-oh eh-lehk-'troh-nee-koh*
emergency	emergencia, la	*lah eh-mehr-'hehn-see·ah*
emperor	emperador, el	*ehl ehm-peh-rah-'dohr*

employee	empleado, el (la empleada)	*ehl ehm-pleh-'ah-doh (lah ehm-pleh-'ah-dah)*
encouragement	ánimo, el	*ehl 'ah-nee-moh*
engine	motor, el	*ehl moh-'tohr*
engineer	ingeniero, el (la ingeniera)	*ehl een-heh-nee-'eh-roh (lah een-heh-nee-'eh-rah)*
English as a second language	inglés como segundo idioma, el	*ehl een-'glehs 'koh-moh seh-'goon-doh ee-dee-'oh-mah*
English literature	literatura en inglés, la	*lah lee-teh-rah-'too-rah ehn een-'glehs*
enrollment	matrícula, la	*lah mah-'tree-koo-lah*
entrance	entrada, la	*lah ehn-'trah-dah*
envelope	sobre, el	*ehl 'soh-breh*
environment	ambiente, el	*ehl ahm-bee-'ehn-teh*
equipment	equipo, el	*ehl eh-'kee-poh*
eraser	borrador, el	*ehl boh-rrah-'dohr*
escalator	escalera mecánica, la	*lah eh-skah-'leh-rah meh-'kah-nee-kah*
essay	ensayo, el	*ehl ehn-'sah-yoh*
European history	historia de Europa, la	*lah ee-'stoh-ree·ah deh eh·oo-'roh-pah*
evacuation	evacuación, la	*lah eh-vah-koo-ah-see-'ohn*
evaluations	evaluaciones, las	*lahs eh-vah-loo-ah-see-'oh-nehs*
event	evento, el	*ehl eh-'vehn-toh*
evidence	evidencia, la	*lah eh-vee-'dehn-see·ah*
exam	exámen, el	*ehl ehk-'sah-meh*
example	ejemplo, el	*ehl eh-'hehm-ploh*
excellent	excelente	*ehk-seh-'lehn-teh*
exercise	ejercicio, el	*ehl eh-hehr-'see-see·oh*
exit	salida, la	*lah sah-'lee-da*
expensive	caro(a)	*'kah-roh(ah)*
explosion	explosión, la	*lah ehk-sploh-see-'ohn*
expulsion	expulsión, la	*lah ehk-spool-see-'ohn*
extension	extensión, la	*lah ehk-stehn-see-'ohn*
eye	ojo, el	*ehl 'oh-hoh*
face	cara, la	*lah 'kah-rah*
facilitator	facilitador, el (la facilitadora)	*ehl fah-see-lee-tah-'dohr (lah fah-see-lee-tah-'doh-rah)*
fact	hecho, el	*ehl 'eh-choh*
factory	fábrica, la	*lah 'fah-bree-kah*
failure	fracaso, el	*ehl frah-'kah-soh*
fair	justo(a)	*'hoo-stoh(ah)*
fall (season)	otoño, el	*ehl oh-'toh-nyoh*
family	familia, la	*lah fah-'mee-lee·ah*

fan	ventilador, el	*ehl vehn-tee-lah-'dohr*
fantastic	fantástico(a)	*fahn-'tah-stee-koh(ah)*
far	lejos	*'leh-hohs*
fat	gordo(a)	*'gohr-doh(ah)*
father	padre, el	*ehl 'pah-dreh*
faucet	grifo, el	*ehl 'gree-foh*
fax	fax, el	*ehl fahks*
feather	pluma, la	*lah 'ploo-mah*
February	febrero	*feh-'breh-roh*
feeling	sentimiento, el	*ehl sehn-tee-mee-'ehn-toh*
fence	cerca, la	*lah 'sehr-kah*
festival	festival, el	*ehl feh-stee-'vahl*
fever	fiebre, la	*lah fee-'eh-breh*
few	pocos(as)	*'poh-kohs(ahs)*
field	campo, el	*ehl 'kahm-poh*
fifth	quinto(a)	*'keen-toh(ah)*
fight	pelea, la	*lah peh-'leh-ah*
file	archivo, el	*ehl ahr-'chee-voh*
file (computer)	fichero, el	*ehl fee-'cheh-roh*
film	película, la	*lah peh-'lee-koo-lah*
finance	finanzas, las	*lahs fee-'nahn-sahs*
fine	bien	*'bee·ehn*
finger	dedo, el	*ehl 'deh-doh*
fire	incendio, el	*ehl een-'sehn-dee·oh*
fire department	departamento de bomberos, el	*ehl deh-pahr-tah-'mehn-toh deh bohm-'beh-rohs*
fire drill	simulacro de incendio, el	*ehl see-moo-'lah-kroh deh een-'sehn-dee·oh*
fire extinguisher	extintor, el	*ehl ehks-teen-'tohr*
firearm	arma de fuego, el	*ehl 'ahr-mah deh 'fweh-goh*
firefighter	bombero, el (la bombera)	*ehl bohm-'beh-roh (lah bohm'beh-rah)*
fireworks	fuegos artificiales, los	*lohs 'fweh-gohs ahr-tee-fee-see-'ah-lehs*
first	primero(a)	*pree-'meh-roh(ah)*
fish (in water)	pez, el	*ehl pehs*
fish (out of the water)	pescado, el	*ehl peh-'skah-doh*
fishbowl	pecera, la	*lah peh-'seh-rah*
flag	bandera, la	*lah bahn-'deh-rah*
flashlight	linterna, la	*lah leen-'tehr-nah*
flood	inundación, la	*lah een-oon-dah-see·'ohn*
floor	piso, el	*ehl 'pee-soh*
flower	flor, la	*lah flohr*
flyer	hoja informativa, la	*lah 'oh-hah een-fohr-mah-'tee-vah*

folder	libreta, la	*lah lee-'breh-tah*
food	comida, la	*lah koh-'mee-dah*
foot	pie, el	*ehl pee-'eh*
football	fútbol americano, el	*ehl 'foot-bohl ah-meh-ree-'kah-noh*
for	para, por	*'pah-rah, pohr*
foreign	extranjero(a)	*ehks-trahn-'heh-roh(ah)*
forest	bosque, el	*ehl 'boh-skeh*
fork	tenedor, el	*ehl teh-neh-'dohr*
form	formulario, el	*ehl fohr-moo-'lah-ree·oh*
formula	fórmula, la	*lah 'fohr-moo-lah*
fountain	fuente, la	*lah 'fwehn-teh*
fourth	cuarto(a)	*'kwahr-toh(ah)*
fraction	fracción, la	*lah frahk-see-'ohn*
free	gratis	*'grah-tees*
freedom	libertad, la	*lah lee-behr-'tahd*
freezer	congelador, el	*ehl kohn-heh-lah-'dohr*
frequently	frecuentemente	*freh-kwehn-teh-'mehn-teh*
Friday	viernes	*vee-'ehr-nehs*
friend	amigo, el (la amiga)	*ehl ah-'mee-goh (lah ah-'mee-gah)*
friendly	amistoso(a)	*ah-mee-'stoh-soh(ah)*
friendship	amistad, la	*lah ah-mee-'stahd*
from	de	*deh*
frostbite	congelamiento, el	*ehl kohn-heh-lah-mee-'ehn-toh*
fruit	fruta, la	*lah 'froo-tah*
fun	divertido(a)	*dee-vehr-'tee-doh(ah)*
function	función, la	*lah foon-see-'ohn*
funding	fondos, los	*lohs 'fohn-dohs*
fundraising	recolección de fondos, la	*lah reh-koh-lehk-see-'ohn deh 'fohn-dohs*
funny	chistoso(a)	*chee-'stoh-soh(ah)*
furniture	muebles, los	*lohs 'mweh-blehs*
future	futuro, el	*ehl foo-'too-roh*
game	juego, el	*ehl joo-'eh-goh*
gang	pandilla, la	*lah pahn-'dee-yah*
gang member	pandillero, el (la pandillera)	*ehl pahn-dee-'yeh-roh (lah pahn-dee-'yeh-rah)*
garage	garaje, el	*ehl gah-'rah-heh*
garden	jardín, el	*ehl hahr-'deen*
gardener	jardinero, el (la jardinera)	*ehl hahr-dee-'neh-roh (lah hahr-dee-'neh-rah)*
gas station	gasolinera, la	*lah gah-soh-lee-'neh-rah*
gate	portón, el	*ehl pohr-'tohn*

generally	generalmente	*heh-neh-rahl-'mehn-teh*
geography	geografía, la	*lah heh-oh-grah-'fee·ah*
geometry	geometría, la	*lah heh-oh-meh-'tree·ah*
gift	regalo, el	*ehl reh-'gah-loh*
girdle	faja, la	*lah 'fah-hah*
girl	niña, la	*lah 'nee-nyah*
girlfriend	novia, la	*lah 'noh-vee·ah*
glass (drinking)	vaso, el	*ehl 'vah-soh*
glass (material)	vidrio, el	*ehl 'vee-dree·oh*
glasses	lentes, los	*lohs 'lehn-tehs*
globe	mundo, el	*ehl 'moon-doh*
glossary	glosario, el	*ehl gloh-'sah-ree·oh*
glove	guante, el	*ehl 'gwahn-teh*
glue	pegamento, el	*ehl peh-gah-'mehn-toh*
goal	meta, la	*lah 'meh-tah*
goat	chivo, el (la chiva)	*ehl 'chee-voh (lah 'chee-vah)*
God	Dios	*'dee·ohs*
godfather	padrino, el	*ehl pah-'dree-noh*
godmother	madrina, la	*lah mah-'dree-nah*
golf	golf, el	*ehl gohlf*
good	bueno(a)	*'bweh-noh(ah)*
good-bye	adiós	*ah-dee-'ohs*
government	gobierno, el	*ehl goh-bee-'ehr-noh*
grades (academic)	notas, las	*lahs 'noh-tahs*
grade (level)	grado, el	*ehl 'grah-doh*
grade school	escuela primaria, la	*lah eh-'skweh-lah pree-'mah-ree·ah*
graduation	graduación, la	*lah grah-doo-ah-see-'ohn*
graffiti	grafiti, el	*ehl grah-'fee-tee*
grammar	gramática, la	*lah grah-'mah-tee-kah*
granddaughter	nieta, la	*lah nee-'eh-tah*
grandfather	abuelo, el	*ehl ah-'bweh-loh*
grandmother	abuela, la	*lah ah-'bweh-lah*
grandson	nieto, el	*ehl nee-'eh-toh*
grape	uva, la	*lah 'oo-vah*
graph	gráfico, el	*ehl 'grah-fee-koh*
grass	pasto, el	*ehl pah-'stoh*
green	verde	*'vehr-deh*
group	grupo, el	*ehl 'groo-poh*
grove	arboleda, la	*lah ahr-boh-'leh-dah*
guest	huésped, el or la	*ehl / lah 'weh-spehd*
guilty	culpable	*kool-'pah-bleh*
gum	chicle, el	*ehl 'chee-kleh*
gym	gimnasio, el	*ehl heem-'nah-see·oh*

gymnastics	gimnasia, la	*lah heem-'nah-see·ah*
hair	pelo, el	*ehl 'peh-loh*
hairbrush	cepillo, el	*ehl seh-'pee-yoh*
half	mitad, la	*lah mee-'tahd*
hall	pasillo, el	*ehl pah-'see-yoh*
ham	jamón, el	*ehl hah-'mohn*
hamburger	hamburguesa, la	*lah ahm-boor-'geh-sah*
hammer	martillo, el	*ehl mahr-'tee-yoh*
hand	mano, la	*lah 'mah-noh*
handcuff	esposas, las	*lahs eh-'spoh-sahs*
handicapped	incapacitado(a)	*een-kah-pah-see-'tah-doh(ah)*
handkerchief	pañuelo, el	*ehl pah-nyoo-'eh-loh*
handsome	guapo(a)	*'gwah-poh(ah)*
hanger	gancho, el	*ehl 'gahn-choh*
happy	contento(a)	*kohn-'tehn-toh(ah)*
harassment	acoso, el	*ehl ah-koh-soh*
hard	duro(a)	*'doo-roh(ah)*
hard drive	disco duro, el	*ehl 'dees-koh 'doo-'roh*
harm	daño, el	*ehl 'dah-nyoh*
hat	sombrero, el	*ehl sohm-'breh-roh*
he	él	*ehl*
head	cabeza, la	*lah kah-'beh-sah*
headache	dolor de cabeza, el	*ehl doh-'lohr deh kah-'beh-sah*
headphones	audífonos, los	*lohs ow-'dee-foh-nohs*
health	salud, la	*lah sah-'lood*
health care	cuidado de la salud, el	*ehl kwee-'dah-doh deh lah sah-'lood*
healthy	sano(a)	*'sah-noh(ah)*
hearing aids	audífonos, los	*lohs ow-'dee-foh-nohs*
heart	corazón, el	*ehl koh-rah-'sohn*
heat	calor, el	*ehl kah-'lohr*
heat stroke	prostración, la	*lah proh-strah-see-'ohn*
heater	calentador, el	*ehl kah-lehn-tah-'dohr*
heating	calefacción, la	*lah kah-leh-fahk-see-'ohn*
height	estatura, la	*lah eh-stah-'too-rah*
help	ayuda, la	*lah ah-'yoo-dah*
helper	ayudante, el (la ayudanta)	*ehl ah-yoo-'dahn-teh (lah ah-yoo-'dahn-tah)*
helpful	servicial	*sehr-vee-see-'ahl*
hen	gallina, la	*lah gah-'yee-nah*
her	su	*soo*
here	aquí; acá	*ah-'kee; ah-'kah*
hi	hola	*'oh-lah*

hiccup	hipo, el	*ehl 'ee-poh*
high school	escuela secundaria, la	*lah eh-'skweh-lah seh-koon-'dah-ree·ah*
highway	carretera, la	*lah kah-rreh-'teh-rah*
hill	cerro, el	*ehl 'seh-rroh*
hip	cadera, la	*lah kah-'deh-rah*
his	su	*soo*
hoe	azadón, el	*ehl ah-sah-'dohn*
hole	hoyo, el	*ehl 'oh-yoh*
holiday	día feriado, el	*ehl 'dee·ah feh-ree-'ah-doh*
home	casa, la	*lah 'kah-sah*
home page	pagina inicial, la	*lah 'pah-hee-nah ee-nee-see-'ahl*
honesty	honradez, la	*lah ohn-rah-'dehs*
hope	esperanza, la	*lah eh-speh-'rahn-sah*
horn	bocina, la	*lah boh-'see-nah*
horse	caballo, el	*ehl kah-'bah-yoh*
hospital	hospital, el	*ehl oh-spee-'tahl*
hot	caliente	*kah-lee-'ehn-teh*
hot dog	perrito caliente, el	*ehl peh-'rree-toh kah-lee-'ehn-teh*
hour	hora, la	*lah 'oh-rah*
house	casa, la	*lah 'kah-sah*
housing	vivienda, la	*lah vee-vee-'ehn-dah*
how	cómo	*'koh-moh*
how many	cuántos	*'kwahn-tohs*
how much	cuánto	*'kwahn-toh*
humanities	humanidades, las	*lahs oo-mah-nee-'dah-dehs*
humid	húmedo	*'oo-meh-doh*
hunger	hambre, el	*ehl 'ahm-breh*
hurricane	huracán, el	*ehl oo-rah-'kahn*
husband	esposo, el	*ehl eh-'spoh-soh*
hydrant	la llave de incendios, la	*lah 'yah-veh deh een-'sehn-dee·ohs*
I	yo	*yoh*
I.D.	identificación, la	*lah ee-dehn-tee-fee-kah-see-'ohn*
ice	hielo, el	*ehl 'yeh-loh*
ice cream	helado, el	*ehl eh-'lah-doh*
ice hockey	hockey, el	*ehl 'hoh-kee*
idea	idea, la	*lah ee-'deh-ah*
if	si	*see*
illness	enfermedad, la	*lah ehn-fehr-meh-'dahd*
important	importante	*eem-pohr-'tahn-teh*

in	en	*ehn*
in front of	en frente de	*ehn 'frehn-teh deh*
inch	pulgada, la	*lah pool-'gah-dah*
incomplete	incompleto(a)	*een-kohm-'pleh-toh(ah)*
incorrect	incorrecto(a)	*een-koh-'rrehk-toh(ah)*
independence	independencia, la	*lah een-deh-pehn-'dehn-see·ah*
individualized	individualizado(a)	*een-dee-vee-doo-ah-lee-'sah-doh(ah)*
industrial arts	artes industriales, las	*lahs 'ahr-tehs een-doos-tree ah-lehs*
industry	industria, la	*lah een-'doo-stree·ah*
infection	infección, la	*lah een-fehk-see-'ohn*
information	información, la	*lah een-fohr-mah-see-'ohn*
injury	herida, la	*lah eh-'ree-dah*
inside	adentro	*ah-'dehn-troh*
institute	instituto, el	*ehl een-stee-'too-toh*
institution	institución, la	*lah een-stee-too-see-'ohn*
instruction	instrucción, la	*lah een-strook-see-'ohn*
instructor	instructor, el (la instructora)	*ehl een-strook-'tohr (lah een-strook-'toh-rah)*
instrument	instrumento, el	*ehl een-stroo-'mehn-toh*
insurance	seguro, el	*ehl seh-'goo-roh*
integration	integración, la	*lah een-teh-grah-see-'ohn*
interesting	interesante	*een-teh-reh-'sahn-teh*
interpreter	intérprete, el or la	*ehl / lah een-'tehr-preh-teh*
interview	entrevista, la	*lah ehn-treh-'vee-stah*
jacket	chaqueta, la	*lah chah-'keh-tah*
jail	cárcel, la	*lah 'kahr-sehl*
janitor	conserje, el	*ehl kohn-'sehr-heh*
January	enero	*eh-'neh-roh*
jar	jarra, la	*lah 'hah-rrah*
jello	gelatina, la	*lah heh-lah-'tee-nah*
jewelry	joyas, las	*lahs 'hoh-yahs*
joke	chiste, el	*ehl 'chee-steh*
journalism	periodismo, el	*ehl peh-ree·oh-'dees-moh*
juice	jugo, el	*ehl 'hoo-goh*
July	julio	*'hoo-lee·oh*
jump rope	cuerda para brincar, la	*lah 'kwehr-dah 'pah-rah breen-'kahr*
June	junio	*'hoo-nee·oh*
jungle	selva, la	*lah 'sehl-vah*
just	apenas	*ah-'peh-nahs*
justice	justicia, la	*lah hoo-'stee-see·ah*

juvenile court	tribunal de menores, el	*ehl tree-boo-'nahl deh meh-'noh-rehs*
key	llave, la	*lah 'yah-veh*
keyboard	teclado, el	*ehl teh-'klah-doh*
kind	amable	*ah-'mah-bleh*
kindness	bondad, la	*lah bohn-'dahd*
kite	cometa, la	*lah koh-'meh-tah*
knee	rodilla, la	*lah roh-'dee-yah*
knife	cuchillo, el	*ehl koo-'chee-yoh*
labels	etiquetas, las	*lahs eh-tee-'keh-tahs*
laboratory	laboratorio, el	*ehl lah-boh-rah-'toh-ree·oh*
lady (Mrs.)	señora, la (Sra.)	*lah seh-'nyoh-rah*
lake	lago, el	*ehl 'lah-goh*
lamp	lámpara, la	*lah 'lahm-pah-rah*
land	terreno, el	*ehl teh-'rreh-noh*
language	lenguaje, el; idioma, el	*ehl lehn-'gwah-heh; ehl ee-dee-'oh-mah*
laptop	computadora portátil, la	*lah kohm-poo-tah-'doh-rah pohr-'tah-teel*
large room	salón, el	*ehl sah-'lohn*
latch	cerrojo, el	*ehl seh-'rroh-hoh*
late	tarde	*'tahr-deh*
later	más tarde	*'mahs 'tahr-deh*
law	ley, la	*lah leh·ee*
lawn	césped, el	*ehl 'seh-spehd*
lawnmower	cortadora de césped, la	*lah kohr-tah-'doh-rah deh 'seh-spehd*
lawyer	abogado, el (la abogada)	*ehl ah-boh-'gah-doh (lah ah-boh-'gah-dah)*
leader	líder, el *or* la	*ehl / lah 'lee-dehr*
league	liga, la	*lah 'lee-gah*
left	izquierda	*ees-kee-'ehr-dah*
leg	pierna, la	*lah pee-'ehr-nah*
legal guardian	tutor legal, el (la tutora legal)	*ehl too-'tohr leh-'gahl (lah too-'toh-rah leh-'gahl)*
lemon	limón, el	*ehl lee-'mohn*
lemonade	limonada, la	*lah lee-moh-'nah-dah*
length	largo, el	*ehl 'lahr-goh*
lens	lente, el	*ehl 'lehn-teh*
less	menos	*'meh-nohs*
lesson	lección, la	*lah lehk-see-'ohn*
letter (alphabet)	letra, la	*lah 'leh-trah*
letter (mail)	carta, la	*lah 'kahr-tah*
lettuce	lechuga, la	*lah leh-'choo-gah*

level	nivel, el	*ehl nee-'vehl*
librarian	bibliotecario, el (la bibliotecaria)	*ehl bee-blee·oh-teh-'kah-ree·oh (lah beeb-lee·oh-teh-'kah-ree·ah)*
library	biblioteca, la	*lah bee-blee·oh-'teh-kah*
license	licencia, la	*lah lee-'sehn-see·ah*
light	luz, la	*lah loos*
line	línea, la	*lah 'lee-neh-ah*
lip	labio, el	*ehl 'lah-bee·oh*
liquor	licor, el	*ehl lee-'kohr*
list	lista, la	*lah 'lee-stah*
little	pequeño(a)	*peh-'keh-nyoh(ah)*
liver	hígado, el	*ehl 'ee-gah-doh*
loan	préstamo, el	*ehl 'preh-stah-moh*
lobby	vestíbulo, el	*ehl veh-'stee-boo-loh*
lock	candado, el	*ehl kahn-'dah-doh*
locker	armario, el	*ehl ahr-'mah-ree·oh*
loiterer	holgazán, el (la holgazana)	*ehl ohl-gah-'sahn (lah ohl-gah-'sah-nah)*
loneliness	soledad, la	*lah soh-leh-'dahd*
long	largo(a)	*'lahr-goh(ah)*
lost	perdido(a)	*pehr-'dee-doh(ah)*
lot	lote, el	*ehl 'loh-teh*
lotion	loción, la	*lah loh-see-'ohn*
loud	ruidoso(a)	*roo-ee-'doh-soh(ah)*
loudspeaker	altoparlante, el	*ehl ahl-toh-pahr-'lahn-teh*
lounge	salón, el	*ehl sah-'lohn*
love	amor, el	*ehl ah-'mohr*
lunch	almuerzo, el	*ehl ahl-moo-'ehr-soh*
lungs	pulmones, los	*lohs pool-'moh-nehs*
machine	máquina, la	*lah 'mah-kee-nah*
machinery	maquinaria, la	*lah mah-kee-'nah-ree·ah*
magazine	revista, la	*lah reh-'vee-stah*
magnet	imán, el	*ehl ee-'mahn*
magnifying glass	lupa, la	*lah 'loo-pah*
mail carrier	cartero, el *or* la	*ehl / lah kahr-'teh-roh*
mailbox	buzón, el	*ehl boo-'sohn*
main office	oficina principal, la	*lah oh-fee-'see-nah preen-see-'pahl*
maintenance	mantenimiento, el	*ehl mahn-teh-nee-mee-'ehn-toh*
makeup	maquillaje, el	*ehl mah-kee-'yah-heh*
mall	centro commercial, el	*ehl 'sehn-troh koh-mehr-see-'ahl*

man	hombre, el	*ehl 'ohm-breh*
many	muchos(as)	*'moo-chohs(ahs)*
map	mapa, el	*ehl 'mah-pah*
March	marzo	*'mahr-soh*
mark	marca, la	*lah 'mahr-kah*
marker	marcador, el	*ehl mahr-kah-'dohr*
market	mercado, el	*ehl mehr-'kah-doh*
marvelous	maravilloso(a)	*mah-rah-vee-'yoh-soh(ah)*
mat	tapete, el	*ehl tah-'peh-teh*
match	fósforo, el	*ehl 'fohs-foh-roh*
material	materia, la	*lah mah-'teh-ree·ah*
mathematics	matemáticas, las	*lahs mah-teh-'mah-tee-kahs*
May	mayo	*'mah-yoh*
maybe	quizás	*kee-'sahs*
mayonnaise	mayonesa, la	*lah mah-yoh-'neh-sah*
mechanic	mecánico, el *or* la	*ehl / lah meh-'kah-nee-koh*
medal	medalla, la	*lah meh-'dah-yah*
media	medios de comunicación, los	*lohs 'meh-dee·ohs deh koh-moo-nee-kah-see-'ohn*
medicine	medicina, la	*lah meh-dee-'see-nah*
meeting	reunión, la	*lah reh-oo-nee-'ohn*
member	miembro, el *or* la	*ehl / lah mee-'ehm-broh*
memo	memorándum, el	*ehl meh-moh-'rahn-doom*
memory	memoria, la	*lah meh-'moh-ree·ah*
mentor	mentor, el (la mentora)	*ehl mehn-'tohr (lah mehn-'toh-rah)*
menu	menú, el	*ehl meh-'noo*
merry-go-round	caballitos, los	*lohs kah-bah-'yee-tohs*
message	recado, el/mensaje, el	*ehl reh-'kah-doh / ehl mehn-'sah-heh*
metal	metal	*meh-'tahl*
meter (length)	metro, el	*ehl 'meh-troh*
meter (parking)	parquímetro, el	*ehl pahr-'kee-meh-troh*
method	método, el	*ehl 'meh-toh-doh*
microphone	micrófono, el	*ehl mee-'kroh-foh-noh*
microscope	microscopio, el	*ehl mee-kroh-'skoh-pee·oh*
microwave	horno de microonda, el	*ehl 'ohr-noh deh mee-kroh-'ohn-dah*
midnight	medianoche, la	*lah meh-dee·ah-'noh-cheh*
mile	una milla	*'oo-nah 'mee-yah*
milk	leche, la	*lah 'leh-cheh*
mine	mío(a)	*'mee·oh(ah)*
minor	menor de edad, el *or* la	*ehl / lah meh-'nohr deh eh-'dahd*

mirror	espejo, el	*ehl eh-'speh-hoh*
mister (Mr.)	señor, el (Sr.)	*ehl seh-'nyohr*
mittens	mitones, los	*lohs mee-'toh-nehs*
model	modelo, el	*ehl moh-'deh-loh*
modeling clay	plastilina, la	*lah plah-stee-'lee-nah*
modified	modificado(a)	*moh-dee-fee-'kah-doh (ah)*
module	módule, el	*ehl 'moh-doo-loh*
Monday	lunes	*'loo-nehs*
money	dinero, el	*ehl dee-'neh-roh*
monitor	monitor, el	*ehl moh-nee-'tohr*
monster	monstruo, el or la	*ehl / lah 'mohn-stroo-oh*
month	mes, el	*ehl mehs*
moon	luna, la	*lah 'loo-nah*
mop	trapeador, el	*ehl trah-peh-ah-'dohr*
more	más	*mahs*
mother	madre, la	*lah 'mah-dreh*
motion	movimiento, el	*ehl moh-vee-mee-'ehn-toh*
motorcycle	motocicleta, la	*lah moh-toh-see-'kleh-tah*
mountain	montaña, la	*lah mohn-'tah-nyah*
mouth	boca, la	*lah 'boh-kah*
movie theater	cine, el	*ehl 'see-neh*
much	mucho(a)	*'moo-choh(ah)*
mud	lodo, el	*ehl 'loh-doh*
museum	museo, el	*ehl moo-'seh-oh*
music	música, la	*lah 'moo-see-kah*
mustard	mostaza, la	*lah moh-'stah-sah*
mute	mudo(a)	*'moo-doh(ah)*
my	mi	*mee*
name	nombre, el	*ehl 'nohm-breh*
napkin	servilleta, la	*lah sehr-vee-'yeh-tah*
narrow	estrecho(a)	*eh-'streh-choh(ah)*
nation	nación, la	*lah nah-see-'ohn*
nationality	nacionalidad, la	*lah nah-see·oh-nah-lee-'dahd*
nausea	náusea, la	*lah 'now-seh-ah*
near	cerca	*'sehr-kah*
necessary	necesario(a)	*neh-seh-'sah-ree·oh(ah)*
neck	cuello, el	*ehl 'kweh-yoh*
necklace	collar, el	*ehl koh-'yahr*
needs	necesidades, las	*lahs neh-seh-see-'dah-dehs*
neighbor	vecino, el	*ehl veh-'see-noh*
neighborhood	barrio, el	*ehl 'bah-rree·oh*
nephew	sobrino, el	*ehl soh-'bree-noh*
nervous	nervioso(a)	*nehr-vee-'oh-soh(ah)*
net	red, la	*lah rehd*

never	nunca	'noon-kah
newspaper	periódico, el	ehl peh-ree-'oh-dee-koh
next to	al lado de	ahl 'lah-doh deh
nice	simpático(a)	seem-'pah-tee-koh(ah)
niece	sobrina, la	lah soh-'bree-nah
ninth	noveno(a)	noh-'veh-noh(ah)
non-fiction	no ficción, la	lah noh feek-see-'ohn
noon	mediodía, el	ehl meh-dee·oh-'deeah
north	norte	'nohr-teh
nose	nariz, la	lah nah-'rees
note	nota, la	lah 'noh-tah
notebook	cuaderno, el	ehl kwah-'dehr-noh
notice	anuncio, el; aviso, el	ehl ah-'noon-see·oh; ehl ah-soh
novel	novela, la	lah noh-'veh-lah
November	noviembre	noh-vee-'ehm-breh
now	ahora	ah-'oh-rah
number	número, el	ehl 'noo-meh-roh
nurse	enfermera, la (el enfermero)	lah ehn-fehr-'meh-rah (ehl ehn-fehr-'meh-roh)
nursery	guardería, la	lah gwahr-deh-'ree·ah
nursing bottle	biberón, el	ehl bee-beh-'rohn
objectives	objetivos, los	lohs ohb-heh-'tee-vohs
occupation	ocupación, la	lah oh-koo-pah-see-'ohn
ocean	océano, el	ehl oh-'seh-ah-noh
October	octubre	ohk-'too-breh
of	de	deh
office	oficina, la	lah oh-fee-'see-nah
official	oficial, el or la	ehl / lah oh-fee-see-'ahl
old	viejo(a)	vee-'eh-hoh(ah)
older	mayor	mah-'yohr
on	en	ehn
once	una vez	'oo-nah vehs
onion	cebolla, la	lah seh-'boh-yah
online	en línea	ehn 'lee-neh-ah
operator	operario, el (la operaria)	ehl oh-peh-'rah-ree·oh (lah oh-peh-'rah-ree·ah)
opinion	opinión, la	lah oh-pee-nee-'ohn
opposite	de frente de	deh 'frehn-the deh
or	o	oh
orange (color)	anaranjado(a)	ah-nah-rahn-'hah-doh(ah)
orange (fruit)	naranja, la	lah nah-'rahn-hah
orchard	huerta, la	lah 'wehr-tah
orchestra	orquesta, la	lah ohr-'keh-stah

organization	organización, la	*lah ohr-gah-nee-sah-see·'ohn*
organized	organizado(a)	*ohr-gah-nee-'sah-doh(ah)*
orientation	orientación, la	*lah oh-ree-ehn-tah-see·'ohn*
ounce	onza, la	*lah 'ohn-sah*
our	nuestro(a)	*'nweh-stroh(ah)*
outdoors	afueras, las	*lahs ah-'fweh-rahs*
outside	afuera	*ah-'fweh-rah*
outstanding	destacado(a); sobresaliente	*deh-stah-'kah-doh(ah); soh-breh-sah-lee-'ehn-teh*
oven	horno, el	*ehl 'ohr-noh*
over	sobre	*'soh-breh*
overcoat	abrigo, el	*ehl ah-'bree-goh*
overdose	sobredosis, la	*lah soh-breh-'doh-sees*
overtime	sobretiempo, el	*ehl soh-breh-'tee-'ehm-poh*
owner	dueño, el (la dueña)	*ehl 'dweh-nyoh (lah 'dweh-nyah)*
pacifier	chupete, el	*ehl choo-'peh-teh*
pack	paquete, el	*ehl pah-'keh-teh*
page	página, la	*lah 'pah-hee-nah*
pain	dolor, el	*ehl doh-'lohr*
paint	pintura, la	*lah peen-'too-rah*
paintbrush	brocha, la	*lah 'broh-chah*
painter	pintor, el (la pintora)	*ehl peen-'tohr (lah peen-'toh-rah)*
painting	pintura, la	*lah peen-'too-rah*
pair	par, el	*ehl pahr*
pajamas	pijama, el	*ehl pee-'yah-mah*
pan	sartén, el	*ehl sahr-'tehn*
panties	bragas, las	*lahs 'brah-gahs*
pants	pantalones, los	*lohs pahn-tah-'loh-nehs*
paper	papel, el	*ehl pah-'pehl*
parade	desfile, el	*ehl dehs-'fee-leh*
paragraph	parrafo, el	*ehl 'pah-rrah-foh*
parent	padre, el	*ehl 'pah-dreh*
park	parque, el	*ehl 'pahr-keh*
parking lot	estacionamiento, el	*ehl eh-stah-see·oh-nah-mee-'ehn-toh*
partner	socio, el (la socia)	*ehl 'soh-see·oh (lah 'soh-see·ah)*
party	fiesta, la	*lah fee-'eh-stah*
pass	permiso, el; pase, el	*ehl pehr-'mee-soh; ehl 'pah-seh*
password	contraseña, la	*lah kohn-trah-'sehn-yah*
passenger	pasajero, el (la pasajera)	*ehl pah-sah-'heh-roh (lah pah-sah-'heh-rah)*

patience	paciencia, la	*lah pah-see-'ehn-see·ah*
payment	pago, el	*ehl 'pah-goh*
peace	paz, la	*lah pahs*
peach	melocotón, el	*ehl meh-loh-koh-'tohn*
pear	pera, la	*lah 'peh-rah*
pedestrian	peatón, el (la peatona)	*ehl peh-ah-'tohn (lah peh-ah-'toh-nah)*
pen	lapicero, el; la pluma	*ehl lah-pee-'seh-roh; lah 'ploo-mah*
pencil	lápiz, el	*ehl 'lah-pees*
pencil sharpener	sacapuntas, el	*ehl sah-kah-'poon-tahs*
people	gente, la	*lah 'hehn-teh*
pepper	pimienta, la	*lah pee-mee-'ehn-tah*
percentage	porcentaje, el	*ehl pohr-sehn-'tah-heh*
performance	rendimiento, el	*ehl rehn-dee-mee-'ehn-toh*
permit	permiso, el	*ehl pehr-'mee-soh*
person	persona, la	*lah pehr-'soh-nah*
personality	personalidad, la	*lah pehr-soh-nah-lee-'dahd*
personnel	personal, el	*ehl pehr-soh-'nahl*
pet	mascota, la	*lah mah-'skoh-tah*
pharmacy	farmacia, la	*lah fahr-'mah-see·ah*
philosophy	filosofía, la	*lah fee-loh-soh-'fee·ah*
phone call	llamada, la	*lah yah-'mah-dah*
photo	foto, la	*lah 'foh-toh*
photocopier	fotocopiadora, la	*lah foh-toh-koh-pee·ah-'doh-rah*
physical education	educación física, la	*lah eh-doo-kah-see·'ohn 'fee-see-kah*
physician	médico, el *or* la	*ehl / lah 'meh-dee-koh*
physics	física, la	*lah 'fee-see-kah*
pickpocket	carterista, el *or* la	*ehl / lah kahr-teh-'ree-stah*
picnic	merienda campestre, la	*lah meh-ree-'ehn-dah*
picture frame	marco, el	*ehl 'mahr-koh*
pictures	dibujos, los	*lohs dee-'boo-hohs*
pie	pastel, el	*ehl pah-'stehl*
pig	cerdo, el (la cerda)	*ehl 'sehr-doh (lah 'sehr-dah)*
pin	alfiler, el	*ehl ahl-fee-'lehr*
pipe	tubería, la	*lah too-beh-'ree·ah*
place	lugar, el	*ehl loo-'gahr*
plan	plan, el	*ehl plahn*
planet	planeta, el	*ehl plah-'neh-tah*
plant	planta, la	*lah 'plahn-tah*
plastic	plástico, el	*ehl 'plah-stee-koh*
plate	plato, el	*ehl 'plah-toh*

play (theater)	drama, el	*ehl 'drah-mah*
player	jugador, el (la jugadora)	*ehl hoo-gah-'dohr (lah hoo-gah-'doh-rah)*
playground	campo de recreo, el	*ehl 'kahm-poh deh reh-'kreh-oh*
playing cards	baraja, la	*lah bah-'rah-hah*
playpen	corral de juego, el	*ehl koh-'rrahl deh 'hweh-goh*
please	por favor	*pohr fah-'vohr*
pliers	alicate, el	*ehl ah-lee-'kah-teh*
plumber	plomero, el (la plomera)	*ehl ploh-'meh-roh (lah ploh-'meh-rah)*
plumbing	tubería, la	*lah too-beh-'ree·ah*
podium	podio, el	*ehl poh-dee·oh*
poetry	poesía, la	*lah poh-eh-'see·ah*
point	punto, el	*ehl 'poon-toh*
poisoning	envenenamiento, el	*ehl ehn-veh-neh-nah-mee-'ehn-toh*
pole	poste, el	*ehl 'poh-steh*
police	policía, la	*lah poh-lee-'see·ah*
police officer	agente de policía, el *or* la	*ehl / lah ah-'hehn-teh deh poh-lee-'see·ah*
police station	estación de policía, la	*lah eh-stah-see-'ohn deh poh-lee-'see·ah*
polite	cortés	*kohr-'tehs*
political science	ciencias políticas	*see-'ehn-see·ahs poh-'lee-'tee-kahs*
politics	política, la	*lah poh-'lee-tee-kah*
pollution	contaminación, la	*lah kohn-tah-mee-nah-see-'ohn*
pond	charca, la	*lah 'chahr-kah*
pool	piscina, la	*lah pee-'see-nah*
poor	pobre	*'poh-breh*
population	población, la	*lah poh-blah-see-'ohn*
porch	portal, el	*ehl pohr-'tahl*
portrait	retrato, el	*ehl reh-'trah-toh*
post office	correo, el	*ehl koh-'rreh-oh*
poster	cartel, el	*ehl kahr-'tehl*
pot	olla, la	*lah 'oh-yah*
potato	papa, la	*lah 'pah-pah*
potato chips	papitas, las	*lahs pah-'pee-tahs*
potty	vasinica, la	*lah vah-see-'nee-kah*
pound	libra, la	*lah 'lee-brah*
poverty	pobreza, la	*lah poh-'breh-sah*
powder	polvo, el	*ehl 'pohl-voh*
practice	práctica, la	*lah 'prahk-tee-kah*

preferences	preferencias, las	*lahs preh-feh-'rehn-see·ahs*
pregnancy	embarazo, el	*ehl ehm-bah-'rah-soh*
prescription	receta médica, la	*lah reh-'seh-tah 'meh-dee-kah*
president	presidente, el	*ehl preh-see-'dehn-teh*
pretty	bonito(a)	*boh 'nee-toh(ah)*
principal	director, el (la directora)	*ehl dee-rehk-'tohr (lah dee-rehk-'toh-rah)*
principle	principio, el	*ehl preen-'see-pee·oh*
prism	prisma, el	*ehl 'prees-mah*
private	privado(a)	*pree-'vah-doh(ah)*
privilege	privilegio, el	*ehl pree-vee-'leh-hee·oh*
prize	premio, el	*ehl 'preh-mee·oh*
problem	problema, el	*ehl proh-'bleh-mah*
procedure	procedimiento, el	*ehl proh-seh-dee-mee-'ehn-toh*
process	proceso, el	*ehl proh-'seh-soh*
procrastination	retraso, el	*ehl reh-'trah-soh*
program	programa, el	*ehl proh-'grah-mah*
program (computer)	programación, la	*lah proh-grah-mah-see-'ohn*
programmer	programador, el (la programadora)	*ehl proh-grah-mah-'dohr (lah proh-grah-mah-'doh-rah)*
project	proyecto, el	*ehl proh-yehk-'toh*
projector	proyector, el	*ehl proh-yehk-'tohr*
promotion	promoción, la	*lah proh-moh-see-'ohn*
property	propiedad, la	*lah proh-pee-eh-'dahd*
prostitute	prostituta, la	*lah proh-stee-'too-tah*
psychiatrist	psiquiatra, el *or* la	*ehl/lah see-kee-'ah-trah*
psychologist	psicólogo, el (la psicóloga)	*ehl see-'koh-loh-goh (lah see-'koh-loh-gah)*
psychology	psicología, la	*lah see-koh-loh-'hee·ah*
puberty	pubertad, la	*lah poo-behr-'tahd*
public	público, el	*ehl 'poob-lee-koh*
public relations	relaciones públicas, las	*lahs reh-lah-see-'oh-nehs 'poob-lee-kahs*
punctual	puntual	*poon-too-'ahl*
punishment	castigo, el	*ehl kah-'stee-goh*
purple	morado(a)	*moh-'rah-doh(ah)*
puzzle	rompecabezas, el	*ehl rohm-peh-kah-'beh-sahs*
question	pregunta, la	*lah preh-'goon-tah*
quickly	rápidamente	*'rah-pee-dah-'mehn-teh*
quiet	quieto(a)	*kee-'eh-toh(ah)*
quiz	cuestionario, el	*ehl kweh-stee·oh-'nah-ree·oh*
rabbit	conejo, el (la coneja)	*ehl koh-'neh-hoh (lah koh-'neh-hah)*
race (competition)	carrera, la	*lah kah-'rreh-rah*

race (people)	raza, la	*lah 'rah-sah*
rack (shelf)	estante, el	*ehl eh-'stahn-teh*
racket	raqueta, la	*lah rah-'keh-tah*
racquetball	frontón con raqueta, el	*ehl frohn-'tohn kohn rah-'keh-tah*
raffle	sorteo, el	*ehl sohr-'teh-oh*
raid	incursión, la	*lah een-koor-see·'ohn*
railroad track	vía del ferrocarril, la	*lah 'vee·ah dehl feh-rroh-kah-'rreel*
rain	lluvia, la	*lah 'yoo-vee·ah*
raincoat	impermeable, el	*ehl eem-pehr-meh-'ah-bleh*
rake	rastrillo, el	*ehl rah-'stree-yoh*
ramp	rampa, la	*lah 'rahm-pah*
rape	violación, la	*lah vee·oh-lah-see·'ohn*
rate	tasa, la	*lah 'tah-sah*
rattle	sonajero, el	*ehl soh-nah-'heh-roh*
reading	lectura, la	*lah lehk-'too-rah*
ready	listo(a)	*'lee-stoh(ah)*
reason	razón, la	*lah rah-'sohn*
receipt	recibo, el	*ehl reh-'see-boh*
receptionist	recepcionista, el *or* la	*ehl / lah reh-sehp-see·oh-'nee-stah*
recommendation	recomendación, la	*lah reh-koh-mehn-dah-see·'ohn*
records	registro, el	*ehl reh-'hee-stroh*
rectangle	rectangulo, el	*ehl rehk-'tahn-goo-loh*
red	rojo(a)	*'roh-hoh(ah)*
red-headed	pelirrojo(a)	*peh-lee-'rroh-hoh(ah)*
refrigerator	refrigerador, el	*ehl reh-free-heh-rah-'dohr*
regime	régimen, el	*ehl 'reh-hee-mehn*
region	región, la	*lah reh-hee-'ohn*
registration	inscripción, la	*lah een-skreep-see·'ohn*
relationship	relación, la	*lah reh-lah-see·'ohn*
relative	pariente, el *or* la	*ehl / lah pah-ree-'ehn-teh*
relaxed	relajado(a)	*reh-lah-'hah-doh(ah)*
religion	religión, la	*lah reh-lee-hee·'ohn*
report	reporte, el	*ehl reh-'pohr-teh*
rescue	rescate, el	*ehl reh-'skah-teh*
research	investigación, la	*lah een-veh-stee-gah-see·'ohn*
resource	recurso, el	*ehl reh-'koor-soh*
respect	respeto, el	*ehl reh-'speh-toh*
responsibility	responsabilidad, la	*lah reh-spohn-sah-bee-lee-'dahd*
restaurant	restaurante, el	*ehl reh-stah·oo-'rahn-teh*

restroom	servicio, el; baño, el	*ehl sehr-'vee-see·oh; ehl 'bah-nyoh*
result	resultado, el	*ehl reh-sool-'tah-doh*
retirement	jubilación, la	*lah hoo-bee-lah-see·'ohn*
reward	recompensa, la	*lah reh-kohm-'pehn-sah*
rhyme	rima, la	*lah 'ree-mah*
ribbon	cinta meritoria, la	*lah 'seen-tah meh-ree-'toh-ree·ah*
rice	arroz, el	*ehl ah-'rrohs*
rich	rico(a)	*'ree-koh(ah)*
right	derecha, la	*lah deh-'reh-chah*
ring	anillo, el	*ehl ah-'nee-yoh*
riot	disturbio, el	*ehl dee-'stoor-bee·oh*
risk	riesgo, el	*ehl ree-'ehs-goh*
river	río, el	*ehl 'ree·oh*
road	camino, el	*ehl kah-'mee-noh*
robbery	robo, el	*ehl 'roh-boh*
room	salón, el; cuarto, el	*ehl sah-'lohn; ehl 'kwahr-toh*
rope	soga, la	*lah 'soh-gah*
rough	áspero(a)	*'ah-speh-roh(ah)*
row	fila, la	*lah 'fee-lah*
rude	grosero(a)	*groh-'seh-roh(ah)*
rug	alfombra, la	*lah ahl-'fohm-brah*
rule; ruler	regla, la	*lah 'reh-glah*
rust	herrumbre, la	*lah eh-'rroom-breh*
sad	triste	*'tree-steh*
safe	seguro(a)	*seh-'goo-roh(ah)*
safety	seguridad, la	*lah seh-goo-ree-'dahd*
safety glasses	lentes de seguridad, los	*lohs 'lehn-tehs deh seh-goo-ree-'dahd*
salad	ensalada, la	*lah ehn-sah-'lah-dah*
salesperson	vendedor, el (la vendedora)	*ehl vehn-deh-'dohr (lah vehn-deh-'doh-rah)*
salt	sal, la	*lah sahl*
sample	muestra, la	*lah 'mweh-strah*
sand	arena, la	*lah ah-'reh-nah*
sandals	sandalias, las	*lahs sahn-'dah-lee·ahs*
sandbox	cajón de arena, el	*ehl kah-'hohn deh ah-'reh-nah*
satisfactory	satisfactorio(a)	*sah-tees-fahk-'toh-ree·oh(ah)*
Saturday	sábado	*'sah-bah-doh*
saw	serrucho, el	*ehl seh-'rroo-choh*
scarf	bufanda, la	*lah boo-'fahn-dah*
scene	escena, la	*lah eh-'seh-nah*
schedule	horario, el	*ehl oh-'rah-ree·oh*

scholarship	beca, la	*lah 'beh-kah*
school	escuela, la	*lah eh-'skweh-lah*
school bus	autobús escolar, el	*ehl ow-toh-'boos eh-skoh-'lahr*
science	ciencia, la	*lah see-'ehn-see·ah*
scissors	tijeras, las	*lahs tee-'heh-rahs*
score	calificación, la; cuenta, la	*lah kah-lee-fee-kah-see·'ohn; lah 'kwehn-tah*
scrape	rasguño, el	*ehl rahs-'goo-nyoh*
screen	pantalla, la	*lah pahn-'tah-yah*
screwdriver	atornillador, el	*ehl ah-tohr-nee-yah-'dohr*
sea	mar, el	*ehl mahr*
search engine	buscador, el	*ehl boos-kah-'dohr*
seat	asiento, el	*ehl ah-see-'ehn-toh*
second	segundo(a)	*seh-'goon-doh(ah)*
secret	secreto, el	*ehl seh-'kreh-toh*
secretary	secretario, el (la secretaria)	*ehl seh-kreh-'tah-ree·oh (lah seh-kreh-'tah-ree·ah)*
section	sección, la	*lah sehk-see·'ohn*
security	seguridad, la	*lah seh-goo-ree-'dahd*
security guard	guardia de seguridad, el *or* la	*ehl / lah 'gwahr-dee·ah deh seh-goo-ree-'dahd*
seesaw	subibaja, el	*ehl soo-bee-'bah-hah*
seminar	seminario, el	*ehl seh-mee-'nah-ree·oh*
September	septiembre	*sehp-tee-'ehm-breh*
serious	serio(a)	*'seh-ree·oh(a)*
server	servidor, el	*ehl sehr-vee-'dohr*
set	juego, el	*ehl 'hweh-goh*
settings	ajustes, los	*lohs ah-'hoos'-tehs*
seventh	séptimo(a)	*'sehp-tee-moh(ah)*
sewage	desagüe, el	*ehl dehs-'ah-gweh*
sex	sexo, el	*ehl 'sehk-soh*
shallow	bajo(a)	*'bah-hoh(ah)*
she	ella	*'eh-yah*
sheep	oveja, la	*lah oh-'veh-hah*
sheet	hoja, la	*lah 'oh-hah*
shelf	repisa, la	*lah reh-'pee-sah*
shelter	refugio, el; amparo, el	*ehl reh-'foo-hee·oh; ehl ahm-'pah-roh*
shirt	camisa, la	*lah kah-'mee-sah*
shock	postración, la	*lah poh-strah-see·'ohn*
shoe	zapato, el	*ehl sah-'pah-toh*
shooting	disparo, el	*ehl dee-'spah-roh*
short (in height)	bajo(a)	*'bah-hoh(ah)*
short (in length)	corto(a)	*'kohr-toh(ah)*
shorts	calzoncillos, los	*lohs kahl-sohn-'see-yohs*

shoulder	hombro, el	*ehl 'ohm-broh*
shovel	pala, la	*lah 'pah-lah*
show	espectáculo, el	*ehl eh-spehk-'tah-koo-loh*
shy	tímido(a)	*'tee-mee-doh(ah)*
sick	enfermo(a)	*ehn-'fehr-moh(ah)*
side	lado, el	*ehl 'lah-doh*
sidewalk	acera, la	*lah ah-'seh-rah*
sign	letrero, el	*ehl leh-'treh-roh*
sign language	lenguaje de sordomudos, el	*ehl lehn-'gwah-heh deh sohr-doh-'moo-dohs*
signal	señal, la	*lah seh-'nyahl*
signature	firma, la	*lah 'feer-mah*
silence	silencio, el	*ehl see-'lehn-see-oh*
silverware	cubiertos, los	*lohs koo-bee-'ehr-tohs*
sink	lavamanos, el	*ehl lah-vah-'mah-nohs*
siren	sirena, la	*lah see-'reh-nah*
sister	hermana, la	*lah ehr-'mah-nah*
site	sitio, el	*ehl 'see-tee·oh*
sixth	sexto(a)	*'sehks-toh(ah)*
skateboards	patinetas, las	*lahs pah-tee-'neh-tahs*
skates	patines, los	*lohs pah-'tee-nehs*
skill	habilidad, la	*lah ah-bee-lee-'dahd*
skin	piel, la	*lah pee-'ehl*
skirt	falda, la	*lah 'fahl-dah*
sled	trineo, el	*ehl tree-'neh-oh*
slide (microscope)	muestra en transparencia, la	*lah 'mweh-strah ehn trahns-pah-'rehn-see·ah*
slide (playground)	tobogán, el	*ehl toh-boh-'gahn*
slip	combinación, la	*lah kohm-bee-nah-see-'ohn*
slippers	zapatillas, las	*lahs sah-pah-'tee-yahs*
slowly	lentamente	*lehn-tah-'mehn-teh*
small	pequeño(a)	*peh-'keh-nyoh(ah)*
smartboard	pizarra interactiva, la	*lah pee-'sah-rrah een-teh-rahk-tee-vah*
smile	sonrisa, la	*lah sohn-'ree-sah*
smoke detector	detector de humo, el	*ehl deh-tehk-'tohr deh 'oo-moh*
smooth	liso(a)	*'lee-soh(ah)*
snack	merienda, la	*lah meh-ree-'ehn-dah*
sneeze	estornudo, el	*ehl eh-stohr-'noo-doh*
snow	nieve, la	*lah nee-'eh-veh*
soap	jabón, el	*ehl hah-'bohn*
soccer	fútbol, el	*ehl 'foot-bohl*
social security	seguro social, el	*ehl seh-'goo-roh soh-see-'ahl*

social studies	estudios sociales, los	*lohs eh-'stoo-dee·ohs soh-see·'ah-lehs*
social worker	trabajador (la trabajadora) social, el	*ehl trah-bah-hah-'dohr (lah trah-bah-hah-'doh-rah) soh-see·'ahl*
sociology	sociología, la	*lah soh-see·oh-loh-'hee·ah*
socks	calcetines, los	*lohs kahl-seh-'tee-nehs*
sofa	sofá, el	*ehl soh-'fah*
soft	blando(a); suave	*'blahn-doh(ah); 'swah-veh*
soft drink	refresco, el	*ehl reh-'freh-skoh*
softball	sófbol, el	*ehl 'sohf-bohl*
software	programa, el	*ehl proh-'grah-mah*
solar system	sistema solar, el	*ehl see-'steh-mah soh-'lahr*
soldier	soldado, el *or* la	*ehl / lah sohl-'dah-doh*
solution	solución, la	*lah soh-loo-see·'ohn*
some	unos(as)	*'oo-nohs(ahs)*
sometimes	a veces	*ah-'veh-sehs*
son	hijo, el	*ehl 'ee-hoh*
song	canción, la	*lah kahn-see·'ohn*
soon	pronto	*'prohn-toh*
sound	sonido, el	*ehl soh-'nee-doh*
soup	sopa, la	*lah 'soh-pah*
sour	agrio(a)	*'ah-gree·oh(ah)*
south	sur	*soor*
space	espacio, el	*ehl eh-'spah-see·oh*
spaceship	nave espacial, la	*lah 'nah-veh eh-spah-see·'ahl*
speaker (person)	orador, el (la oradora)	*ehl oh-rah-'dohr (lah oh-rah-'doh-rah)*
speaker (stereo)	altoparlante, el	*ehl 'ahl-toh-pahr-'lahn-teh*
special education	educación especial, la	*lah eh-doo-kah-see·'ohn eh-speh-see·'ahl*
specialist	especialista, el *or* la	*ehl / lah eh-speh-see·ah-'lee-stah*
speech	discurso, el	*ehl dee-'skoor-soh*
speech pathologist	patologo del habla	*pah-'toh-loh-goh dehl 'ah-blah*
speed	velocidad, la	*lah veh-loh-see-'dahd*
sphere	esfera, la	*lah eh-'sfeh-rah*
spinach	espinaca, la	*lah eh-spee-'nah-kah*
spirit	espíritu, el	*ehl eh-'spee-ree-too*
sponge	esponja, la	*lah eh-'spohn-hah*
sponsor	patrocinador, el (la patrocinadora)	*ehl pah-troh-see-nah-'dohr (lah pah-troh-see-nah-'doh-rah)*
spoon	cuchara, la	*lah koo-'chah-rah*

sport	deporte, el	*ehl deh-'pohr-teh*
sportcoat	saco, el	*ehl 'sah-koh*
sprain	torcedura, la	*lah tohr-seh-'doo-rah*
spring	primavera, la	*lah pree-mah-'veh-rah*
sprinkler	rociadora, la	*lah roh-see·ah-'doh-rah*
square	cuadrado, el	*ehl kwah-'drah-doh*
stadium	estadio, el	*ehl eh-'stah-dee·oh*
staff	funcionarios, los	*lohs foon-see·oh-'nah-ree·ohs*
stairs	escalera, la	*lah eh-skah-'leh-rah*
stand	soporte, el	*ehl soh-'pohr-teh*
stapler	engrapadora, la	*lah ehn-grah-pah-'doh-rah*
star	estrella, la	*lah eh-'streh-yah*
state	estado, el	*ehl eh-'stah-doh·oh*
stationery	objetos de escritorio, los	*lohs ohb-'heh-tohs deh eh-skree-'toh-ree·oh*
statue	estatua, la	*lah eh-'stah-too-ah*
steak	bistec, el	*ehl bee-'stehk*
step	paso, el	*ehl 'pah·soh*
stepfather	padrastro, el	*ehl pah-'drah-stroh*
stepmother	madrastra, la	*lah mah-'drah-strah*
steps	escalones, los	*lohs eh-skah-'loh-nehs*
stick	palo, el	*ehl 'pah-loh*
sticker	etiqueta, la	*lah eh-tee-'keh-tah*
stockings	medias, las	*lahs 'meh-dee·ahs*
stomach	estómago, el	*ehl eh-'stoh-mah-goh*
stomachache	dolor de estómago, el	*ehl doh-'lohr deh eh-'stoh-mah-goh*
stone	piedra, la	*lah pee-'eh-drah*
stool	banquillo, el	*ehl bahn-'kee-yoh*
stop sign	señal de parada, la	*lah seh-'nyahl deh pah-'rah-dah*
storage	depósito, el	*ehl deh-'poh-see-toh*
store	tienda, la	*lah tee-'ehn-dah*
storm	tormenta, la	*lah tohr-'mehn-tah*
story	cuento, el	*ehl 'kwehn-toh*
storybook	libro de cuentos, el	*ehl 'lee-broh deh 'kwehn-tohs*
stove	estufa, la	*lah eh-'stoo-fah*
strange	raro(a)	*'rah-roh(ah)*
stranger	desconocido, el (la desconocida)	*ehl dehs-koh-noh-'see-doh (lah dehs-koh-noh-'see-dah)*
strategy	estrategia, la	*lah eh-strah-'teh-hee·ah*
strawberry	fresa, la	*lah 'freh-sah*
stream	arroyo, el	*ehl ah-'rroh-yoh*
street	calle, la	*lah 'kah-yeh*
strike	huelga, la	*lah 'wehl-gah*

string	hilo, el	*ehl 'ee-loh*
stroller	carrito de bebé, el	*ehl kah-'rree-toh deh beh-'beh*
strong	fuerte	*'fwehr-teh*
student	alumno, el (la alumna); el *or* la estudiante	*ehl ah-'loom-noh (lah ah-'loom-nah); ehl / lah eh-stoo-dee-'ahn-teh*
study	estudio, el	*ehl eh-'stoo-dee·oh*
stuffed animal	animal de peluche, el	*ehl ah-nee-'mahl deh peh-'loo-cheh*
subject	tema, el	*ehl 'teh-mah*
subway	metro, el	*ehl 'meh-troh*
suggestion	sugerencia, la	*lah soo-heh-'rehn-see·ah*
suit	traje, el	*ehl 'trah-heh*
sum	suma, la	*lah 'soo-mah*
summary	resumen, el	*ehl reh-'soo-mehn*
summer	verano, el	*ehl veh-'rah-noh*
sun	sol, el	*ehl sohl*
Sunday	domingo	*doh-'meen-goh*
sunglasses	lentes de sol, los	*lohs 'lehn-tehs deh sohl*
sunny	soleado(a)	*soh-leh-'ah-doh(ah)*
sunstroke	insolación, la	*lah een-soh-lah-see-'ohn*
suntan lotion	bronceador, el	*ehl broh-seh-ah-'dohr*
superintendent	superintendente, el *or* la	*ehl / lah soo-pehr-een-tehn-'dehn-teh*
supermarket	supermercado, el	*ehl soo-pehr-mehr-'kah-doh*
supervision	supervisión, la	*lah soo-pehr-vee-see-'ohn*
supervisor	supervisor, el (la supervisora)	*ehl soo-pehr-vee-'sohr (lah soo-pehr-vee-'soh-rah)*
supplies	materiales, los; provisiones, las	*lohs mah-teh-ree-'ah-lehs; lahs proh-vee-see-'oh-nehs*
support	apoyo, el	*ehl ah-'poh-yoh*
sure	seguro(a)	*seh-'goo-roh(ah)*
surname	apellido, el	*ehl ah-peh-'yee-doh*
surprised	sorprendido(a)	*sohr-prehn-'dee-doh(ah)*
suspect	sospechoso, el (la sospechosa)	*ehl soh-speh-'choh-soh (lah soh-speh-'choh-sah)*
suspension	suspensión, la	*lah soo-spehn-see-'ohn*
sweater	suéter, el	*ehl 'sweh-tehr*
sweatsuit	sudadera, la	*lah soo-dah-'deh-rah*
sweet	dulce	*'dool-seh*
sweetheart	querido(a)	*keh-'ree-doh(ah)*
swing	columpio, el	*ehl koh-'loom-pee·oh*
switch	interruptor, el	*ehl een-teh-rroop-'tohr*
T-shirt	camiseta, la	*lah kah-mee-'seh-tah*
table	mesa, la	*lah 'meh-sah*

tablet	tableta	*tah-'bleh-tah*
talcum powder	talco, el	*ehl 'tahl-koh*
tall	alto(a)	*'ahl-toh(ah)*
tape	cinta, la	*lah 'seen-tah*
tardiness	tardanza, la	*lah tahr-'dahn-sah*
tantrums	tener rabietas	*teh-'nehr rah-bee-'eh-tahs*
tattoo	tatuaje, el	*ehl tah-too-'ah-heh*
tea	té, el	*ehl teh*
teacher	maestro, el (la maestra); profesor, el (la profesora)	*ehl mah-'eh-stroh (lah mah-'eh-strah); ehl proh-feh-'sohr (lah proh-feh-'soh-rah)*
teacher's aide	ayudante (la ayudanta) de maestro, el	*ehl ah-yoo-'dahn-teh (lah ah-yoo-'dahn-tah) deh mah-'eh-stroh*
team	equipo, el	*ehl eh-'kee-poh*
technician	técnico, el *or* la	*ehl/lah'tehk-nee-koh*
technique	técnica, la	*lah 'tehk-nee-kah*
teenager	muchacho, el (la muchacha)	*ehl moo-'chah-choh (lah moo-'chah-chah)*
teeth	· dientes, los	*lohs dee-'ehn-tehs*
telephone	teléfono, el	*ehl teh-'leh-foh-noh*
telescope	telescopio, el	*ehl teh-leh-'skoh-pee·oh*
television	televisor, el	*ehl teh-leh-vee-'sohr*
tennis	tenis, el	*ehl 'teh-nees*
tennis shoes	tenis, los	*lohs 'teh-nees*
tenth	décimo(a)	*'deh-see-moh(ah)*
term	período, el	*ehl peh-'ree·oh-doh*
test	prueba, la; examen, el	*lah proo-'eh-bah; ehl ehk-'sah-mehn*
test tube	tubo de ensayo, el	*ehl 'too-boh deh ehn-'sah-yoh*
textbook	libro de texto, el	*ehl 'lee-broh deh 'tehks-toh*
thanks	gracias	*'grah-see·ahs*
that	ese(a)(o)	*'eh-seh(ah)(oh)*
theater	teatro, el	*ehl teh-'ah-troh*
their	su(s)	*soo(s)*
theme	tema, el	*ehl 'teh-mah*
then	entonces	*ehn-'tohn-sehs*
theory	teoría, la	*lah teh-oh-'ree·ah*
therapist	terapeuta, el *or* la	*ehl/lah teh-rah-peh-'oo-tah*
therapy	terapia, la	*lah teh-'rah-pee·ah*
there	allá; allí	*ah-'yah; ah-'yee*
thermometer	termómetro, el	*ehl tehr-'moh-meh-troh*
thermostat	termostato, el	*ehl tehr-moh-'stah-toh*
these	estos(as)	*'eh-stohs(as)*

they	ellos(as)	'eh-yohs(as)
thick	grueso(a)	groo-'eh-soh(ah)
thief	ladrón, el (la ladrona)	ehl lah-'drohn (lah lah-'droh-nah)
thin	delgado(a)	dehl-'gah-doh(ah)
third	tercero(a)	tehr-'seh-roh(ah)
this	este(a)	'eh-steh(ah)
those	esos(as)	'eh-sohs(ahs)
thought	pensamiento, el	ehl pehn-sah-mee-'ehn-toh
threat	cumpoter amenaza, la	lah ah-meh-'nah-sah
throat	garganta, la	lah gahr-'gahn-tah
thumbtack	tachuela, la	lah tah-choo-'eh-lah
thumb-sucking	chuparse el dedo	choo-'pahr-seh ehl 'deh-doh
Thursday	jueves	'hweh-vehs
ticket	boleto, el	ehl boh-'leh-toh
tie	corbata, la	lah kohr-'bah-tah
time	hora, la	lah 'oh-rah
tired	cansado(a)	kahn-'sah-doh(ah)
title	título, el	ehl 'tee-too-loh
to	a	ah
today	hoy	'oh·ee
toe	dedo, el	ehl 'deh-doh
toilet	excusado, el	ehl ehk-skoo-'sah-doh
toilet paper	papel higiénico, el	ehl pah-'pehl ee-hee-'eh-nee-koh
tomato	tomate, el	ehl toh-'mah-teh
tomato sauce	salsa de tomate, la	lah 'sahl-sah deh toh-'mah-teh
tomorrow	mañana	mah-'nyah-nah
tongue	lengua, la	lah 'lehn-gwah
tonight	esta noche	'eh-stah 'noh-cheh
tool	herramienta, la	lah eh-rrah-mee-'ehn-tah
toolbar	barra de herramientas, la	lah 'bah-rrah deh eh-rrah-mee-'ehn-tahs
top	trompo, el	ehl 'trohm-poh
topic	asunto, el	ehl ah-'soon-toh
tornado	tornado, el	ehl tohr-'nah-doh
tournament	torneo, el	ehl tohr-'neh-oh
tow truck	grúa, la	lah 'groo-ah
towel	toalla, la	lah toh-'ah-yah
tower	torre, la	lah 'toh-rreh
toy	juguete, el	ehl hoo-'geh-the
toy dishes	los platos de juguete	lohs 'plah-tohs deh hoo-'geh-teh
track and field	atletismo, el	ehl aht-leh-'tees-moh

tractor	tractor, el	*ehl trahk-'tohr*
trade union	sindicato, el	*ehl seen-dee-'kah-toh*
traffic signal	semáforo, el	*ehl seh-'mah-foh-roh*
tragedy	tragedia, la	*lah trah-'heh-dee·ah*
train	tren, el	*ehl trehn*
trainer	entrenador, el (la entrenadora)	*ehl ehn-treh-nah-'dohr (lah ehn-treh-nah-'doh-rah)*
training	entrenamiento, el	*ehl ehn-treh-nah-mee-'ehn-toh*
transcript	transcripción, la	*lah trahn-skreep-see-'ohn*
transfer	transferencia, la	*lah trahns-feh-'rehn-see·ah*
translator	traductor, el (la traductora)	*ehl trah-dook-'tohr (lah trah-dook-'toh-rah)*
transparency	diapositiva, la	*lah dee·ah-poh-see-'tee-vah*
transportation	transporte, el	*ehl trahns-'pohr-teh*
trash can	bote para basura, el	*ehl 'boh-teh 'pah-rah bah-'soo-rah*
tray	bandeja, la	*lah bahn-'deh-hah*
treadmill	caminadora, la	*lah cah-mee-nah-'dohr-ah*
tree	árbol, el	*ehl 'ahr-bohl*
trespasser	intruso, el (la intrusa)	*ehl een-'troo-soh (lah een-'troo-sah)*
trespassing	intrusión, la	*lah een-'troo-see-'ohn*
trick	truco, el	*ehl 'troo-koh*
tricycle	triciclo, el	*ehl tree-'see-kloh*
trigonometry	trigonometría, la	*lah tree-goh-noh-meh-'tree·ah*
trip	viaje, el	*ehl vee-'ah-heh*
trophy	trofeo, el	*ehl troh-'feh-oh*
truck	camión, el	*ehl kah-mee-'ohn*
trust	confianza, la	*lah kohn-fee-'ahn-sah*
tub	tina, la	*lah 'tee-nah*
tube	tubo, el	*ehl 'too-boh*
Tuesday	martes	*'mahr-tehs*
tuna	atún, el	*ehl ah-'toon*
tune	tono, el	*ehl 'toh-noh*
tunnel	túnel, el	*ehl 'too-nehl*
turkey	pavo, el (la pava)	*ehl 'pah-voh (lah 'pah-vah)*
turtle	tortuga, la	*lah tohr-'too-gah*
tutor	tutor, el (la tutora)	*ehl too-'tohr (lah too-'toh-rah)*
typing	escribir a máquina, el	*ehl eh-skree-'beer ah 'mah-kee-nah*
U.S. history	historia de los Estados Unidos, la	*lah ee-'stoh-ree·ah deh lohs eh-'stah-dohs oo-'nee-dohs*
ugly	feo(a)	*'feh-oh(ah)*
umbrella	paraguas, el	*ehl pah-'rah-gwahs*

uncle	tío, el	*ehl 'tee·oh*
underground	subterráneo(a)	*soob-teh-'rrah-neh-oh(ah)*
underwear	ropa interior, la	*lah 'roh-pah een-teh-ree-'ohr*
unemployment	desempleo, el	*ehl dehs-ehm-'pleh-oh*
uniform	uniforme, el	*ehl oo-nee-'fohr-meh*
unit	unidad, la	*lah oo-nee-'dahd*
universe	universo, el	*ehl oo-nee-'vehr-soh*
university	universidad, la	*lah oo-nee-vehr-see-'dahd*
up	arriba	*ah-'rree-bah*
upset	enojado(a)	*eh-noh-'hah-doh(ah)*
urgent	urgente	*oor-'hehn-teh*
urinal	orinal, el	*ehl oh-ree-'nahl*
usually	usualmente	*oo-soo-ahl-'mehn-teh*
vacations	vacaciones, las	*lahs vah-kah-see-'oh-nehs*
vaccination	vacunación, la	*lah vah-koo-nah-see-'ohn*
valley	valle, el	*ehl 'vah-yeh*
value	valor, el	*ehl vah-'lohr*
vase	florero, el	*ehl floh-'reh-roh*
vegetables	vegetales, los	*lohs veh-heh-'tah-lehs*
vest	chaleco, el	*ehl chah-'leh-koh*
vice-principal	subdirector, el (la subdirectora)	*ehl soob-dee-rehk-'tohr (lah soob-dee-rehk-'toh-rah)*
victim	víctima, la	*lah 'veek-tee-mah*
video	vídeo, el	*ehl 'vee-deh-oh*
videogame	videojuego, el	*ehl vee-deh-oh-hoo-'eh-goh*
violation	violación, la	*lah vee·oh-lah-see-'ohn*
violence	violencia, la	*lah vee·oh-'lehn-see·ah*
visitor	visitante, el or la	*ehl / lah vee-see-'tahn-teh*
vitamins	vitaminas, las	*lahs vee-tah-'mee-nahs*
vocabulary	vocabulario, el	*ehl voh-kah-boo-'lah-ree·oh*
voice	voz, la	*lah vohs*
volleyball	vóleibol, el	*ehl 'voh-leh·ee-bohl*
volume	volumen, el	*ehl voh-'loo-mehn*
volunteer	voluntario, el (la voluntaria)	*ehl voh-loon-'tah-ree·oh (lah voh-loon-'tah-ree·ah)*
wages	sueldo, el	*ehl 'swehl-doh*
wagon	vagón, el	*ehl vah-'gohn*
wall	pared, la	*lah pah-'rehd*
war	guerra, la	*lah 'geh-rrah*
warehouse	almacén, el	*ehl ahl-mah-'sehn*
warm	tibio(a)	*'tee-bee·oh(ah)*
warm (weather)	templado	*tehm-'plah-doh*
warning	advertencia, la	*lah ahd-vehr-'tehn-see·ah*
washer	lavadora, la	*lah lah-vah-'doh-rah*

waste	desperdicios, los	*lohs dehs-pehr-'dee-see·ohs*
wastebasket	cesto de basura, el	*ehl 'seh-stoh deh bah-'soo-rah*
watch	reloj, el	*ehl reh-'loh*
water	agua, el	*ehl 'ah-gwah*
water fountain	bebedero, el	*ehl beh-beh-'deh-roh*
water polo	polo acuático, el	*ehl 'poh-loh ah-'kwah-tee-koh*
we	nosotros(as)	*noh-'soh-trohs(as)*
weak	débil	*'deh-beel*
wealth	riqueza, la	*lah ree-'keh-sah*
weather	tiempo, el	*ehl tee-'ehm-poh*
website	sitio web, el	*ehl 'see-tee·oh web*
Wednesday	miércoles	*mee-'ehr-koh-lehs*
week	semana, la	*lah seh-'mah-nah*
weight	peso, el	*ehl 'peh-soh*
weights	pesas, las	*lahs 'peh-sahs*
welcome	bienvenidos(as)	*bee·ehn-veh-'nee-dohs(ahs)*
welfare	bienestar social, el	*ehl bee·ehn-eh-'stahr soh-see-'ahl*
west	oeste	*oh-'eh-steh*
wet	mojado(a)	*moh-'hah-doh(ah)*
wetting	orinarse	*oh-ree-'nahr-seh*
what	qué	*keh*
wheelbarrow	carretilla, la	*lah kah-rreh-'tee-yah*
wheelchair	silla de ruedas, la	*lah 'see-yah deh 'rweh-dahs*
when	cuándo	*'kwahn-doh*
where	dónde	*'dohn-deh*
which	cuál	*kwahl*
whistle	silbato, el	*ehl seel-'bah-toh*
white	blanco(a)	*'blahn-koh(ah)*
whiteboard	pizarron, el	*ehl pee-sah-'rrohn*
who	quién	*kee-'ehn*
whose	de quién	*deh kee-'ehn*
why	por qué	*pohr keh*
wide	ancho(a)	*'ahn-choh(ah)*
wife	esposa, la	*lah eh-'spoh-sah*
wind	viento, el	*ehl vee-'ehn-toh*
window	ventana, la	*lah vehn-'tah-nah*
winter	invierno, el	*ehl een-vee-'ehr-noh*
wire	alambre, el	*ehl ah-'lahm-breh*
with	con	*kohn*
without	sin	*seen*
witness	testigo, el *or* la	*ehl / lah teh-'stee-goh*
woman	mujer, la	*lah moo-'hehr*
wood	madera, la	*lah mah-'deh-rah*

word	palabra, la	*lah pah-'lah-brah*
work	trabajo, el	*ehl trah-'bah-hoh*
workshop	taller, el	*ehl tah-'yehr*
world	mundo, el	*ehl 'moon-doh*
worried	preocupado(a)	*preh-oh-koo-'pah-doh(ah)*
worse	peor	*peh-'ohr*
wrench	llave inglesa, la	*lah 'yah-veh een-'gleh-sah*
wrestling	lucha libre, la	*lah 'loo-chah 'lee-breh*
wrist	muñeca, la	*lah moo-'neyh-kah*
writing	escritura, la	*lah eh-skree-'too-rah*
wrong	equivocado(a)	*eh-kee-voh-'kah-doh(ah)*
year	año, el	*ehl 'ah-nyoh*
yearbook	anuario, el	*ehl ah-noo-'ah-ree·oh*
yellow	amarillo(a)	*ah-mah-'ree-yoh(ah)*
yes	sí	*see*
yesterday	ayer	*ah-'yehr*
yet	todavía	*toh-dah-'vee·ah*
you (singular, informal)	tú	*too*
you (plural, formal and informal)	ustedes	*oo-'steh-dehs*
you (singular, formal)	usted	*oo-'stehd*
young	joven	*'hoh-vehn*
younger	menor	*meh-'nohr*
your	su(s)	*soo(s)*
zip code	zona postal, la	*lah 'soh-nah poh-'stahl*
zipper	cierre, el	*ehl see-'eh-rreh*
zone	zona, la	*lah 'soh-nah*
zoo	zoológico, el	*ehl soh-oh-'loh-hee-koh*

SPANISH-ENGLISH DICTIONARY

➤ The gender of Spanish nouns is indicated by the article (el or la).

➤ When a noun can be either masculine or feminine, it is shown in the masculine form and then in the feminine form: adulto, el (la adulta).

➤ All adjectives are shown in the masculine form. An (a) is added to remind you of the feminine ending.

a	to	*ah*
a veces	sometimes	*ah-'veh-sehs*
abajo	down	*ah-'bah-hoh*
abogado, el (la abogada)	lawyer	*ehl ah-boh-'gah-doh (lah ah-boh-'gah-dah)*
aborto, el	abortion	*ehl ah-'bohr-toh*
abrigo, el	overcoat	*ehl ah-'bree-goh*
abril	April	*ah-'breel*
abuela, la	grandmother	*lah ah-'bweh-lah*
abuelo, el	grandfather	*ehl ah-'bweh-loh*
aburrido(a)	bored	*ah-boo-rree-doh(ah)*
abuso, el	abuse	*ehl ah-'boo-soh*
academia, la	academy	*lah ah-kah-'deh-mee·ah*
accidente, el	accident	*ehl ahk-see-'dehn-teh*
acción, la	action	*lah ahk-see·'ohn*
acera, la	sidewalk	*lah ah-'seh-rah*
acné, el	acne	*ehl ahk-'neh*
acondicionador de aire, el	air conditioner	*ehl ah-kohn-dee-see·oh-nah-'dohr deh 'ah·ee-reh*
acoso, el	harassment	*ehl ah-koh-soh*
actitud, la	attitude	*lah ahk-tee-'tood*
actividad, la	activity	*lah ahk-tee-vee-'dahd*
acuario, el	aquarium	*ehl ah-'kwah-ree·oh*
adelante	ahead	*ah-deh-'lahn-teh*
adentro	inside	*ah-'dehn-troh*
ADHD	ADHD	*ah deh hache deh*
adicción, la	addiction	*lah ah-deek-see·'ohn*
adiós	good-bye	*ah-dee-'ohs*
adjunto, el	attachment	*ehl ahd-'hoon-toh*
administración, la	administration	*lah ahd-mee-nee-strah-see·'ohn*
administrador, el (la administradora)	administrator	*ehl ahd-mee-nee-strah-'dohr (lah ahd-mee-nee-strah-'doh-rah)*
admisiones, las	admissions	*lahs ahd-mee-see·'oh-nehs*

adulto, el (la adulta)	adult	*ehl ah-'dool-toh (lah ah-'dool-tah)*
advertencia, la	warning	*lah ahd-vehr-'tehn-see·ah*
aeropuerto, el	airport	*ehl ah-eh-roh-'pwehr-toh*
afroamericano(a), el *or* la	African-American	*ehl / lah ah-froh-ah-meh-ree-'kah-noh(ah)*
afuera	outside	*ah-'fweh-rah*
afueras, las	outdoors	*lahs ah-'fweh-rahs*
agencia, la	agency	*lah ah-'hehn-see·ah*
agente de polica, el *or* la	police officer	*ehl / lah ah-'hehn-teh deh poh-lee 'see·ah*
agosto	August	*ah-'goh-stoh*
agrio(a)	sour	*'ah-gree·oh(ah)*
agua, el	water	*ehl 'ah-gwah*
ahora	now	*ah-'oh-rah*
ajedrez, el	chess	*ehl ah-heh-'drehs*
ajustes, los	settings	*lohs ah-'hoos'-tehs*
al lado de	next to	*ahl 'lah-doh deh*
alambre, el	wire	*ehl ah-'lahm-breh*
alarma, la	alarm	*lah ah-'lahr-mah*
alcohol, el	alcohol	*ehl ahl-koh-'ohl*
alergias, las	allergies	*lahs ah-'lehr-hee·ahs*
alfabeto, el	alphabet	*ehl ahl-fah-'beh-toh*
alfiler, el	pin	*ehl ahl-fee-'lehr*
alfombra, la	rug	*lah ahl-'fohm-brah*
álgebra, el	algebra	*ehl 'ahl-heh-'brah*
algodón, el	cotton	*ehl ahl-goh-'dohn*
alicate, el	pliers	*ehl ah-lee-'kah-teh*
aliento, el	breath	*ehl ah-lee-'ehn-toh*
allá; allí	there	*ah-'yah; ah-'yee*
almacén, el	warehouse	*ehl ahl-mah-'sehn*
almuerzo, el	lunch	*ehl ahl-moo-'ehr-soh*
altavoz, el	bullhorn	*ehl ahl-tah-'vohs*
alternativa, la	alternative	*lah ahl-tehr-nah-'tee-vah*
alto(a)	tall	*'ahl-toh(ah)*
altoparlante, el	speaker (stereo); loudspeaker	*ehl ahl-toh-pahr-'lahn-teh*
alumno, el (la alumna); el *or* la estudiante	student	*ehl ah-'loom-noh (lah ah-'loom-nah); ehl / lah eh-stoo-dee-'ahn-teh*
amable	kind	*ah-'mah-bleh*
amarillo(a)	yellow	*ah-mah-'ree-yoh(ah)*
ambiente, el	environment	*ehl ahm-bee-'ehn-teh*
ambulancia, la	ambulance	*lah ahm-boo-'lahn-see·ah*

amenaza, la	threat	*lah ah-meh-'nah-sah*
amigo, el (la amiga)	friend	*ehl ah-'mee-goh (lah ah-'mee-gah)*
amistad	friendship	*ah-mee-'stahd*
amistoso(a)	friendly	*ah-mee-'stoh-soh(ah)*
amor, el	love	*ehl ah-'mohr*
amparo, el	shelter	*ehl ahm-'pah-roh*
ampolla, la	blister	*lah ahm-'poh-yah*
anaranjado(a)	orange (color)	*ah-nah-rahn-'hah-doh(ah)*
ancho(a)	wide	*'ahn-choh(ah)*
anfiteatro, el	arena	*ehl ah-fee-teh-'ah-troh*
anillo, el	ring	*ehl ah-'nee-yoh*
animal de peluche, el	stuffed animal	*ehl ah-nee-'mahl deh peh-'loo-cheh*
animal, el	animal	*ehl ah-nee-'mahl*
ánimo, el	encouragement	*ehl 'ah-nee-moh*
año, el	year	*ehl 'ah-nyoh*
antes	before	*'ahn-tehs*
anuario, el	yearbook	*ehl ah-noo-'ah-ree·oh*
anuncio, el	announcement; bulletin; notice	*ehl ah-'noon-see·oh*
apartamento, el	apartment	*ehl ah-pahr-tah-'mehn-toh*
apellido, el	surname	*ehl ah-peh-'yee-doh*
apenas	just	*ah-'peh-nahs*
aplicación, la	application (computer)	*lah ah-plee-kah-see-'ohn*
apoyo, el	support	*ehl ah-'poh-yoh*
aquí; acá	here	*ah-'kee; ah-'kah*
árbol, el	tree	*ehl 'ahr-bohl*
arboleda, la	grove	*lah ahr-boh-'leh-dah*
archivo, el	archive	*ehl ahr-'chee-voh*
área, el	area	*ehl 'ah-reh-ah*
arena, la	sand	*lah ah-'reh-nah*
arete, el	earring	*ehl ah-'reh-teh*
argumento, el	argument	*ehl ahr-goo-'mehn-toh*
arma de fuego, el	firearm	*ehl 'ahr-mah deh 'fweh-goh*
armario, el	cupboard; locker	*ehl ahr-'mah-ree·oh*
arquitecto, el *or* la	architect	*ehl ahr-kee-'tehk-toh*
arriba	up	*ah-'rree-bah*
arroyo, el	stream	*ehl ah-'rroh-yoh*
arroz, el	rice	*ehl ah-'rrohs*
arte, el	art	*ehl 'ahr-teh*
artes industriales, las	industrial arts	*lahs 'ahr-tehs een-doos-tree-'ah-lehs*
artículo, el	article	*ehl ahr-'tee-koo-loh*
asamblea, la	assembly	*lah ah-sahm-'bleh-ah*

ascensor, el	elevator	*ehl ah-sehn-'sohr*
asiento, el	seat	*ehl ah-see-'ehn-toh*
asistencia, la	attendance	*lah ah-see-'stehn-see·ah*
asistente, el (la asistenta)	assistant	*ehl ah-see-'stehn-teh (lah ah-see-'stehn-tah)*
asociado, el (la asociada)	associate	*ehl ah-soh-see-'ah-doh (lah ah-soh-see-'ah-dah)*
áspero(a)	rough	*'ah-speh-roh(ah)*
aspirina, la	aspirin	*lah ah-spee-'ree-nah*
astronomía, la	astronomy	*lah ah-stroh-noh-'mee·ah*
asunto, el	topic	*ehl ah-'soon-toh*
asustado(a)	afraid	*ah-soo-'stah-doh(ah)*
atlas, el	atlas	*ehl 'aht-lahs*
atletismo, el	track and field	*ehl aht-leh-'tees-moh*
atornillador, el	screwdriver	*ehl ah-tohr-nee-yah-'dohr*
atún, el	tuna	*ehl ah-'toon*
audiencia, la	audience	*lah ow-dee-'ehn-see·ah*
audífonos, los	headphones; hearing aids	*lohs ow-'dee-foh-nohs*
auditorio, el	auditorium	*ehl ow-dee-'toh-ree·oh*
ausencia, la	absence	*lah ow-'sehn-see·ah*
autismo	autism	*ow-'tees-moh*
autobús, el	bus	*ehl ow-toh-'boos*
autobús escolar, el	school bus	*ehl ow-toh-'boos eh-skoh-'lahr*
autor, el (la autora)	author	*ehl ow-'tohr, lah ow-'toh-rah*
avanzado(a)	advanced	*ah-vahn-'sah-doh(ah)*
avenida, la	avenue	*lah ah-veh-'nee-dah*
avión, el	airplane	*ehl ah-vee-'ohn*
aviso, el	notice	*ehl ah 'vee-soh*
ayer	yesterday	*ah-'yehr*
ayuda, la	assistance; help	*lah ah-'yoo-dah*
ayudante, el (la ayudanta)	aide; helper	*ehl ah-yoo-'dahn-teh (lah ah-yoo-'dahn-tah)*
ayudante (la ayudanta) de maestro, el	teacher's aide	*ehl ah-yoo-'dahn-teh (lah ah-yoo-'dahn-tah) deh mah-'eh-stroh*
azadón, el	hoe	*ehl ah-sah-'dohn*
azul	blue	*ah-'sool*
babero, el	bib	*ehl bah-'beh-roh*
bacinete, el	bassinet	*ehl bah-see-'neh-teh*
bádminton, el	badminton	*ehl 'bahd-meen-tohn*
baile, el	dance	*ehl 'bah-ee-leh*
bajo(a)	short (in height); shallow	*'bah-hoh(ah)*
balcón, el	balcony	*ehl bahl-'kohn*
balde, el	bucket	*ehl 'bahl-deh*

bancas, las	benches	lahs 'bahn-kahs
banco, el	bank	ehl 'bahn-koh
banda, la	band	lah 'bahn-da
bandeja, la	tray	lah bahn-'deh-hah
bandera, la	flag	lah bahn-'deh-rah
baño, el	restroom; bathroom	ehl 'bah-nyoh
banquete, el	banquet	ehl bahn-'keh-teh
banquillo, el	stool	ehl bahn-'kee-yoh
baraja de juguete, la	playing cards	lah bah-'rah-hah deh hoo-'geh-teh
barato(a)	cheap	bah-'rah-toh(ah)
barbilla, la	chin	lah bahr-'bee-yah
barco, el	boat	ehl 'bahr·koh
barra de herramientas, la	toolbar	lah 'bah-rrah deh eh-rrah-mee·'ehn-tahs
barrio, el	neighborhood	ehl 'bah-rree·oh
básquetbol, el	basketball	ehl 'bah-skeht-bohl
bata de bano, la	bathrobe	lah 'bah-tah deh 'bahn-yoh
batalla, la	battle	lah bah-'tah-yah
bate, el	bat	ehl 'bah-teh
baúl, el	chest (trunk)	ehl bah-'ool
bebé, el or la	baby	ehl / lah beh-'beh
bebedero, el	water fountain	ehl beh-beh-'deh-roh
beca, la	scholarship	lah 'beh-kah
béisbol, el	baseball	ehl 'beh·ees-bohl
bello(a)	beautiful	'beh-yoh(ah)
beneficios, los	benefits	lohs beh-neh-'fee-see·ohs
biberón, el	nursing bottle	ehl bee-beh-'rohn
biblioteca, la	library	lah bee-blee·oh-'teh-kah
bibliotecario, el (la bibliotecaria)	librarian	ehl bee-blee·oh-teh-'kah-ree·oh (lah beeb-lee·oh-teh-'kah-ree·ah)
bicicleta, la	bicycle	lah bee-see-'kleh-tah
bien	fine	'bee·ehn
bienestar social, el	welfare	ehl bee·ehn-eh-'stahr soh-see-'ahl
bienvenidos(as)	welcome	bee·ehn-veh-'nee-dohs(ahs)
bilingüe	bilingual	bee-'leen-gweh
biografía, la	biography	lah bee·oh-grah-'fee·ah
biología, la	biology	lah bee·oh-loh-'hee·ah
bistec, el	steak	ehl bee-'stehk
blanco(a)	white	'blahn-koh (ah)
blando(a); suave	soft	'blahn-doh(ah); 'swah-veh
blusa, la	blouse	lah 'bloo-sa

boca, la	mouth	*lah 'boh-kah*
bocina, la	horn	*lah boh-'see-nah*
boleto, el	ticket	*ehl boh-'leh-toh*
bolsa, la	bag	*lah 'bohl-sah*
bomba, la	bomb	*lah 'bohm-bah*
bombero, el (la bombera)	firefighter	*ehl bohm-'beh-roh (lah bohm-'beh-rah)*
bondad, la	kindness	*lah bohn-'dahd*
bonito(a)	pretty	*boh-'nee-toh(ah)*
borracho, el (la borracha)	drunkard	*ehl boh-'rrah-choh (lah boh-'rrah-chah)*
borrador, el	eraser	*ehl boh-rrah-'dohr*
bosque, el	forest	*ehl 'boh-skeh*
bota, la	boot	*lah 'boh-tah*
bote para basura, el	trash can	*ehl 'boh-teh 'pah-rah bah-'soo-rah*
boxeo, el	boxing	*ehl bohk-'seh-oh*
bragas, las	panties	*lahs 'brah-gahs*
brazalete, el	bracelet	*ehl brah-sah-'leh-teh*
brazo, el	arm	*ehl 'brah-soh*
brocha, la	brush; paintbrush	*lah 'broh-chah*
bronceador, el	suntan lotion	*ehl broh-seh-ah-'dohr*
bueno(a)	good	*'bweh-noh(ah)*
bufanda, la	scarf	*lah boo-'fahn-dah*
buscador, el	search engine	*ehl boos-kah-'dohr*
buzón, el	mailbox	*ehl boo-'sohn*
caballete, el	easel	*ehl kah-bah-'yeh-teh*
caballitos, los	merry-go-round	*lohs kah-bah-'yee-tohs*
caballo, el	horse	*ehl kah-'bah-yoh*
cabeza, la	head	*lah kah-'beh-sah*
cable, el	cable	*ehl 'kah-bleh*
cadena, la	chain	*lah kah-'deh-nah*
cadera, la	hip	*lah kah-'deh-rah*
café	brown	*kah-'feh*
café, el	coffee	*ehl kah-'feh*
cafetería, la	cafeteria	*lah kah-feh-teh-'ree·ah*
caja, la	box	*lah 'kah-hah*
cajero, el (la cajera)	cashier	*ehl kah-'heh-roh (lah kah-'heh-rah)*
cajón de arena, el	sandbox	*ehl kah-'hohn deh ah-'reh-nah*
cajón, el	drawer	*ehl kah-'hohn*
calcetines, los	socks	*lohs kahl-seh-'tee-nehs*
calculadora, la	calculator	*lah kahl-koo-lah-'doh-rah*

cálculo, el	calculus; calculation	*ehl 'kahl-koo-loh*
calefacción, la	heating	*lah kah-leh-fahk-see-'ohn*
calendario, el	calendar	*ehl kah-lehn-'dah-ree·oh*
calentador, el	heater	*ehl kah-lehn-tah-'dohr*
caliente	hot	*kah-lee-'ehn-teh*
calificación, la	score	*lah kah-lee-fee-kah-see·'ohn*
calle, la	street	*lah 'kah-yeh*
callejón, el	alley	*ehl kah-yeh-'hohn*
calor, el	heat	*ehl kah-'lohr*
calvo(a)	bald	*'kahl-voh(ah)*
calzoncillos, los	shorts	*lohs kahl-sohn-'see-yohs*
cama, la	bed	*lah 'kah-mah*
cambio, el	change	*ehl 'kahm-bee·oh*
caminadora, la	treadmill	*lah cah-mee-nah-'dohr-ah*
camino, el	road	*ehl kah-'mee-noh*
camión, el	truck	*ehl kah-mee·'ohn*
camisa, la	shirt	*lah kah-'mee-sah*
camiseta, la	T-shirt	*lah kah-mee-'seh-tah*
campamento, el	camp	*ehl kahm-pah-'mehn-toh*
campana, la	bell	*lah kahm-'pah-nah*
campo de recreo, el	playground	*ehl 'kahm-poh deh reh-'kreh-oh*
campo, el	campus; field	*ehl 'kahm-poh*
canasta, la	basket	*lah kah-'nah-stah*
cancha, la	court (tennis)	*lah 'kahn-chah*
canción, la	song	*lah kahn-see·'ohn*
candado, el	lock	*ehl kahn-'dah-doh*
cansado(a)	tired	*kahn-'sah-doh(ah)*
capacidad, la	capacity	*lah kah-pah-see-'dahd*
capitán, el (la capitana)	captain	*ehl kah-pee-'tahn (lah kah-pee-'tah-nah)*
capítulo, el	chapter	*ehl kah-'pee-too-loh*
cara, la	face	*lah 'kah-rah*
cárcel, la	jail	*lah 'kahr-sehl*
cargador, el	charger	*ehl kahr-gah-'dohr*
carnaval, el	carnival	*ehl kahr-nah-'vahl*
carne, la	beef	*lah 'kahr-neh*
caro(a)	expensive	*'kah-roh(ah)*
carpintero, el (la carpintera)	carpenter	*ehl kahr-peen-'teh-roh (lah kahr-peen-'teh-rah)*
carrera, la	race (competition)	*lah kah-'rreh-rah*
carreta, la	cart	*lah kah-'rreh-tah*
carretera, la	highway	*lah kah-rreh-'teh-rah*
carretilla, la	wheelbarrow	*lah kah-rreh-'tee-yah*

carrito de bebé, el	stroller	*ehl kah-'rree-toh deh beh-'beh*
carro, el	car	*ehl 'kah-rroh*
·carta, la	letter (mail)	*lah 'kahr-tah*
cartel, el	poster	*ehl kahr-'tehl*
carterista, el (la carterista)	pickpocket	*ehl kahr-teh-'ree-stah (lah kahr-teh-'ree-stah)*
cartero, el *or* la	mail carrier	*ehl / lah kahr-'teh-roh*
cartón, el	cardboard	*ehl kahr-'tohn*
casa de muñecas, la	dollhouse	*lah 'kah-sah deh moo-'nyeh-kahs*
casa, la	house; home	*lah 'kah-sah*
casete, el	cassette	*ehl kah-'seh-teh*
castigo corporal, el	corporal punishment	*ehl kah-'stee-goh kohr-poh-'rahl*
castigo, el	punishment	*ehl kah-'stee-goh*
cebolla, la	onion	*lah seh-'boh-yah*
celular, el	cell phone	*ehl seh-loo-'lahr*
cementerio, el	cemetery	*ehl seh-mehn-'teh-ree·oh*
cena, la	dinner	*lah 'seh-nah*
centavo, el	cent	*ehl sehn-'tah-voh*
centro, el	center; downtown	*ehl 'sehn-troh*
centro commercial, el	mall	*ehl 'sehn-troh koh-mehr-see-'ahl*
cepillo, el	hairbrush	*ehl seh-'pee-yoh*
cerca	near	*'sehr-kah*
cerca, la	fence	*lah 'sehr-kah*
cerdo, el (la cerda)	pig	*ehl 'sehr-doh (lah 'sehr-dah)*
cerebro, el	brain	*ehl seh-'reh-broh*
ceremonia, la	ceremony	*lah seh-reh-'moh-nee·ah*
cerro, el	hill	*ehl 'seh-rroh*
cerrojo, el	latch	*ehl seh-'rroh-hoh*
certificado, el	certificate	*ehl sehr-tee-fee-'kah-doh*
césped, el	lawn	*ehl 'seh-spehd*
cesto de basura, el	wastebasket	*ehl 'seh-stoh deh bah-'soo-rah*
chaleco, el	vest	*ehl chah-'leh-koh*
chaqueta, la	jacket	*lah chah-'keh-tah*
charca, la	pond	*lah 'chahr-kah*
cheque, el	check	*ehl 'cheh-keh*
chicle, el	gum	*ehl 'chee-kleh*
chiste, el	joke	*ehl 'chee-steh*
chistoso(a)	funny	*chee-'stoh-soh(ah)*
chivo, el (la chiva)	goat	*ehl 'chee-voh (lah 'chee-vah)*
chocolate, el	chocolate	*ehl choh-koh-'lah-teh*

chofer de autobús, el or la	bus driver	ehl / lah choh-'fehr deh ow-toh-'boos
chofer, el or la	driver	ehl / lah choh-'fehr
chuparse el dedo	thumb-sucking	choo-'pahr-seh ehl 'deh-doh
chupete, el	pacifier	ehl choo-'peh-teh
ciego(a)	blind	see-'eh-goh(ah)
ciencia del mundo, la	earth science	lah see-'ehn-see·ah dehl 'moon-doh
ciencia, la	science	lah see-'ehn-see·ah
ciencias políticas	political science	see-'ehn-see·ahs poh-'lee-'tee-kahs
cierre, el	zipper	ehl see-'eh-rreh
cigarrillos, los	cigarettes	lohs see-gah-'rree-yohs
cine, el	movie theater	ehl 'see-neh
cinta, la	tape	lah 'seen-tah
cinta meritoria, la	ribbon (of merit)	lah 'seen-tah meh-ree-'toh-ree·ah
cinturón, el	belt	ehl seen-too-'rohn
cita, la	appointment	lah 'see-tah
ciudad, la	city	lah see-oo-'dahd
clase, la	class; classroom	lah 'klah-seh
clima, el	climate	ehl 'klee-mah
clínica, la	clinic	lah 'klee-nee-kah
club, el	club	ehl kloob
cobija, la	blanket	lah koh-'bee-hah
cocinero, el (la cocinera)	cook	ehl koh-see-'neh-roh (lah koh-see-'neh-rah)
código, el	code	ehl 'koh-dee-goh
código telefonico	area code	'koh-dee-goh teh-leh-'foh-nee-koh
codo, el	elbow	ehl 'koh-doh
collar, el	necklace	ehl koh-'yahr
color, el	color	ehl koh-'lohr
colores, los	colors	lohs koh-'loh-rehs
columpio, el	swing	ehl koh-'loom-pee·oh
combinación, la	slip	lah kohm-bee-nah-see-'ohn
comentario, el	comment	ehl koh-mehn-'tah-ree·oh
cometa, la	kite	lah koh-'meh-tah
comida, la	food	lah koh-'mee-dah
comité, el	committee	ehl koh-mee-'teh
cómo	how	'koh-moh
cómodo(a)	comfortable	'koh-moh-doh(ah)
compañero, el (la compañera)	companion, acquaintance	ehl kohm-pah-'nyeh-roh (lah kohm-pah-'nyeh-rah)

comportamiento, el	behavior; conduct	*ehl kohm-pohr-tah-mee-'ehn-toh*
computadora, la	computer	*lah kohm-poo-tah-'doh-rah*
computadora portátil, la	laptop	*lah kohm-poo-tah-'doh-rah pohr-'tah-teel*
comunicación, la	communication	*lah koh-moo-nee-kah-see-'ohn*
con	with	*kohn*
concepto, el	concept	*ehl kohn-'sehp-toh*
concurso, el	contest	*ehl kohn-'koor-soh*
condado, el	county	*ehl kohn-'dah-doh*
conejo, el (la coneja)	rabbit	*ehl koh-'neh-hoh (lah koh-'neh-hah)*
conferencia, la	conference	*lah kohn-feh-'rehn-see·ah*
confianza, la	trust	*lah kohn-fee-'ahn-sah*
conflicto, el	conflict	*ehl kohn-'fleek-toh*
confundido(a)	confused	*kohn-foon-'dee-doh(ah)*
congelador, el	freezer	*ehl kohn-heh-lah-'dohr*
congelamiento, el	frostbite	*ehl kohn-heh-lah-mee-'ehn-toh*
cono, el	cone	*ehl 'koh-noh*
consejero, el (la consejera)	counselor	*ehl kohn-seh-'heh-roh (lah kohn-seh-'heh-rah)*
consejo, el	counseling	*ehl koh-'seh-hoh*
consentimiento, el	consent	*ehl kohn-sehn-tee-mee-'ehn-toh*
conserje, el	janitor	*ehl kohn-'sehr-heh*
consultor, el (la consultora)	consultant	*ehl kohn-sool-'tohr (lah kohn-sool-'toh-rah)*
contacto, el	contact	*ehl kohn-'tahk-toh*
contaminación, la	pollution	*lah kohn-tah-mee-nah-see·'ohn*
contenido, el	content	*ehl kohn-teh-'nee-doh*
contento(a)	happy	*kohn-'tehn-toh(ah)*
contra	against	*'kohn-trah*
contraseña, la	password	*lah kohn-trah-'sehn-yah*
contrato, el	contract	*ehl kohn-'trah-toh*
contusión, la	bruise	*lah kohn-too-see·'ohn*
convención, la	convention	*lah kohn-vehn-see·'ohn*
copiadora, la	copier	*lah koh-pee·ah-'doh-rah*
corazón, el	heart	*ehl koh-rah-'sohn*
corbata, la	tie	*lah kohr-'bah-tah*
coro, el	choir	*ehl 'koh-roh*
corral de juego, el	playpen	*ehl koh-'rrahl deh 'hweh-goh*
correcto(a)	correct	*koh-'rrehk-toh(ah)*
correo, el	post office	*ehl koh-'rreh-oh*

correo electrónico, el	email	*ehl koh-'rreh-oh eh-lehk-'troh-nee-koh*
correr a campo traviesa, el	cross country	*ehl koh-'rrehr ah 'kahm-poh trah-vee-'eh-sah*
cortadora de césped, la	lawnmower	*lah kohr-tah-'doh-rah deh 'seh-spehd*
cortadura, la	cut	*lah kohr-tah-'doo-rah*
corte, la	court (law); courthouse	*lah 'kohr-teh*
cortés	polite	*kohr-'tehs*
corto(a)	short (in length)	*'kohr-toh(ah)*
costa, la	coast	*lah 'koh-stah*
costo, el	cost	*ehl 'koh-stoh*
costumbre, la	custom	*lah koh-'stoom-breh*
creativo(a)	creative	*kreh-ah-'tee-voh(ah)*
crédito, el	credit	*ehl 'kreh-dee-toh*
creencia, la	belief	*lah kreh-'ehn-see·ah*
crema, la	cream	*lah 'kreh-mah*
criadero, el	nursey	*ehl kree·ah-'deh-roh*
crimen, el	crime	*ehl 'kree-mehn*
criminal, el *or* la	criminal	*ehl/lah kree-mee-'nahl*
cruce de peatones, el	crosswalk	*ehl 'kroo-seh deh peh-ah-'toh-nehs*
cuaderno, el	notebook	*ehl kwah-'dehr-noh*
cuadrado, el	square	*ehl kwah-'drah-doh*
cuál	which	*kwahl*
cuándo	when	*'kwahn-doh*
cuánto	how much	*'kwahn-toh*
cuántos	how many	*'kwahn-tohs*
cuarto(a)	fourth	*'kwahr-toh(ah)*
cuarto, el	room	*ehl 'kwahr-toh*
cubiertos, los	silverware	*lohs koo-bee-'ehr-tohs*
cubito, el	(play) block	*ehl koo-'bee-toh*
cuchara, la	spoon	*lah koo-'chah-rah*
cuchillo, el	knife	*ehl koo-'chee-yoh*
cuello, el	neck	*ehl 'kweh-yoh*
cuenta, la	bill; score	*lah 'kwehn-tah*
cuento, el	story	*ehl 'kwehn-toh*
cuerda para brincar, la	jump rope	*lah 'kwehr-dah 'pah-rah breen-'kahr*
cuerpo, el	body	*ehl 'kwehr-poh*
cuestionario, el	quiz	*ehl kweh-stee·oh-'nah-ree·oh*
cueva, la	cave	*lah 'kweh-vah*
cuidado de la salud, el	health care	*ehl kwee-'dah-doh deh lah sah-'lood*

cuidado, el	care	*ehl kwee-'dah-doh*
culpable	guilty	*kool-'pah-bleh*
cultura, la	culture	*lah kool-'too-rah*
cuna, la	crib	*lah 'koo-nah*
cuna mecedora, la	cradle	*lah 'ko-nah meh-seh-'doh-rah*
cupón, el	coupon	*ehl koo-'pohn*
curita, la	Band Aid®	*lah koo-'ree-tah*
curso, el	course	*ehl 'koor-soh*
daño, el	harm	*ehl 'dah-nyoh*
datos, los	data	*lohs 'dah-tohs*
de	from; of	*deh*
de frente de	opposite	*deh 'frehn-teh deh*
de quién	whose	*deh kee-'ehn*
débil	weak	*'deh-beel*
décimo(a)	tenth	*'deh-see-moh(ah)*
dedo, el	finger; toe	*ehl 'deh-doh*
delantal, el	apron	*ehl deh-lahn-'tahl*
delgado(a)	thin	*dehl-'gah-doh(ah)*
delicioso(a)	delicious	*deh-lee-see-'oh-soh(ah)*
delicuente, el *or* la	delinquent	*ehl / lah deh-leen-'kwehn-teh*
dentista, el (la dentista)	dentist	*ehl dehn-'tee-stah (lah dehn-'tee-stah)*
departamento de bomberos, el	fire department	*ehl deh-pahr-tah-'mehn-toh deh bohm-'beh-rohs*
departamento, el	department	*ehl deh-pahr-tah-'mehn-toh*
dependiente, el (la dependienta)	clerk	*ehl deh-pehn-dee-'ehn-teh (lah deh-pehn-dee-'ehn-tah)*
deporte, el	sport	*ehl deh-'pohr-teh*
deportes competitivos, los	competitive athletics	*lohs deh-'pohr-tehs kohm-peh-tee-'tee-vohs*
depósito, el	bin; storage	*ehl deh-'poh-see-toh*
derecho(a)	right	*lah deh-'reh-choh(ah)*
derechos civiles, los	civil rights	*lohs deh-'reh-chohs see-'vee-lehs*
desagüe, el	sewage	*ehl dehs-'ah-gweh*
desastre, el	disaster	*ehl deh-'sah-streh*
desayuno, el	breakfast	*ehl deh-sah-'yoo-noh*
descanso, el	break	*ehl deh-'skahn-soh*
desconocido, el (la desconocida)	stranger	*ehl dehs-koh-noh-'see-doh (lah dehs-koh-noh-'see-dah)*
descripción, la	description	*lah deh-skreep-see-'ohn*
descubrimiento, el	discovery	*ehl deh-skoo-bree-mee-'ehn-toh*
descuidado(a)	careless	*dehs-kwee-'dah-doh(ah)*
desempleo, el	unemployment	*ehl dehs-ehm-'pleh-oh*

desfile, el	parade	*ehl dehs-'fee-leh*
desierto, el	desert	*ehl deh-see-'ehr-toh*
desperdicios, los	waste	*lohs dehs-pehr-'dee-see·ohs*
después	afterward	*deh-'spwehs*
destacado(a); sobresaliente	outstanding	*deh-stah-'kah-doh(ah); soh-breh-sah-lee-'ehn-teh*
detector de humo, el	smoke detector	*ehl deh-tehk-'tohr deh 'oo-moh*
detención, la	detention	*lah deh-tehn-see-'ohn*
detrás	behind	*deh-'trahs*
día, el	day	*ehl 'dee·ah*
día feriado, el	holiday	*ehl 'dee·ah feh-ree-'ah-doh*
diagrama, el	chart	*ehl dee·ah-'grah-mah*
diapositiva, la	transparency	*lah dee·ah-poh-see-'tee-vah*
dibujos animados, los	cartoons	*lohs dee-'boo-hohs ah-nee-'mah-dohs*
dibujos, los	pictures	*lohs dee-'boo-hohs*
diccionario, el	dictionary	*ehl deek-see·oh-'nah-ree·oh*
diciembre	December	*dee-see-'ehm-bre*
dientes, los	teeth	*lohs dee-'ehn-tehs*
diferencia, la	difference	*lah dee-feh-'rehn-see·ah*
difícil	difficult	*dee-'fee-seel*
dinero, el	money	*ehl dee-'neh-roh*
Dios	God	*dee·'ohs*
dirección, la	address	*lah dee-rehk-see·'ohn*
director (la directora) del departamento, el	chairperson	*ehl dee-rehk-'tohr (lah dee-rehk-'toh-rah) dehl deh-pahr-tah-'mehn-toh*
director, el (la directora)	director; principal	*ehl dee-rehk-'tohr (lah dee-rehk-'toh-rah)*
discapacidad, la	disability	*lah dees-cah-pah-'see-dad*
disciplina, la	discipline	*lah dee-see-'plee-nah*
disco, el	disk	*ehl 'dee-skoh*
discos compactos, los	CDs	*lohs 'dee-skohs kohm-'pahk-tohs*
disco duro, el	hard drive	*ehl 'dees-koh 'doo-'rohsetting*
discriminación, la	discrimination	*lah dee-skree-mee-nah-see·'ohn*
discurso, el	speech	*ehl dee-'skoor-soh*
discusión, la	argument	*lah dees-koo-see·'ohn*
disfraz, el	costume	*ehl dees-'frahs*
disparo, el	shooting	*ehl dee-'spah-roh*
disponible	available	*dee-spoh-'nee-bleh*
dispuesto(a)	cooperative	*dee-'spweh-stoh(ah)*
disputa, la	altercation	*lah dee-'spoo-'tah*

distancia, la	distance	*lah dee-'stahn-see·ah*
distribuidor, el (la distribuidora)	dispenser	*ehl dee-stree-boo-ee-'dohr (lah dee-stree-boo-ee-'doh-rah)*
distrito, el	district	*ehl dee-'stree-toh*
disturbio, el	disturbance; riot	*ehl dee-'stoor-bee·oh*
divertido(a)	fun	*dee-vehr-'tee-doh(ah)*
división, la	division	*lah dee-vee-see-'ohn*
divorcio, el	divorce	*ehl dee-'vohr-see·oh*
doble, el	double	*ehl 'doh-bleh*
docena, la	dozen	*lah doh-'seh-nah*
doctor, el (la doctora)	doctor	*ehl dohk-'tohr (lah dohk-'toh-rah)*
dólar, el	dollar	*ehl 'doh-lahr*
dolor de cabeza, el	headache	*ehl doh-'lohr deh kah-'beh-sah*
dolor de espalda, el	backache	*ehl doh-'lohr deh eh-'spahl-dah*
dolor de estómago, el	stomachache	*ehl doh-'lohr deh eh-'stoh-mah-goh*
dolor, el	pain	*ehl doh-'lohr*
domingo	Sunday	*doh-'meen-goh*
dónde	where	*'dohn-deh*
dormitorio, el	bedroom; dormitory	*ehl dohr-mee-'toh-ree·oh*
drama, el	drama; play (theater)	*ehl 'drah-mah*
droga, la	drug	*lah 'droh-gah*
drogadicto, el (la drogadicta)	drug addict	*ehl drohg-ah-'deek-toh (lah drohg-ah-'deek-tah)*
dueño, el (la dueña)	owner	*ehl 'dweh-nyoh (lah 'dweh-nyah)*
dulce	sweet	*'dool-seh*
dulces, los	candy	*lohs 'dool-sehs*
duro(a)	hard	*'doo-roh(ah)*
economía, la	economics	*lah eh-koh-noh-'mee·ah*
edad, la	age	*lah eh-'dahd*
edificio, el	building	*ehl eh-dee-'fee-see·oh*
educación especial, la	special education	*lah eh-doo-kah-see-'ohn eh-speh-see-'ahl*
educación física, la	physical education	*lah eh-doo-kah-see-'ohn 'fee-see-kah*
educador, el (la educadora)	educator	*ehl eh-doo-kah-'dohr (lah eh-doo-kah-'doh-rah)*
ejemplo, el	example	*ehl eh-'hehm-ploh*
ejercicio, el	exercise	*ehl eh-hehr-'see-see·oh*
él	he	*ehl*

agente de policía, el *or* la	police officer	*ehl/lah ah-'hehn-teh deh poh-lee-'see·ah*
elección, la	election	*lah eh-lehk-see-'ohn*
electricidad, la	electricity	*lah eh-lehk-tree-see-'dahd*
electrodoméstico, el	appliance	*ehl eh-lehk-troh-doh-'meh-stee-koh*
ella	she	*'eh-yah*
ellos(as)	they	*'eh-yohs(as)*
embarazo, el	pregnancy	*ehl ehm-bah-'rah-soh*
emblema, el	badge	*ehl ehm-'bleh-mah*
emergencia, la	emergency	*lah eh-mehr-'hehn-see·ah*
emperador, el	emperor	*ehl ehm-peh-rah-'dohr*
empleado, el (la empleada)	employee	*ehl ehm-pleh-'ah-doh (lah ehm-pleh-'ah-dah)*
en	at; in; on	*ehn*
en frente de	in front of	*ehn 'frehn-teh deh*
en línea	online	*ehn 'lee-neh-ah*
enchufe, el	electrical outlet	*ehl ehn-'choo-feh*
encima	above	*ehn-'see-mah*
encuadernador, el	binder	*ehl ehn-kwah-dehr-nah-'dohr*
enero	January	*eh-'neh-roh*
enfermedad, la	illness	*lah ehn-fehr-meh-'dahd*
enfermera, la (el enfermero)	nurse	*lah ehn-fehr-'meh-rah (ehl ehn-fehr-'meh-roh)*
enfermo(a)	sick	*ehn-'fehr-moh*
enfoque, el	approach	*ehl ehn-'foh-keh*
engrapadora, la	stapler	*lah ehn-grah-pah-'doh-rah*
enojado(a)	angry; upset	*eh-noh-'hah-doh(ah)*
ensalada, la	salad	*lah ehn-sah-'lah-dah*
ensayo, el	essay	*ehl ehn-'sah-yoh*
enseñanza de conducir, la	driver's education	*lah ehn-seh-'nyahn-sah deh kohn-doo-'seer*
entonces	then	*ehn-'tohn-sehs*
entrada, la	entrance	*lah ehn-'trah-dah*
entrada para carros, la	driveway	*lah ehn-'trah-dah 'pah-rah 'kah-rrohs*
entrenador, el (la entrenadora)	trainer; coach	*ehl ehn-treh-nah-'dohr (lah ehn-treh-nah-'doh-rah)*
entrenamiento, el	training	*ehl ehn-treh-nah-mee-'ehn-toh*
entrevista, la	interview	*lah ehn-treh-'vee-stah*
envenenamiento, el	poisoning	*ehl ehn-veh-neh-nah-mee-'ehn-toh*
equilibrio, el	balance	*ehl eh-kee-'lee-bree·oh*
equipo, el	team; equipment	*ehl eh-'kee-poh*
equivocado(a)	wrong	*eh-kee-voh-'kah-doh(ah)*

eructo, el	burp	*ehl eh-'rook-toh*
escalera, la	stairs	*lah eh-skah-'leh-rah*
escalera mecánica, la	escalator	*lah eh-skah-'leh-rah meh-'kah-nee-kah*
escalones, los	steps	*lohs eh-skah-'loh-nehs*
escena, la	scene	*lah eh-'seh-nah*
escoba, la	broom	*lah eh-'skoh-bah*
escribir a máquina, el	typing	*ehl eh-skree-'beer ah 'mah-kee-nah*
escritorio, el	desk	*ehl ehs-kree-'toh-ree·oh*
escritura, la	writing	*lah eh-skree-'too-rah*
escuela, la	school	*lah eh-'skweh-lah*
escuela primaria, la	grade school	*lah eh-'skweh-lah pree-'mah-ree·ah*
escuela secundaria, la	high school	*lah eh-'skweh-lah seh-koon-'dah-ree·ah*
ese(a)(o)	that	*'eh-seh(ah)(oh)*
esfera, la	sphere	*lah eh-'sfeh-rah*
esos(as)	those	*'eh-sohs(ahs)*
espacio, el	space	*ehl eh-'spah-see·oh*
espalda, la	back	*lah eh-'spahl-dah*
especialista, el *or* la	specialist	*ehl / lah eh-speh-see·ah-'lee-stah*
espectáculo, el	show	*ehl eh-spehk-'tah-koo-loh*
espejo, el	mirror	*ehl eh-'speh-hoh*
esperanza, la	hope	*lah eh-speh-'rahn-sah*
espinaca, la	spinach	*lah eh-spee-'nah-kah*
espíritu, el	spirit	*ehl eh-'spee-ree-too*
esponja, la	sponge	*lah eh-'spohn-hah*
esposa, la	wife	*lah eh-'spoh-sah*
esposas, las	handcuffs	*lahs eh-'spoh-sahs*
esposo, el	husband	*ehl eh-'spoh-soh*
esquina, la	corner	*lah eh-'skee-nah*
esta noche	tonight	*'eh-stah 'noh-cheh*
estación de policía, la	police station	*lah eh-stah-see-'ohn deh poh-lee-'see·ah*
estacionamiento, el	parking lot	*ehl eh-stah-see·oh-nah-mee-'ehn-toh*
estadio, el	stadium	*ehl eh-'stah-dee·oh*
estado, el	state	*ehl eh-'stah-doh*
estante, el	shelf, rack	*ehl eh-'stahn-teh*
estatua, la	statue	*lah eh-'stah-too-ah*
estatura, la	height	*lah eh-stah-'too-rah*
este	east	*'eh-steh*
este(a)	this	*'eh-steh(ah)*

estómago, el	stomach	*ehl eh-'stoh-mah-goh*
estornudo, el	sneeze	*ehl eh-stohr-'noo-doh*
estos(as)	these	*'eh-stohs(ahs)*
estrategia, la	strategy	*lah eh-strah-'teh-hee·ah*
estrecho(a)	narrow	*eh-'streh-choh(ah)*
estrella, la	star	*lah eh-'streh-yah*
estuche, el	kit	*ehl eh-'stoo-cheh*
estudiante, el *or* la	student	*ehl / lah eh-stoo-dee-'ahn-teh*
estudio, el	study	*ehl eh-'stoo-dee·oh*
estudios sociales, los	social studies	*lohs eh-'stoo-dee·ohs soh-see-'ah-lehs*
estufa, la	stove	*lah eh-'stoo-fah*
etiqueta, la	sticker; label	*lah eh-tee-'keh-tah*
evacuación, la	evacuation	*lah eh-vah-koo-ah-see-'ohn*
evaluación, la	assessment; evaluation	*lah eh-vah-loo-ah-see-'ohn*
evento, el	event	*ehl eh-'vehn-toh*
evidencia, la	evidence	*lah eh-vee-'dehn-see·ah*
examen, el	test; exam	*ehl ehk-'sah-meh*
excelente	excellent	*ehk-seh-'lehn-teh*
excusado, el	toilet	*ehl ehk-skoo-'sah-doh*
explosión, la	explosion	*lah ehk-sploh-see-'ohn*
expulsión, la	expulsion	*lah ehk-spool-see-'ohn*
extensión, la	extension	*lah ehk-stehn-see-'ohn*
extintor, el	fire extinguisher	*ehl ehks-teen-'tohr*
extranjero(a)	foreign	*ehks-trahn-'heh-roh(ah)*
fábrica, la	factory	*lah 'fah-bree-kah*
fácil	easy	*'fah-seel*
facilitador, el (la facilitadora)	facilitator	*ehl fah-see-lee-tah-'dohr (lah fah-see-lee-tah-'doh-rah)*
faja, la	girdle	*lah 'fah-hah*
falda, la	skirt	*lah 'fahl-dah*
familia, la	family	*lah fah-'mee-lee·ah*
fantástico(a)	fantastic	*fahn-'tah-stee-koh(ah)*
farmacia, la	pharmacy	*lah fahr-'mah-see·ah*
fax, el	fax	*ehl fahks*
febrero	February	*feh-'breh-roh*
fecha, la	date	*lah 'feh-chah*
fecha límite, la	deadline	*lah 'feh-chah 'lee-mee-teh*
felicitaciones, las	congratulations	*lahs feh-lee-see-tah-see-'oh-nehs*
feo(a)	ugly	*'feh-oh(ah)*
festival, el	festival	*ehl feh-stee-'vahl*
fichero, el	file (computer)	*ehl fee-'cheh-roh*
fiebre, la	fever	*lah fee-'eh-breh*

fiesta, la	party	*lah fee-'eh-stah*
fila, la	row	*lah 'fee-lah*
filosofía, la	philosophy	*lah fee-loh-soh-'fee·ah*
finanzas, las	finance	*lahs fee-'nahn-sahs*
firma, la	signature	*lah 'feer-mah*
física, la	physics	*lah 'fee-see-kah*
flecha, la	arrow	*lah 'fleh-chah*
flor, la	flower	*lah flohr*
florero, el	vase	*ehl floh-'reh-roh*
folleto, el	brochure	*ehl foh-'yeh-toh*
fondos, los	funding	*lohs 'fohn-dohs*
fórmula, la	formula	*lah 'fohr-moo-lah*
formulario, el	form	*ehl fohr-moo-'lah-ree·oh*
fósforo, el	match	*ehl 'fohs-foh-roh*
foto, la	photo	*lah 'foh-toh*
fotocopiadora, la	photocopier	*lah foh-toh-koh-pee·ah-'doh-rah*
fracaso, el	failure	*ehl frah-'kah-soh*
fracción, la	fraction	*lah frahk-see-'ohn*
fraude, el	cheating	*ehl 'frow-deh*
frecuentemente	frequently	*freh-kwehn-teh-'mehn-teh*
fresco	cool	*'frehs-koh*
fresa, la	strawberry	*lah 'freh-sah*
frijoles, los	beans	*lohs free-'hoh-lehs*
frío(a)	cold	*'free·oh(ah)*
frontón con raqueta, el	racquetball	*ehl frohn-'tohn kohn rah-'keh-tah*
fruta, la	fruit	*lah 'froo-tah*
fuegos artificiales, los	fireworks	*lohs 'fweh-gohs ahr-tee-fee-see·'ah-lehs*
fuente, la	fountain	*lah 'fwehn-teh*
fuerte	strong	*'fwehr-teh*
fuerzas armadas, las	armed forces	*lahs 'fwehr-sahs ahr-'mah-dahs*
función, la	function	*lah foon-see·'ohn*
funcionarios, los	staff	*lohs foon-see·oh-'nah-ree·ohs*
fútbol americano, el	football	*ehl 'foot-bohl ah-meh-ree-'kah-noh*
fútbol, el	soccer	*ehl 'foot-bohl*
futuro, el	future	*ehl foo-'too-roh*
gabinete, el	cabinet	*ehl gah-bee-'neh-teh*
galardón, el	award	*ehl gah-lahr-'dohn*
galleta, la	cookie	*lah gah-'yeh-tah*
gallina, la	hen	*lah gah-'yee-nah*

gancho, el	hanger	*ehl 'gahn-choh*
garaje, el	garage	*ehl gah-'rah-heh*
garganta, la	throat	*lah gahr-'gahn-tah*
gasolinera, la	gas station	*lah gah-soh-lee-'neh-rah*
gato, el (la gata)	cat	*ehl 'gah-toh (lah 'gah-tah)*
gelatina, la	jello	*lah heh-lah-'tee-nah*
generalmente	generally	*heh-neh-rahl-'mehn-teh*
gente, la	people	*lah 'hehn-teh*
geografía, la	geography	*lah heh-oh-grah-'fee·ah*
geometría, la	geometry	*lah heh-oh-meh-'tree·ah*
gimnasia, la	gymnastics	*lah heem-'nah-see·ah*
gimnasio, el	gym	*ehl heem-'nah-see·oh*
gis, el	crayon	*ehl hees*
globo, el	balloon	*ehl 'gloh-boh*
glosario, el	glossary	*ehl gloh-'sah-ree·oh*
gobierno, el	government	*ehl goh-bee-'ehr-noh*
golf, el	golf	*ehl gohlf*
gordo(a)	fat	*'gohr-doh(ah)*
gorra, la	cap	*lah 'goh-rrah*
gracias	thanks	*'grah-see·ahs*
grado, el	degree (measurement); grade (level)	*ehl 'grah-doh*
graduación, la	graduation	*lah grah-doo-ah-see-'ohn*
gráfico, el	graph	*ehl 'grah-fee-koh*
grafiti, el	graffiti	*ehl grah-'fee-tee*
gramática, la	grammar	*lah grah-'mah-tee-kah*
grande	big	*'grahn-de*
gratis	free	*'grah-tees*
grifo, el	faucet	*ehl 'gree-foh*
grosero(a)	rude	*groh-'seh-roh(ah)*
grúa, la	tow truck	*lah 'groo-ah*
grueso(a)	thick	*groo-'eh-soh(ah)*
grupo, el	group	*ehl 'groo-poh*
guante, el	glove	*ehl 'gwahn-teh*
guapo(a)	handsome	*'gwah-poh(ah)*
guardería, la	nursery	*lah gwahr-deh-'ree·ah*
guardia de seguridad, el *or* la	security guard	*ehl/lah 'gwahr-dee·ah deh seh-goo-ree-'dahd*
guardia del tráfico, el *or* la	crossing guard	*ehl/lah 'gwahr-dee·ah dehl 'trah-fee-koh*
guerra, la	war	*lah 'geh-rrah*
habilidad, la	skill	*lah ah-bee-lee-'dahd*
hacha, el	ax	*ehl 'ah-chah*
hambre, el	hunger	*ehl 'ahm-breh*

hamburguesa, la	hamburger	*lah ahm-boor-'geh-sah*
hecho, el	fact	*ehl 'eh-choh*
helado, el	ice cream	*ehl eh-'lah-doh*
herida, la	injury	*lah eh-'ree-dah*
hermana, la	sister	*lah ehr-'mah-nah*
hermano, el	brother	*ehl ehr-'mah-noh*
herramienta, la	tool	*lah eh-rrah-mee-'ehn-tah*
herrumbre, la	rust	*lah eh-'rroom-breh*
hielo, el	ice	*ehl 'yeh-loh*
hígado, el	liver	*ehl 'ee-gah-doh*
hija, la	daughter	*lah 'ee-ha*
hijo, el	son	*ehl 'ee-hoh*
hilo, el	string	*ehl 'ee-loh*
hipo, el	hiccup	*ehl 'ee-poh*
historia de Europa, la	European history	*lah ee-'stoh-ree·ah deh eh·oo-'roh-pah*
historia de los Estados Unidos, la	U.S. history	*lah ee-'stoh-ree·ah deh lohs eh-'stah-dohs oo-'nee-dohs*
hockey, el	ice hockey	*ehl 'hoh-kee*
hoja informativa, la	flyer	*lah 'oh-hah een-fohr-mah-'tee-vah*
hoja, la	sheet	*lah 'oh-hah*
hola	hi	*'oh-lah*
holgazán, el (la holgazana)	loiterer	*ehl ohl-gah-'sahn (lah ohl-gah-'sah-nah)*
hombre, el	man	*ehl 'ohm-breh*
hombro, el	shoulder	*ehl 'ohm-broh*
honradez, la	honesty	*lah ohn-rah-'dehs*
hora, la	hour; time	*lah 'oh-rah*
horario, el	schedule	*ehl oh-'rah-ree·oh*
horno de microonda, el	microwave	*ehl 'ohr-noh deh mee-kroh-'ohn-dah*
horno, el	oven	*ehl 'ohr-noh*
hospital, el	hospital	*ehl oh-spee-'tahl*
hoy	today	*'oh·ee*
hoyo, el	hole	*ehl 'oh-yoh*
huelga, la	strike	*lah 'wehl-gah*
huerta, la	orchard	*lah 'wehr-tah*
huésped, el *or* la	guest	*ehl / lah 'weh-spehd*
huevo, el	egg	*ehl 'weh-voh*
humanidades, las	humanities	*lahs oo-mah-nee-'dah-dehs*
húmedo	humid	*'oo-meh-doh*
huracán, el	hurricane	*ehl oo-rah-'kahn*
idea, la	idea	*lah ee-'deh-ah*

identificación, la	I.D.	lah ee-dehn-tee-fee-kah-see·'ohn
idioma, el	language	ehl ee-dee-'oh-mah
iglesia, la	church	lah ee-'gleh-see·ah
imán, el	magnet	ehl ee-'mahn
impermeable, el	raincoat	ehl eem-pehr-meh-'ah-bleh
importante	important	eem-pohr-'tahn-teh
incapacitado(a)	handicapped	een-kah-pah-see-'tah-doh(ah)
incendio, el	fire	ehl een-'sehn-dee·oh
incompleto(a)	incomplete	een-kohm-'pleh-toh(ah)
incorrecto(a)	incorrect	een-koh-'rrehk-toh(ah)
incursión, la	raid	lah een-koor-see·'ohn
independencia, la	independence	lah een-deh-pehn-'dehn-see·ah
individualizado(a)	individualized	een-dee-vee-doo-ah-lee-'sah-doh(ah)
industria, la	industry	lah een-'doo-stree·ah
infección, la	infection	lah een-fehk-see·'ohn
información, la	information	lah een-fohr-mah-see·'ohn
ingeniero, el (la ingeniera)	engineer	ehl een-heh-nee-'eh-roh (lah een-heh-nee-'eh-rah)
inglés como segundo idioma, el	English as a second language	ehl een-'glehs 'koh-moh seh-'goon-doh ee-dee-'oh-mah
inscripción, la	registration	lah een-skreep-see·'ohn
insolación, la	sunstroke	lah een-soh-lah-see·'ohn
institución, la	institution	lah een-stee-too-see·'ohn
instituto, el	institute	ehl een-stee-'too-toh
instrucción, la	instruction	lah een-strook-see·'ohn
instructor, el (la instructora)	instructor	ehl een-strook-'tohr (lah een-strook-'toh-rah)
instrumento, el	instrument	ehl een-stroo-'mehn-toh
integracion, la	integration	lah een-teh-grah-see·'ohn
interesante	interesting	een-teh-reh-'sahn-teh
intérprete, el or la	interpreter	ehl / lah een-'tehr-preh-teh
interruptor, el	switch	ehl een-teh-rroop-'tohr
intruso, el (la intrusa)	trespassing	ehl een-'troo-soh (lah een-'troo-sah)
inundación, la	flood	lah een-oon-dah-see·'ohn
investigación, la	research	lah een-veh-stee-gah-see·'ohn
invierno, el	winter	ehl een-vee-'ehr-noh
irrespetuoso(a)	disrespectful	ee-reh-speh-too-'oh-soh(ah)
izquierdo(a)	left	ees-kee-'ehr-doh(ah)
jabón, el	soap	ehl hah-'bohn
jamón, el	ham	ehl hah-'mohn
jardín, el	garden	ehl hahr-'deen

jardinero, el (la jardinera)	gardener	*ehl hahr-dee-'neh-roh (lah hahr-dee-'neh-rah)*
jarra, la	jar	*lah 'hah-rrah*
joven	young	*'hoh-vehn*
joyas, las	jewelry	*lahs 'hoh-yahs*
jubilación, la	retirement	*lah hoo-bee-lah-see-'ohn*
juego de damas, el	checkers	*ehl 'hoo·ee-goh deh 'dah-mahs*
juego, el	game; set	*ehl 'joo·eh-goh*
jueves	Thursday	*'hweh-vehs*
jugador, el (la jugadora)	player	*ehl hoo-gah-'dohr (lah hoo-gah-'doh-rah)*
jugo, el	juice	*ehl 'hoo-goh*
juguete, el	toy	*ehl hoo-'geh-teh*
julio	July	*'hoo-lee·oh*
junio	June	*'hoo-nee·oh*
junta de educación	Board of Education	*lah 'hoon-tah deh eh-doo-kah-see-'ohn*
junta, la	council	*lah 'hoon-tah*
justicia, la	justice	*lah hoo-'stee-see·ah*
justo(a)	fair	*'hoo-stoh(ah)*
labio, el	lip	*ehl 'lah-bee·oh*
laboratorio, el	laboratory	*ehl lah-boh-rah-'toh-ree·oh*
lado, el	side	*ehl 'lah-doh*
ladrón, el (la ladrona)	thief	*ehl lah-'drohn (lah lah-'droh-nah)*
lago, el	lake	*ehl 'lah-goh*
lámpara, la	lamp	*lah 'lahm-pah-rah*
lapicero, el; pluma, la	pen	*ehl lah-pee-'seh-roh; lah 'ploo-mah*
lápiz, el	pencil	*ehl 'lah-pees*
largo(a)	long	*'lahr-goh(ah)*
largo, el	length	*ehl 'lahr-goh*
lavadora, la	washer	*lah lah-vah-'doh-rah*
lavamanos, el	sink	*ehl lah-vah-'mah-nohs*
lavaplatos, el	dishwasher	*ehl lah-vah-'plah-tohs*
lección, la	lesson	*lah lehk-see-'ohn*
leche, la	milk	*lah 'leh-cheh*
lechuga, la	lettuce	*lah leh-'choo-gah*
lectura, la	reading	*lah lehk-'too-rah*
lejos	far	*'leh-hohs*
lengua, la	tongue	*lah 'lehn-gwah*
lenguaje de sordomudos, el	sign language	*ehl lehn-'gwah-heh deh sohr-doh-'moo-dohs*
lenguaje, el; idioma, el	language	*ehl lehn-'gwah-heh; ehl ee-dee-'oh-mah*

lentamente	slowly	*lehn-tah-'mehn-teh*
lente, el	lens	*ehl 'lehn-teh*
lentes de seguridad, los	safety glasses	*lohs 'lehn-tehs deh seh-goo-ree-'dahd*
lentes de sol, los	sunglasses	*lohs 'lehn-tehs deh sohl*
lentes, los	glasses	*lohs 'lehn-tehs*
letra, la	letter (alphabet)	*lah 'leh-trah*
letrero, el	billboard; sign	*ehl leh-'treh-roh*
ley, la	law	*lah leh·ee*
libertad, la	freedom	*lah lee-behr-'tahd*
libra, la	pound	*lah 'lee-brah*
librería, la	bookstore	*lah lee-breh-'ree·ah*
libreta, la	folder	*lah lee-'breh-tah*
libro de cuentos, el	storybook	*ehl 'lee-broh deh 'kwehn-tohs*
libro de texto, el	textbook	*ehl 'lee-broh deh 'tehks-toh*
libro, el	book	*ehl 'lee-broh*
licencia, la	license	*lah lee-'sehn-see·ah*
licenciatura, la	degree (college)	*lah lee-sehn-see·ah-'too-rah*
licor, el	liquor	*ehl lee-'kohr*
licuadora, la	blender	*lah lee-kwah-'doh-rah*
líder, el *or* la	leader	*ehl/lah'lee-dehr*
liga, la	league	*lah 'lee-gah*
limón, el	lemon	*ehl lee-'mohn*
limonada, la	lemonade	*lah lee-moh-'nah-dah*
limpiador, el	duster	*ehl leem-pee·ah-'dohr*
limpio(a)	clean	*'leem-pee·oh(ah)*
línea, la	line	*lah 'lee-neh-ah*
linterna, la	flashlight	*lah leen-'tehr-nah*
liso(a)	smooth	*'lee-soh(ah)*
lista, la	list	*lah 'lee-stah*
listo(a)	clever; ready	*'lee-stoh(ah)*
literatura en inglés, la	English literature	*lah lee-teh-rah-'too-rah ehn een-'glehs*
llamada, la	phone call	*lah yah-'mah-dah*
llave de incendios, la	hydrant	*lah 'yah-veh deh een-'sehn-dee·ohs*
llave inglesa, la	wrench	*lah 'yah-veh een-'gleh-sah*
llave, la	key	*lah 'yah-veh*
lluvia, la	rain	*lah 'yoo-vee·ah*
loción, la	lotion	*lah loh-see·'ohn*
lodo, el	mud	*ehl 'loh-doh*
lote, el	lot	*ehl 'loh-teh*
lucha libre, la	wrestling	*lah 'loo-chah 'lee-breh*
lugar, el	place	*ehl loo-'gahr*

luna, la	moon	*lah 'loo-nah*
lunes	Monday	*'loo-nehs*
lupa, la	magnifying glass	*lah 'loo-pah*
luz, la	light	*lah loos*
madera, la	wood	*lah mah-'deh-rah*
madrastra, la	stepmother	*lah mah-'drah-strah*
madre, la	mother	*lah 'mah-dreh*
madrina, la	godmother	*lah mah-'dree-nah*
maestro, el (la maestra); profesor, el (la profesora)	teacher	*'ehl mah-'eh-stroh (lah mah-'eh-strah); ehl proh-feh-'sohr (lah proh-feh-'soh-rah)*
maíz, el	corn	*ehl mah-'ees*
malo(a)	bad	*'mah-loh(ah)*
mañana	tomorrow	*mah-'nyah-nah*
mano, la	hand	*lah 'mah-noh*
mantenimiento, el	maintenance	*ehl mahn-teh-nee-mee-'ehn-toh*
manzana, la	apple	*lah mahn-'sah-nah*
mapa, el	map	*ehl 'mah-pah*
maquillaje, el	makeup	*ehl mah-kee-'yah-heh*
máquina, la	machine	*lah 'mah-kee-nah*
maquinaria, la	machinery	*lah mah-kee-'nah-ree·ah*
mar, el	sea	*ehl mahr*
maravilloso(a)	marvelous	*mah-rah-vee-'yoh-soh(ah)*
marca, la	mark	*lah 'mahr-kah*
marcador, el	marker	*ehl mahr-kah-'dohr*
marco, el	picture frame	*ehl 'mahr-koh*
mareos, los	dizziness	*lohs mah-'reh-ohs*
martes	Tuesday	*'mahr-tehs*
martillo, el	hammer	*ehl mahr-'tee-yoh*
marzo	March	*'mahr-soh*
más	more	*mahs*
más tarde	later	*'mahs tahr-deh*
mascota, la	pet	*lah mah-'skoh-tah*
matemáticas, las	mathematics	*lahs mah-teh-'mah-tee-kahs*
materia, la	material	*lah mah-'teh-ree·ah*
materiales, los; provisiones, las	supplies	*lohs mah-teh-ree-'ah-lehs; lahs proh-vee-see-'oh-nehs*
matrícula, la	enrollment	*lah mah-'tree-koo-lah*
mayo	May	*'mah-yoh*
mayonesa, la	mayonnaise	*lah mah-yoh-'neh-sah*
mayor	older	*mah-'yohr*
mecánico, el *or* la	mechanic	*ehl / lah meh-'kah-nee-koh*
medalla, la	medal	*lah meh-'dah-yah*

mediodía, el	noon	*ehl men-dee·oh-'deeah*
medianoche, la	midnight	*lah meh-dee·ah-'noh-cheh*
medias, las	stockings	*lahs 'meh-dee·ahs*
medicina, la	medicine	*lah meh-dee-'see-nah*
médico, el *or* la	physician	*ehl / lah 'meh-dee-koh*
medios de comunicación, los	media	*lohs 'meh-dee·ohs deh koh-moo-nee-kah-see-'ohn*
mejilla, la	cheek	*lah meh-'hee-yah*
mejor	better	*meh-'hohr*
melocotón, el	peach	*ehl meh-loh-koh-'tohn*
memorándum, el	memo	*ehl meh-moh-'rahn-doom*
memoria, la	memory	*lah meh-'moh-ree·ah*
mendigo, el	beggar	*ehl mehn-'dee-goh*
menor	younger	*meh-'nohr*
menor de edad, el *or* la	minor	*ehl / lah meh-'nohr deh eh-'dahd*
menos	less	*'meh-nohs*
mensaje, el	message	*ehl mehn-'sah-heh*
mentor, el (la mentora)	mentor	*ehl mehn-'tohr (lah mehn-'toh-rah)*
menú, el	menu	*ehl meh-'noo*
mercado, el	market	*ehl mehr-'kah-doh*
merienda, la	snack	*lah meh-ree-'ehn-dah*
merienda campestre, la	picnic	*lah meh-ree-'ehn dah kahm-'peh-streh*
mes, el	month	*ehl mehs*
mesa, la	table	*lah 'meh-sah*
meta, la	goal	*lah 'meh-tah*
metal	metal	*meh-'tahl*
método, el	method	*ehl 'meh-toh-doh*
metro, el	meter (length); subway	*ehl 'meh-troh*
mi(s)	my	*mee(s)*
micrófono, el	microphone	*ehl mee-'kroh-foh-noh*
microscopio, el	microscope	*ehl mee-kroh-'skoh-pee·oh*
miembro, el *or* la	member	*ehl / lah mee-'ehm-broh*
miércoles	Wednesday	*mee-'ehr-koh-lehs*
milla	mile	*'oo-nah 'mee-yah*
mío(a)	mine	*'mee·oh(ah)*
mitad, la	half	*lah mee-'tahd*
mitones, los	mittens	*lohs mee-'toh-nehs*
mochila, la	backpack	*lah moh-'chee-lah*
modelo, el	model	*ehl moh-'deh-loh*
modificado(a)	modified	*moh-dee-fee-'kah-doh(ah)*
módule, el	module	*ehl 'moh-doo-loh*

mojado(a)	wet	*moh-'hah-doh(ah)*
monitor, el	monitor	*ehl moh-nee-'tohr*
monstruo, el *or* la	monster	*ehl / lah 'mohn-stroo-oh*
montaña, la	mountain	*lah mohn-'tah-nyah*
morado(a)	purple	*moh-'rah-doh(ah)*
moreno(a)	brunette; dark-haired	*moh-'reh-noh(ah)*
mostaza, la	mustard	*lah moh-'stah-sah*
motocicleta, la	motorcycle	*lah moh-toh-see-'kleh-tah*
motor, el	engine	*ehl moh-'tohr*
movimiento, el	motion	*ehl moh-vee-mee-'ehn-toh*
muchacho, el	teenager	*ehl moo-'chah-choh*
(la muchacha)		*(lah moo-'chah-chah)*
mucho(a)	much	*'moo-choh(ah)*
muchos(as)	many	*'moo-chohs(ahs)*
mudo(a)	mute	*'moo-doh(ah)*
muebles, los	furniture	*lohs 'mweh-blehs*
muerte, la	death	*lah 'mwehr-teh*
muestra en transparencia,	slide (microscope)	*lah 'mweh-strah ehn trahns-*
la		*pah-'rehn-see·ah*
muestra, la	sample	*lah 'mweh-strah*
mujer, la	woman	*lah moo-'hehr*
muletas, las	crutches	*lahs moo-'leh-tahs*
mundo, el	world; globe	*ehl 'mon-doh*
muñeca, la	doll; wrist	*lah moo-'nyeh-kah*
municipio, el	city hall	*ehl moo-nee-'see-pee·oh*
museo, el	museum	*ehl moo-'seh-oh*
música, la	music	*lah 'moo-see-kah*
nacimiento, el	birth	*ehl nah-see-mee-'ehn-toh*
nación, la	nation	*lah nah-see·'ohn*
nacionalidad, la	nationality	*lah nah-see·oh-nah-lee-'dahd*
naranja, la	orange (fruit)	*lah nah-'rahn-hah*
nariz, la	nose	*lah nah-'rees*
náusea, la	nausea	*lah 'now-seh-ah*
nave espacial, la	rocket	*lah 'nah-veh eh-spah-see-'ahl*
navegador, el	browser	*ehl nah-veh-gah-'dohr*
Navidad, la	Christmas	*lah nah-vee-'dahd*
necesario(a)	necessary	*neh-seh-'sah-ree·oh(ah)*
necesidades, las	needs	*lahs neh-seh-see-'dah-dehs*
negro(a)	black	*'neh-groh(ah)*
nervioso(a)	nervous	*nehr-vee-'oh-soh(ah)*
nieta, la	granddaughter	*lah nee-'eh-tah*
nieto, el	grandson	*ehl nee-'eh-toh*
nieve, la	snow	*lah nee-'eh-veh*
niña, la	girl	*lah 'nee-nyah*

niño, el	boy	*ehl 'nee-nyoh*
nivel, el	level	*ehl nee-'vehl*
no ficción, la	non-fiction	*lah noh feek-see-'ohn*
nombre, el	name	*ehl 'nohm-breh*
norte	north	*'nohr-teh*
nosotros(as)	we	*noh-'soh-trohs(as)*
nota, la	grade (academic); note	*lah 'noh-tah*
noticia, la	notice	*lah noh-'tee-see·ah*
novela, la	novel	*lah noh-'veh-lah*
noveno(a)	ninth	*noh-'veh-noh(ah)*
novia, la	girlfriend; bride	*lah 'noh-vee·ah*
noviembre	November	*noh-vee-'ehm-breh*
novio, el	boyfriend; groom	*ehl 'noh-vee·oh*
nuestro(a)	our	*'nweh-stroh(ah)*
número, el	number	*ehl 'noo-meh-roh*
nunca	never	*'noon-kah*
o	or	*oh*
objetivo, el	objective	*ehl ohb-heh-'tee-voh*
objetos de escritorio, los	stationery	*lohs ohb-'heh-tohs deh eh-skree-'toh-ree·oh*
océano, el	ocean	*ehl oh-'seh-ah-noh*
octavo(a)	eighth	*ohk-'tah-voh (ah)*
octubre	October	*ohk-'too-breh*
ocupación, la	occupation	*lah oh-koo-pah-see-'ohn*
ocupado(a)	busy	*oh-koo-'pah-doh(ah)*
oeste	west	*oh-'eh-steh*
oficial, el *or* la	official	*ehl / lah oh-fee-see-'ahl*
oficina, la	office	*lah oh-fee-'see-nah*
oficina principal, la	main office	*lah oh-fee-'see-nah preen-see-'pahl*
ojo, el	eye	*ehl 'oh-hoh*
olla, la	pot	*lah 'oh-yah*
onza, la	ounce	*lah 'ohn-sah*
operario, el (la operaria)	operator	*ehl oh-peh-'rah-ree·oh (lah oh-peh-'rah-ree·ah)*
opinión, la	opinion	*lah oh-pee-nee-'ohn*
orador, el (la oradora)	speaker (person)	*ehl oh-rah-'dohr (lah oh-rah-'doh-rah)*
oreja, la	ear	*lah oh-'reh-hah*
organización, la	organization	*lah ohr-gah-nee-sah-see-'ohn*
organizado(a)	organized	*ohr-gah-nee-'sah-doh(ah)*
orientación, la	orientation	*lah oh-ree-ehn-tah-see-'ohn*
orinal, el	urinal	*ehl oh-ree-'nahl*
orinarse	wetting	*oh-ree-'nahr-seh*

orquesta, la	orchestra	*lah ohr-'keh-stah*
otoño, el	fall (season)	*ehl oh-'toh-nyoh*
oveja, la	sheep	*lah oh-'veh-hah*
paciencia, la	patience	*lah pah-see-'ehn-see·ah*
padrastro, el	stepfather	*ehl pah-'drah-stroh*
padre, el	father; parent	*ehl 'pah-dreh*
padrino, el	godfather	*ehl pah-'dree-noh*
página, la	page	*lah 'pah-hee-nah*
página inicial, la	home page	*loh 'pah-hee-nah ee-nee-see-'ahl*
pago, el	payment	*ehl 'pah-goh*
país, el	country	*ehl pah-'ees*
pájaro, el	bird	*ehl 'pah-hah-roh*
pala, la	shovel	*lah 'pah-lah*
palabra, la	word	*lah pah-'lah-brah*
palo, el	stick	*ehl 'pah-loh*
pañal, el	diaper	*ehl pah-'nyahl*
pandilla, la	gang	*lah pahn-'dee-yah*
pandillero, el (la pandillera)	gang member	*ehl pahn-dee-'yeh-roh (lah pahn-dee-'yeh-rah)*
pantalla, la	screen	*lah pahn-'tah-yah*
pantalones, los	pants	*lohs pahn-tah-'loh-nehs*
pañuelo, el	handkerchief	*ehl pah-nyoo-'eh-loh*
papa, la	potato	*lah 'pah-pah*
papel, el	paper	*ehl pah-'pehl*
papel higiénico, el	toilet paper	*ehl pah-'pehl ee-hee-'eh-nee-koh*
papitas, las	potato chips	*lahs pah-'pee-tahs*
paquete, el	pack	*ehl pah-'keh-teh*
par, el	pair	*ehl pahr*
para	for	*'pah-rah,*
parada de autobús, la	bus stop	*lah pah-'rah-dah deh ow-toh-'boos*
paraguas, el	umbrella	*ehl pah-'rah-gwahs*
pared, la	wall	*lah pah-'rehd*
pariente, el *or* la	relative	*ehl / lah pah-ree-'ehn-teh*
parque, el	park	*ehl 'pahr-keh*
parque de atracciones, el	amusement park	*ehl 'pahr-keh deh ah-trahk-see-'oh-nehs*
parquímetro, el	meter (parking)	*ehl pahr-'kee-meh-troh*
parrafo, el	paragraph	*ehl 'pah-rrah-foh*
pasajero, el (la pasajera)	passenger	*ehl pah-sah-'heh-roh (lah pah-sah-'heh-rah)*
pase, el	pass	*ehl 'pah-seh*

pasillo, el	aisle; hall	*ehl pah-'see-yoh*
paso, el	step	*ehl 'pah-soh*
pastel, el	pie	*ehl pah-'stehl*
pasto, el	grass	*ehl pah-'stoh*
patines, los	skates	*lohs pah-'tee-nehs*
patinetas, las	skateboards	*lahs pah-tee-'neh-tahs*
pato, el (la pata)	duck	*ehl 'pah-toh (lah 'pah-tah)*
patólogo del habla	speech pathologist	*pah-'toh-loh-goh dehl 'ah-blah*
patrocinador, el (la patrocinadora)	sponsor	*ehl pah-troh-see-nah-'dohr (lah pah-troh-see-nah-'doh-rah)*
pavo, el (la pava)	turkey	*ehl 'pah-voh (lah 'pah-vah)*
paz, la	peace	*lah pahs*
peatón, el (la peatona)	pedestrian	*ehl peh-ah-'tohn (lah peh-ah-'toh-nah)*
pecera, la	fishbowl	*lah peh-'seh-rah*
pecho, el	chest (body)	*ehl 'peh-choh*
pegamento, el	glue	*ehl peh-gah-'mehn-toh*
peine, el	comb	*ehl 'peh·ee-neh*
pelea, la	fight	*lah peh-'leh-ah*
película, la	film	*lah peh-'lee-koo-lah*
peligro, el	danger	*ehl peh-'lee-groh*
peligroso(a)	dangerous	*peh-lee-'groh-soh(ah)*
pelirrojo(a)	red-headed	*peh-lee-'rroh-hoh(ah)*
pelo, el	hair	*ehl 'peh-loh*
pelota, la	ball	*lah peh-'loh-tah*
pensamiento, el	thought	*ehl pehn-sah-mee-'ehn-toh*
peor	worse	*peh-'ohr*
pequeño(a)	little; small	*peh-'keh-nyoh(ah)*
pera, la	pear	*lah 'peh-rah*
perdido(a)	lost	*pehr-'dee-doh(ah)*
periódico, el	newspaper	*ehl peh-ree-'oh-dee-koh*
periodismo, el	journalism	*ehl peh-ree·oh-'dees-moh*
período, el	term	*ehl peh-'ree·oh-doh*
permiso, el	permit; pass	*ehl pehr-'mee-soh*
pero	but	*'peh-roh*
perrito caliente, el	hot dog	*ehl peh-'rree-toh kah-lee-'ehn-teh*
perro, el (la perra)	dog	*ehl 'peh-rroh (lah 'peh-rrah)*
persona, la	person	*lah pehr-'soh-nah*
personal, el	personnel	*ehl pehr-soh-'nahl*
personalidad, la	personality	*lah pehr-soh-nah-lee-'dahd*
pesas, las	weights	*lahs 'peh-sahs*

pescado, el	fish (out of the water)	*ehl peh-'skah-doh*
peso, el	weight	*ehl 'peh-soh*
pestillo, el	deadbolt	*ehl peh-'stee-yoh*
pez, el	fish (in water)	*ehl pehs*
pie, el	foot	*ehl 'pee-eh*
piedra, la	stone	*lah pee-'eh-drah*
piel, la	skin	*lah pee-'ehl*
pierna, la	leg	*lah pee-'ehr-nah*
pijama, el	pajamas	*ehl pee-'yah-mah*
pila, la	battery	*lah 'pee-lah*
pimienta, la	pepper	*lah pee-mee-'ehn-tah*
pintor, el (la pintora)	painter	*ehl peen-'tohr (lah peen-'toh-rah)*
pintura, la	paint; painting	*lah peen-'too-rah*
piscina, la	pool	*lah pee-'see-nah*
piso, el	floor	*ehl 'pee-soh*
pizarrón, el	whiteboard	*ehl pee-sah-'rrohn*
pizarra interactiva, la	smartboard	*lah pee-'sah-rrah een-teh-rahk-tee-vah*
plan de estudios, el	curriculum	*ehl plahn deh eh-'stoo-dee·ohs*
plan, el	plan	*ehl plahn*
planeta, el	planet	*ehl plah-'neh-tah*
planta, la	plant	*lah 'plahn-tah*
plástico, el	plastic	*ehl 'plah-stee-koh*
plastilina, la	modeling clay	*lah plah-stee-'lee-nah*
plátano, el	banana	*ehl 'plah-tah-noh*
plato, el	plate	*ehl 'plah-toh*
plato hondo, el	bowl	*ehl 'plah-toh 'ohn-doh*
los platos de juguete	toy dishes	*lohs 'plah-tohs deh hoo-'geh-teh*
playa, la	beach	*lah 'plah-yah*
plaza, la	courtyard	*lah 'plah-sah*
plomero, el (la plomera)	plumber	*ehl ploh-'meh-roh (lah ploh-'meh-rah)*
pluma, la	feather; pen	*lah 'ploo-mah*
población, la	population	*lah poh-blah-see-'ohn*
pobre	poor	*'poh-breh*
pobreza, la	poverty	*lah poh-'breh-sah*
pocos(as)	few	*'poh-kohs(ahs)*
podio, el	podium	*ehl poh-dee·oh*
poesía, la	poetry	*lah poh-eh-'see·ah*
policía, la	police	*lah poh-lee-'see·ah*
política, la	politics	*lah poh-'lee-tee-kah*
pollo, el	chicken	*ehl 'poh yoh*

polo acuático, el	water polo	*ehl 'poh-loh ah-'kwah-tee-koh*
polvo, el	powder	*ehl 'pohl-voh*
por	for	*pohr*
por favor	please	*pohr fah-'vohr*
por qué	why	*pohr keh*
porcentaje, el	percentage	*ehl pohr-sehn-'tah-heh*
portal, el	porch	*ehl pohr-'tahl*
portón, el	gate	*ehl pohr-'tohn*
poste, el	pole	*ehl 'poh-steh*
postre, el	dessert	*ehl 'poh-streh*
práctica, la	practice	*lah 'prahk-tee-kah*
preferencias, las	preferences	*lahs preh-feh-'rehn-see·ahs*
pregunta, la	question	*lah preh-'goon-tah*
premio, el	prize	*ehl 'preh-mee·oh*
preocupado(a)	worried	*preh-oh-koo-'pah-doh(ah)*
presidente, el (la presidenta)	president	*ehl preh-see-'dehn-teh (lah preh-see-'dehn-tah)*
préstamo, el	loan	*ehl 'preh-stah-moh*
presupuesto, el	budget	*ehl preh-soo-'pweh-stoh*
primavera, la	spring	*lah pree-mah-'veh-rah*
primero(a)	first	*pree-'meh-roh(ah)*
primo, el (la prima)	cousin	*ehl 'pree-moh (lah 'pree-mah)*
principio, el	principle	*ehl preen-'see-pee·oh*
prisma, el	prism	*ehl 'prees-mah*
privado(a)	private	*pree-'vah-doh(ah)*
privilegio, el	privilege	*ehl pree-vee-'leh-hee·oh*
problema, el	problem	*ehl proh-'bleh-mah*
procedimiento, el	procedure	*ehl proh-seh-dee-mee-'ehn-toh*
proceso, el	process	*ehl proh-'seh-soh*
producto químico, el	chemical	*ehl proh-'dook-toh 'kee-mee-koh*
profundo(a)	deep	*proh-'foon-doh(ah)*
programa, el	program; software	*ehl proh-'grah-mah*
programación, la	program (computer)	*lah proh-grah-mah-see-'ohn*
programador, el (la programadora)	programmer	*ehl proh-grah-mah-'dohr (lah proh-grah-mah-'doh-rah)*
promedio, el	average	*ehl proh-'meh-dee·oh*
promoción, la	promotion	*lah proh-moh-see-'ohn*
pronto	soon	*'prohn-toh*
propiedad, la	property	*lah proh-pee-eh-'dahd*
prostituta, la	prostitute	*lah proh-stee-'too-tah*
postración, la	heat stroke; shock	*lah poh-strah-see-'ohn*
provisiones, las	supplies	*lahs proh-vee-see-'oh-nehs*
proyecto, el	project	*ehl proh-yehk-'toh*

proyector, el	projector	*ehl proh-yehk-'tohr*
prueba, la	test	*lah proo-'eh-bah;*
psicología, la	psychology	*lah see-koh-loh-'hee·ah*
psicólogo, el (la psicóloga)	psychologist	*ehl see-'koh-loh-goh (lah see-'koh-loh-gah)*
psiquiatra, el *or* la	psychiatrist	*ehl / lah see-kee-'ah-trah*
pubertad, la	puberty	*lah poo-behr-'tahd*
público, el	public	*ehl 'poob-lee-koh*
puente, el	bridge	*ehl 'pwehn-teh*
puerta, la	door	*lah 'pwehr-tah*
pulgada, la	inch	*lah pool-'gah-dah*
pulmones, los	lungs	*lohs pool-'moh-nehs*
punto, el	point	*ehl 'poon-toh*
puntual	punctual	*poon-too-'ahl*
pupitre, el	desk	*ehl poo-'pee-treh*
qué	what	*keh*
quemadura, la	burn	*lah keh-mah-'doo-rah*
querido, el	sweetheart	*ehl keh-'ree-doh*
quién	who	*kee-'ehn*
quieto(a)	quiet	*kee-'eh-toh(ah)*
química, la	chemistry	*lah 'kee-mee-kah*
quinto(a)	fifth	*'keen-toh(ah)*
quizás	maybe	*kee-'sahs*
rama, la	branch	*lah 'rah-mah*
rampa, la	ramp	*lah 'rahm-pah*
rápidamente	quickly	*'rah-pee-dah-mehn-teh*
raqueta, la	racket	*lah rah-'keh-tah*
raro(a)	strange	*'rah-roh(ah)*
rasguño, el	scrape	*ehl rahs-'goo-nyoh*
rastrillo, el	rake	*ehl rah-'stree-yoh*
raza, la	race (people)	*lah 'rah-sah*
razón, la	reason	*lah rah-'sohn*
recado, el	message	*ehl reh-'kah-doh*
recepcionista, el *or* la	receptionist	*ehl / lah reh-sehp-see·oh-'nee-stah*
receta médica, la	prescription	*lah reh-'seh-tah 'meh-dee-kah*
recibo, el	receipt	*ehl reh-'see-boh*
recogedor de basura, el	dustpan	*ehl reh-koh-heh-'dohr deh bah-'soo-rah*
recolección de fondos, la	fundraising	*lah reh-koh-lehk-see-'ohn deh 'fohn-dohs*
recomendación, la	recommendation	*lah reh-koh-mehn-dah-see-'ohn*
recompensa, la	reward	*lah reh-kohm-'pehn-sah*

rectangulo, el	rectangle	*ehl rehk-'tahn-goo-loh*
recurso, el	resource	*ehl reh-'koor-soh*
red, la	net	*lah rehd*
rendimiento, el	performance	*ehl rehn-dee-mee-'ehn-toh*
refresco, el	soft drink	*ehl reh-'freh-skoh*
refrigerador, el	refrigerator	*ehl reh-free-heh-rah-'dohr*
refugio, el	shelter	*ehl reh-'foo-hee·oh*
regalo, el	gift	*ehl reh-'gah-loh*
régimen, el	regime	*ehl 'reh-hee-mehn*
región, la	region	*lah reh-hee-'ohn*
registro, el	records	*ehl reh-'hee-stroh*
regla, la	rule; ruler	*lah 'reh-glah*
relación, la	relationship	*lah reh-lah-see-'ohn*
relaciones públicas, las	public relations	*lahs reh-lah-see-'oh-nehs 'poob-lee-kahs*
relajado(a)	relaxed	*reh-lah-'hah-doh(ah)*
religión, la	religion	*lah reh-lee-hee-'ohn*
reloj, el	clock; watch	*ehl reh-'loh*
reporte, el	report	*ehl reh-'pohr-teh*
rescate, el	rescue	*ehl reh-'skah-teh*
respeto, el	respect	*ehl reh-'speh-toh*
responsabilidad, la	responsibility	*lah reh-spohn-sah-bee-lee-'dahd*
respuesta, la	answer	*lah reh-'spweh-stah*
restaurante, el	restaurant	*ehl reh-stah·oo-'rahn-teh*
resultado, el	result	*ehl reh-sool-'tah-doh*
resumen, el	summary	*ehl reh-'soo-mehn*
retraso, el	delay; procrastination	*ehl reh-'trah-soh*
retrato, el	portrait	*ehl reh-'trah-toh*
reunión, la	meeting	*lah reh-oo-nee-'ohn*
revés, al	backwards	*ahl reh-'vehs*
revista, la	magazine	*lah reh-'vee-stah*
rico(a)	rich	*'ree-koh(ah)*
riesgo, el	risk	*ehl ree-'ehs-goh*
rima, la	rhyme	*lah 'ree-mah*
río, el	river	*ehl 'ree·oh*
riqueza, la	wealth	*lah ree-'keh-sah*
robo, el	robbery	*ehl 'roh-boh*
rociadora, la	sprinkler	*lah roh-see·ah-'doh-rah*
rodilla, la	knee	*lah roh-'dee-yah*
rojo(a)	red	*'roh-hoh(ah)*
rompecabezas, el	puzzle	*ehl rohm-peh-kah-'beh-sahs*
ropa interior, la	underwear	*lah 'roh-pah een-teh-ree-'ohr*
ropa, la	clothing	*lah 'roh-pah*

rubio(a)	blond	*'roo-bee·oh(ah)*
ruidoso(a)	loud	*roo-ee-'doh-soh(ah)*
sábado	Saturday	*'sah-bah-doh*
sacapuntas, el	pencil sharpener	*ehl sah-kah-'poon-tahs*
saco, el	sportcoat	*ehl 'sah-koh*
sal, la	salt	*lah sahl*
salida, la	exit	*lah sah-'lee-da*
salón, el	large room; lounge	*ehl sah-'lohn*
salsa de tomate, la	tomato sauce	*lah 'sahl-sah deh toh-'mah-teh*
salud, la	health	*lah sah-'lood*
sandalias, las	sandals	*lahs sahn-'dah-lee·ahs*
sangre, la	blood	*lah 'sahn-greh*
sano(a)	healthy	*'sah-noh(ah)*
sartén, el	pan	*ehl sahr-'tehn*
satisfactorio	satisfactory	*sah-tees-fahk-'toh-ree·oh*
secadora, la	dryer	*lah seh-kah-'doh-rah*
sección, la	section	*lah sehk-see-'ohn*
seco(a)	dry	*'seh-koh (ah)*
secretario, el (la secretaria)	secretary	*ehl seh-kreh-'tah-ree·oh (lah seh-kreh-'tah-ree·ah)*
secreto, el	secret	*ehl seh-'kreh-toh*
segundo(a)	second	*seh-'goon-doh(ah)*
seguridad, la	safety; security	*lah seh-goo-ree-'dahd*
seguro(a)	safe; sure	*seh-'goo-roh(ah)*
seguro, el	insurance	*ehl seh-'goo-roh*
seguro social, el	social security	*ehl seh-'goo-roh soh-see-'ahl*
selva, la	jungle	*lah 'sehl-vah*
semáforo, el	traffic signal	*ehl seh-'mah-foh-roh*
semana, la	week	*lah seh-'mah-nah*
seminario, el	seminar	*ehl seh-mee-'nah-ree·oh*
señal de parada, la	stop sign	*lah seh-'nyahl deh pah-'rah-dah*
señal, la	signal	*lah seh-'nyahl*
señor, el (Sr.)	mister (Mr.)	*ehl seh-'nyohr*
señora, la (Sra.)	lady (Mrs.)	*lah seh-'nyoh-rah*
sentimiento, el	feeling	*ehl sehn-tee-mee-'ehn-toh*
septiembre	September	*sehp-tee-'ehm-breh*
séptimo(a)	seventh	*'sehp-tee-moh(ah)*
serio(a)	serious	*'seh-ree·oh(ah)*
serrucho, el	saw	*ehl seh-'rroo-choh*
servicial	helpful	*sehr-vee-see-'ahl*
servicio, el	restroom	*ehl sehr-'vee-see·oh*
servidor, el	server	*ehl sehr-vee-'dohr*

servilleta, la	napkin	*lah sehr-vee-'yeh-tah*
sexo, el	sex	*ehl 'sehk-soh*
sexto(a)	sixth	*'sehks-toh(ah)*
si	if	*see*
sí	yes	*see*
siempre	always	*see-'ehm-preh*
silbato, el	whistle	*ehl seel-'bah-toh*
silencio, el	silence	*ehl see-'lehn-see·oh*
silla de ruedas, la	wheelchair	*lah 'see-yah deh 'rweh-dahs*
silla, la	chair	*lah 'see-yah*
sillón, el	armchair	*ehl see-'yohn*
simpático	nice	*seem-'pah-tee-koh*
simulacro de incendio, el	fire drill	*ehl see-moo-'lah-kroh deh een-'sehn-dee·oh*
simulacro, el	drill (exercise)	*ehl see-moo-'lah-kroh*
sin	without	*seen*
sindicato, el	trade union	*ehl seen-dee-'kah-toh*
sirena, la	siren	*lah see-'reh-nah*
sistema solar, el	solar system	*ehl see-'steh-mah soh-'lahr*
sitio, el	site	*ehl 'see-tee·oh*
sitio web, el	website	*ehl 'see-tee·oh web*
sobre, el	envelope	*ehl 'soh-breh*
sobredosis, la	overdose	*lah soh-breh-'doh-sees*
sobresaliente	outstanding	*soh-breh-sah-lee-'ehn-'teh*
sobretiempo, el	overtime	*ehl soh-breh-tee-'ehm-poh*
sobrina, la	niece	*lah soh-'bree-nah*
sobrino, el	nephew	*ehl soh-'bree-noh*
socio, el (la socia)	partner	*ehl 'soh-see·oh (lah 'soh-see·ah)*
sociología, la	sociology	*lah soh-see·oh-loh-'hee·ah*
sofá, el	sofa	*ehl soh-'fah*
sófbol, el	softball	*ehl 'sohf-bohl*
soga, la	rope	*lah 'soh-gah*
sol, el	sun	*ehl sohl*
soldado, el *or* la	soldier	*ehl / lah sohl-'dah-doh*
soleado(a)	sunny	*soh-leh-'ah-doh(ah)*
soledad, la	loneliness	*lah soh-leh-'dahd*
solicitud, la	application	*lah soh-lee-see-'tood*
solución, la	solution	*lah soh-loo-see-'ohn*
sombrero, el	hat	*ehl sohm-'breh-roh*
sonajero, el	rattle	*ehl soh-nah-'heh-roh*
sonido, el	sound	*ehl soh-'nee-doh*
sonrisa, la	smile	*lah sohn-'ree-sah*
sopa, la	soup	*lah 'soh-pah*

soporte, el	stand	*ehl soh-'pohr-teh*
sordo(a)	deaf	*'sohr-doh(ah)*
sorprendido(a)	surprised	*sohr-prehn-'dee-doh(ah)*
sorteo, el	raffle	*ehl sohr-'teh-oh*
sospechoso, el	suspect	*ehl soh-speh-'choh-soh*
(la sospechosa)		*(lah soh-speh-'choh-sah)*
sostén, el	brassiere	*ehl soh-'stehn*
su	her; his	*soo*
su(s)	their; your	*soo(s)*
subdirector, el	vice-principal	*ehl soob-dee-rehk-'tohr*
(la subdirectora)		*(lah soob-dee-rehk-'toh-rah)*
subibaja, el	seesaw	*ehl soo-bee-'bah-hah*
subterráneo(a)	underground	*soob-teh-'rrah-neh-oh(ah)*
sucio(a)	dirty	*'soo-see·oh(ah)*
sudadera, la	sweatsuit	*lah soo-dah-'deh-rah*
sueldo, el	wages	*ehl 'swehl-doh*
sueño, el	dream	*ehl 'sweh-nyoh*
suéter, el	sweater	*ehl 'sweh-tehr*
sugerencia, la	suggestion	*lah soo-heh-'rehn-see·ah*
suma, la	sum	*lah 'soo-mah*
superintendente,	superintendent	*ehl / lah soo-pehr-een-tehn-*
el *or* la		*'dehn-teh*
supermercado, el	supermarket	*ehl soo-pehr-mehr-'kah-doh*
supervisión, la	supervision	*lah soo-pehr-vee-see-'ohn*
supervisor, el	supervisor	*ehl soo-pehr-vee-'sohr*
(la supervisora)		*(lah soo-pehr-vee-'soh-rah)*
sur	south	*soor*
suspensión, la	suspension	*lah soo-spehn-see-'ohn*
tablero de anuncios, el	bulletin board	*ehl tah-'bleh-roh deh ah-*
		'noon-see·ohs
tableta	tablet	*tah-'bleh-tah*
tachuela, la	thumbtack	*lah tah-choo-'eh-lah*
taladro, el	drill (tool)	*ehl tah-'lah-droh*
talco, el	talcum powder	*ehl 'tahl-koh*
taller, el	workshop	*ehl tah-'yehr*
tambor, el	drum	*ehl tahm-'bohr*
tapete, el	mat	*ehl tah-'peh-teh*
tardanza, la	tardiness	*lah tahr-'dahn-sah*
tarde	late	*'tahr-deh*
tarea, la	assignment	*lah tah-'reh-ah*
tarjeta, la	card	*lah tahr-'heh-tah*
tasa, la	rate	*lah 'tah-sah*
tatuaje, el	tattoo	*ehl tah-too-'ah-heh*
taza, la	cup	*lah 'tah-sah*

tazón, el	beaker	*ehl tah-'sohn*
té, el	tea	*ehl teh*
teatro, el	theater	*ehl teh-'ah-troh*
teclado, el	keyboard	*ehl teh-'klah-doh*
técnica, la	technique	*lah 'tehk-nee-kah*
técnico, el *or* la	technician	*ehl / lah 'tehk-nee-koh*
tela, la	cloth	*lah 'teh-lah*
teléfono, el	telephone	*ehl teh-'leh-foh-noh*
telescopio, el	telescope	*ehl teh-leh-'skoh-pee·oh*
televisor, el	television (set)	*ehl teh-leh-vee-'sohr*
tema, el	subject; theme	*ehl 'teh-mah*
temblor, el	earthquake	*ehl tehm-'blohr*
templado	warm (weather)	*tehm-'plah-doh*
temprano(a)	early	*tehm-'prah-noh(ah)*
tenedor, el	fork	*ehl teh-neh-'dohr*
tener rabietas	tantrums	*the-nehr rah-bee-'eh-tahs*
tenis, el	tennis	*ehl 'teh-nees*
tenis, los	tennis shoes	*lohs 'teh-nees*
teoría, la	theory	*lah teh-oh-'ree·ah*
terapeuta, el *or* la	therapist	*ehl / lah teh-rah-peh-'oo-tah*
terapia, la	therapy	*lah teh-'rah-pee·ah*
tercero(a)	third	*tehr-'seh-roh(ah)*
termómetro, el	thermometer	*ehl tehr-'moh-meh-troh*
termostato, el	thermostat	*ehl tehr-moh-'stah-toh*
terraza, la	deck	*lah teh-'rrah-sah*
terreno, el	land	*ehl teh-'rreh-noh*
testigo, el *or* la	witness	*ehl / lah teh-'stee-goh*
tía, la	aunt	*lah 'tee·ah*
tibio(a)	warm	*'tee-bee·oh(ah)*
tiempo, el	weather	*ehl tee-'ehmpoh*
tienda, la	store	*lah tee-'ehn-dah*
tierra, la	dirt	*lah tee-'eh-rrah*
tijeras, las	scissors	*lahs tee-'heh-rahs*
timbre, el	buzzer	*ehl 'teem-breh*
tímido(a)	shy	*'tee-mee-doh(ah)*
tía, la	aunt	*lah 'tee·ah*
tina, la	tub	*lah 'tee-nah*
tío, el	uncle	*ehl 'tee·oh*
título, el	title	*ehl 'tee-too-loh*
tiza, la	chalk	*lah 'tee-sah*
toalla, la	towel	*lah toh-'ah-yah*
tobillo, el	ankle	*ehl toh-'bee-yoh*
tobogán, el	slide (playground)	*ehl toh-boh-'gahn*
tocador de DVD, el	DVD player	*ehl toh-kah-'dohr deh DVD*

todavía	yet	toh-dah-'vee·ah
todo(a) (os) (as)	all	'toh-doh(ah) (ohs) (ahs)
tomate, el	tomato	ehl toh-'mah-teh
tono, el	tune	ehl 'toh-noh
torcedura, la	sprain	lah tohr-seh-'doo-rah
tormenta, la	storm	lah tohr-'mehn-tah
tornado, el	tornado	ehl tohr-'nah-doh
torneo, el	tournament	ehl tohr-'neh-oh
torre, la	tower	lah 'toh-rreh
torta, la	cake	lah 'tohr-tah
tortuga, la	turtle	lah tohr-'too-gah
tos, la	cough	lah tohs
trabajador (la trabajadora) social, el	social worker	ehl trah-bah-hah-'dohr (lah trah-bah-hah-'doh-rah) soh-see-'ahl
trabajo, el	work	ehl trah-'bah-hoh
tractor, el	tractor	ehl trahk-'tohr
traductor, el (la traductora)	translator	ehl trah-dook-'tohr (lah trah-dook-'toh-rah)
tragedia, la	tragedy	lah trah-'heh-dee·ah
traje, el	suit	ehl 'trah-heh
traje de baño, el	bathing suit	ehl 'trah-heh deh 'bahn-yoh
transcripción, la	transcript	lah trahn-skreep-see-'ohn
transferencia, la	transfer	lah trahns-feh-'rehn-see·ah
transporte, el	transportation	ehl trahns-'pohr-teh
trapeador, el	mop	ehl trah-peh-ah-'dohr
traste, el	dish	ehl 'trah-steh
tren, el	train	ehl trehn
tribunal de menores, el	juvenile court	ehl tree-boo-'nahl deh meh-'noh-rehs
triciclo, el	tricycle	ehl tree-'see-kloh
trigonometría, la	trigonometry	lah tree-goh-noh-meh-'tree·ah
trineo, el	sled	ehl tree-'neh-oh
triste	sad	'tree-steh
trofeo, el	trophy	ehl troh-'feh-oh
trompo, el	top	ehl 'trohm-poh
truco, el	trick	ehl 'troo-koh
tú	you (singular, informal)	too
tubería, la	pipe; plumbing	lah too-beh-'ree·ah
tubo de ensayo, el	test tube	ehl 'too-boh deh ehn-'sah-yoh
tubo, el	tube	ehl 'too-boh
tumulto, el	disturbance	ehl too-'mool-toh
túnel, el	tunnel	ehl 'too-nehl
tutor, el (la tutora)	tutor	ehl too-'tohr (lah too-'toh-rah)

tutor (la tutora) legal, el	legal guardian	*ehl too-'tohr leh-'gahl (lah too-'toh-rah leh-'gahl)*
una vez	once	*'oo-nah vehs*
unidad, la	unit	*lah oo-nee-'dahd*
uniforme, el	uniform	*ehl oo-nee-'fohr-meh*
universidad, la	university; college	*lah oo-nee-vehr-see-'dahd*
universo, el	universe	*ehl oo-nee-'vehr-soh*
unos(as)	some	*'oo-nohs(ahs)*
urgente	urgent	*oor-'hehn-teh*
usted	you (singular, formal)	*oo-'stehd*
ustedes	you (plural, formal and informal)	*oo-'steh-dehs*
usualmente	usually	*oo-soo-ahl-'mehn-teh*
uva, la	grape	*lah 'oo-vah*
vaca, la	cow	*lah 'vah-kah*
vacaciones, las	vacation	*lahs vah-kah-see-'oh-nehs*
vacunación, la	vaccination	*lah vah-koo-nah-see-'ohn*
vagón, el	wagon	*ehl vah-'gohn*
valle, el	valley	*ehl 'vah-yeh*
valor, el	value	*ehl vah-'lohr*
vasinica, la	potty	*lah vah-see-'nee-kah*
vaso, el	glass (drinking)	*ehl 'vah-soh*
vecino, el (la vecina)	neighbor	*ehl veh-'see-noh (lah veh-'see-nah)*
vegetales, los	vegetables	*lohs veh-heh-'tah-lehs*
vela, la	candle	*lah 'veh-lah*
velocidad, la	speed	*lah veh-loh-see-'dahd*
vendaje, el	bandage	*ehl vehn-'dah-heh*
vendedor, el (la vendedora)	salesperson	*ehl vehn-deh-'dohr (lah vehn-deh-'doh-rah)*
vendedor (la vendedora) de drogas, el	drug dealer	*ehl vehn-deh-'dohr (lah ven-deh-'doh-rah) deh 'droh-gahs*
ventana, la	window	*lah vehn-'tah-nah*
ventilador, el	fan	*ehl vehn-tee-lah-'dohr*
verano, el	summer	*ehl veh-'rah-noh*
verde	green	*'vehr-deh*
vestíbulo, el	lobby	*ehl veh-'stee-boo-loh*
vestido, el	dress	*ehl veh-'stee-doh*
vía del ferrocarril, la	railroad track	*lah 'vee·ah dehl feh-rroh-kah-'rreel*
viaje, el	trip	*ehl vee·'ah-heh*
víctima, la	victim	*lah 'veek-tee-mah*
vídeo, el	video	*ehl 'vee-deh-oh*

videojuego, el	videogame	*ehl vee-deh-oh-hoo-'eh-goh*
vidrio, el	glass (material)	*ehl 'vee-dree·oh*
viejo(a)	old	*vee-'eh-hoh(ah)*
viento, el	wind	*ehl vee-'ehn-toh*
viernes	Friday	*vee-'ehr-nehs*
violación, la	rape; violation	*lah vee·oh-lah-see-'ohn*
violencia, la	violence	*lah vee·oh-'lehn-see·ah*
visitante, el *or* la	visitor	*ehl / lah vee-see-'tahn-teh*
vitaminas, las	vitamins	*lahs vee-tah-'mee-nahs*
vivienda, la	housing	*lah vee-vee-'ehn-dah*
vocabulario, el	vocabulary	*ehl voh-kah-boo-'lah-ree·oh*
vóleibol, el	volleyball	*ehl voh-'leh·ee-bohl*
volumen, el	volume	*ehl voh-'loo-mehn*
voluntario, el (la voluntaria)	volunteer	*ehl voh-loon-'tah-ree·oh (lah voh-loon-'tah-ree·ah)*
voz, la	voice	*lah vohs*
y	and	*ee*
ya	already	*yah*
yo	I	*yoh*
zanahoria, la	carrot	*lah sah-nah-'oh-ree·ah*
zanja, la	ditch	*lah 'sahn-hah*
zapatillas, las	slippers	*lahs sah-pah-'tee-yahs*
zapato, el	shoe	*ehl sah-'pah-toh*
zona, la	zone	*lah 'soh-nah*
zona postal, la	zip code	*lah 'soh-nah poh-'stahl*
zoológico, el	zoo	*ehl soh-oh-'loh-hee-koh*

TRACKS